Fear in early modern society

STUDIES IN EARLY MODERN
EUROPEAN HISTORY

This exciting new series aims to publish
challenging and innovative research in all areas
of early modern continental history.
The editors are committed to encouraging work
that engages with current historiographical
debates, adopts an interdisciplinary
approach, or makes an original contribution
to our understanding of the period.

SERIES EDITORS
William G. Naphy and Penny Roberts

EDITORIAL ADVISORY BOARD
Professor N. Z. Davis, Professor Brian Pullan,
Professor Joseph Bergin and
Professor Robert Scribner

Already published in the series

The rise of Richelieu   Joseph Bergin

A city in conflict: Troyes during the French wars of religion
Penny Roberts

Forthcoming

*Narratives of witchcraft in early modern Germany:
fabrication, feud and fantasy*   Alison Rowlands

The Duke of Lerma: a political life   Patrick Williams

FEAR
in early modern society

EDITED BY WILLIAM G. NAPHY
AND PENNY ROBERTS

Manchester University Press

Manchester and New York

distributed exclusively in the USA by St. Martin's Press

Copyright © Manchester University Press 1997

While copyright in the volume as a whole is vested in Manchester University Press, copyright in individual chapters belongs to their respective authors, and no chapter may be reproduced wholly or in part without the express permission in writing of both author and publishers.

Published by Manchester University Press
Oxford Road, Manchester M13 9NR, UK

Distributed exclusively in the USA
by St. Martin's Press, Inc., 175 Fifth Avenue, New York, NY10010, USA

Distributed exclusively in Canada by
UBC Press, University of British Columbia, 63214 Memorial Road,
Vancouver, BC, Canada V6T 1Z2

British Library Cataloguing-in-Publication Data
A catalogue record is available from the British Library

Library of Congress Cataloging-in-Publication Data applied for

ISBN   0 7190 4866 4 *hardback*
         0 7190 5205 X *paperback*

First published 1997

01   00   99   98   97   10   9   8   7   6   5   4   3   2   1

Typeset in Monophoto Perpetua with Albertus
by Northern Phototypesetting Co Ltd, Bolton
Printed in Great Britain
by Bell & Bain Ltd, Glasgow

Contents

Contributors

Will Coster received his D.Phil. in History from the University of York. He is the author of *Kinship and Inheritance in Early Modern England: Three Yorkshire Parishes*, numerous articles and the forthcoming *Spiritual Kinship in Early Modern England*. He is Lecturer in History and Director of the Institute for the Study of War and Society at De Montfort University, Bedford.

Raingard Eßer was, until recently, lecturer at the Department of Economic History at the London School of Economics and is now attached to the University of Gießen, where she is completing her *Habilitationsschrift*. She is the author of *Niederländische Exulanten im England des 16. und frühen 17. Jahrhunderts*.

David Gentilcore received his Ph.D. from the University of Cambridge, before going on to a research fellowship at the Wellcome Unit for the History of Medicine and Churchill College, Cambridge. He is the author of *From Bishop to Witch: the System of the Sacred in Early Modern Terra d'Otranto*, and his current project is a book entitled *Healers and Healing in Early Modern Italy*. He is Wellcome Research Fellow and Honorary Lecturer at Leicester University.

Mark Jenner is Lecturer in the History Department of the University of York. He has published on various aspects of the history of early modern gender, medicine and, in particular, on early modern London. A revised version of his Oxford D.Phil. thesis on *Early Modern Conceptions of 'Cleanliness' and 'Dirt'* is forthcoming. He is currently working on a project on the 'Medical History of London Water, 1500–1830' funded by the Wellcome Trust, some of the findings of which will appear in an article in the forthcoming P. Griffiths and M. Jenner, eds, *Londinopolis: Studies in the Cultural and Social History of Early Modern London*.

Beat A. Kümin graduated from Berne University and wrote a Cambridge (Corpus Christi College) Ph.D. thesis on the late medieval English parish. He is a Research Fellow of Magdalene College, Cambridge and author of *The Shaping of a Community: The Rise and Reformation of the English Parish c.1400–1560*, editor of *Reformations Old and New* and co-editor of *The Parish in English Life 1400–1600*.

Karin Maag is a Postdoctoral Fellow funded by the Social Sciences and Humanities Research Council of Canada. She is also a fellow of the St Andrews Reformation Studies Institute, and an Honorary Lecturer in the Department of Modern History at St Andrews University. Her research interests focus on higher education and the training of ministers. She is the author of *Seminar or University? The Genevan*

Academy and Reformed Higher Education, as well as various articles and essays.

Peter Marshall was educated at University College, Oxford, and is now Lecturer in History at the University of Warwick. He is the author of a number of articles on aspects of the Reformation in England and of *The Catholic Priesthood and the English Reformation*.

P. G. Maxwell-Stuart received his Ph.D. in Humanity at the University of St Andrews. He has published widely on Classical subjects and is about to publish *A Chronicle of the Popes*. Forthcoming publications also include a translation of Martin del Río's *Investigations into Magic*, and an edited collection of *Documents on the Occult Sciences in Early Modern Europe*. He is a Research Fellow in the Department of History and Economic History at the University of Aberdeen, and an Honorary Fellow of the Institute of Reformation Studies at the University of St Andrews.

William Naphy received his Ph.D. in Reformation History from the University of St Andrews. He is the author of *Calvin and the Consolidation of the Genevan Reformation* and the forthcoming *Plagues, Poisons and Potions: Conspiratorial Plague-Spreading in the Western Alps, 1530–1645*, as well as editor and translator of *Documents on the Continental Reformation*. He is lecturer in Late Medieval and Early Modern European History at the University of Aberdeen.

Penny Roberts received her Ph.D. from the University of Birmingham in 1992. She is author of *A City in Conflict: Troyes during the French Wars of Religion*, a number of articles and essays on the wars of religion, and 'Arson, conspiracy and rumour in early modern Europe', in *Continuity and Change*, 12 (1997), 9–29. Her current research is on the practical application of the edicts of pacification, and a textbook on the French wars for Macmillan. She is Lecturer in History at the University of Warwick.

Andrew Spicer received his Ph.D. from the University of Southampton. In addition to various essays and articles his publications include the forthcoming *The French-Speaking Reformed Community and their Church, 1567–c.1620*. His current research relates to the impact of the Reformation upon church architecture. He presently teaches at Stonyhurst College, Lancashire.

Bruce Taylor was educated at the University of Manchester and at Oxford where he received his D.Phil. in 1996. He is the author of the forthcoming *Armatures of Reform: The Mercedarian Order in the Spanish Golden Age* and co-editor of *Learning and Society in Spain from Humanism to the Enlightenment: The Expansion of University Culture, 1300–1800*. He is currently Vicente Canada Blanch Research Fellow at the University of Manchester.

Abbreviations

AC Nantes	Archives Communales de Nantes
ACV	Archivio della Curia Vescovile
AD Aube	Archives Départementales de l'Aube
AEG	Archives d'État de Genève
AM Rennes	Archives Municipales de Rennes
BL	British Library
BM Troyes	Bibliothèque Municipale de Troyes
BN Paris	Bibliothèque Nationale, Paris
BRO	Bristol Record Office
CLRO	Corporation of London Record Office
CO	E. Cunitz and E. Baum, eds, *Joannis Calvini Opera* (Corpus Reformatorum, 29–87; Berlin, 1863–1900)
CRO	Cambridgeshire Record Office
CSPD	*Calendar of State Papers Domestic*
CSPS	*Calender of State Papers Scottish*
CUL	Cambridge University Library
CWA	Churchwardens' Accounts
CWTM	Yale Edition of the *Complete Works of St Thomas More*
CYCR	City of York Chamberlains' Rolls
CYHB	City of York House Books
DNB	*Dictionary of National Biography*
GkS	Gammel könhelig Samling
GL	Guildhall Library (London)
HRO	Hampshire Record Office
HZ	*Historische Zeitschrift*
JCCC	Journal of the Court of Common Council
LPL	Lambeth Palace Library (London)
MDG	Mémoires et documents de la Société d'histoire et d'archéologie de Genève
P&P	*Past and Present*
PC	Procès criminels
PH	Pièces historiques
PRO	Public Record Office
Processus	Biblioteca Comunale dell'Archiginnasio, Bologna, *Fondo Ospedali*
PS	Parker Society

RC	Registres du Conseil de Genève
RZ	Rijksarchief in Zeeland
RCP	Royal College of Physicians
SCJ	*Sixteenth Century Journal*
SHR	*Scottish Historical Review*
SPODRLC	Society for the Publication of Original Documents relating to Lancashire and Cheshire
SR	*Scottish Review*
SRO	Scottish Record Office
STAZ	Staatsarchiv Zürich
SufRO	Suffolk Record Office
SUL	Sheffield University Library
SZ	Stakenvan Zeeland
TRHS	*Transactions of the Royal Historical Society*
Versoris	Nicolas Versoris, *Livre de raison de Me. Nicolas Versoris, avocat au Parlement de Paris, 1519–30*, ed. G. Fagniez (Paris, 1885)
YCA	York City Archives

Note Place of publication is London unless otherwise stated.

Introduction

PENNY ROBERTS AND WILLIAM G. NAPHY

Historians have broadly accepted that the fourteenth to eighteenth centuries witnessed a 'climate of fear' or 'unease', that fear was all-pervasive and omnipresent within society, and that the population of Europe at this time experienced unprecedented levels of anxiety and pessimism.[1] In order to support this theory, emphasis has been given to the momentous and unsettling changes that accompanied this transitional period from the medieval to the modern world. The Black Death and the subsequent pandemic of plague (biological/demographic change); papal schism, heresy and Reformation (religious change); international warfare and the rise of nation–states (political change); the shift from feudalism to capitalism, proto-industrialisation, the 'expropriation' of the peasantry, increasing urbanisation, the rise of the bourgeoisie (socio-economic change); have all been seen to play a part. The geographical and astronomical discoveries of the period and the Renaissance questioning of established knowledge, with their challenge to former orthodoxies, are only thought to have added to this increased sense of instability and insecurity. Finally, the 'witch craze' is seen as the most dramatic and unpleasant manifestation of this collective anxiety in operation. Yet, like the witch craze, what might be termed the 'great fear' theory has been subject to scrutiny, qualification and revision in recent years.[2]

It is not the purpose of this volume to refute or endorse the assertion that the early modern period was somehow different in its level of fearfulness to those that came before and after. Indeed, it might be argued that interpretations of its significance have largely been distorted by the exponential growth in documentary evidence, in particular of a personal nature, surviving from these centuries, as has been shown to be the case for the debate concerning the emergence of the 'modern' family and parental affection.[3] Moreover, it is evident that all periods might be so labelled, and that fear is a constant phenomenon throughout history. Accepted as a natural part of existence, fear is seen as part of the survival instinct and desire for security.⁴ Even our own century, with its better understanding of why and how tragedies occur, and its medical and technological advances, has been termed 'the age of anxiety'.⁵ In this context, few can doubt the devastating impact of two world wars, the threat of nuclear destruction or germ warfare, and the spread of AIDS. Moreover, in a way mirroring one of the major preoccupations of earlier centuries, our age is fast becoming dominated by almost apocalyptic expectations of the planet's demise through global warming, pollution and over-population. On a less global level, deepseated fears are still manifest in our concerns about crime, unemployment and terrorism. Finally, although death has in many ways been distanced and sanitised, it can still strike suddenly and inexplicably. Whilst divine action has been replaced by human, biological and socio-economic forces as an explanation for what occurs, it is clear that fear is not a state that can be overcome, only reduced or curbed. It is clear also that, in any age, fear permeates society from top to bottom, from the king down. In this context, the fear of overthrow can be as powerful as the fear of destitution.⁶

To say the least, then, fear in early modern society is a problematic subject. But we should perhaps begin with a clarification of what precisely is meant by fear in the context of this volume. Most importantly, we are concerned with dealing with fear as an historical phenomenon, not as a psychological or instinctual condition, although these factors may inform our understanding of what constitutes fear. In broad terms fear is most often defined in relation or juxtaposition to anxiety. It is generally agreed that anxiety represents a general uncertainty about the future, whilst fear is more specific, immediate and focused, and, therefore, assailable. As Bouwsma sums it up, 'because the object of fear is concrete and may be dealt with by some appropriate action, fear can be reduced or overcome'.⁷ It is thus very much fear, in its more specific and varied forms, that will be discussed in this volume, and in particular the strategies used to reduce or overcome it. The intention is thus to move away from the tendency of much of the historiography to treat fear in a rather abstract and often ill-defined way, which has resulted in a relative neglect of detailed studies of the objects of fear and the interaction of individuals, communities and authorities in dealing with them. What we are primarily concerned with, then, is in a sense the logistics of fear: the ways in which people in the early modern period coped with, and took precautions against, what they feared, from the more practical (fire, flood, plague) to the more intangible (death, witchcraft, fear itself).⁸ Such fears could be individually held, but were more often collective, and therefore more volatile and consequential.⁹ The object, or threat, could be external (nature, foreigners, soldiers) or internal (illness, religious or ethnic minorities), the means by which to tackle it religious or practical.

Whilst spiritual remedies, such as the intercession of saints, were sought, measures were introduced to deal with or guard against further damage according to the nature of the threat, as in the case of dam-building, fire-breaks and the slaughter of plague-carrying animals. More sophisticated still were the strategies used by local communities to circumvent the more harmful effects of central government encroachment into their lives, or the imposition of a garrison.[10] Rather different from this opposition between central and local interest, city authorities could take measures against the danger posed by the ignorance of the masses under their jurisdiction, risking tension between popular and elite.[11]

Yet in many cases we see that fear resulted in the uniting of society behind a common interest, and occasionally against a common enemy, identified most often with marginals and outsiders. When a calamity, such as a fire or outbreak of plague, occurred, the authorities could feed on people's fears, as well as deflecting their discontent, by naming scapegoats. As a result, those accused fulfilled a stereotype of an evildoer drawn from those groups perceived to pose the greatest threat to society, thereby justifying their persecution and prosecution.[12] Jews, lepers, witches, vagrants, the poor, heretics and foreigners were all targeted as scapegoats at various points in the late medieval and early modern periods.[13] They were blamed for the poisoning of wells, the spread of disease, arson, subsistence crises and other misfortunes. An important social function was served by the provision of an explanation for the tragedy that had occurred, the identification, capture and punishment of the supposed culprits, as a result of which collective anxieties were assuaged.[14] This scapegoating, then, indicates the ability of fear to act as a unifying factor, reinforcing solidarities between social groups, and encouraging co-operation. Yet, only in the most extreme cases did the unifying power of fear result in the persecution of marginal groups. Thus fear need not be seen simply as a negative force; it could also be dynamic, leading to positive action, such as popular protest, as well as practical measures to deal with the object of fear.[15]

Whilst eschewing the wider debate about the level of fear, we have been keen to engage with both the more traditional and much newer debates regarding particular types and sources of fear in the early modern period. Fear of death, that most fundamental of human anxieties, and the associated concerns about purgatory, hell and damnation, burial rites, and in a Protestant context, reprobation, have been the focus of several historical studies of these centuries.[16] The depiction of the emergence of Protestantism as a means to overcome fears regarding salvation is flawed by the evident inability of the 'new' faith to eradicate such concerns. Predestination did not necessarily, in practice, bring reassurance and certainty.[17] This volume explores fears in both Catholic and Protestant contexts and reveals, in this regard, little of a confessional divide.[18] Both faiths were also heavily immersed in eschatology, embodying perhaps the greatest fear of all.[19] Furthermore, in a religious age it was perhaps inevitable that both fears and their remedies were perceived in terms of divine providence.

A more recent debate has focused on attitudes to nature and natural forces, as well as changing perceptions of the animal kingdom in the medieval and early modern periods, and the fears associated with them.[20] Exploring reactions to flood, as well as to dogs as agents of contagion, we hope to build on these early foundations. Out of all the animals that have integrated with human society, cats seem to have had a particularly rough deal in this period, in particular as sources of rituals involving fires and sorcery.[21] It has, of course, proved impossible to include all aspects of fear in one volume, and consequently there are several that we were forced to leave out due to lack of space or a willing contributor. Thus famine might have accompanied fire, flood and plague, or crime contributed to the marginality debate. Nor has the gender issue been as well covered as we would have liked. Primarily this may reflect that the 'fear' of women was too inextricably entangled with other sources of anxiety, and we were concerned that any analysis of it threatened to draw our discussion back into the uncertainties of the psychological or instinctual sphere. Moreover, some of the essays do focus on fears which eventually led to the persecution of women.[22] Finally, as the word implies, misogyny involves hatred of women rather than fear of them. Though the two impulses are often intertwined, we were loath to attempt to quantify 'feelings' in favour of examining their manifestations in concrete situations. Despite such omissions, however, we feel that some aspect of most types of fear are thoroughly treated and believe the conclusions of each study to be more widely applicable: from the scourge of plague to the less obvious concerns about lack of educational provision, from procuring the King's death by magical means to the practical measures that were taken to reduce the threats that accompanied everyday life, from the disease of fear to the fear of contagion, from the enemy within to the threat of external encroachment.

Many of the fears that are examined in this volume are discussed in an urban context: fire, flood, poison/plague, soldiers, ignorance, outside authority. Bouwsma posited a strong connection between the anxiety of this period and increased urbanisation.[23] But such an association may be more apparent than real, as a consequence (once again) of the burgeoning of surviving documentation from this period, much of it urban, and the fact that the towns had a more literate population, combined with the increase in the keeping of diaries, memoirs, letters in which such emotions are more likely to be to the fore than in official sources. It surely would be implausible to claim, however, that rural fear was any less prevalent or pervasive, as indeed several studies have shown.[24] Nevertheless, towns would have provided an ideal breeding ground for the kind of rumours that led to the development of collective fears about the security of the community. It is worth underlining the significance of rumour in a society with poor communications and low literacy rates – in a predominantly oral culture.[25] Interestingly, the language and images used to describe the spread of fear, and the rumour that often preceded it, correlate with many of the sources of fear itself, comparing it to the contagion of disease and consuming by fire.

In addition to differentiating between fear and anxiety, it is perhaps necessary for us to delineate between fear and panic. If 'fear is concrete ... and can be reduced and overcome', then panic ought to be seen as the sudden, relatively short-lived, and ultimately uncontrollable equivalent of fear; in effect, at the other extreme from anxiety. In this context it may prove fruitful to consider the so-called witch craze, for our findings also support much of the debate that has qualified recent reassessments of this peculiarly early modern occurrence.[26] Witch-hunting was a phenomenon (a panic, we may allow) which affected different areas of Europe, at diverse times and to varying degrees. It has become the focus of historiographical interest because of the sensational nature (and number, if now far fewer than was once thought) of the executions which resulted. Our essays have tried to focus on fears which were a persistent concern to early modern people, fears which preoccupied their thoughts, influenced their actions and guided those of their governments (sometimes incurring regular expenditure). In this regard, witchcraft and its role in deciding an individual's good or bad fortune sits well with such everyday concerns; but the diabolical conspiracy theory that drove the major trials does not. In addition, if we look at the entire period during which witch-hunting took place on a significant scale, and compare the rate of execution and the geographical spread for infanticide (a manifestation of the female fear of the shame and ostracisation that increasingly accompanied illegitimacy) and for sodomy, it becomes clear that these crimes were more consistently considered as heinous by early modern society, and the local 'witch' more readily indulged.[27] Thus, the death of a new-born infant and sexual deviance are perhaps more easily classifiable as fears than witchcraft (at least in its diabolical form), if one were to plot them on a continuum between anxiety/concern and panic/terror.

One conclusion that can be drawn is the efficacy of the remedies and strategies employed, demonstrating that fears were not unassailable, and that society was not impotent in the face of them, as some historians have tended to portray in the past. There was much that could be done to assuage fear; people were not paralysed by it as Muchembled would have us believe.[28] It is clear, too, that the authorities exercised restraint in trying those believed to be responsible for inflicting harm on society, as in Geneva, despite rumours of plague-spreading.[29] Indeed, the ability of the authorities to contain or 'manage' fear may have proved crucial in preventing an anxious situation from turning into one of panic. In this sense, fear can be seen as a sort of index of institutional health, reflecting the efficacy of local or central government in curbing the negative effects of fear.[30] This might be on a daily basis, as with fire and educational provision, and to a lesser extent, flood, plague, foreigners and the garrisoning of soldiers. The Church had an important role to play, too, in reassuring the faithful and providing them with the means to overcome their fears about salvation, disease and divine providence (in the form of fire, flood, illness, etc.). A further recourse existed in that contemporaries also discussed fear with regard to its debilitating effects, which in itself was a kind of therapy, what might be termed dealing with the fear of fear.[31]

It is questionable quite how far people had an awareness of momentous changes taking place over four centuries, which mostly would have only gradually permeated society. It is also possible to dispute the claim that it was only at the end of the eighteenth century that society was able to come to terms with these changes and learned to cope effectively with them. The essays in this volume show that throughout the early modern period people were well equipped to deal with their fears, however irrational they might now appear to us. Indeed, what emerges is an altogether more rational society that approached its problems, whether they were of an everyday or exceptional nature, in an organised, disciplined and preconceived way. Although society was more vulnerable than today, the response to fear was in general measured and responsible. Panics could and did occur, but day-to-day fear was a respected but not invincible enemy.

Notes

1 J. Delumeau, *La Peur en Occident: XIVe–XVIIIe siècles* (Paris, 1978), 15 and 19. His ideas were foreshadowed by, among others, L. Febvre, *The Problem of Unbelief in the Sixteenth Century: The Religion of Rabelais* (1982), and J. Huizinga, *The Waning of the Middle Ages* (1955). More recent works that have pursued this theme include, R. Muchembled, *Popular Culture and Elite Culture in France, 1400–1750* (1985); W. J. Bouwsma, 'Anxiety and the formation of early modern culture', in B. C. Malament, ed., *After the Reformation* (Manchester, 1980), 215–46; D. Crouzet, *Les Guerriers de Dieu: la Violence au Temps des Troubles de Religion* (Paris, 1990).

2 Bouwsma, 'Anxiety', 215–16, on the difficulties of categorising any one period; S. Clark, 'French historians and early modern popular culture', *P&P*, 100 (1983), 62–99, largely a critique of Muchembled. On witches, see most recently, R. Briggs, *Witches and Neigh-*

bours: The Social and Cultural Context of European Witchcraft (1996); J. Sharpe, *Instruments of Darkness: Witchcraft in England, 1550–1750* (1996).

3 The main exponents of this view were L. Stone, *The Family, Sex and Marriage in England, 1500–1800* (1977), and P. Ariès, *Centuries of Childhood* (1962). Their conclusions have been widely challenged; for example see R. A. Houlbrooke, *The English Family, 1450–1700* (1984), esp. 6–7 and 13–14, A. MacFarlane's review of Stone in *History and Theory*, 18 (1979), 103–26, and A. Wilson's of Ariès, *History and Theory*, 19 (1980), 132–53.

4 Delumeau, *La Peur*, 9; P. Mannoni, *La Peur* (Paris, 1982), 3. For a comparable approach to this volume on the modern period see, S. Dunant and R. Porter, *The Age of Anxiety* (1996).

5 W. H. Auden (1947), under 'anxiety' in the *Chambers Dictionary*.

6 Maxwell-Stuart, Ch. 12, this volume.

7 Bouwsma, 'Anxiety', 218, 222; Mannoni, *La Peur*, pp. 39–47; for Freud's definition see Gentilcore, Ch. 11, this volume, p. 190.

8 On fire (Roberts), flood (Eßer), plague (Naphy and Jenner), soldiers (Coster); death/burial (Spicer and Marshall), witchcraft (Maxwell-Stuart), fear (Gentilcore), all in this volume.

9 As it happens, for the chapters in this volume, the practical/intangible division corresponds with the collective/individual, though this would not be true in all contexts, e. g. for witchcraft. Kümin and Maag (Chs 7 and 8) fall into the collective category.

10 Kümin and Coster, Chs 7 and 6, this volume.

11 Maag, Ch. 8, this volume.

12 The classic text regarding such theories is Georges Lefebvre, *The Great Fear of 1789* (New York, 1973), in this case, gangs of brigands. C. Gauvard, 'Rumeur et stéréotypes à la fin du moyen âge', and C. Beaune, 'La rumeur dans le *Journal* du bourgeois de Paris', both in M. Balard, *La Circulation des nouvelles au moyen âge* (Paris, 1994), 157–77, 191–203.

13 For further discussion of conspiracy theories and their role in early modern society, see C. Ginzburg, 'Présomptions sur le sabbat', *Annales*, 39 (1984), 341–54; 'Le démon du soupçon' with M. Gauchet, *Histoire*, 84 (1985), 48–56; D. Groh, 'La tentation des théories de conspiration', *Storia della Storiografia*, 14 (1988), 96–118. For a stimulating study of the origins of the persecution of such groups in the medieval period, see R. I. Moore, *The Formation of a Persecuting Society: Power and Deviance in Western Europe, 950–1250* (Oxford, 1987). In an English context, the activities of Catholics were most feared: see R. Clifton, 'Fear of popery', in C. Russell, ed., *Origins of the English Civil War* (1973), 144–67, and P. Lake, 'Anti-popery: the structure of a prejudice', in R. Cust and A. Hughes, eds, *Conflict in Early Stuart England* (1989).

14 On collective fears see esp. Delumeau, *La Peur*, passim.

15 Mannoni, *La Peur*, 109–22; Delumeau, *La Peur*, 16–17.

16 Notably J. Delumeau, *Sin and Fear: The Emergence of a Western Guilt Culture, 13th–18th centuries*, E. Nicholson, trans. (New York, 1990); P. Camporesi, *The Fear of Hell: Images of Damnation and Salvation in Early Modern Europe*, L. Byatt, trans. (Oxford, 1990); C. M. N. Eire, *From Madrid to Purgatory: The Art and Craft of Dying in Sixteenth-Century Spain* (Cambridge, 1995). Marshall and Spicer, Chs 9 and 10, this volume.

17 Delumeau, *Sin and Fear*, 536–54.

18 Esp. Gentilcore, Eßer, Maag, Marshall, Spicer and Taylor, Chs 11, 4, 8, 9, 10 and 5, this volume.

19 R. W. Scribner, *For the Sake of Simple Folk: Popular Propaganda for the German Reformation* (Oxford, 1994); Crouzet, *Les Guerriers*.

20 K. Thomas, *Man and the Natural World: Changing Attitudes in England, 1500–1800* (1983); V. Fumagalli, *Landscapes of Fear: Perceptions of Nature and the City in the Middle Ages* (Stanford and London, 1994); B. Bennassar, ed., *Les Catastrophes naturelles dans l'Europe medié-*

vale et moderne (Paris, 1996). Jenner and Eßer, Chs 3 and 4, this volume.

21 Jenner, Roberts and Maxwell-Stuart, Chs 3, 1 and 12, this volume. R. Darnton, *The Great Cat Massacre and Other Episodes in French Cultural History* (1984).

22 Notably, Naphy and Maxwell-Stuart, whereas arson was largely a 'male' crime (Chs 2 and 12, this volume).

23 Bouwsma, 'Anxiety', esp. 225–31.

24 Notably, Muchembled, *Popular Culture*, and Lefebvre, *Fear*, as well as much of the recent work on witchcraft.

25 On the role of rumour, see Delumeau, *La Peur*, 147, 171–80; Mannoni, *La Peur*, 102–4.

26 Briggs, *Witches*, is an excellent guide to this reassessment.

27 It is significant that infanticide and sodomy both had far higher rates of execution than witchcraft: e.g. the Paris *Parlement* executed only 20 per cent of those it tried for witchcraft compared with 70 per cent for infanticide. See A. F. Soman, 'The Parlement of Paris and the Great Witch Hunt (1565–1640)', *SCJ*, 9 (1978), 31–44. Cf. E. W. Monter, who gives thirty deaths in sixty-two sodomy trials, 1555–1678 in his 'Sodomy and heresy in early modern Switzerland', *Journal of Homosexuality*, 6: 1/2 (Fall/Winter 1980/81), 51 n. 7; he also found that rates of execution for sodomy and infanticide were about the same. For general information on social and judicial attitudes to homosexuality see J. Boswell, *Christianity, Social Tolerance, and Homosexuality* (1980) and C. Spencer, *Homosexuality, A History* (1995). There are many works relating to women, sex and sexuality which touch upon infanticide, among other issues. One might suggest: on Italy and England, J. G. Turner, ed., *Sexuality and Gender in Early Modern Europe* (Cambridge, 1993); on Francophone areas, J. R. Farr, *Authority and Sexuality in Early Modern Burgundy* (Oxford, 1995); on England, Stone, *The Family*; on Scotland, R. Mitchison and L. Leneman, *Sexuality and Social Control, Scotland 1660–1780* (Oxford, 1989); and, on Germany, L. Roper, *Oedipus and the Devil. Witchcraft, Sexuality and Religion in Early Modern Europe* (1994).

28 Muchembled, *Popular Culture*, esp. ch. 1, 'A world of insecurity and fears', 14–42, and the attack on this approach by Clark, 'French historians and early modern popular culture', that it is 'founded on error' (78).

29 Naphy, Ch. 2, this volume.

30 Mannoni, *La Peur*, 113.

31 Gentilcore and Marshall, Chs 11 and 9, this volume.

1

Agencies human and divine: fire in French cities, 1520–1720

PENNY ROBERTS

> always insatiable and unjust ... it devours all, and respects neither
> churches nor royal palaces; whence doubtless comes that just fear
> which seizes the mind at the first news of fire or of conflagration.[1]

As this extract from Nicolas de Lamare's monumental treatise on the policing of Paris so vividly evokes, the fear of fire was a very real and constant
factor in the early modern European city, of concern to both authorities
and citizenry alike. The urban environment was extremely vulnerable to
destruction by fire and its impact could be devastating. A blaze could break
out without warning at any time and was a more regular and indiscrimi-
nate threat than either plague or famine, though not so rapacious in terms
of lives. Although the death toll was usually low, overnight an urban fire
could destroy livelihoods built up over many years or generations and
reduce even the wealthy to extreme poverty. For since fire primarily threatened property, it indiscriminately targeted both rich and poor. As such it
was often interpreted as a judgement from God, playing on the association
of fire with both hell and purgatory, as well as with purification.[2] Preachers exploited incidents of urban devastation by fire as a prompt to call for
moral reform and spiritual reflection. Fire was also a regular and effective
weapon in the armoury of early modern armies, used to both reduce and
demoralise the enemy; alternatively it could be employed by towns for
defensive purposes.[3] Thus, both the risk and consequently the fear of fire
were increased during periods of prolonged conflict with foreign powers.
Indeed, whether at the hands of God or of man, as Friedrichs states, 'of all
the elements ... that most persistently threatened the well-being of the
early modern city. The most dangerous element was fire.'[4]

On a more practical level, the destruction of property rendered many
destitute, forced to rely on handouts from the authorities. The cost of
reconstruction and relief to the victims, as well as the impact in the loss

and disruption of trade, were burdensome, and as a result fire prevention remained at the top of the municipal authorities' agenda. Their priority was to ensure that measures were taken to prevent fires breaking out in the first place, or if they did so to limit their progress, and these became increasingly sophisticated over time. Although the fear of fire could not be eradicated whilst major tragedies still occurred, the practical initiatives taken did go some way to alleviating concern. More worrying still was the possibility of arson, and a wide variety of measures were also introduced to counter this threat, as well as to bring the perpetrators to justice. Yet the identification of those held responsible usually reveals more about the prejudices and fears of those who wielded authority in the early modern city than it does about their ability to solve such crimes. Indeed, an exploration of the means by which the authorities in French cities sought to prevent, combat and mitigate the effects of conflagration, and how successful they were in this endeavour, exposes the persistence of such conservative attitudes alongside the more practical developments in fire-fighting methods.[5]

The frequency and danger of urban fires in this period is easily explained by the fact that wood was both the primary building material and the main source of fuel. Chimneys, too, were usually constructed of wood with the obvious attendant risks this entailed. The chief cause of urban conflagrations was the proximity of buildings, since flames could easily jump from one to another even across streets, in the narrowest of which the eaves could nearly touch. Even in wider thoroughfares inflammable substances piled in the street could aid dispersal. The risk was further heightened during the drier summer months when the timbers burned more easily, as well as during electrical storms when lightning might strike an exposed steeple or chimney-stack. In addition, all dwellings were kept warm and lit by a fire, and food cooked on a stove. Candles, lanterns and torches were used to light the residents' way at night both between and within buildings. Certain trades required furnaces (glassworkers, metalworkers, bakers) or the use of inflammable materials (carpenters and pharmacists). In Nantes in 1724, a fire was believed to have been caused by an unguent made for use in his work by a dentist.[6] Moreover, only a moment's negligence could be enough to allow a blaze to take hold. Fires were a particular hazard during public holiday celebrations or fairs due to the difficulty of policing large crowds and the increased likelihood of accidents and oversights. Vigilance over every unattended flame, candle, stove and lantern was clearly beyond the capabilities of early modern authorities. Nevertheless, they did what they could to combat the problem with specific legislation.

City ordinances stipulated basic precautions to be taken, including the

safe storage of hazardous substances and the provision of water outside each
house. After an incidence of suspected arson a lantern was to be placed outside at night to make concealment more difficult for the arsonists, and the
night-watch or *guet* was increased. Easy access to wells (or later, pumps)
was essential, and their ropes were to be regularly checked. In addition,
buckets and ladders were to be kept in good order by those responsible for
them.[7] The lighting of bonfires in the streets was repeatedly forbidden, even
on customary feast-days, such as at St John's and Corpus Christi, especially
if it was believed that arsonists might use them as a cover for their
activities.[8] Private fires were to be covered, raked over, and enclosed in the
evening, since it was at night when they were left unattended that they presented the greatest hazard. Concern was also expressed regarding the fires
that the members of the night-watch lit to keep themselves warm in the
colder months. Naked flames posed an obvious danger, especially in stables
or near timber, and the use of enclosed lanterns was encouraged. Nor were
lighted substances to be carried from one place to another unless in an
earthen or metallic vessel.[9] Further measures were aimed at the removal of
obstructions and inflammable materials. Workshops, chimneys, houses and
wells were to be kept clean; city streets and the naves of churches where
construction was going on were to be cleared. Following a fire in Troyes
in 1524, the cathedral chapter ordered the removal of the wood provided
for new stalls, as well as forbidding the ringing of the church bell because
it might alarm the people, and a month later decided to destroy the wooden
chimneys of their chapter houses before the city council had them torn
down.[10]

As a consequence of the particular risks their work entailed, those
trades that were specifically targeted in the fire prevention regulations,
notably metalworkers, leatherworkers, glassworkers and bakers, had their
workshops exposed to regular inspection. Over time the official net came
to be cast more widely, and activities deemed hazardous were less readily
tolerated. Nicolas de Lamare, for instance, expressed his irritation with
those who risked the safety of the Parisian citizenry by having baking ovens
and forges in their private houses.[11] Different groups were specified at different times and in different places according to where the greatest risk was
perceived to lie, but a common pattern emerges in the measures taken to
control their activities. Prohibition was the favoured weapon of the authorities; in Nantes in the early eighteenth century, candlemakers were forbidden to melt wax, whilst in Rennes the drying of gunpowder and smoking
of grain were of greater concern.[12] In Paris in the same period, there were
repeated admonitions to anyone involved with the storage of highly inflammable materials such as straw, or using fire regularly in their work, to take

all necessary precautions or risk heavy fines. A leatherworker was duly punished 'for having lit a fire for working on his leathers in the alleyway of the
house where he lives, causing a fire risk'.[13] Proprietors of *magasins de char-
bon* also faced stiff penalties, whilst it was ordered that cannon powder was
not to be stored near residential or public buildings. Of especial concern to
the Parisian magistrates was the uncomfortable proximity of the wooden
stalls and shops growing up beneath the *palais de justice* itself. Storing flammable materials and burning noxious substances, they posed both a fire and
a health hazard and were, therefore, threatened with demolition.[14] The pro-
posal that all these workshops should relocate their trade facilities from the
centre to the outskirts of the capital met with little success, despite the fact
that for many such enterprises it made sense to move to a more rural,
forested area, and thus closer to a more immediate and plentiful supply of
fuel.[15]

Two further locations frequently cited as trouble spots in fire regulations were port cities and bridges. Ports with their resident fleets and ship-
building yards were especially vulnerable, both to accidental and intentional
damage.[16] Naval regulations provided strict guidelines, and stern penalties,
for those on board ship who were careless with naked flames.[17] Bridges,
again usually constructed of wood, produced some spectacular fires in Paris
in the early modern period. Although de Lamare points out that since the
sixth century there had only been four major fires on Parisian bridges, and
only two in recent times, nevertheless, their impact proved traumatic. In
1621 the Pont Marchand to the Pont-au-Change was destroyed, and in April
1718, 'the cruellest ... of our age' on the Petit Pont saw twenty houses
burned down and fourteen demolished, though the inhabitants had feared
much worse since the fire had initially threatened to spread to the Hôtel-
Dieu and Notre-Dame.[18] It had reputedly been caused by a burning boat that
became stuck in the timber reinforcements of the bridge, which dated from
1627 when Louis XIII had needed to transport his cannons across the river
for his expedition to La Rochelle. Since then the planks had been added to
by the inhabitants of the bridge to make cellars for their houses, inadver-
tently providing a ready source of fuel for the blaze.

The most obvious long-term solution to fire prevention was to raze
wooden structures and replace them with less flammable materials.
Throughout the period admonitions to build in stone rather than wood were
issued, but only towards the end do we find injunctions which suggest that
such guidelines were regularly adhered to. Replacing plank coverings with
tiles or slates was one such measure, but the bulk of the regulations concerned the construction of chimneys.[19] Chimneys were increasingly to be
built in stone, and masons and carpenters were ordered to comply with

strict safety standards. Regular inspections of properties were carried out to ensure that they conformed to these standards, with crafts made responsible for supervising and checking on their members. The standardisation covered the materials used to build the chimney and its surround (including the use of metal rather than wooden fastenings), and the widths and thicknesses of the linings, all designed to prevent any fire that did break out from spreading to adjoining houses. The height of the chimney above the roof and the ease of access for cleaning were also matters of concern.[20] Chimney-cleaning was stipulated to be undertaken twice a year, in the spring and autumn, and it is in this period that chimney-sweeps emerge as a craft group with official privileges.[21]

As smoking grew in popularity during the early modern period it was reflected in additional provisions in fire prevention measures, urging smokers to be careful to extinguish their pipes safely. Equally, the proliferation of firearms in the seventeenth century added a further dimension to those concerns already addressed by legislation. Restrictions were placed on the storage of gunpowder and the throwing of fireworks and fuses, and specific prohibitions on the use of firearms in public places and on feast days.[22] Parents and employers were to be held responsible for the activities of their children and employees, suggesting that the young were the most likely to behave irresponsibly with firearms in the street, especially in the carnival atmosphere of public holidays that combined both high spirits and heavy drinking.[23] It is clear from the regulations that the possibility of starting a fire in this way, when the authorities would be otherwise preoccupied by the general festivities, was as much a cause for concern as the danger of inflicting personal injury.

Even the most vigilant and well-regulated regime could not hope to prevent all fires taking hold, and so provision also had to be made for dealing with them when they did break out. Basic advice to individual citizens that vinegar, snow, manure, urine or damp cloths could all prove useful in putting out a fire, evidently only addressed the problem of small-scale blazes. Even shouting for help or ringing bells when a fire had spread or was first detected would only be effective if there was some formal provision for further action to be taken.[24] Thus, the organisation of a rudimentary fire-fighting 'service' also came to be developed and supervised by the authorities. In the sixteenth century those employed for this purpose were drawn primarily from the building trade: carpenters, roofers, joiners and, increasingly, masons. This was also the occupational group against whom most of the regulations for fire prevention were aimed because of the nature of their craft, just as leatherworkers were targeted during outbreaks of plague for fear that the hides that they worked with might be a source of infection. Frequent orders were issued for carpenters to remove timbers from blocking streets because they acted as an obstruction, but primarily because they presented a serious fire hazard. At the same time, however, it was the building trades to whom the authorities looked to observe and enforce safety guidelines when constructing houses. Moreover, they were given the responsibility of discharging fire-fighting duties not just because their trades were the most vulnerable, but because they were able to provide the tools necessary to tear down buildings and thus to provide fire-breaks, the most effective and decisive way to prevent a blaze from spreading. The articles of the city of Strasbourg, issued in the early eighteenth century, stated that in the event of a fire all apprentice carpenters were expected to turn out, even visiting foreigners, as well as chimney-sweeps with their tools.[25] It was believed that such organisation and the construction of a firebreak saved the Hôtel-Dieu from destruction when the Petit Pont was set alight in 1718.[26] Yet, even with such tools, the rapid demolition of any building was no easy or quick task, and careful calculation had to be made regarding the speed and direction of the fire, inevitably provoking the antagonism of any whose house was condemned as a result.

Despite the evident concern of the authorities, this system was initially organised on a fairly *ad-hoc* basis, and its participants often paid in kind. This was the case in Troyes in the 1530s when fish, butter, bread, eggs, and an all-expenses-paid dinner, including wine, at the house of a member of the municipal elite, were provided.[27] Certain locations were specified for the storage of fire-fighting equipment, such as buckets, kept in forty houses in Troyes as well as at the town hall and the house of the *cordeliers*. Rewards were given to those who alerted the authorities to a blaze, as did a group of boys in 1588 and some roofers in 1593. In Nantes in 1547 payments were made to those who had provided the torches, buckets and hooks necessary for tackling a fire in the city suburbs.[28] Compensation was also provided for those who were injured in the course of carrying out their duties, as was the carpenter, Jacob Villote, who broke his leg and was awarded 100 *sols* for sustenance and 20 *sols* for his treatment, to cover medicines and the cost of surgeons.[29] Surprisingly little is recorded regarding the rescue or injury of those whose homes had burned down, suggesting that casualties were low because the progress of a fire was slow enough to allow time to escape, except for the old or infirm who required assistance.[30] In this regard, would-be-pillagers who arrived after the fact took the greatest risk.[31]

Although the fire-fighting system was gradually to become more formalised and regulated during the seventeenth century, the basic provision and apportioning of responsibility essentially remained the same. Hatchets of a regulated size were to be provided by all households in Rennes, and by the 1720s all those who paid over 300 *livres* in rent per annum were obliged to provide a regulation leather bucket (priced at 6 *livres* in 1735), whilst master craftsmen were not to be received until they agreed to do so at their own expense. If a bucket was destroyed during a fire, then the nearest dozen houses to the blaze were to cover the costs of a replacement. The buckets and other fire-fighting equipment, which bore the arms of the city, were to be kept at the town hall and returned there within twenty-four hours of a fire being extinguished. Copper tokens would be distributed during a fire to those who came to collect their equipment so that defaulters could be identified and punished.[32] In Nantes in the 1720s, six leather buckets were provided for each craft; a list was made of householders responsible for them, and regular checks on their condition were carried out.[33] Similarly a list of names and addresses of those responsible for fire-fighting was regularly kept, so that those who failed to turn up in the event of a fire could be reprimanded. At the same time substantial financial rewards and public recognition of their service were given to those who distinguished themselves whilst fighting a blaze.[34]

It is notable that, as the methods of combating fire developed, the duties involved were increasingly borne by all trades. As well as the obligation of carpenters and masons to provide their hatchets and hammers, coopers supplied vessels for carrying water, and carters, barrowmen and street porters provided transport and drew the water.[35] Metalworkers' tools were also required in some instances, presumably for much the same purpose as builders' tools.[36] The responsibility for the inspection and advice about the purchase of the essential leather buckets was undertaken by a master shoemaker in Rennes, a position much sought after.[37] De Lamare acknowledged that 'the most essential workers during fires are masons, labourers, carpenters and roofers', but he also included 'the city archers, the night watch and their officers'. Such groups were expected to keep order during fires, guarding against the collapse of buildings and protecting vulnerable property from the pillaging that often accompanied a fire, as opportunists took advantage of the ensuing chaos.[38] A hazard of a different kind was presented during a fire by people throwing their possessions out of windows or attics into the street; householders were advised to carry bulky wooden furniture to public places far from the blaze.[39] The property of fire-fighters also needed to be safeguarded, and as a consequence identifying marks were placed on their tools and commissioners made a record of these in case they went missing during a fire. In Rennes craftsmen were told that if any tools were damaged, lost or burned, then this must be reported immediately in order that replacements could be paid for by the community.[40] Buckets could also be stolen, and in one such case the river porters between Nantes and Orléans were suspected and their boats subsequently searched.[41]

The introduction of pumps (an innovation first developed in Flanders) at the end of the seventeenth century allowed for a more efficient and reliable flow of water that could be directed more effectively against a blaze. Paris established thirteen public pumps in October 1699, and in 1722 brought in seventeen more. Each had four wheels and was easy to manoeuvre, based on those already in use in London and Strasbourg; the Germans had reputedly developed the most advanced models, with metal rather than perishable leather used for the pipes.[42] Pumps represented both a long-term investment and a considerable short-term municipal expense, each costing over a thousand *livres*. In Rennes an additional burden was involved in the construction of a special building behind the town hall to house the city pump at an estimated cost of 331 *livres*; after the fire in 1720, four more were ordered from Holland, with eight men assigned to each (figure 1).[43] When the city sought information about the latest machines in 1735 it was sent a description and some illustrations of the models available, along with their prices and uses. The main feature was the ability to provide a constant flow of water by all but the smallest and cheapest version, which was suitable only for small fires but could also be used to water plants. In their search for the latest innovations, the authorities even obtained a recipe for a grease with which to preserve leather hose-pipes, to be applied twice a year.[44]

The introduction of pumps also resulted in a reorganisation and further regulation, including more regular pay, for those designated to man and look after the new equipment. In Strasbourg, each craft was put in charge of two pumps.[45] The team in charge of the Parisian pumps was to practise its drill regularly and its members were to be fined if they did not turn up, though a reward was no longer to be given to those who were first there or any penalty to those last on the scene of a fire, so as not to cause disputes.[46] In Strasbourg, 50 *livres* was the fine if there was a tocsin, 25 if not.[47] Pumps were to be checked twice a year; the locations of public pumps under the charge of the various craft groups was to be posted up; taps in squares were provided to prevent the need to dig up paving. In return for their service on the pumps, the team in Rennes were exempted from the onerous obligations of guard duty and from lodging soldiers. However, if they abandoned their duty during a fire they faced imprisonment.[48] Once again rewards, public recognition on posters, and compensation were granted to those who served their city well: 78 *livres* to carpenters, roofers and others in Nantes in 1752.[49] When a man died falling off a third storey whilst oper-

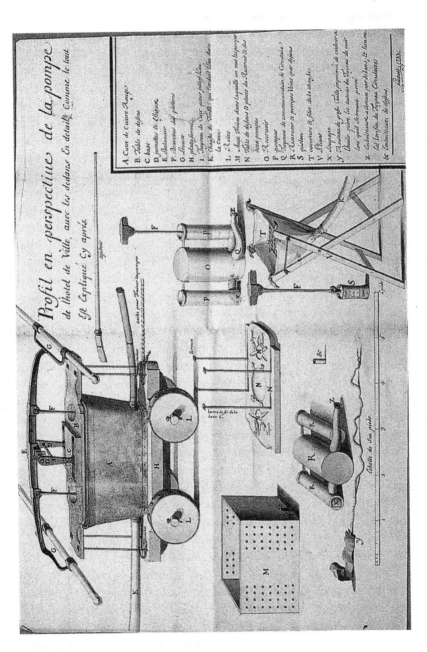

Diagram of the municipal pump at Rennes, by Huguet, 1722 (Archives municipales de Rennes)

ating a pump in 1724, his family received 450 *livres* from the municipality in compensation.[50]

In drawing up and updating their fire-prevention measures urban authorities looked to the experience of other cities for guidance, hoping to learn how best to avoid a similar calamity befalling them, just as Nantes looked to Rennes after the 'great' fire of 1720.[51] In this regard, the preventative measures subsequently introduced by the authorities of the devastated town were of particular interest. Alternatively, copies of another city's regulations might be requested or otherwise obtained, as Nantes did those of Strasbourg at the beginning of the eighteenth century.[52] The Strasbourg articles are particularly detailed and this may well be the reason for Nantes, at the other side of the country, having put them on file. The 1717 provisions list the instructions for and duties of forty named men responsible for fighting fires in the city: six were put in charge of wells, four were to look after those in danger and guard against pillage, ten were to man the pumps, four to clean wells and draw water, seven to carry water, four to chase off any rabble, and five to ensure that the rest were all pulling their weight and report any problems back to the commissioners.[53] The most curious provision in the articles is the prohibition against attaching lighted materials to the tails of dogs and cats or to swallows. Cats in particular are cited, along with wind, as a common means of spreading fire.[54] In other contexts in early modern France, bags containing live cats might be thrown on to bonfires as part of the ritual celebrations on feast-days.[55] As with firearms regulations, the main anxiety was the potential fire hazard rather than any injury sustained by the unfortunate animals concerned.

As we have seen, one of the primary concerns of the authorities, and doubtless also of the citizenry, was the safeguarding of property during fires, hence the repeated measures introduced against pillage. In the aftermath of the fire of 1720 in Rennes, inhabitants were requested to return all property taken during the fire to the town hall. The authorities were especially fearful that property recovered or stolen from the still smouldering ruins and transported elsewhere might be the cause of a second fire.[56] However, the most pressing problem regarding loss of property was the provision of relief for those left homeless or destitute. Following the fire on the Petit Pont in Paris in 1718, a collection was made for the victims, and the proceeds distributed according to need and the extent of the losses suffered, ranging from 30 *livres* to a *servante* to more than 12,000 *livres* to a cloth merchant. The total distributed was 111,898 *livres* 9 *sols* 9 *deniers*.[57] It was common for the Church to provide for the homeless in the immediate aftermath of such a tragedy, and in this case six months' shelter was granted in the Hôpital Saint-Louis.[58] A report was made of the damage done, with a list of houses completely destroyed or demolished and the names of their former occupants. In Nantes, as a consequence of a fire in 1682 which began at a chandler's, eleven houses were destroyed, eight gutted and twelve knocked down. Sixty-four families were ruined with losses of more than 150,000 *livres* estimated.[59] In 1724 parish collections were made and prayers said for the repose of the dead.[60] A further cause for concern was the destruction of grain supplies, especially at a time of dearth.[61] Not only did local individuals and congregations contribute to the relief of fire victims, but cities also gave donations to assist other urban communities, as in the case of Rennes and Châteaudun, devastated in the 1720s. Reconstruction was usually undertaken with royal aid, the Crown often allocating the revenue from particular taxes when approached by the authorities for assistance.[62] For instance, 10,000 *livres* were granted for the rebuilding of walls, bridges and other parts of the city of Troyes in 1524.[63]

The most destructive, or 'great' fires, as they were known, entered the popular memory and came to be seen as a landmark or watershed in the history and fortunes of a town, and are still viewed as such, in some cases, centuries later. The fire in Bourges in 1487, for example, is thought to have marked a downturn in the city's commercial prosperity because of the enormous cost of rebuilding at a time of economic adversity.[64] The deforestation and consequent steep rise in the price of wood for construction over the course of the sixteenth century made the cost of even the most basic building material formidable.[65] Indeed, in order to encourage victims of the fire to have their properties repaired or rebuilt, and to keep the part of town affected from falling into permanent decay, some form of coercion was often necessary.[66] The intention was to restore the life of the city to normal as soon as possible. Of additional concern was the danger posed by falling chimneys, obscured wells and debris accumulating in the city ditches. Carters in Rennes were threatened with fines if they failed to deposit materials within the designated area, whilst victims of the fire of 1720 were allowed to retrieve materials from the ditches for the purposes of rebuilding as long as they did not cause an obstruction.[67] Recycling is also evident following the fire in Troyes in 1524, when new church bells were cast from the molten metal left by the burning-down of the Belfroy gate.[68] The need to remove debris and rebuild following a fire also provided the opportunity to include additional safety measures, such as leaving greater distance between buildings and from walls. This policy reflected official awareness of the hazards, but as with construction in stone, often proved difficult to enforce, because of the pressures on urban space as populations and trade grew.

In the years following the fire of 1720, the city authorities in Rennes seized the opportunity presented by the destruction to undertake an ambitious and well-documented rebuilding programme. Several proposals were put forward 'to retrieve this unfortunate town from the ashes' without overburdening either the royal or public purse.[69] The favoured solution was the *tontine*, an innovation of the 1650s, whereby an association was formed whose members pooled their capital and in return received rent for their lifetime, in this case from the houses built as a result of their initial investment. It was envisaged that most of the participants would be those who had lost property in the fire, for whom it would reduce the expense of rebuilding, combined with outside assistance. The conditions and regulations were strict but designed to protect all parties. Building was to begin within six months of signing the agreement and only materials from the public store were to be used. Special access was granted to the royal forests to obtain the necessary wood, despite the protests of other interested parties, including the Navy; supplies of other materials were sought out, and the navigability of the rivers by which they would be transported assessed.

Architects and engineers come to the fore as town-planners, directors of the rebuilding project, and even as supervisors of fire-fighting in these documents, reflecting the rise of the profession and status of architect since the sixteenth century.[70] The substantial payments made to them continued up to 1738, an indication of the careful planning that went into the project, as well as the enormity of the task. Firstly, a detailed report was made of the location and measurements of all properties in the town, and a corresponding plan indicating those houses burned down and in need of replacement.[71] The man in charge of the programme at Rennes, *Sieur* Robelin, was able to make suggestions of both a practical and aesthetic nature to improve the layout of the city. These, of course, included measures to make the new houses less vulnerable to fire by decreasing the amount of timbers common to adjoining houses, reducing the number of partitions, restricting the number of storeys to two, roofing with tiles rather than wood, widening streets, as well as by suggesting ways to improve drainage and thus reduce contagion.[72] The town council looked at these proposals with due consideration for the cost and convenience to the inhabitants of undertaking such modifications. Petitions were also received from individual householders and religious houses who sought to reap some benefit from the damage inflicted on their property by suggesting improvements that might be made during the rebuilding. On the basis of the proposals for future fire prevention, the city approached the Crown for relief and measures to facilitate the provision of the necessary materials and labour. Of particular concern were the heavy impositions on the sale of drink, which had forced prices up and were believed to be deterring workers from seeking employment in the city.[73]

The deposition of an eye-witness to the fire, Pierre Villet, records that all had performed their duties as required, but that the speed and extent of the fire meant that firebreaks could not be created fast enough to prevent its spread. The deposition was both an opportunity to give a general report on the cause and course of the fire, as well as a more personal account of the difficulties faced and losses sustained.[74] In the months following the fire, two comprehensive *procès-verbaux* were conducted, the first a list of the owners, location, dimensions and estimated cost of the properties burned down or demolished, and the other a detailed ledger of the movable possessions destroyed.[75] The value of the individual losses ranged from 30 *livres* to a hefty 200,000 *livres*, claimed by the Marquis de Coëtmadeuc, to a total of 2,527,947 *livres*. A number of municipal and royal officials figure in the list, including the mayor and officials in both the *présidial* and *parlement*, which suggests that the claims would have received a sympathetic hearing.[76] Victims were particularly concerned about the destruction of title-deeds and other valuable family papers, as well as merchandise and other wares, especially textiles and books. More unusually, the church of Saint-Sauveur reported the loss of its parish register for the year 1720, and requests were made to the inhabitants of the parish to report any family baptisms, marriages or burials for that year to the rector so that records could be kept up to date.[77] The authorities had to make sure both that the claims for compensation were honest (some, for example, tried to claim for an entire house rather than just the one floor on which they had lived), and that those left homeless were not exploited by greedy landlords charging excessive rents. Householders were also expected, and eventually ordered, to take responsibility for the demolition of the unstable ruins of their houses left behind by the fire.[78]

Investigations into the causes of a fire and the effectiveness of the techniques used to combat it were undertaken so that the authorities could learn what measures they should take in future in order to be better prepared. In doing so, it was important to establish who or what was responsible for a fire. The household where the fire had begun was ultimately blamed for negligence, unless it could be proved that it was the result of an act of war, lightning or arson: that is, an outside agency, human or divine. The assumption that a divine agency was responsible was used by both Catholics and Protestants to argue that a fire was a sign that God was displeased with the citizenry and had sent this calamity to chastise them. Thus, the appropriate response was for the people to amend their ways and address the abuses that had incurred divine wrath. As a result, attempts were made to divert or quench fires through prayer or the use of the relics of a local saint, as was the case with those of Saint-Loup at Troyes in 1524.[79] The blaze could

also be followed by sermons designed to make some religious capital out of
the event, by encouraging greater displays of piety, congregational solidarity and generosity to the victims. Thus, natural forces such as lightning or
a strong wind acted as both a practical explanation for a fire and yet could
also be interpreted as having a supernatural origin. Even when other elements were present, fires were frequently explained in religious terms as
part of people's attempts to understand the tragedy that had befallen them.

A more evidently human agency was involved in instances of arson.
This could arise from private quarrels or could even, in certain circumstances, be believed to form part of an international conspiracy due to its
role as a weapon of war. The authorities encouraged the citizenry to inform
on their neighbours if they were negligent with regard to the usual fire precautions, but to do so 'amiablement'.[80] However, disputes between neighbours often seem to have arisen from a long-established enmity between the
parties concerned. Cases brought before the courts focused on the risks to
the safety of the life and property of the plaintiff due to either negligence
or malice, and culminated in accusations of deliberate fire-setting. In 1569,
a furbisher from Troyes tried to have one of his neighbours, a Huguenot
printer named Dureau, evicted because 'several times and for the last two
weeks fires had been lit at night in the said Dureau's house', threatening the
safety of properties nearby.[81] The 'great' fire in 1524, which destroyed up
to a quarter of the town, was said to have been the result of a disagreement
over the ownership of the house in which the fire started. A long lawsuit
conducted in the courts had decided in one man's favour but the losing party
was said to have threatened that his rival would never be allowed to enjoy
it.[82] Such accusations could be used to shift the blame for a fire on to another
(much as insurance claims can be exploited today), a ruse of which the
authorities were well aware. In July 1525, following a fire at Montargis, suspicion fell on the *vidame* of Chartres who was said to have harboured a
grudge against the inhabitants.[83] There was also concern that, as well as
being a weapon of vengeance, arson could be used as a means to cover up
evidence of other crimes.[84] It could certainly represent a more organised
criminal activity, and some appear to have made something of a career out
of it. On 20 May 1557, a twenty-four-year-old student from Amiens studying at the University of Paris was burned alive for setting fire to property
and for extortion – demanding money from others not to burn their houses
down. This individual was nicknamed *le cappitaine des bouttefeux*, 'the fire-
setters' captain', and his victims were doubtless relieved to see his reign of
terror brought to an end.[85]

Fire, as we have seen, was hazardous enough without the involvement
of wilful and malicious intent. The seriousness with which arson was viewed

is reflected in the harshness of the penalties meted out to its perpetrators, usually burning at the stake, thus equating it with those crimes that society considered most heinous: sodomy, witchcraft and heresy. This was not only because deliberate fire-setting was harder to guard against, but also because it put the whole community at risk. As a crime against the community it was associated with marginals, outsiders and the poor, especially vagrants, reinforcing both existing prejudices and community solidarity as a result of prosecution. Following the fire in Troyes in 1524 vagabonds were targeted and imprisoned in Paris, 'through suspicion and through fear'.[86] Blame could also be directed at enemy agents of foreign powers, as in the case of the Troyes fire, when Germans and Flemings were the main suspects, or as religious tensions grew, the Huguenots, common targets in the 1560s. Suspicion was cast on their activities during this decade in the cities of Dijon, Paris, Sens and Troyes.[87] As late as 1621, when the Pont Marchand to the Pont-au-Change in Paris burned down, Protestants were suspected, though the subsequent investigation found no proof to support this accusation.[88] Better documented are the reports of Reformed churches being burned down by Catholic arsonists, a regular occurrence in Brittany in the seventeenth century. The church at Cleusné near Rennes was repeatedly torched in 1613, 1654, 1661 and 1675.[89] Catholic churches in Protestant strongholds suffered a similar fate.

De Lamare believed that attitudes had been more relaxed in earlier centuries, when arson was not equated with conspiracy but was seen as the work of individuals who were simply ordered to pay compensation to the victims.[90] Arson was often more readily suspected than proven in the early modern period, and scares were probably more common than actual instances of deliberate fire-setting.[91] Nevertheless, the authorities were obliged to take all necessary precautions to prevent the danger or recurrence of arson. As a result of such fears, a curfew was imposed, and visitations made, especially to innkeepers who might be lodging strangers, a regular precaution when there was any possibility of an outside threat.[92] In 1524, following the fire in Troyes when a conspiracy was suspected, the Parisian authorities increased the night-watch, and citizens blocked up external entrances and windows to guard against arsonists throwing fireballs inside.[93] A reward and amnesty were offered to any of the conspirators who gave away their accomplices. By the early eighteenth century there was felt to be less risk of arson because of the introduction of a continuous guard at night and street lighting, so that the same precautions were no longer deemed necessary.[94]

Arson generated the most tangible fears with regard to fires in early modern French cities. It undermined all the efforts of the authorities to safeguard the citizenry and their property, efforts which became embodied in lists of regulations, fines for their contravention, and modifications to them as circumstances changed and experience was gained. Only so much could be done to prevent fires, as present-day domestic tragedies reflect, and, considering the limitations of technology and communications in the early modern city, fire-fighting is one area of urban life in which the authorities seem to have been as well prepared and efficiently organised as was possible, given the circumstances of the time. Methods remained fairly primitive, though the introduction of new pumps from Flanders made the job easier, and much still depended on the speed and efficiency of the human response. Authorities and citizenry worked together in a common interest in combating fire and the fire-setter, and relief efforts reflect a national concern for the victims. The King was petitioned for aid and, in turn, extended sympathy to the plight of his subjects. Conspiracy theories involving arson reveal the potential for panic that lay beneath the orderly regulations for fire prevention, but as far as possible the authorities sought to maintain calm, and the measures taken to deal with arson were in general as practical as the more regular provision. The fear of fire was combated by a sensible and effective means of dealing with the danger through regulations introduced by municipal authorities and dutifully observed by the majority of the citizenry. It was a danger that threatened the whole community, whose members were therefore expected to take responsibility for it, and it could both test and reinforce communal solidarities.[95] Whilst the provision of relief might override some of the existing tensions between different interest groups within society, the seeking of a scapegoat when suspicion of arson was aroused only served to strengthen the marginalisation of certain members of the urban community. As a result, fire in French cities in the early modern period, and the fears that accompanied it, generated trust and suspicion, solidarity and discrimination in equal measure.

Notes

1 Nicolas de Lamare, *Traité de la police* (Paris, 1705–38), 4: 136.
2 For a lengthier discussion of contemporary attitudes to purgatorial fire, see Marshall, Ch. 9, this volume.
3 For more on fire's defensive uses, see Coster, Ch. 6, this volume.
4 Christopher R. Friedrichs, *The Early Modern City, 1450–1750* (1995), 276.
5 Whilst the literature on urban fires in England in the early modern period is quite extensive, their French counterparts have been comparatively neglected: see, e.g., E. L. Jones, S. Porter and M. Turner, *A Gazetteer of English Urban Fire Disasters, 1500–1900* (Hist. Geog. Research Series, 13, 1984); M. Farr, ed., *The Great Fire of Warwick*, Dugdale Society, 36 (1992); Christopher Dyer, 'The great fire of Shipston-on-Stour', *Warwickshire History*, 8 (1992/93), 179–94; C. J. Kitching, 'Fire disasters and fire relief in sixteenth-century England; the Nantwich fire of 1583', *Bulletin of the Institute of Historical Research*, 54 (1981), 171–87; David Underdown, *Fire from Heaven* (1992). Many of the same pat-

terns emerge, and indeed it is clear that cities looked both at home and abroad for lessons on how fires might best be prevented. For a brief but useful comparative analysis see Friedrichs, *The Early Modern City*, 276–81.

6 AC Nantes, DD 369, no. 18.

7 BM Troyes, collection Boutiot, AA 32, folder 2, no. 1, 1532; AC Nantes, DD 330.

8 For example, Versoris, 147.

9 AC Nantes, DD 332, no. 4, articles 12 and 13, fol. 2.

10 AD Aube, G 1283.

11 De Lamare, *Traité de la police*, 4: 150.

12 AC Nantes, DD 331, 1720–85; AM Rennes, folder 236, 56 regulations of 1721.

13 BN Paris, MS fr. 21682, fos. 88–9, 1736; and for the other regulations, fos. 72–100.

14 BN Paris, MS fr. 21682, fos. 102–6.

15 H. Heller, *Labour, Science and Technology in France, 1500–1620* (Cambridge, 1996), 15–19 on the growth of rural-based industry in the sixteenth century. A similar suggestion was made at Rennes following the fire there in 1720: AM Rennes, folder 231; and folder 236, for restrictions on ovens.

16 BN Paris, MS fr. 21681, fos. 137–41, e.g. Marseille.

17 E. Sue, ed., *Correspondance de Henri d'Escoubleau de Sourdis* (Paris, 1839), 3: 345.

18 De Lamare, *Traité de la police*, 4: 159–60.

19 AC Nantes, DD 329; AM Rennes, folder 236.

20 AM Rennes, folder 236, 56 regulations for 1721.

21 BN Paris, MS fr. 21681, fos. 17–23; and 87–9 on privileges for *rammonneurs de cheminees*.

22 E.g. AM Rennes, folder 236, 1721.

23 BN Paris, MS fr. 21681, fos. 157–9, 165–6 and 180–1, and 21682, fos. 1–70.

24 As in the copy of the Strasbourg articles at AC Nantes, DD 332, no. 4, article 30, fol. 5r; articles 32 and 33.

25 AC Nantes, DD 332, no. 4, articles 72 and 73, fol. 12r. In 1721, Nantes's master roofers and carpenters were told to respond to the city tocsin with their apprentices and tools: AC Nantes, DD 328; cf. AM Rennes, folder 236, where any who disobeyed orders were to be imprisoned.

26 De Lamare, *Traité de la police*, 4: 158.

27 BM Troyes, Boutiot, AA 32, folder 2, no. 1.

28 AM Nantes, BB 3, no. 7, 2 Dec. 1547.

29 BM Troyes, Boutiot, AA 32, folder 2, no. 2.

30 In AM Rennes, folder 230, 22 Jan. 1721, Pierre Villet reported the problems of getting his aged mother to safety.

31 BN Paris, collection Dupuy, MS 698, fos. 28v–29r, Nicolas Pithou reporting on the fate of pillagers during the fire in Troyes in 1524.

32 AM Rennes, folders 231, 236 and 568 (formerly 698).

33 AC Nantes, DD 327.

34 E.g. AC Nantes, DD 369, nos. 65–7.

35 AC Nantes, DD 332, no. 4, articles 60–7, fos. 9–11; AM Rennes, folder 236, 1721.

36 AC Nantes, DD 369, no. 4 (1682).

37 AM Rennes, folder 236, supplication from master shoemaker to replace the late inspector; report of the master shoemaker, 1736.

38 BN Paris, MS fr. 21681, 25r; AC Nantes, DD 369, no. 4.

39 AM Rennes, folder 236, 56 regulations of 1721.

40 AM Rennes, folder 236.

41 AC Nantes, DD 369, no. 31.

42 De Lamare, *Traité de la police*, 4: 157.

43 AM Rennes, folder 236, 'Pompes et pompiers (1702–39)', 1702 and 1721.

44 AM Rennes, folder 236, 'pompes à boyaux', 1735; 'composition d'une graisse pour con-

server les tuyaux de cuir des pompes destinés aux incendies', 24 Apr. 1727.
45 AC Nantes, DD 332, no. 4, article 39, fol. 6.
46 E.g. BN Paris, MS fr. 21681, fos. 50–3 and 24v–25r.
47 AC Nantes, DD 332, no. 4, article 24, fol. 4.
48 AM Rennes, folder 236, 1721.
49 AC Nantes, DD 369, no. 66; also 65 (1739) and 67 (1766).
50 AC Nantes, DD 369, nos. 17, 23 and 25.
51 AM Rennes, folder 236.
52 AC Nantes, DD 332, no. 4 (originally 1688 and 1693), 107 articles, 19 fos.
53 AC Nantes, DD 332, nos. 3 and 6, 6 fos. (1717).
54 AC Nantes, DD 332, no. 4, article 17, fol. 3r, and article 12, fol. 2r.
55 E.g. on St John's Day, in the hope that such rituals would appease divine wrath; see J. Goudsblom, *Fire and Civilization* (1992), 133.
56 AM Rennes, folder 230, registers of the Parlement, 2 and 11 Jan. 1721.
57 BN Paris, MS fr. 21682, fos. 207–19.
58 De Lamare, *Traité de la police*, 4: 161–2.
59 AC Nantes, DD 369, no. 4.
60 AC Nantes, DD 369, no. 7.
61 As in Troyes in 1524, BM Troyes, Boutiot, A 6, fos. 172–8, council deliberations May–June 1524. Archives Nationales Paris, X²ᵃ reg. 76, fos. 300–1.
62 AC Nantes, DD 369, nos. 1–3, 1557; AM Troyes, Boutiot, A 6, fos. 172–8, town council deliberations, May–June 1524.
63 *Catalogue des actes de François Ier* (Paris, 1887–1908), 1: 380, no. 2020.
64 B. Chevalier, *Les Bonnes villes de France du XIVe au XVIe siècle* (Paris, 1982), 188.
65 Heller, *Labour, Science and Technology*, 86.
66 *Catalogue des actes de François Ier*, 1: 435, no. 2301; 457, no. 2420.
67 AM Rennes, folder 235, esp. 1721 and 1728.
68 T. Boutiot, *Histoire de la ville de Troyes* (Marseille, 1977), 3: 323.
69 AM Rennes, folder 231, 'Réédification et rétablissement de la ville (1720–23)'. The collection is not numbered and so dates are used as far as possible to indicate the different pieces.
70 AM Rennes, folders 231 and 236. Heller, *Labour, Science and Technology*, 87–8.
71 AM Rennes, folders 230, 2 Aug. 1722, and 231.
72 AM Rennes, folder 231, 27 Aug. 1722.
73 AM Rennes, folder 231, report to King, 1721, 4 fos. This despite the fact that the fire was believed to have been caused by the carelessness of a drunken carpenter.
74 AM Rennes, folder 230, 22 Jan. 1721.
75 AM Rennes, folder 696 (formerly 566), 10 Mar. 1721, 204 fos.; folder 697 (formerly 567), 27 Mar. 1721, 156 fos.
76 AM Rennes, folder 697, e.g. from fos. 144v (30 *livres*), 29r (Coëtmadeuc), 59v (mayor), 8r and 146r (*parlement*).
77 AM Rennes, folders 230, 27 Jan. 1721, and 697, fol. 127r.
78 AM Rennes, folder 230, 21 Jan. and 30 June 1721, 26 Sept. 1722, 14 Nov. 1723.
79 BN Paris, Dupuy, MS 698, fol. 28r; N. Desguerrois, *La Saincteté Chréstienne* (Troyes, 1637), 417. Cf. BN Paris, MS fr. 21682, fos. 141–2 and 203–6.
80 AC Nantes, DD 332, no. 4, article 23, fol. 4r.
81 AD Aube, G 1286, deliberations of the cathedral chapter (1569–72), 22 Aug. 1569.
82 BN Paris, Dupuy, MS 698, fos. 27 and 29.
83 Versoris, pp. 174–5.
84 J. R. Ruff, *Crime, Justice and Public Order in Old Regime France: The Sénéchaussées of Libourne and Bazas, 1696–1789* (1984), 139.
85 BN Paris, MS fr. 3952, fol. 138.
86 V. L. Bourrilly, ed., *Journal d'un bourgeois de Paris sous le règne de François Ier* (Paris, 1910),

200.

87 On Sens and Troyes, see BM Troyes, Boutiot, A 13, 15 Apr. 1562; and BB 14, folder
i, no. 25; on Paris, B. B. Diefendorf, *Beneath the Cross: Catholics and Huguenots in Sixteenth-century Paris* (Oxford, 1991), 80; and on Dijon, M. P. Holt, 'Wine, community
and Reformation in sixteenth-century Burgundy', *P&P*, 138 (1993), 62.

88 De Lamare, *Traité de la police*, 4: 159.

89 AM Rennes, folders 344 (1601–54) and 345 (1661–1720). J.-Y. Carluer, *Protestants et
Bretons: la mémoire des hommes et des lieux* (Carrières-sous-Poissy, 1993), 87–93.

90 BN Paris, MS fr. 21682, fos. 147–54.

91 On arson scares in this period, see P. Roberts, 'Arson, conspiracy and rumour in early
modern Europe', *Continuity and Change*, 12 (1997), 9–29.

92 E.g. BM Troyes, Boutiot, AA 32, folder 2, no. 1.

93 Versoris, 142; Michel Félibien, *Histoire de la ville de Paris* (Paris, 1725), 2: 952; *Journal
d'un bourgeois de Paris*, 200.

94 De Lamare, *Traité de la police*, 4: 137.

95 Cf. community action and reaction in the face of plague and flood; see William Naphy
and Raingard Eßer, Chs 2 and 4, this volume.

2

Plague-spreading and a magisterially controlled fear

WILLIAM G. NAPHY

Intentional, conspiratorial plague-spreading was an enduring and recurring threat to societies in the Western Alps. Aristocratic, ecclesiastical, republican and monarchical regimes were all threatened. Religious divisions seemingly had no effect on governmental approaches nor inter-communal co-operation. Catholics, Calvinists, Lutherans and Zwinglians happily and enthusiastically worked together to identify, prosecute and execute the conspirators for over a century (c.1530–1645). However, the only major treatment of this phenomenon is by Monter.[1] His study is a statistical examination of the incidence of witchcraft and judicial responses to it.[2] He believes that the accused plague-spreaders were involved in 'a terrifying form of diabolical activity'.[3]

On 4 June 1543, two servant girls, who washed linens and fumigated infected houses (*cureuses*) in the Rhône were arrested on the suspicion that they were wilfully spreading plague.[4] The authorities became even more concerned when a Bernese jurist at Thonon sent Geneva's magistrates information obtained under torture from one Bernard Dallinge, a male linen-washer from Cervens in Savoy. He confessed that he had assisted a certain Jean Dunant (alias Lentille) – then working as a private linen-washer and barber-surgeon in Geneva – in preparing an ointment for spreading the plague.[5]

An investigation was begun by the Lieutenant, Geneva's chief legal officer. All subsequent prosecutions sprang from details extracted from Lentille. The assumption of the authorities was that Lentille, and the others, were guilty, although their investigation failed to produce significant corroborative evidence against the barber-surgeon.[6] Lentille's markedly short confession was enough. After lengthy and fatal torture, he supposedly uttered but one phrase: 'If you want to clean up everything, then seize everyone from the hospital.' Given such sound advice, the magistrates acted quickly and decisively.[7]

Lentille was accused of removing a putrefying foot from a corpse exposed on the city's gibbet. He then cooked the foot to remove the fat and combined this with secretions collected from the pustules of deceased plague victims.[8] He was also accused of making various powders by similar repulsive means.[9] The resulting ointment could be applied to walls, windowsills, doorposts, objects left on the pathway and, as powder, could be placed in food.[10] When touched, or ingested, plague would be contracted. The conspirators, as fumigators and linen-washers, would then be able to enter the homes of their victims and loot the valuables.[11] Also, by prolonging the plague outbreak they would secure their jobs as plague workers. It is clear from the records that their salaries and terms of employment were very good indeed.[12] Their position was strong enough to bargain with the magistrates, ensuring that their heirs would be paid for any quarter in which they worked and died. Such an arrangement was unheard-of in Geneva.[13]

Who were these people accused of attempting to destroy Geneva by plague? The *typical* plague-spreader of 1545 was a woman, fairly poor, with no local family connections, a hospital worker (*cureuse*), a Genevan resident with no civic rights and a Savoyard.[14] Indeed, the early regulations from 1505 on fumigators make it clear that this hiring profile was intentional.[15]

Finally, it was alleged that these conspirators had bound themselves by an oath: 'to give their bodies and souls to the Devil and, under pain of three applications of the *strappado*, to declare nothing'.[16] One might well compare the words of the pastors. At the onset of plague they were asked to provide a minister for the victims. In their response, which shocked and angered their citizen employers – the pastors were also foreigners – the ministers said that they would rather 'to go to the Devil'.[17] This 'demonic' reference eerily echoes the supposed oath of the plague-spreaders.

However, no contemporary writer, chronicler, council minute or court document explicitly identifies plague-spreading – a form of conspiratorial poisoning – with witchcraft.[18] For example, two women prosecuted in 1545 also confessed to attending a Sabbath. They were condemned as plague-spreaders *and* witches: the official verdict is quite clear that this is an additional charge. All subsequent histories continued to view the crime as a poison conspiracy.[19] When does this identification of plague-spreading with witchcraft enter the historiography? In 1899, Doumergue published his monumental, some would say definitive biography of Calvin.[20] In it he discussed the plague-spreaders.[21] His next section related cases of witchcraft in nearby Peney. His transition sentence between these two events says, 'Sadly, the affair of the plague-spreaders was followed almost immediately

by that of the witches. Is there a great deal of difference between them?'
After this, the historiographical identification of plague-spreading and witchcraft is both consistent and unanimous.

However, there is another consideration. Is this in fact a forfeit oath?
In fact, a careful reading of the council records yields another version:
'[They swore,] under pain of the three applications of the *strappado* and
giving their bodies and souls to the Devil, to declare nothing.'[22] So much
for being 'technically in league with the Devil'.[23]

This phenomenon, however, has another side: the magistrates. Time
and again, they were forced to react to a grave threat to communal safety.
Inevitably, the appearance of plague led to the appointment of hospital
workers, then accusations, prosecutions and executions. Although this essay
will focus on the two outbreaks of the 1540s and 1570s, the story begins in
1530 with the first appearance of plague-spreading.

The 1530 event which first attracted magisterial interest was the dropping of a handkerchief. The hospital's barber-surgeon, Caddo, was noted
dropping – most probably by accident – a handkerchief on the roadway. It
gave off an horrific stench. Immediately, the doctor was accused of endan-
gering public health. Under questioning and torture, he implicated his wife,
a few workers and the hospital's father-confessor in a plague-spreading conspiracy. The case was brief, the executions quick. The city alerted the towns
and villages in its vicinity of the danger – case closed.[24]

Any lessons which might have been learned and passed on were swept
aside in the subsequent political, social and religious conflict. Geneva
declared its independence from Savoy, deposed its Prince-bishop, embraced
the Reformation, and expelled its educated, wealthy Savoyard elite.[25] The
records of the trial remained but the magistracy was altered beyond recognition.

The question to be examined here is how the affair was next brought to the
State's attention, how the magistrates reacted and what, if any, steps they
took to control the situation. Although the (aforesaid) June 1543 investigation is considered the first action taken, the magistrates were already
alerted. On 5 May 1543, Lausanne's authorities wrote to report the arrest
of a suspected plague-spreader.[26]

Plague had been present in Geneva since September 1542. An *hospi-
talier*, barber-surgeon, guard and minister were arranged to serve the
infected. No attempt was made at this early date to hire any cleaners or
fumigators. Basic precautions were taken: repairs were made to the plague-
hospital, a separate cemetery was opened, servants hired, even spies dis-
patched to Nyon to watch Germans suspected of being infected.[27] Not until

a fortnight later does one see male and female servants being hired who might be fumigators. Private fumigators are mentioned in November; the city ruled that the cleaning of infected houses should be at the owner's expense. Within four days, however, the city was forced to confront the issue of state-employed fumigators and their salaries. According to 'the ancient usage' the fumigators were assured that their salaries would be paid to their heirs should they die on the job.[28] This set the stage for the later accusations of plague-spreading both for larcenous profit and secure employment. This provision guaranteeing wages – a health and life-insurance policy – was unique. No other state employees were in a strong enough position to gain, or more accurately, extract this concession.

When did the magistrates begin to evidence unease about the fumigators? Unintentional plague propagation was an immediate and obvious concern. For example, the fumigator Angellin Berthier was investigated for chatting with a healthy young lady as early as December 1542.[29] This initial problem was allowed to die away as the preliminary bout of plague had abated by the end of February 1543 and the workers were sent home.[30] By mid-April, though, plague returned.[31]

Intentional plague-spreading seems to have come to the magistrates' attention that month when François Boulat was arrested and tortured seven times. He confessed nothing but was kept jailed while being investigated.[32] The case languished and in no way discouraged the State from hiring a large number of linen-washers. In May there was a rumour that fumigators were entering non-infected houses; a report was ordered. At this point the magistrates assigned two guards to watch the workers. A week later two grave-diggers, Fiollet and Tallien (both later executed), were dismissed without explanation. In a somewhat bizarre twist a barber-surgeon, Bernard Tallien (almost certainly the grave-digger), was asked to examine the body of Jean Pernet, the hospital's deceased barber-surgeon. Two days later, on 4 June, the two young girls were arrested for plague-spreading. On 8 June 1543, extra precautions were ordered at the gates after rumours of nocturnal plague-spreading.[33]

July saw more problems. Jean Grangier, a barber-surgeon, asked for work at the hospital but was considered suspicious because of unspecified associations with Caddo (from 1530). Three days later the city set up guards because grease (graisse) was being smeared on doors. In less than a month, the guard was strengthened – more grease had appeared. This is an important event; for the first time the issue was discussed not only by the Senate (of twenty-five men) but before the larger Council of Two Hundred. No wonder – the grease had caused a 'very great commotion'. Fascinatingly, although the grease had killed people, the magistrates confessed they did not know if this was 'from plague or poison'.[34]

Poor Boulat reappears at this point. One might expect that he would be a likely target for blame in any supposed conspiracy. Rather, it is clear that he had been arrested for unintentional plague-spreading; he had buried a plague victim and then come to Geneva. Despite repeated torture, the city could discover no more and released Boulat five months after his arrest.[35]

In December the plague ceased and with it the State's interest in plague-spreaders and grease.[36] It is worth pausing at this point to reflect on the magistrates' approach to containing the chaos and fear accompanying a major outbreak of plague. The burdens placed on the senators were extreme. They were forced to micro-manage the situation: the Senate had to settle the barber-surgeon's demand for white rather than red wine.[37] Moreover, problems abounded with the fumigators. They had to be continually watched and were constantly wandering about when forbidden.[38] However, these troubles were of a practical, managerial nature and never extended to linen-workers and *engraisseurs*. Nevertheless, plague-spreading or poisoning by grease was a concern and the only aspect of the plague containment campaign taken to the larger council.

The behaviour of the magistracy is obviously reactive. Geneva's rulers were simply responding to events; they seem barely in control. Although troubled by events at the hospital, the magistrates did not seem overly suspicious.[39] Nor was there any perceived threat from the fumigators beyond fear of petty theft and accidental plague-spreading. More importantly, there is no hint that the senators or citizens suspected a conspiracy. It is crucial to realise that the appearance of grease did not immediately or necessarily recall the conspiracy of 1530 (even though Grangier proves that the magistrates were aware of the earlier trials). Finally, there is not the slightest notion of any supernatural activity – the perceived threat seems to have been that certain malicious individuals were spreading a poisonous grease. No motives were preconceived, no perpetrators identified, no conspiracy suspected – and no elite 'hidden agenda' apparent.

Although nearby towns were afflicted, Geneva saw no more disease until August 1544. Basic precautions were again instituted. Fumigators were organised and instructed where on the Rhône to wash linens.[40] Chaultemps, the senator responsible for the hospital, complained that the fumigators would 'obey nothing'. He was told to threaten them with jail and punishment.[41] His complaint, as before, was based on problems of management. The situation changed on 5 January 1545 when reports came from Thonon. More details, requested by Geneva, arrived on 22 January and Lentille, a plague-worker (*marron*), fumigator and barber-surgeon, was arrested.[42] Ironically, the arrest coincided with the plague's abatement.

Freed from distraction, the magistracy turned to Lentille's case with enthusiasm and wrote for more information. The officials went so far as to send Lentille to Thonon, through Bernese territory, to confront him with his accuser. Three senators and the Senate's secretary escorted him. The whole Senate was present at the subsequent examination and torture of Lentille upon his return. The city decreed that the investigation to uncover accomplices should proceed 'day by day, hour by hour'.[43] They also appointed 'faithful men' to guard after yet more grease was discovered on doors.[44]

In marked contrast to attitudes apparent in 1543–44, the senators now explicitly suspected the hospital workers. Tyvent Furjod, a guard at the hospital, was 'suspected because of his great familiarity with the fumigators ... who are, for the most part, greasing the doors'; he was investigated. The same day, the city ordered that all the fumigators be rounded up in a street and searched bodily for boxes of grease.[45] Lentille's torture proceeded the same day but he was fatally injured on the third application of the *strappado* and, despite the frantic efforts of three barber-surgeons, died. His one statement, noted above, became the basis for all subsequent prosecutions.[46] The prosecutions followed so swiftly that citizens charged with maintaining the hospital complained that, apart from Furjod (who was suspected) and six patients there was no one left at the hospital – they were all in jail. Other citizens took private action. City guards reported vigilante patrols of *anti-engraisseurs*. Moreover, vagrants and beggars were herded into the cathedral cloister and searched.[47]

The senators also had external concerns. Neighbouring communities wanted details and sent information which might interest Geneva's authorities. Letters arrived from Lyon on 11 March 1545.[48] Catholic Lyon asked about the Genevan cases, and later wrote thanking the city for information and reporting that their careful search of Lyon had failed to uncover any criminals.[49] Another report arrived from Brig (Vallais). However, this letter did not request information but provided it. Brig had also caught a plague-spreader with Genevan connections.[50] Indeed, Petitjean, their prisoner, had confessed under torture to trying 'to depopulate' Geneva. Nine accomplices were named, including Louis Papegay, an innkeeper in Geneva, and Louis Danan (probably the Louis Dunant executed for plague-spreading).[51] Most other names correspond with no known persons.[52] Protestant Geneva replied by rushing off letters to the Bishop of Syon and the Catholic Governor of Vallais for a copy of the transcript.[53]

Within a week the senators had visited the prisoners numerous times and decided to make a judgement 'as quickly as possible'. Also, the senators, for the first time, referred to the phenomenon both as a *conspiracy* and an *enterprise*. The hasty trials were interrupted by the ferocious return of plague in April. Necessity dictated to the city and the poor – although executing fumigators by the handful, the city hired Martinaz, wife of François Dupuis, as a new linen-washer. Indeed, by the cruellest twist of fate, the city had to pay two new fumigators to clean the prison where the inmates were dying of plague.[54] Peculiarly, no orders were issued to guard these new fumigators.

The change in the magistrates' approach to plague-spreading from 1543/44 to 1545 could hardly be more dramatic. What can account for this difference? There is one new element introduced into the situation – conspiracy. Before Lentille's arrest there was a certain complacency about the spreading of grease. Unable to identify even one perpetrator, the magistrates did no more than post guards to stop the crimes and to reassure the populace. Once an individual was identified and a conspiracy explicitly apparent the city moved rapidly and ruthlessly to identify and neutralise all conspirators.

This again highlights the reactive nature of the magisterial approach. Rather than launching a strenuous investigation in 1543–44, the city posted guards. Despite questionable behaviour by the fumigators, the rulers only set them watchers. Even the prosecutions have a reactive element. All stemmed from accusations made by other conspirators – the confession at Thonon led the way. In other words, Geneva failed to make any independent identification, arrest or prosecution. Moreover, the city failed to conclude that the plague-containment system might be inherently flawed. Once the conspirators were identified and eradicated the city happily returned to the previous methods – the *status quo ante*. There was no conclusion that poor, foreign, female plague workers were dangerous or suspicious. If there is some form of stereotyping or scapegoating here it is certainly unintentional, indeed, unconscious.

We now turn our attention to whether or not any lessons had been learned from the previous events by the time of the next plague outbreak in 1567–71. The situation was much more serious, as Geneva faced not only a health crisis but the threat of attack from Savoyard and Imperial armies.[55] Moreover, the city was in the grip of a series of witch prosecutions.[56] Despite these dangers and concerns, no precautions were taken to prevent plague-spreading, no link was made between the witches and possible greasers, and no efforts were made to contain the disease – no fumigators were hired. The 1567 advent of plague was swift and mild; the moment it abated the few servants at the hospital were sacked to save money. However, the respite was short-lived; the plague returned in May 1568.[57]

The city seems to have taken more practical measures than in the 1540s outbreak. The Senate ruled that children born to citizens outwith Geneva in the next three months were legally citizens.[58] The clear implication of this – and a strikingly noticeable difference from the previous outbreaks – is that a significant portion of the elite was contemplating flight to the countryside.

Geneva also began to take active steps to prevent plague-spreading. In June 1568, a patrol was established and it was decreed that lanterns had to be carried after 9 o'clock. This was explicitly to forestall plague-spreading – regardless of the apparent lack of any threat.[59] In other words, this is a proactive approach by the magistrates. But was it? Can it be pure coincidence that the next day the guards reported that three different houses had been greased on the patrol's very first night?[60] There are three possibilities: this was the first appearance of grease; grease had been there but no one had noticed; the new rules were actually a reaction to grease. The latter seems the more plausible.

The magistrates had learned one simple and valuable lesson, however: when in doubt, suspect the fumigators. Rules were approved confining the fumigators at night. Perhaps this explains why the senators felt free to economise and disband the patrol, replacing it with a dozen guards. In the end, after three days of work, the guards reported that they had found neither grease nor greasers. The patrol which had been abandoned was re-established seventeen days later, when rumour spoke of more plague-spreaders.[61] Again, a purely reactive short-term move. While the guards patrolled there was no grease, so the magistrates disbanded the patrol; grease returned and so too the patrols. What does not appear is any connection between the presence of the patrols and the absence of the grease!

Clearly the magistrates had to maintain a delicate balance. Patrols encouraged the populace to think that plague-spreaders were about.[62] Not patrolling invited the appearance of grease and charges of senatorial negligence. A similar concern can be seen in the change forced upon the magistrates in dealing with the fumigators. It made logical sense to confine them at night. However, people did not care for their working in the daytime. After all, during the day the streets were crowded and no one wanted to bump into a fumigator labouring under a burden of infected linens. The Senate was forced to order that fumigators could only operate from 9 p.m. to 3 a.m. Clearly, juggling public sensibilities, good hygiene, and crime prevention was difficult. By October 1568, the plague was lessening, workers were released and the situation calmed. Nevertheless, complaints were made against fumigators and guards posted in response.[63]

Plague returned to the city with spring. The city convened a general council of magistrates, medics, barber-surgeons, and apothecaries on 2 May 1569 to consider a 'Reformation of Medicine'.[64] The new 'Medical Ordinances' were approved and announced throughout Geneva on 11 May.[65] This internal reform was of little help externally and the city found itself increasingly cut off by a *cordon sanitaire*.[66]

By August there were again complaints about the fumigators, but these related only to the basic health regulations: they were washing at a forbidden spot on the Rhône. Plague-spreading was still confined to the unintentional. The death-rate was making disposal of bodies a serious problem with too few mass graves available. Also, the city feared the contagious threat posed by cats and dogs.[67] By September, however, public opinion began to pressurise the senators. People complained about the presence of fumigators but were told to tolerate them. It is clear, though, that the fumigators were viewed with suspicion because of their necessary and legal contact with the infected rather than any conspiratorial threat. Moreover, the magistrates regularly noted the total disregard of the regulations by the general populace. In the end Geneva survived this second year of plague without serious problems with *engraisseurs*. The plague lessened in November. By December, the Senate was discussing cleaning the city to avert the disease's return in spring. Not surprisingly, meetings were held with medics, barber-surgeons and apothecaries, but on this occasion nurses and 'wise women' were consulted as well.[68]

In February, the magistrates braced themselves for more plague. The regular rules were restated. Specific guidelines for fumigators were spelled out. Their advantageous salary and death-benefit package was reaffirmed. For the first time, 'masters of fumigators' were mentioned and housed at public expense. Also, the magistrates attempted to control every aspect of the fumigators' work: nothing was to be done without prior consent. There was no sign of plague or *engraisseurs*, and this is the first evidence of a preventative and proactive policy on a grand scale. In a very real sense, the Senate was preparing Geneva for plague and its attendant threats. A few days later, this trend continued when the Senate began a series of meetings with ministers and medical workers to outline a plan of action and, especially, to care for the poor. This extended to discussions with Gex about co-operative, inter-communal action. By April, the magistrates noted with relief that plague had not returned. The celebration was short-lived, however, as the city was struck in early May.[69]

This outbreak was very serious indeed. The Senate was advised by its health committee that quarantine and seclusion were not working; people should be allowed to flee. The lack of ministers and the scarcity of worshippers resulted in the temporary closure of one of the four city churches. In the midst of these momentous decisions the city was distracted by the fumigators. Apparently they had been overcharging for their services. (They were allowed to ask a fee of those who could afford to pay, thereby augmenting their generous state salaries.) Senator Colland assembled them, read out their names and addresses from the roll – the first mention of such a record book – and forbade excessive charges. Apart from this digression the year passed without note. No plague-spreading was recorded and no other complaints were raised against the fumigators. The plague abated in October and normal sermons were restored the following month. By January there was not a single infected person to be found.[70]

At this point, Geneva had been afflicted by plague for three years. Each outbreak was worse than the last. By 1570, the social fabric was beginning to fray. Despite the length of the outbreak it was not until the end of the third year that the magistrates sat down to consider truly preventative and preparatory measures. More surprising, though, is the lack of plague-spreaders, anti-fumigator activity, paranoia about conspiracies or any attempt to apportion blame. Considering the previous experiences with fumigators, the general dislike and distrust of them, and the isolated appearances of grease in 1567, this fairly calm situation is remarkable. Why is there no mass persecution? If one presupposes that the basic magisterial approach is wholly reactive then the lack of plague-spreaders is due to their absence. That is, the magistrates never seem to have decided actively to seek them out. In 1530 and 1545, Geneva's rulers were presented with *faits accomplis* – plague-spreaders were dropped in their laps. Once a criminal was identified the judicial and prosecutorial system went into overdrive. It was the (accidental) apprehension of an *engraisseur* – greasy-handed – which led to an investigation, not the appearance of grease, nor the rumour of plague-spreaders or even previous bad experiences with fumigators.

Battered and wearied by plague, the city's all-too-brief break drew to a close. The next year proved to be the worst in Geneva's history. Sooner than anticipated, in February, the disease struck. Meetings were held with medical workers. The need for more women in the hospital was noted. The health committee was named. Lengthy regulations were considered.[71] The pre-emptive and proactive approach of 1570 was swept away by the sudden and unexpected return of plague. Geneva returned to a reactive mode.

However, the severity of this outbreak swamped the ability of the magistrates to react. On 7 May they noted the disease's increase and the multitude languishing unaided. By 11 May the harshness of this advent was noted. Now, rumour of *engraisseurs* returned with a vengeance. Guards were posted and 'every foreigner suspected' of being a potential plague-spreader.[72] This seems to be but one manifestation of the anxiety (*angoisse*) which swept the populace. Indeed, Geneva teetered towards collapse. The ministers and medical workers reported that they were overwhelmed by the numbers. The magistrates despairingly asked the ministers how to placate God. With obvious relief, the Senate's secretary recorded that 'good hope' had returned with the plague's lessening. Regulations were relaxed in January 1572.[73]

The city was still clean in mid-March but a fortnight later the disease returned. Thoughts of plague-spreading still centred on the unintentional variety. Grave-diggers were in continual trouble both for their excessive prices and for violating quarantine. However, this outbreak was clearly less virulent and by August had ceased entirely, to the evident joy of magistrates and citizenry. Indeed, the only reference to plague-spreaders in 1572 was by Magdeleine Ros, who said 'the rulers and people here are grease-spreaders'; she was banished for her malicious opinions.[74]

On the surface, the magistrates' behaviour in this lengthy outbreak was identical to that of 1530 and 1545. The reactive predominated. There was a slight drift towards preventative and preparatory action, both relating to plague generally and plague-spreading specifically. However, the change is minimal and only applies to early 1570. In one major area there was a difference. In reality, this outbreak saw the greatest number of prosecutions (115) and executions (44) for plague-spreading. Some may well wonder why no mention of this has been made heretofore. This is because I have been confining my remarks throughout to the magistrates' behaviour and views as apparent from the Senate's deliberations. In both earlier outbreaks the magistrates were so concerned with the phenomenon that they took personal responsibility for the examination, torture and sentencing of the accused. There was no necessary institutional reason for their direct involvement. They were concerned – indeed, afraid – and took complete control. By 1572 the Senate seemed confident enough of the handling of the situation to allow the courts and prosecutorial bureaucracy to deal with the issue. Indeed, reading the Senate's debates one would not be aware that any organised greasing had happened. For example, the secretary did not even note the receipt of a letter warning of a plague-spreader apprehended at Lausanne who had confessed to crimes in Geneva.[75] Thus, there is fear but it is confidently controlled by the magistrates rather than something which controlled them.

This behaviour became the norm by 1614. This final outbreak of plague-spreading is noteworthy for total silence. There is overwhelming evidence of the State's interest in the advance of plague towards Geneva. For example, most neighbouring towns and villages are noted as afflicted.[76] But the magistrates seem to rest secure in their regulations and the ability of the system to cope with the disease and any crimes. From the Senate's records one can barely tell that plague struck. Moreover, there is not a single reference to plague-spreading. Not only had Geneva developed a preventative approach which they trusted, but the magistrates became almost blasé.[77] The 1614 outbreak was less severe, but even taking that into consideration one is struck by the difference in attitude between 1614 and earlier outbreaks. For example on 17 August 1614, after a review of the city's populace, the magistrates decided to expel undesirables before the disease's arrival. The result: 440 people – mostly women – were thrown out (this when the population was between 15,000 and 20,000).[78] Seemingly, this represented the domestic service population. Most were single girls from Geneva's rural hinterland. What is perhaps most noteworthy about this decisive and unprecedented move is that there is no implication that it was associated with any threat of plague-spreading or even the presence of the disease, merely its proximity. It is simply the most obvious manifestation of the magistrates' 'battening down the hatches' as the storm clouds of plague gathered.

Over the course of eighty years the magistracy moved from a purely reactive approach to plague containment to a proactive policy of plague prevention. The move was cautious but continuous. It could be delayed by sudden changes in the situation, such as an unexpected return of plague. However, in preventing or stopping plague-spreading there is little change in policy. The city was wholly dependent on fumigators and the magistrates knew it – as did the fumigators. Any attempt to provide greater oversight for the work of the linen-washers caused problems with the citizenry. In reality, the greatest trouble the rulers faced in controlling the fumigators was that which beset them at every turn: most people ignored the plague regulations. The one substantial development over time is the increasing lack of interest among the city's leading magistrates about engraisseur prosecutions. They quite honestly were not concerned and by 1614 took no collective official notice of the phenomenon. This is symptomatic of the general change from containment to prevention. The leadership increasingly relied on its bureaucratic and judicial system to deal with problems.

A few other points must be made. First, there seems to have been no attempt by magistrates or citizens to scapegoat fumigators specifically. If anyone is 'automatically' suspected of plague-spreading it tends to be strangers or the poor. Experience notwithstanding, the eye of suspicion did not inexorably turn on fumigators. This is symptomatic of the basic feature of plague-spreading which upset the magistrates, conspiracy. This is what frightened them more than anything else. Unless they suspected group activity, they preferred not to disturb the peace of the populace. Once a conspiracy was uncovered they acted swiftly and ruthlessly. Accidental plague-spreading or individual greasing they were content to overlook or control with a few guards. When they thought they faced a concerted attack the whole weight of the State was thrown into the fray. In time, the senators learned that even the threat of conspiratorial plague-spreading could be dealt with by Geneva's governmental system. If nothing else, one can say that the city's rulers had learned how to control fear efficiently and calmly.

Notes

1 E. W. Monter, *Witchcraft in France and Switzerland* (1976).
2 This connection is followed by subsequent authors. See E. Mallet, 'Notice sur les anciennes pestes de Genève', in *Annales d'hygiène publique et de médecine légale*, 14: 2 (1835); A. Arnould, 'Mortalité et épidémie sous l'Ancien Régime dans le Hainaut et quelques régions limitrophes', in *Actes de colloque international de démographie historique* (Liège, 1963); L. Torfs, *Fastes des calamités publiques survenues dans le Pays-Bas* (Paris, 1859–62); H. Boguet, *Discours execrable des sorciers* (Paris, 1980).
3 Monter, *Witchcraft*, 44. See the use of Monter in B. P. Levack, *The Witch-Hunt in Early Modern Europe* (1987), 83f.
4 AEG (all subsequent manuscripts taken from this archive unless noted otherwise), RC 37, fol. 114 (4 June 1543). On fumigation, etc., see J. N. Biraben, *Les Hommes et la peste en France et dans les pays européens et méditerranéens* (Paris, 1975), 2: 177, 180 and C. M. Cipolla, *Cristofano and the Plague* (1973), 31, 49, 85f. Detailed lists of remedies and preventives were published throughout the period, e.g. anon., T. Peynell, trans., *Regimen sanitatis Salerne* (Wyllyam How, 1575); *Margarita Medicinæ* (Nuremberg: F. Peypus, 1516); J. Widmann, *Regimen ... wie man sich in pestilentzischen Lufft* (Strasbourg: M. Schuerer, 1511). See also M. U. Chrisman, *Lay Culture, Learned Culture. Books and Social Change in Strasbourg, 1480–1599* (New Haven, 1982), 129, 137. It is worth noting that the normal contemporary term was *engraisseur* (grease-spreader), then *empoissoneur* (poisoner) and finally, *bouteur de peste* (plague-spreader, cf. boute-feu for arsonist in Roberts', Ch. 1, this volume).
5 F. M. Burgy, 'Les semeurs de peste' (AEG unpublished ms., Oct. 1982), 39f.
6 The one discovery was 'des morceaux d'une matière sembable à la chair un anneau de cuivre avec un sifflet une dentz du ongle pacte de loupt servier'. PC, 1re Sèr[ie] 388, fol. 58.
7 J. A. Gautier, *Histoire de Genève* (Geneva, 1896), 3: 237.
8 Fat from corpses, as well as their teeth, figured in magical practices. J. C. Baroja, *The World of the Witches* (1968), print 16 (caption). Also, Levack, *Witch-Hunt*, pp. 38f (e.g. fat in potions: Kilkenny, Ireland, 1324/5). There were also strict regulations for the control of blood from plague victims. For example, it could not be fed to pigs (Angers, 1410; Chalon-sur-Saône, 1426; Brussels, 1439; Lyons 1472; Paris, 1531; Amiens, 1545). Biraben, *Peste*, 2: 179. See A. C. Kors and E. Peters, eds, *Witchcraft in Europe 1100–1700* (Philadelphia, 1972), 95 on the Inquisition of Toulouse: '[Anne Marie de Georgel] boiled together in a cauldron, over an accursed fire, poisonous herbs and substances taken from the bodies of animals and humans ... to use for her spells.' According to the theologian Filiberto Marchini, the plague could be spread 'humana arte' by hiding powders (derived

from secretions of infected bodies) in clothes and soaps; see G. Calvi, *Histories of a Plague Year* (Oxford, 1989), 65.

9 Cf. Levack, *Witch-Hunt*, 15 for the use of (black) powders to harm cattle.

10 There was a long tradition of associating ointments, poisons, and evil activities. Baroja, *World of the Witches*, 35f, 254f. Cf. Monter, *Witchcraft*, 109–11 on the uses of 'pusset' (diabolical powder).

11 For example, PC 1re Sèr 388 fol. 47v (Lentille); 402, fol. 2v (Bernarde Guillat); 396, fol. 4 (Clauda Mossier); 2e Sèr 627, fol. 1v (Christopha Mermillod). The fear of looting is a concern also apparent in Roberts and Jenner, Chs 1 and 3, this volume.

12 Cf., e.g., six *sols* per day with room and board. RC 64, fol. 177 (23 Dec. 1569). To put this in context, Calvin, on his death in 1564, was receiving 16 *sols* per day. Also see L. Gautier, 'La dernière peste de Genève', MDG, 23 (1888–94), 31.

13 RC 65, fos. 27–8 (17 Feb. 1570).

14 Note the connection between women, ointments and healing/white magic in Levack, *Witch-Hunt*, p. 127. Also, the contemporary link, legally and psychologically, between poverty and the threat of plague-spreading. See A. G. Carmichael, *Plague and the Poor in Renaissance Florence* (Cambridge, 1986), 90, 101 and Biraben, *Peste*, 2: 125–35. Cf. J. Klaits, *Servants of Satan* (Bloomington, 1985), 2.

15 It is clear that the authorities want simply 'two clean women and a man': Nycod Gueynet; his wife, Theveneta; and Guigona, widow of Estienne Marchand. They were to get a good salary of 30 *sols* per month (30 florins per year) plus 2 *sols* per day while cleaning (danger pay, as it were). The barbier at the time got 80 florins per year. See E. Rivoire *et al.*, eds, *Registres du Conseil de Genève* (Geneva, 1916), 6: 241 (12 Mar. 1505), 300 (5 May 1505), 307 (12 June 1506); 8: 407 (3 Jan. 1520).

16 RC 40, fol. 60 (21 Mar. 1545).

17 RC 37, fol. 80 (1 May 1543).

18 M. Roset, *Chroniques de Genève* (Geneva, 1894), 143f, 306–8. Roset is explicit in connecting the 1530 and 1545 cases. He also says (of 1545), 's'adonner corps & âme par parolles expresses au diable'. J. Balard, *Journal* (Geneva, 1854), 271. No mention of the panics is to be found in J. de Jussie, *Levain du Calvinisme* (Geneva, 1865) or A. Froment, *Les Actes et gestes merveilleux* (Geneva, 1854). For Calvin's brief comments see CO, 12: cols. 55 (to Myconius, [27] Mar. 1545) and 62 (to Farel, 25 Apr. 1545).

19 See J. Spon, *Histoire de Genève* (1730; repr. Geneva, 1976), 1: 201–3; J. Picot, *Histoire de Genève* (Geneva, 1811), 1: 405–8 (Picot turns immediately to the Peney witches, but he makes no connection); A. Thourel, *Histoire de Genève* (Geneva, 1833), 2: 199f (Thourel never misses a chance to attack superstition and yet, although condemning the medical ignorance and judicial violence of sixteenth-century Geneva, he never mentions sorcery or witchcraft with plague-spreading); A. J. P. Pictet de Sergey, *Genève, origine et développement de cette république* (Geneva, 1847), 2: 458–60; Gautier, *Histoire*, 3: 235–8 ('les boutepestes n'occupèrent pas seuls le magistrat pendant dette année: ceaux que l'on nommait sorciers l'exercederent aussi'). Cf. 'The plague plots of Geneva', *British Medical Journal: Nova et Vetera*, 2 (July–Dec. 1907), 99f: 'This mention of locks and dead men's limbs introduces an element of magic into the plot, which is in other respects as dull and horrible as possible.'

20 E. Doumergue, *Jean Calvin* (Geneva, 1899).

21 Doumergue, *Calvin*, 6: 46–50 *passim*.

22 RC 40, fol. 45 (11 Mar. 1545).

23 Monter, 47 – he continues with: 'although often lacking *most* [my emphasis; they lack *all*] of the ordinary paraphernalia of witchcraft'.

24 E. Rivoire *et al.*, eds, *Registres du Conseil de Genève* (Geneva, 1931), 11: 435 (29–30 Apr. 1530), 444 (23 June 1530).

25 W. G. Naphy, *Calvin and the Consolidation of the Genevan Reformation* (Manchester, 1994), 12–52.

26 PH 1299.

27 Cf. attitudes to foreigners and outsiders in Coster's, Taylor's and Kümin's Chs 6, 5 and
    7 in this volume as well as the more general ambivalence evidenced towards the 'out-
    side' in Jenner's Ch. 3. Also, Spicer's Ch. 10 for concerns about burial practices in plague
    outbreaks.

28 RC 36, fos. 128 (25 Sept. 1542), 129–30 (26 Sept. 1542), 132–132v (29 Sept. 1542),
    146 (17 Oct. 1547), 59v (3 Nov. 1542), 167 (13 Nov. 1542), 172v (17 Nov. 1542),
    173v (20 Nov. 1542).

29 RC 36, fol. 181v (1 Dec. 1542).

30 RC 37, fol. 21v (23 Feb. 1543).

31 RC 37, fol. 66v (20 Apr. 1543).

32 RC 37, fol. 75v (27 Apr. 1543). Eventually Boulat was executed for plague-spreading.

33 RC 37, fos. 83v (4 May 1543), 91v (14 May 1543), 94v (21 May 1543), 113v (2 June
    1543), 114 (4 June 1543), 120 (8 June 1543).

34 RC 37, fos. 149v (10 July 1543), 154 (13 July 1543), 186v (8 Aug. 1543), 188 (10 Aug.
    1543).

35 RC 37, fol. 227 (24 Sept. 1543).

36 RC 38, fol. 3 (11 Dec. 1543).

37 Compare this level of magisterial involvement in *minutiae* with James VI's interest in a
    seemingly obscure witchcraft trial in Maxwell-Stuart, Ch. 12, this volume.

38 RC 37, fos. 238 (8 Oct. 1543), 248 (22 Oct. 1543).

39 RC 37, fol. 194 (15 Aug. 1543). More worrying, he was accused by his wife of trying
    to give her poisoned bread. RC 38, fol. 6 (14 Dec. 1543). E.g., the barber-surgeons or
    grave-digger Tallien, who replaced Pernet, was suspended for fornicating with a servant.

40 RC 38, fos. 346 (30 Aug. 1544), 377 (18 Sept. 1544), 398 (6 Oct. 1544). The impor-
    tance of water − as a necessary friend and an implacable foe − is well treated in Eßer,
    Ch. 4, this volume.

41 RC 39, fol. 19v (25 Oct. 1544).

42 RC 39, fos. 89v (5 Jan. 1545), 107v (22 Jan. 1545). A *marron(e)* is an 'infirmier − ou
    parfois croque-mort − en temps d'épidémie' in the *Suisse romande*. The word appears in
    the sixteenth century at Yverdon, Lausanne, the Vallais, Vevey, Neuchâtel and Geneva.
    Cf. W. Peirrehumbert, ed., *Dictionnaire historique du parler Neuchâtelois et Suisse romande*
    (Neuchâtel, 1926), 352f and L. Favrat, ed., *Glossaire du patois de la Suisse romande* (Lau-
    sanne, 1866), 82, 239.

43 RC 39, fos. 108 (22 Jan. 1545), 109v (23 Jan. 1545), 114 (26 Jan. 1545), 115v (27 Jan.
    1545: Curtet, DesArts, Dorsière, secr. Beguin), 117v (29 Jan. 1545), 121 (2 Feb. 1545),
    125v (6 Feb. 1545).

44 RC 40, fol. 25v (17 Feb. 1545).

45 RC 40, fos. 25v–26v (17 Feb. 1545).

46 Gautier, *Histoire*, 3: 237.

47 RC 40, fos. 43–43v (9 Mar. 1545).

48 RC 40, fol. 44v (11 Mar. 1545).

49 PH 1347 (7 Mar. 1545): 'poisoniers'.

50 PH 1345 (Mar. 1545). Letters were also received from the Swiss Diet (PH 1357) and
    Gex (PH 1358).

51 PH 1345, fol. 5 (Mar. 1545).

52 PH 1345, fol. 8 (Mar. 1545): also, Jehan Barbier, francois; Jehan Montillion; Glada
    (Clauda) Gelbera Brigot; Glada de Boyra; Cristobla de Dartza; Lautreta Eyim; Jena de
    Marsez.

53 RC 40, fol. 52 (17 Mar. 1545).

54 RC 40, fos. 63–63v (24–25 Mar. 1545), 77v (10 Apr. 1545), 91v (23 Apr. 1545), 93v
    (24 Apr. 1545: Cholex and Ayme desArts's servant girl).

55 Cf. Coster's Ch. 6, this volume, for the effect approaching armies can have on govern-

mental decision-making.

56 RC 62, fol. 158 [155, actually] (6 Feb. 1567); RC 67, fos. 7 (18 Feb. 1568), 17v–18v
    (11 Mar. 1568).
57 RC 63, fos. 24v (18 Mar. 1568), 49 (17 May 1568).
58 RC 63, fos. 58 (1 June 1568), 74 (5 July 1568).
59 RC 63, fol. 59 (3 June 1568).
60 RC 63, fol. 60 (4 June 1568).
61 RC 63, fos. 61v (8 June 1568), 63 (11 June 1568), 70 (28 June 1568), 89v (10 Aug.
    1568).
62 They also placed the population under close governmental scrutiny. See Kümin's essay
    and popular antagonism to governmental intrusion. Also, compare Marshall's essay and
    the astuteness of leaders and elites in understanding – and appreciating – the power of
    fear on ordinary people.
63 RC 63, fos. 122 (27 Oct. 1568), 128 (9 Nov. 1568), 129 (12 Nov. 1568).
64 RC 64, fos. 30 (18 Feb. 1569), 67 (2 May 1569). A governmental committee recom-
    mended the meeting on 29 April 1569 (RC 64, fol. 67).
65 RC 64, fol. 71 (11 May 1569).
66 From Annecy on 26 May 1569 (RC 64, fol. 79) and Gex on 18 July (RC 64, fol. 108v).
    Geneva complained to the Duke of Savoy about the harshness of the blockade which
    clearly had religious, political and military undertones.
67 Cf., Jenner, Ch. 3, this volume.
68 RC 64, fos. 121v (15 Aug. 1569), 125 (25 Aug. 1569), 126 (27 Aug. 1569), 127v (29
    Aug. 1569), 129v (2 Sept. 1569), 148v (27 Oct. 1569), 158 (18 Nov. 1569), 176v (22
    Dec. 1569). The city's willingness to consult women is in marked contrast to the normal
    early modern disdain of authorities for the wisdom (and education) of women. Cf. Maag,
    Ch. 8, this volume.
69 RC 65, fos. 27–28v (17, 13 [20] Feb. 1570), 30v (23 Feb. 1570), 34–34v (28 Feb.
    1570), 40v (10 Mar. 1570), 45 (20 Mar. 1570), 54v (3 Apr. 1570), 72 (2 May 1570).
70 RC 65, fos. 122v (20 July 1570), 126v (28 July 1570), 148v (28 Sept. 1570), 149v (2
    Oct. 1570), 151v (5 Oct. 1570), 172v (20 Nov. 1570), 192v (2 Jan. 1571).
71 RC 66, fos. 35 (20 Feb. 1571), 50v (29 Mar. 1571), 55v (12 Apr. 1571), 59 (19 Apr.
    1571), 60v (23 Apr. 1571).
72 Compare attitudes to outsiders in Taylor, Coster and Kümin, Chs 5, 6 and 7, this
    volume.
73 RC 66, fos. 67 (7 May 1571), 68v (11 May 1571), 79 (7 June 1571), 102–102v (20/21
    Aug. 1571), 104v (27 Aug. 1571), 112v (12 Sept. 1571), 130 (22 Oct. 1571), 164 (4
    Jan. 1572).
74 RC 67, fos. 37 (11 Mar. 1572), 47 (25 Mar. 1572), 78v (20 May 1572), 86 (2 June
    1572), 96v–97 (19 June 1572), 101v (26 June 1572), 128v (15 Aug. 1572), 182v (17
    Oct. 1572).
75 PH 1907 (27 June 1571).
76 At Vevey, RC 112, fol. 10v (7 Jan. 1614); Thonon, RC 112, fol. 25 (19 Jan. 1614);
    Vaud, RC 112, fol. 40 (2 Feb. 1614); Burgundy, RC 112, fol. 44–44v (11 Feb. 1614);
    Chablais, Lausanne, Morges, RC 112, fos. 70–70v (15 Mar. 1614).
77 Compare this institutional complacency with the personal trauma associated with disease
    in Gentilcore, Ch. 11, this volume essay.
78 For the complete list see RC 112, fos. 228v–236 (17 Aug. 1614).

3

The Great Dog Massacre[1]

MARK S. R. JENNER

> Historiography writes the history of society, not of man ... . Example:
> In the years that followed the 1968 Russian invasion of Czechoslova-
> kia, the reign of terror against the public was preceded by officially
> organised massacres of dogs. An episode totally forgotten and without
> importance for a historian.[2]

There are, perhaps, three ways of writing the history of fear.[3] Firstly, one
can explore whether some cultures are more fearful than others. Nine-
teenth- and early twentieth-century anthropologists such as Frazer and
Tylor often followed Lucretius in arguing that 'primitive societies' were
driven, by their fear of a capricious and dangerous world over which they
had little technological control, into adopting particular magical and religious practices. Other scholars have argued (like Freud's *Civilisation and its
Discontents*) that the mentalities of earlier societies were characterised by an
emotionality which was controlled or repressed by the growth of modern
civilisation.

   A number of influential historians of early modern Europe have written in a similar vein. Some have developed the insights of Norbert Elias,
and have traced the increasing social and psychic control which was (they
argue) produced by increasingly elaborate codes of civility and by the growing interconnectedness of early modern society.[4] Many have argued that
pre-industrial society was particularly fearful. '[F]ear, the child of ignorance
was always lodged in ... [their] hearts', wrote Lucien Febvre of sixteenth-
century people, while Robert Muchembled pronounced that 'fears, real and
imaginary ... were the devoted companions of the anemic men of the
time'.[5] In his massive histories of fear in early modern Europe Jean
Delumeau has concurred, arguing that 'fear, whether hidden or openly
manifested, was present everywhere', and further suggesting that the Reformation and Counter-Reformation accentuated fears of damnation, and
helped create a culture particularly likely to be convulsed by panics.[6] How-

ever, these approaches have long come under fierce and justified criticism. As early as 1934 the British anthropologist A. M. Hocart declared, when reviewing a book of James Frazer's, that 'When the anthropology of anthropologists comes to be written, future generations will have to explain why the first quarter of the twentieth century was so fascinated by fear, why that emotion was made to account for everything, for weddings, funerals, for religion itself.'[7] Most philosophers and anthropologists writing in the last thirty years would dismiss such reductive and intellectualist accounts of the origin and nature of religion.[8] In a more political vein other anthropologists and cultural critics have stressed how such characterisations of 'primitive' societies replicate the imperialist categories which rendered indigenous peoples as 'childlike' and needing to be governed by Westerners.[9] Historians outlining what they see as the peculiar fearfulness of early modern society risk being equally condescending and imperialist in their representations of the past.[10]

Furthermore, this approach assumes that emotions are isolable entities and that fear is the same all over the world.[11] It does not investigate how cultures possess their own specific emotional lexicons and thus experience anxiety in different ways. Nor does it recognise the ways in which emotion is specific to particular contexts or relationships, that, in Geertz's formulation, 'emotions are cultural artefacts', and that consequently attempts (like Delumeau's) to trace the rise or decline of fear or anxiety within societies are at the very least epistemologically questionable.[12] Much recent work on the history and anthropology of the emotions has emphasised the cultural and discursive construction of sentiment, often focusing upon the culturally specific narratives or analogies by which individuals understood or represented particular emotional states.[13] Michael MacDonald, for instance, has brilliantly demonstrated the ways in which the life of the Italian reformer Francis Spira provided a model by which Puritans and nonconformists articulated a sense of religious despair.[14]

This chapter is less ambitious. Unlike Gentilcore's contribution to this collection, it neither situates phrases such as 'sore afraid' within the emotional categories of early modern England, nor discusses fear with reference to early modern understandings of the passions. It explicates neither the experiences nor the context of the individuals whose cause of death the London Bills of Mortality described as 'frighted'.[15]

Rather, it investigates the anxieties and reasoning behind one little-explored aspect of the early modern attempts to combat plague – the large-scale slaughter of dogs and cats. The methodology adopted is thus related to the third approach to the history of fear: the historical sociology of risk. For, putting aside the question of whether every society experiences the same fear, few would dispute that cultures separated by time or space fear different things, or that different groups within a particular society are likely to exhibit varying anxieties. Concerns about environmental degradation or the threat of nuclear war, for instance, have fluctuated considerably over the last fifty years and have been shown to be very unevenly spread within contemporary society.[16]

Moreover, various scholars have demonstrated how the fear that particular animals may give you a fatal disease changes over time. A number of studies have suggested that this sense of danger is often produced by the activities of elite (often medical) groups. Naomi Rogers has argued, for instance, that early twentieth-century public health propaganda not only promulgated a version of germ theory but also instilled a new horror of the fly which transformed it 'from a friendly domestic insect into a threat to health and hearth'.[17] Drawing upon Marxisant labelling theory and/or upon the Durkheimian analyses of Mary Douglas, other historians have interpreted campaigns against 'dangerous creatures' as forms of medico-moral panic, expressing either perceived crises within the social order or the anxieties of particular social groups.[18] Kathleen Kete, for instance, has argued that the discourses produced around rabies in nineteenth-century France articulated wider anxieties about the pressures of urban society, and has noted the pronounced class and gender dimensions to policies introduced to combat rabies.[19] More generally, some anthropologists, sociologists, and even (Milan Kundera notwithstanding) historians, have begun to explore the ways in which discourses about animals and other aspects of the 'natural world' articulate social relationships or political ideologies or even function as ways of imagining society.[20] In a similar spirit, this chapter will explore the mental world in which the dog and cat were feared as possible vectors of disease.

Rats symbolise plague and pestilence in the iconography of popular history and in contemporary lay medical belief. When, for instance, the film, *Interview with a Vampire*, represented plague in New Orleans, the scenery crawled with rats. The York Dungeon promises a rat-filled evocation of the Black Death. Camus's *La Peste* opens with the corpses of rats. Although other wild rodents are now recognised as important vectors of the disease, the eradication of rats has been an important part of the response to plague since the early twentieth century. When, for instance, a Cardiff flour-mill worker died of bubonic plague in 1901, the corporation immediately doubled the number of rat-catchers; the instructions against a possible outbreak of plague issued by the Local Government Board recommended the destruction of rats wherever an epidemic was suspected. From around 1907 the Indian Imperial authorities instigated a new drive against rats, offering a bounty for every rat's tail brought in.[21] Such measures continue today. During the recent outbreak of plague in Surat, India, in September and October 1994, for instance, a similar payment was offered for every dead rodent. Partly because of this powerful association with terrible pestilence (as well as with Orwellian nightmare), the rat has thus become a standard figure of horror within contemporary Western mass culture.

However, rats did not possess the same symbolic power in England before the early twentieth century. By the 1850s sewer rats could provoke horrified fascination among Henry Mayhew's readers, but the mid-nineteenth-century naturalist, Francis Buckland, reckoned that rats actually contributed to general health because they ate the 'concentrated cholera' represented by the sewage and market refuse all over Victorian cities. He was far more interested in describing the ferocity and cannibalistic tendencies of the black rat (an immigrant from France, apparently) when compared with the more placid, native English rat.[22] Furthermore, for Buckland and many male Victorians the rat was a creature of sport. The combat between dogs and rats, famously described in *London Labour and London Poor*, was a frequent feature of nineteenth-century English folk art.[23]

Nor do rats seem to have provoked particular horror in sixteenth- or seventeenth-century England. They were simply viewed as destructive vermin, whose eradication was highly desirable. 'Every Countryman almost is sensible of the great injuries and annoyances they receive from' rats and mice, wrote John Worlidge, before listing a variety of methods by which they could be captured or otherwise eradicated.[24] 'Vermine will destroy, (if they be not destroyed) more in ... . Barnes ... then the art and industry of man can improove in them', opined one correspondent of Samuel Hartlib's. He recommended that sheep intermittently be folded in barns to drive them away because rats and mice could not abide the smell of sheep.[25] City-dwellers waged a similar though more prosaic war against the pests. In 1666, for instance, Hull Trinity House paid 'for mortaring holes in the sail chamber where rats got in'; in 1640–41 the Chamberlain of London paid 2s to a 'ratkiller' for 'laying of bayts to destroy Rattes in the Chamber'.[26] Such rat-catchers were familiar figures within the Cries of London,[27] while many householders purchased ratsbane to kill unwanted rodents. Thus, for instance, in 1600 the alleged poisoner Sir Walter Leveson was said to have bought such poison ostensibly 'to kill rats in his chamber at Lambeth'.[28]

However, rats and mice were not generally associated with disease or pestilence. The appearance of remarkable numbers of such creatures or the sudden death of large numbers of them was sometimes held to presage it. Thomas Lodge's *Treatise of the Plague*, for instance, stated that when 'Rats,

Moules, and other creatures, (accustomed to live under ground) forsake their holes, it is a token of corruption in the same' and a sign that plague was imminent. Significantly, the passage also noted that 'any increase of such creatures as are engendered of putrifaction, as wormes ... flies, gnattes, eales, serpents, toades, frogs and such like' was a forewarning of corruption in earth and water which might lead to plague.[29] The annals of the College of Physicians similarly noted how the plague in London in 1563 was preceded by an epidemic of woodlice, while a report to the Royal Society remarked upon the 'extraordinary Number of Spiders' which had appeared the year before plague struck Danzig (Gdansk).[30] Outbreaks of pestilence consequently did not provoke special efforts to kill rats or mice (or frogs for that matter), because any increase in or unusual behaviour by such creatures was not seen as *causing* or *spreading* the disease, even though they might be signs of its imminent arrival

Instead, when plague was feared English civic authorities gave order for the slaughter of large numbers of cats and (especially) dogs. In the summer of 1563, for instance, the Lord Mayor of London commanded that no dog be allowed out of any house without a lead on pain of a 3s 4d fine for the owner and death for the dog.[31] In 1592 an even sterner mayoral proclamation declared that

> noe person ... shall kepe any dogg, or bitche, but such as they will keepe within there owne doores, withowt suffering them to goe loose in the streets, not ledd in slippe or lyne, nor within there owne doores making howling or other annoyaunce to there neyghbours. And that the Common hunts man shall have speciall chardge to kill every dogg or Bitch, as shalbe found loose in any streete or lane ... And if he be remisse and negligent, and wittingly spare and shewe favour in not killing any such dogge or Bitche, he shall loose his place and service, and suffer Imprisonmente.[32]

The dog-killers were to carry away the dead animals and to bury them at least four feet deep in fields outside the city.[33] Such orders were generally one of the first official responses to any rise in plague deaths in the London Bills of Mortality. In May 1603, for example, Giovanni Carlo Scaramelli, the Venetian Secretary in England, informed his masters that plague had killed thirty-six people in nine London parishes. There was, he wrote, 'dread of disease spreading ... but no steps have been taken as yet, except to kill the dogs and mark the houses'.[34]

Although these regulations often also ordered the impounding and slaughter of cats, pigs, conies and even pigeons not kept indoors,[35] in practice dogs were singled out. Huge numbers were killed. The London Chamber accounts of 1584–86, for instance, not years of particularly high plague mortality, record payments for killing 1,882 dogs.[36] In times of pestilence the numbers rose accordingly. After an order for the slaughter of dogs in May 1636, the Chamberlain of the City paid for the killing of '310 dozen' (3,720) dogs over that plague-stricken summer;[37] during the last major outbreak of plague in the capital in 1665 he paid for the slaughter of at least 4,380 animals.[38] The same policy was followed in suburban communities. The parish of St Margaret's, Westminster, for instance, paid for the killing of 502 dogs during the 1603 epidemic, while the vestry of St Martin-in-the-Fields employed one Daniell Stocken of Westminster to 'kill the dogges of this p[ar]ishe' in the epidemic of 1592–93.[39]

This extermination policy became routinised. One of the official duties of the common hunt and his men within the City of London was to kill dogs when the Lord Mayor and aldermen reckoned that it was necessary. Specific individuals were appointed as 'dog-killers'.[40] By the early seventeenth century they were sufficiently well established for John Taylor, the Water Poet, to comment on their plague-time profits alongside those of apothecaries and coffin makers:

> the Dog-killers greate gaines abounds
> For Brayning brawling currs, and foisting hounds.[41]

This policy was not a metropolitan peculiarity. Ipswich employed a dog-killer in the plague of 1585–86; during the 1597 epidemic in Newcastle upon Tyne two men claimed a civic bounty for killing at least 150 animals. In the plague year of 1625 the Mayor of Leicester ordered that any dogs or cats 'founde abroade' in the streets should be killed, while in 1645 the civic authorities of York commanded that all dogs and cats within the infected areas of the city should be killed.[42] The phenomenon entered metaphorical parlance. In an anti-Quaker riot of the 1650s one magistrate described the sect as being 'like dogs in time of plague. They are to be killed as they go up and down the streets, that they do not infect.'[43]

Nor was the phenomenon confined to England. When Edinburgh was afflicted by plague in 1512, a royal proclamation commanded that all stray dogs, cats and pigs be killed. During an epidemic in 1515 the magistracy in Middleburg commanded that all dogs wandering in the streets should be rounded up, herded on to a ship and drowned. Dogs were killed by official order in the Florentine plague of 1494; they were particularly blamed for an epidemic in Amiens in 1596.[44] The orders promulgated against plague in Rome and Naples in 1656–57 commanded that all dogs and cats in the streets should be killed, while there were fierce debates among doctors during the Marseilles epidemic of 1719–21 about the efficacy of the dog-slaughter policy.[45]

A number of historians have remarked upon this phenomenon. Keith Thomas noted that dogs and cats were killed 'as a sanitary measure' in time of epidemic.[46] Rather strangely, Ronald Hutton commends the practice, seemingly implying that early modern people associated fleas with the disease. F. P. Wilson, Brian Pullan and Paul Slack have commented (with considerably more clinical justification) on the irony of how, in trying to combat bubonic plague by killing dogs and cats, sixteenth- and seventeenth-century people were exterminating natural enemies of the plague's main vector – the rat.[47]

However, scholars have not investigated the cultural logic of such sanitary measures; they have not considered why dogs and cats should have become creatures viewed with such fear in times of epidemic. Instead much of the historiography of plague has played a rather pointless game of 'hunt the rat' through the medical texts of early modern Europe, searching for someone who can be claimed to have had the prescience to identify what modern science has seen as the major rodent vector of *Yersinia Pestis*. Even Paul Slack's magisterial study of plague in early modern England comments that 'Only Mayerne noted that rats and other vermin "running from house to house and creeping over stuff may receive and carry the infection".'[48]

In following this rather limited and medical materialist approach, and by using historical demographers' findings about particular epidemics to adjudicate between 'the rival rat-flea and human-flea theories of the transmission of human plague',[49] historians of plague have (often unwittingly) become enmeshed in epidemiological debates of the early twentieth century. For between around 1900 and around 1940 there was considerable medical dispute (notably, it seems between various national schools) about the relative importance of rat to human as opposed to human to human transmission in epidemics of bubonic plague and about which insects were the principal vectors of *Y. Pestis*.[50] Doctors debating these issues spent a great deal of time studying the ecology and behaviour of rodents and of fleas, but they also studied medieval and early modern plagues, sometimes engaging in historical research in order to substantiate arguments about the nature of the disease. Any mention of rats or mice in historical sources thus became a counter in debates about the nature of the disease and in the related disputes about whether pre-industrial epidemics, not least the Black Death, were 'really' or entirely bubonic plague.[51]

The changing relations between humankind and rodent populations is an important question and has clear implications for historical demography, but this should not squeeze out cultural approaches to the history of plague.[52] We need also to ask how early modern people understood the notion of contagion, how they experienced and articulated the fear of the disease spreading and how it was that dogs in particular became the object of fear and were thus killed in such large numbers.

Now dogs and cats *can* catch plague either by eating rodents which have died of the disease, or, like humans, by being bitten by an infected flea.[53] Some animals may thus indeed have succumbed to plague before being hit on the head. The annals of the College of Physicians, for instance, record that in 1563, after the entire household of a certain citizen had died, three dogs belonging to that family also died of the disease. Consequently it was ordered that all dogs and cats should be killed to prevent the spread of the contagion.[54] However, modern clinical research has shown that dogs, cats and their fleas are singularly ineffective vectors of the plague;[55] such investigations do not and cannot explain why dogs and cats were singled out as vectors by early modern communities with no access to laboratory methods. They do not account for the *plausibility* of the notion that the animals might spread the disease. To understand fully such questions we need to examine the visibility of dogs in early modern culture and the ways in which their treatment articulated wider (human) relationships.[56]

It is worth stressing that civic authorities were not sacrificing dogs and cats in order to ward off divine punishment and the advance of the disease, as when in 1796 a group of Würtemberg villagers buried their village bull alive in an effort to halt an outbreak of foot-and-mouth disease.[57] Nor in England, at least, do they seem to have been operating on an analogy between mad dogs and the spread of plague.[58] They were following long-established medical warnings that dogs could spread the infection. In the early 1480s Marsilio Ficino suggested that plague could be spread by dogs and cats, while in the 1590s Simon Kellwaye reckoned that plague 'may ... come by dogs, cattes, pigs, and weasels which are prone and apt to receive and carie the infection from place to place'. Unsurprisingly he recommended that magistrates, 'Suffer not any dogs, cattes, or pigs, to runne about the streetes.'[59] A decade later the French author Nicolas Ellain complained of this 'great harm done to man by pet dogs'.[60] In 1618 Maurice de Tolon urged that no women or children, dogs or cats be permitted to go with the sick to pesthouses in the fields,[61] while in 1631 one Florentine physician translated this fear into a cosmological principle in which the constellation of the Dog was an omen of plague and in which dogs symbolised death.[62]

As is clear from the canine casualty figures quoted above, dogs were very abundant in early modern towns. In 1590 the Common Council of London complained that 'there are at present an exceeding greate and unnecessarie number of ... . Dogges and bitches ... very noysome and dangerous for many respects not to be suffered'. Keith Thomas has, for instance, commented on the extraordinary numbers of dogs appearing in many topographical representations of seventeenth- and eighteenth-century England.[63] Some of these animals were pets. Pepys, for example, records ferocious rows with his wife over her inadequately house-trained puppy and also noted the grief of Mrs Penington after her pet dog died. In the late seventeenth century one finds newspaper advertisements for lost or stolen dogs; in November 1675, for instance, an announcement was inserted in the *London Gazette* offering a £20 reward for the return of a missing black spaniel.[64]

However, such pet-keeping was largely an elite (and often female) pastime. The majority of dogs were kept at least partly for utilitarian reasons. Most farms would have required a dog to help with the animals, while aristocrats were expected to maintain and to care for large packs of hounds. George Gascoigne, for instance, waxed lyrical on the qualities required of the 'Good keeper of hounds', who 'should be gratious, curteous, and gentle, loving his dogs of a naturall disposition' and who should attend to their needs the very first thing in the morning.[65]

In and around cities dogs were used for guarding the house and for work turning spits in large kitchens. Butchers in particular kept large and fierce dogs, sometimes for baiting animals before slaughter. However, it is likely that many urban dogs were not particularly closely tied to one household. Certainly nineteenth-century commentators complained that the dogs of the poor were turned out to fend for themselves for much of the day; few labouring households could afford to feed an animal when it could scavenge at least part of its own living.[66]

Consequently English towns regulated dogs from the Middle Ages, if not before. In medieval Winchester, for instance, butchers' dogs were to be chained up for much of the day. During the late fourteenth and fifteenth centuries mayors of London issued proclamations against permitting dogs to wander the streets without a guard;[67] similar provisions were general in early modern towns.[68] Such regulations were not without foundation. Sessions records contain a fair number of prosecutions for anti-social dogs. In 1612, for instance, the Middlesex justices had to deal with one Ann Fisher of Saffron Hill, 'for not reforminge of a Curste Mastie Dogge wch hath thrice bitten one Thomas Dallyn ... who goeth ... in greete danger of the said ... dogge'.[69]

Canine slaughter in time of epidemic was in part an extension of this habitual regulation. As we have seen, the London plague orders particularly singled out for death dogs which howled or otherwise annoyed their neighbours. In other words, without the slightest contemporary medical justification, those dogs deemed a nuisance were also treated as the likeliest to spread the infection. The slaughter policy thus at one level marked an intensification of household regulation and of the norms of good neighbourliness. Just as Robert Darnton demonstrated that a story about the killing and torture of cats could be a rich cultural historical source with which to explore the psychodynamics of the eighteenth-century bourgeois household,[70] so the slaughter of dogs can illuminate the maintenance of order in early modern towns, for, to adapt the axioms of Lévi-Strauss and S. J. Tambiah, dogs in early modern England were good to think with and good to prohibit.[71]

For dogs were not just ubiquitous, they also carried an extraordinary variety of emphatically anthropocentric meanings. M. P. Tilley records 113 proverbial uses of 'dog' in sixteenth- and seventeenth-century England.[72] As Jean-Claude Schmitt demonstrated, in folklore and popular culture hounds could epitomise suprahuman loyalty, selflessness and obedience.[73] Within learned culture the *Odyssey* memorialised the faithfulness of Ulysses' dog, Argus, which alone recognised and greeted his master after his long absence before expiring. As Pope rendered it in the early eighteenth century,

> When wise *Ulysses*, from his native coast
> Long kept by wars, and long by tempests tost,
> Arriv'd at last, poor, old, disguis'd, alone,
> To all his friends, and ev'n his Queen unknown ...
> Scorn'd by those slaves his former bounty fed,
> Forgot of all his own domestic crew;
> The faithful Dog alone his rightful Master knew![74]

The extent to which dogs provided metaphors for aspects of human conduct and character, even before the English began figuring themselves as the Bulldog, indicates just how far they were privileged creatures. They lived close to human beings and often carried human names; they were, in Lévi-Strauss's formulation, metonymical humans.[75] Despite Vesalius' polemical juxtaposition of a canine and a human skull in illustrations of *De Humani Corporis Fabrica*, in order to show how Galenic anatomy had incorrectly used a dog as the basis for human anatomy, in many experiments during the seventeenth and early eighteenth centuries canine bodies acted in the place of human ones.[76]

In part, precisely this privileged status with regard to humans meant that they were easily understood to share diseases with humans. They shared human spaces, food and names; they could thus readily be imagined as the means by which infection was communicated. When Alderman Micklethwaite and his son were commanded to remain in their home in York because their servants used to visit the house of a suspected plague victim, they were also ordered to kill their dogs and cats as part of this household isolation.[77] Furthermore, animals had widely acknowledged therapeutic uses in early modern England. Unlike contemporary medical teaching, which suggests that pets reduce stress and thus heart disease, early modern doctors believed in the possibility of a more direct physical exchange between animal and human. The humanist physician, John Caius, noted when discussing small spaniels in his *Of Englishe Dogges* (a development of Gesner's natural history) that

> we find that these litle dogs are good to asswage the sicknesse of the stomacke being oftentimes thereunto applyed as a plaster preservative, or borne in the bosom of the diseased ... person, which effect is performed by theyr moderate heate. Moreover the disease ... chaungeth his place and entreth (though it be not precisely marcked) into the dogge, which be no untruthe, experience can testify, for these kinde of dogges sometimes fall sicke, and somtime die, without any harme outwardly inforced, which is an argument that the disease of the ... owner ... entreth into the dogge by operation of heate intermingled and infected.[78]

The possibility that infection could pass from human to other animal through the operation of heat underpinned that (to modern eyes) most bizarre of therapies found in medical texts from Dioscorides onwards – the application of live animals to the body of the plague victim. The College of Physicians, for instance, recommended that one should take a live cockerel, hen or pigeon, hold it firmly by the beak and remove its tail feathers. Then one should press the bird 'hard to the Blotch or swelling, and so keepe them at that part untill they die, and by this meanes draw out the poison'.[79]

But the slaughter of dogs also articulated a reordering of society in time of plague. As is well known, aristocratic and royal portraiture, such as Titian's portrait of the Emperor Charles V and many Van Dyck portraits of Caroline courtiers, regularly displayed the magisterial character of the subject by representing them with a masterful hand upon the head of a well-disciplined and obedient hound.

Plague challenged precisely these uncomplicated lines of authority. Colin Jones has recently noted the paradoxical parallels between a plague-stricken city and one in carnival – both with the conventional hierarchies of good order and government overturned.[80] The slaughter of dogs represented a ferocious reinstation of magisterial authority, whereby the hand resting upon the canine head has become a club beating out its brains. To put it another way, the slaughter of dogs was also an acting-out of the necessary repression of human bestiality at a time when sinfulness was being punished. For canine qualities were not always painted as positively as Pope represented Argus. One was 'as greedy as a dog', 'as idle as a dog'.[81] Dogs symbolised lust – in one London ecclesiastical court case a woman was said to be 'worse than anie salte bitche which the dogge followethe up and downe the streete'.[82] In an image taken from the book of Proverbs, a life of repeated sin was often characterised as resembling a dog returning to its vomit.[83] In his *Dictionary*, Samuel Johnson developed these anthropocentric and anti-canine sentiments. As Ronald Paulson has put it, 'Johnson's dog is simply part of man, his baser or less fortunate ... aspect.'[84] Dogs thus symbolised the beastly aspects of human nature which religion and civil government sought to train, master and control.

Moreover, crucially it was *dogs* that they slaughtered, not other members of the canine commonwealth.[85] Ladies' lap-dogs and the hounds of the gentry were specifically excluded from these regulations. When the aldermen of London sent the dog-killers into action in 1590 they excepted 'greyhounds, spanyelles and hounds' from the cull.[86] Social difference and monetary value was thus respected and their difference was alleged also to be expressed in a superior character. As Katherine Philips wrote of the Irish Greyhound, a lion amongst dogs,

> This Dog hath so himself subdu'd,
> That hunger cannot make him rude:
> And his behaviour does confess
> True Courage dwells with Gentleness.[87]

Dogs, curs, the less valuable and less restrained creatures of the middling and lower sort were not seen in such a positive light. They lived a liminal lifestyle, regularly traversing the threshold between the domestic interior of house and shop and the more public world of the street. The dog-whippers employed in many urban churches and cathedrals sought to control the problem posed by large numbers of these creatures literally transgressing the boundaries of human or sacred space.[88] Like the *cureuses* of Geneva discussed by Naphy, in the eyes of civic authorities they were incompletely integrated into the fabric of society. Like the sale of second-hand clothes, the movement of dogs and other semi-domestic animals such as pigs or cats thus provided a way of understanding the social exchanges which spread the plague.[89] Such creatures were a *visible* source of disorder in a way that rodents and lap-dogs were not.

This anxiety about the wandering dog was part of a wider anxiety about relationships consequent upon epidemic. Within medical and civic discourse all interaction was dangerous; unregulated social intercourse, especially through unknown media such as hackney carriages, water-bearers or itinerants (human or canine) was especially to be feared.[90] This anxiety was articulated in a variety of ways. Some medical commentators suggested that dogs and cats could carry the disease because their fur attracted the sticky miasma from which it originated.[91] Others attributed it to canine diet. One anonymous plague pamphlet warned the reader to

> suffer no Dogs nor Cats to come into your houses, nor to keepe any your selves, (except you dwell in some open place of the Ayre) for they be very dangerous, and most apt (of any kind of thing) to take infection of sicknesse, and to bring it home to their maisters house; by reason that they run from place to place and from one house to another, continually feeding upon the uncleanest things that are cast forth into the streets.[92]

The language in which this concern was expressed echoed the frequent precepts against beggars and vagrants that were said to 'wander up and downe the streets' and whose expulsion from the city was a regular theme of plague regulations. As William Empson noted, late sixteenth- and early seventeenth-century texts often used canine metaphors to describe vagrants. In Harman's *Caveat for Common Cursitors*, for instance, the rogue was said to rise in the morning and to shake his ears, while upright-men (another variety of rogue) and their harlots were said to shelter in barns 'where they couch comely together, and it were dog and bitch'.[93] Householders were similarly ordered to ensure that servants and apprentices were kept within doors on holidays, to ensure that they did not 'wander abroad in the streetes'. The slaughter of dogs was thus more than an extension of the policy of household isolation that played so important a part in the response to plague. Dogs in streets were not simply breaking sanitary regulations. They were quite literally masterless. In London in 1563 and 1584–86 they were allowed out so long as they were on a leash and thus visibly and physically fixed within a particular social relationship.[94] Their slaughter was a symbolic warning to the rest of the population.

In August 1665, at the height of the plague in London, Samuel Pepys mused in his diary that the epidemic was 'making us more cruel to one another then we are [to] dogs'.[95] This chapter develops this parallel. For although English national and local government never enforced its plague policy with regard to humans with quite the sanguinary enthusiasm that they displayed towards wayward canines, considerable force was required to sustain the deeply unpopular policies of household isolation and segregation which were the keystone of their response to the plague. It is to this overall context of the coercive exercise of authority and of social differentiation that we should look when we try to understand these dog massacres. They were not based upon simple ignorance, nor were they the febrile panic reactions of a terrified generation unable to control their environment. Rather, they articulated a variety of fears about human relationships with each other, with the bestial aspects of humankind and with the wider world.

Notes

1 In preparing this chapter I have benefited from discussions with Justin Champion, David Harley, Bill Naphy, Dave Peacock, Margaret Pelling, Lyndal Roper, Bertrand Taithe and Sir Keith Thomas. My thanks to Simon Ditchfield for reading and commenting on a draft. I wish to express my particular and heartfelt thanks to Patricia Greene for her encouragement and careful commentary on the chapter.

2 Milan Kundera, 'Dialogue on the art of the novel', in *The Art of the Novel* (1988), 37.

3 For an overview of the history of the emotions, see P. N. Stearns and C. Z. Stearns, 'Emotionology: clarifying the history of emotions and emotional standards', *American Historical Review*, 90 (1985), 813–36.

4 N. Elias, *The Civilizing Process* (Oxford, 1979–82) and *The Court Society* (Oxford, 1983); G. Vigarello, *Le Corps Redressé* (Paris, 1978), partly translated as 'The upward training of the body from the age of chivalry to courtly civility', in D. Feher, ed., *Fragments for the History of the Human Body* (New York, 1989), 2: 148–99; P. Spierenburg, *The Broken Spell* (1991).

5 L. Febvre, *The Problem of Unbelief in the Sixteenth Century* (1982), 407; R. Muchembled, *Popular Culture and Elite Culture in France 1450–1750* (Baton Rouge, 1985), 22. One should stress that Febvre's approach to historical psychology was multi-faceted; see P. Burke, ed., *A New Kind of History; from the Writings of Lucien Febvre* (1973).

6 J. Delumeau, *La Peur en Occident: XIVe–XVIIIe siècles* (Paris, 1978), *passim*, esp. 31, and *Sin and Fear. The Emergence of Western Guilt Culture 13th–18th Centuries* (New York, 1990). On the propensity to panic, see also G. Lefebvre, *The Great Fear of 1789* (1973).

7 A. M. Hocart, 'Fear and the anthropologists', *Nature*, 29 (Sept. 1934), pp. 475–6. This passage is quoted in H. Kuklick, *The Savage Within. The Social History of British Anthropology, 1885–1945* (Cambridge, 1991), 119.

8 For an extremely perceptive discussion of these themes and their relevance to historians' use of the term 'popular culture', see S. Clark, 'French historians and early modern popular culture', *P&P*, 100 (1983), 62–99. See also E. E. Evans-Pritchard, *Theories of Primitive Religion* (Oxford, 1965) and (for a demonstration that these problematic strands are not peculiar to French historiography) H. Geertz, 'An anthropology of religion and magic', *Journal of Interdisciplinary History*, 6 (1975–76), 71–89.

9 See T. Asad, ed., *Anthropology and the Colonial Encounter* (1973); J. Clifford and G. E. Marcus, eds, *Writing Culture* (1986).

10 Cf. Hans-Peter Duerr's ferocious critique of Norbert Elias, *Nachtheit und Scham* (Frankfurt, 1988).

11 See, for instance, Delumeau's universalising discussion of the physiological signs of fear and his evident debt to existentialist strands of French thought, *La Peur*, 13–20.

12 C. Geertz, *The Interpretation of Cultures* (1973), 81.

13 See, e.g., S. Hallam, 'Some constructivist observations on "anxiety" and its history', in T. R. Sarbin and J. I. Kitsure, eds, *Constructing the Social* (1994); C. Lutz, *Unnatural Emotions* (Chicago, 1988). For an excellent overview of the anthropology of emotion, see C. Lutz and G. M. White, 'The anthropology of emotions', *Annual Review of Anthropology*, 15 (1986), 405–36. There appears to be within anthropology a heated ongoing debate between broadly social constructivist and realist approaches to selfhood and emotions. For a recent review of the field, J. Leavitt, 'Meaning and feeling in the anthropology of the emotions', *American Ethnologist*, 23 (1996), 514–39.

14 M. MacDonald, '*The Fearefull Estate of Francis Spira*: narrative, identity, and emotion in early modern England', *Journal of British Studies*, 31 (1992), 32–61.

15 M. MacDonald, *Mystical Bedlam* (Cambridge, 1981), esp. 157–8, 181–2. According to the annual bill of mortality for 1665 twenty-three people died 'frighted' that year. It is reproduced in J. A. I. Champion, ed., *Epidemic Disease in London* (1995), 37.

16 See, e.g., M. Douglas and A. Wildalsky, *Risk and Culture* (Los Angeles, 1982).

17 N. Rogers, 'Germs with legs: flies, disease, and the new public health', *Bulletin of the*

History of Medicine, 63 (1989), 599–617, esp. 601. See also the forthcoming Manchester University Ph.D. thesis of Val Whitehouse.

18 See S. Cohen, *Folk Devils and Moral Panics* (1980); M. Douglas, *Purity and Danger* (1966), esp. ch. 3. These approaches have become very influential within the history of public health as historians seek to understand the social and political reasons by which particular environments come to be deemed unhealthy, e.g. M. Jenner, 'The politics of London air: John Evelyn's *Fumifugium* and the Restoration', *Historical Journal*, 38 (1995), 535–51; C. Hamlin, 'Environmental sensibility in Edinburgh, 1839–1840: the "Fetid Irrigation" controversy', *Journal of Urban History*, 20 (1994), 311–39.

19 K. Kete, *The Beast in the Boudoir* (Los Angeles, 1995), ch. 6 and '*La Rage* and the bourgeoisie: the cultural context of rabies in the French nineteenth century', *Representations*, 22 (1988), 89–107. The parallels between these events and the British Dangerous Dogs Act are readily apparent.

20 Anthropological studies include R. Bulwer, 'Why the cassowary is not a bird', *Man*, new ser., 2 (1967), 5–25; M. Douglas, 'Animals in Lele religious symbolism', *Africa*, 27 (1957), 46–57; E. Leach, 'Animal categories and verbal abuse', in E. H. Lenneberg, ed., *New Directions in the Study of Language* (1964). Historical studies of these themes include D. Harraway, *Primate Visions* (1989); S. Schama, *Landscape and Memory* (1995); H. Ritvo, *The Animal Estate* (1987); Kete, *The Beast*. See also T. Ingold, ed., *What is an Animal?* (1988) and S. Baker, *Picturing the Beast* (Manchester, 1993).

21 J. F. D. Shrewsbury, *A History of Bubonic Plague in the British Isles* (Cambridge, 1970), 535–6, 540–1; I. J. Catanach, 'Plague and the tensions of Empire: India 1896–1918', in D. Arnold, ed., *Imperial Medicine and Indigenous Societies* (Manchester, 1988), 162. For an up-to-date summary of rodents and epidemiology, see N. G. Gratz, 'Rodents as carriers of disease', in A. P. Buckle and R. H. Smith, eds, *Rodent Pests and their Control* (Wallingford, 1994), 85–108.

22 C. Herbert, 'Rat worship and taboo in Mayhew's London', *Representations*, 23 (1988) 1–24; F. Buckland, *Curiosities of Natural History First Series* (1900), 56–148, esp. 81.

23 H. Mayhew, *London Labour and London Poor* (1861), 3: 7–13; Peter Moores Foundation, *British Folk Art Collection* (1993), 7–8.

24 J. Worlidge, *Systema Agriculturae* (1675; facsimile: Los Angeles, 1970), 210. Cf. the 'dislike' of rats and mice for eating grain, but the absence of concern about them as vectors of disease, noted in a modern survey of hygienic practices and health in Lesotho: R. Feachem *et al.*, *Water, Health and Development* (1978), 128.

25 SUL, Hartlib MS 64/9/1. Most householders preferred more traditional, carnivorous forms of pest control; see, e.g., the thirteenth-century *mundus inversus* marginal drawing of a rat hanging two cats reproduced in Shrewsbury, *Bubonic Plague*, facing 225.

26 D. Woodward, *Men at Work. Labourers and Building Craftsmen in the Towns of Northern England, 1450–1750* (Cambridge, 1995), 4; CLRO, City Cash 1/4 fol. 43v.

27 Sir F. Bridge, *The Old Cryes of London* (1921), 49, 67.

28 *CSPD 1598–1601*, 400.

29 T. Lodge, *A Treatise of the Plague* in *The Complete Works of Thomas Lodge* (1883), 4: 21. This is a reworking of Francois Val);riole's 1566 *Traité de la Peste*, E. Cuvelier, 'A treatise of the plague de Thomas Lodge (1603): traduction d'un ouvrage médicale français', *Etudes Anglaises*, 21 (1968), 395–403.

30 RCP, Annals vol. I, fol. 22; *Philosophical Transactions*, 28 (1713; facsimile: New York, 1963), 105; J. Pringle, *A Rational Enquiry into the Nature of the Plague* (1722), 4.

31 CLRO, JCCC 18, fol. 136.

32 CLRO, JCCC 23, fol. 130v. Cf. CLRO, Repertory of the Court of Aldermen, 22, fol. 201.

33 *Ibid.*, fos. 126v, 130v.

34 *Calendar of State Papers Venetian 1603–07*, 42. On modes of reading bills of mortality, see

J. C. Robertson, 'Reckoning with London: interpreting the *Bills of Mortality* before John Graunt', *Urban History*, 23 (1996), 325–50.

35 In June 1630, for instance, the city fathers of Norwich employed one John Campe to kill 'Doggs, hoggs, Catts & tame Doves' found in the streets, *Minutes of the Norwich Court of Mayoralty 1630–1631*, W. L. Sachse, ed., Norfolk Record Society, 15 (1942), 61.

36 *Chamber Accounts of the Sixteenth Century*, B. R. Masters, ed., London Record Society, 20 (1984), 46, 93 (Items 107, 238). The Common Hunt was an officer within the Lord Mayor's household with general responsibility for maintaining the Mayor's hounds, B. R. Masters, 'The Lord Mayor's household before 1600', in A. E. J. Hollaender and W. Kellaway, eds, *Studies in London History* (1969), 99–101.

37 CLRO, City Cash 1/2 fol. 54.

38 W. G. Bell, *The Great Plague of London* (1951), 102. Bell's estimate should be regarded as a minimum as he assumes that the dog-killers were paid 2d per animal, as in 1563. However, this rate of pay was subsequently reduced and the true level of canine mortality may have been far higher.

39 F. P. Wilson, *The Plague in Shakespeare's London* (Oxford, 1927), 39; J. V. Kitto, ed., *St. Martin-in-the-Fields. The Accounts of the Churchwardens 1525–1603* (1901), 453 and n.

40 Cf. B. Jonson, *Bartholomew Fair*, 2: 1.15–16, where Justice Overdo talks of the Lord Mayor, who in August adopted the guise of a dog-killer in order to investigate wrong-doing incognito.

41 J. Taylor, 'The Fearefull Summer', in *All the Workes of John Taylor the Water Poet 1630*, intro. by V. E. Neuberg (facsimile: 1977), 61. 'Foisting' means farting.

42 *Poor Relief in Elizabethan Ipswich*, J. Webb, ed., SufRO, 9 (1966), 116–17; Woodward, *Men at Work*, 197; *Records of the Borough of Leicester 1603–1688*, H. Stocks and W. H. Stevenson, eds (Cambridge, 1923), 260, 235; YCA House Book 36, fol. 151.

43 Quoted in K. Thomas, *Man and the Natural World: Changing Attitudes in England, 1500–1800* (1983), 47.

44 Shrewsbury, *Bubonic Plague*, 166; M. A. van Andel, 'Plague regulations in the Netherlands', *Janus*, 21 (1916), 436–7; A. Carmichael, *Plague and the Poor in Renaissance Florence* (Cambridge, 1986), 105; J. N. Biraben, *Les Hommes et la peste* (Paris, 1976), 2: 25.

45 L. F. Hirst, *The Conquest of Plague* (Oxford, 1953), 409; *Mercurius Politicus*, 323 (14–21 Aug. 1656), facsimile reprint, *The English Revolution III Newsbooks 5*, 13: 378; J. B. Bertrand, *A Historical Relation of the Plague at Marseilles in the Year 1720* (1805; repr. with an intro. by J. N. Biraben, n. p., 1973), 134–5, 210.

46 Thomas, *Natural World*, 105.

47 R. Hutton, *The Restoration* (Oxford, 1985), 228; Wilson, *Plague in Shakespeare's London*, 36–40; B. Pullan, 'Plague and perceptions of the poor in early modern Italy', in T. Ranger and P. Slack, eds, *Epidemics and Ideas* (Cambridge, 1992), 120; P. Slack, *The Impact of Plague in Tudor and Stuart England* (1985), 27. Despite its title, L. Wilkinson, *Animals and Disease. An Introduction to the History of Comparative Medicine* (Cambridge, 1992) does not discuss these themes.

48 Slack, *Impact of Plague*, 238–9.

49 L. Bradley, 'The most famous of all English plagues. A detailed analysis of the plague at Eyam, 1665–66', in *The Plague Reconsidered*, Local Population Studies, supplement (1977), 77–8.

50 These debates are extensively reviewed in Hirst, *Conquest of Plague*. Hirst's account is both full and compelling, but he was personally involved in these entomological and epidemiological disputes and his account is inevitably partisan. The subject requires fresh historical investigation. See H. Kupferschmidt, *Die Epidemiologie der Pest*, in Gesnerus, supplement (1993).

51 There is an ongoing historical debate on these points. See, for instance, J. A. I. Champion, *London's Dread Visitation. The Social Geography of the Great Plague in 1665* (Historical Geography Research Series, 31, 1995); G. Twigg, *The Black Death* (1984).

52 See C. Jones, 'Plague and its metaphors in early modern France', *Representations*, 53 (1996).

53 See J. H. Rust, Jr, *et al.*, 'The role of domestic animals in the epidemiology of plague', *Journal of Infectious Diseases*, 124: 5 (Nov. 1971), 522–31.

54 RCP, Annals vol. I, fol. 22; calendared in *Historic Manuscripts Commission*, 8th Report, 227a.

55 Hirst, *Conquest of Plague*, 71, 163, 183–7.

56 To argue this is *not* to deny past peoples' capacity to observe and to reason upon physical phenomena around them, cf. P. Richards, 'Natural symbols and natural history: chimpanzees, elephants and experiments in Mende thought', in K. Milton, ed., *Environmentalism: The View from Anthropology* (1993), 144–59.

57 D. Sabean, *Power in the Blood* (Cambridge, 1984), ch. 6, esp. 191–3. On sacrifice and epidemiological crisis more generally, see R. Girard, *Violence and the Sacred* (1977); V. Turner, *The Ritual Process* (1969).

58 In its definition of 'dog-killer', OED suggests incorrectly that during the sixteenth- and seventeenth-century civic dog-killers were primarily ordered to kill mad dogs. However, in a discussion of plague published in 1631 the Florentine physician Alessandro Righi argued that the fury of a mad dog symbolized the raging of the epidemic, G. Calvi, *Histories of a Plague Year* (Oxford, 1989), 59. For discussions of rabies in early modern Britain, see C. F. Mullett, 'Hydrophobia: its history in England to 1800', *Bulletin of the History of Medicine*, 18 (1945), 44–65 and B. Griffin, 'Mad dogs and Irishmen. Dogs and rabies in the 18th and 19th centuries', *Ulster Folklife*, 40 (1994), 1–15.

59 Hirst, *Conquest of Plague*, 412; S. Kellwaye, *A Defensative against the Plague* (1593), fos. 1, 13v.

60 Biraben, *Les Hommes*, 2: 25.

61 Maurice de Tolon, *Preservatifs et remedes contre la peste, ou le capuchin charitable* (Paris, 1618), 92.

62 Calvi, *Plague Year*, 59.

63 CLRO, JCCC 22, fol. 402v; Thomas, *Natural World*, 102. One should note that visual representations of dogs often also performed a range of symbolic or ironic functions.

64 S. Pepys, *Diary*, R. C. Latham and W. Matthews, eds (1970–83), 1: 54 and 284–5, 4: 290, 293; *The London Gazette*, 1040 (4–8 November 1675). For an electronic version of this text, see: http://www.history.rochester.edu/London_Gazette/1040/lgazette.htm

65 G. Gascoigne, *The Noble Arte of Venerie or Hunting* (1611), 30.

66 J. K. Walton, 'Mad dogs and Englishmen', *Journal of Social History*, 13 (1979).

67 D. Keene, *Survey of Medieval Winchester* (Oxford, 1985) 2: 257–8; *Calendar of Letter Book H*, R. R. Sharpe, ed. (1908), 311; *Liber Albus*, H. T. Riley, ed. and trans. (1862), 388–9.

68 E.g., *The Lawes of the Markette* (1562); J. W. F. Hill, *Tudor and Stuart Lincoln* (Cambridge, 1956), 217; *Records of the Borough of Leicester 1509–1603*, M. Bateson, ed. (Cambridge, 1905), 232.

69 *Calendar to the Middlesex Sessions Records*, new ser., W. L Hardy, ed. (1935–41), 1: 185.

70 R. Darnton, 'The Great Cat Massacre', in his *The Great Cat Massacre and other Essays in Cultural History* (1984).

71 I here appropriate the title and some of the methodology of S. J. Tambiah's study of Thailand, 'Animals are good to think with and good to prohibit', *Ethnology*, 8 (1969), 424–59.

72 M. P. Tilley, *Dictionary of the Proverbs in England in the Sixteenth and Seventeenth Centuries* (Ann Arbor, 1950), s.v.

73 J-C. Schmitt, *The Holy Greyhound* (Cambridge, 1983).

74 A. Pope, *Minor Poems*, N. Ault and J. Butt, eds (1954), 51. See also Book 17 of George Chapman's early seventeenth-century *Translation of Homer's Odyssey*. A handy, if revoltingly sentimental, selection of verses on and other literary references to the excellent

qualities of dogs is contained in G. R. Jesse, *Researches into the History of the British Dog* (1866).

75 C. Lévi-Strauss, *The Savage Mind* (1966), 204–8.

76 See, e.g., R. Williamson, 'The plague of Marseilles and the experiments of Professor Anton Deidier on its transmission', *Medical History*, 2 (1968), 237–52. Discussions of human and animals within the history of science and medicine generally become subsumed within the teleology of the rise of humanitarianism. Studies of such ethical themes include A. Guerrini, 'The ethics of animal experimentation in seventeenth-century England', *Journal of the History of Ideas*, 50 (1989), 391–407; A. H. Maehle, 'The ethical discourse on animal experimentation', in A. Wear, J. Geyer-Kordesch and R. French, eds, *Doctors and Ethics* (Amsterdam, 1993); N. A. Rupke, *Vivisection in Historical Perspective* (1990).

77 YCA House Book 35, fol. 149.

78 J. Caius, *Of Englishe Dogges* (1576), 21–2.

79 College of Physicians, *Certain Directions for the Plague* (1636; facsimile: Amsterdam, 1979), sigs. E2–2v.

80 Jones, 'Plague', 97–127.

81 Tilley, *Proverbs*, D434 and D435.

82 L. Gowing, *Domestic Dangers: Women, Words and Sex in Early Modern London* (Oxford, 1996), 67. A version of this insult is noted in Tilley, *Proverbs*, D527. For the sexual meanings of dogs in nineteenth-century art, R. Thomson, '"Les Quat' Pattes": the image of the dog in late nineteenth-century French art', *Art History*, 5 (1982), 323–37.

83 The relevant verse is Proverbs 26:11. See also, Tilley, *Proverbs*, D458.

84 R. Paulson, *Popular and Polite Art in the Age of Hogarth and Fielding* (1979), 50.

85 Cf. I. M. Lewis, 'The spider and the pangolin', *Man*, new ser., 26 (1991), 513–25.

86 CLRO, JCCC 22, fol. 402v. Cf., however, YCA House Book 32, fol. 329v.

87 Katherine Philips, *Selected Poems* (Hull, 1904), 40.

88 For the employment of dog-whippers, see, e.g., J. C. Cox, *Churchwardens' Accounts from the Fourteenth Century to the Close of the Seventeenth Century* (1913), 307–9; L. A. Price, 'Parish constables: a study of administration and peacekeeping, Middlesex, 1603–1625', (University of London Ph.D. Thesis, 1991), 77; C. B. Estabrook, 'In the mist of ceremony: cathedral and community in seventeenth-century Wells', in S. D. Amussen and M. A. Kishlansky, eds, *Political Culture and Cultural Politics in Early Modern England* (Manchester, 1995), 161 n.146.

89 Cf. G. Calvi, 'A metaphor for social exchange: the Florentine plague of 1630', *Representations*, 13 (1986), 139–63.

90 See, for instance, *The Shutting Up Infected Houses ... Soberly Debated* (1665), *passim*.

91 C. M. Cipolla, *Miasmas and Disease* (1992), 4.

92 *Especial Observations and Approved Physical Rules* (1625), sig. Bv.

93 W. Empson, *The Structure of Complex Words* (1952), 160–1; A. V. Judges, ed., *The Elizabethan Underworld* (1965), 70.

94 Cf. P. Griffiths, 'Masterless young people in Norwich, 1560–1645', in P. Griffiths, A. Fox and S. Hindle, eds, *The Experience of Authority in Early Modern England* (1996).

95 Pepys, *Diary*, 4: 201.

4

Fear of water and floods in the Low Countries

RAINGARD EßER

Few areas have inspired human imagination more than the sea.[1] In the Bible the sea is portrayed as a hostile place, inhabited by frightening and evil animals such as serpents and whales. Genesis 1:2 starts with a description of the 'formless' earth when the 'darkness was over the surface of the deep'. In Revelation 13:1, the visionary sees 'a beast coming out of the sea' at the day of the Last Judgement. For the majority of early modern men and women the sea was perceived as a dangerous place, which was associated with disorder, chaos and death. It was that element which men could least control. Fishermen and sailors were in most cases helpless victims of the wind and storms, but might suffer from dead calm, which made a swift return to a safe haven impossible for days or even weeks. For the inhabitants of coastal areas, the sea did not only threaten the collapse of civilised society, but also was a very manifest threat to people's property and lives. Shipwrecks and the drowning of fishermen in the waves were part of the everyday life of all coastal communities. There were few families who did not lose at least one person to the sea. Even for those who stayed on shore the sea remained a constant danger. The inhabitants of coastal areas were prone to humidity-related diseases such as malaria, rheumatism and colds, and, more obviously, suffered frequently from storms and floods.[2]

Research on the history of natural disasters and its effects on man is very much in its infancy. A discipline which is still dominantly interested in the history of political events and their consequences may find the analysis of events caused by nature rather than by mankind a less worthwhile topic for investigation. So far only a handful of studies, most of them inspired by the French *Annales* School, have tried to investigate the relations between man and natural disasters – floods, earthquakes, the eruption of volcanoes, etc. – in early modern Europe.[3] The following study tries to shed further light on this aspect of history. An analysis of the 'disaster-management' in cases of flooding in the early modern Low Countries can add to our understanding of the relations between man and nature. The reactions of contemporaries coming to terms with catastrophes, as well as the practical steps taken to prevent similar disasters in the future, will be at the centre of the discussion. For this purpose a particular example, the All Saints' Flood of 1570, will be studied. The chapter will cover a wide range of sources. Histories and diaries both of contemporaries and later chroniclers will help to illuminate the mental and psychological reactions of an early modern society under the constant threat of floods and its worst result: death by drowning. Official documents as well as tracts and pamphlets concerning dikes and the preservation of dikes will cover the practical side of the above-mentioned 'disaster-management'. They record the precautions taken by town and government authorities to reduce the damaging effects of flooding on the general public.

In spite of contemporary historians' disinterest in natural disasters, it seems that most histories of the Low Countries from the sixteenth century until today mention the famous All Saints' Flood at least in passing.[4] The interpretations of the disaster, however, have changed decisively. The way a witness or a later chronicler depicted the event was influenced by whether his or her comment was part of a private or a public discourse. It was also determined by the political and religious background of the respective writer. 'On the evening of All Saints' Day around nine o'clock a great storm arose caused by north-westerly winds. The waves in the rivers and along the dikes of the provinces were so high that it seemed that another Great Flood would sweep across the land.'[5] Thus Frisia's official historian Pieter Winsemius, in his *Chronique ofte Hist. geschiedenisse van Vrieslant* (1622), described a disaster that devastated large parts of the North Sea coast from Flanders to Denmark in the first days of November 1570. The 'Great Flood' became known among contemporaries and later chroniclers as the *Allerheiligenvloed*, the All Saints' Flood of 1570.

Much has been written in retrospect about the disaster, but only a few contemporary accounts shed any light on what actually happened. The most immediate description of the flood is Jan Fruytier's *Corte beschrijvinghe van den ellendighen ende seer beclaghelicken Watervloet ... 1 november 1570*, a verse chronicle, which was first published after July 1571.[6] Fruytier was then *Requestermaster* of William of Orange. In November 1570 he lived in East Frisia, but went to Holland shortly afterwards. His account, which he regarded as the impressionistic view of an eye-witness rather than as a definitive report of the disaster, is therefore more detailed on the events in the north. Here, the storm and the subsequent floods reached their climax in the middle of the night of 1–2 November, surprising the inhabitants of the coastal villages and farmhouses in their sleep. The majority of the victims were lost on the North German coast, and according to Fruytier, in Frisia alone 20,000 people died. This estimate, however, is undoubtedly much too high. A more detailed analysis taken from various local sources reckons the number of dead to about 3,000.[7] The southern parts of the coastline were hardest hit by the storm and the water on the afternoon of All Saints' Day, a delay which gave the people a better chance of survival than their northern neighbours. Here again, Fruytier's figures, which estimated 8,000–9,000 men, women and children were drowned in Groningen and 3,000 in Zealand, are certainly much too high. A more realistic account gives an estimate of several hundred victims at the most.[8]

A more detailed report of the effects of the flood in the south is given by Andries van der Goes, a wine and beer merchant and royal treasurer for South Holland, resident in Dordrecht, in a letter to his brother-in-law Jacob de Rover in Antwerp.[9] The letter was written on 13 November, less than two weeks after the disaster, which Van der Goes had witnessed in Dordrecht. The first part recounts details of the situation in the city: 'the whole town of Dordrecht was under water'.

Van der Goes's own house was severely affected by the flooding. He reported that his rear yard was knee-deep in water. His two beer-cellars were flooded, spoiling his stock of beer. Fortunately, with the help of rags and other textiles piled at the entrance to his wine-cellars, he managed to prevent the water from getting into his other storehouses and thus saved his wine. In the city, four or five women were drowned. Barrels of wine and other victuals drifted through the streets, which had become waterways.

Between seven and eight o'clock in the evening the flood reached its highest point. There were rumours of fires in Van der Goes's street and elsewhere in the city, but fortunately, these caused no further damage. Van der Goes then continues with a detailed account of the devastation of the land under his supervision in South Holland. Two-thirds of these lands were under water: the land of Stryen, Bonaventura, the Westmaeze and other *polders* around Beyerlandt. In many parts the water overflowed the dikes. Although there were heavy losses of livestock, only a few people died.

In North Holland, the whole Rhineland went under 'so that you could take a boat from Amsterdam to Leyden'. Here, on 6–7 November, the area went through a severe crisis when the Rhine dike between Leiden and Woerden nearly broke. All church bells were rung in Delftland day and night to prevent a catastrophe, and eventually the water fell. In Schieland, Van der Goes's brother, who was the local bailiff, and the dike-count fought against the sea for ten days to prevent the breaching of the dikes which would have put all of Schieland under water. In the coastal town of Scheveningen no less than ninety houses were swept away by the flood, leaving no trace of their existence. A further forty houses were so severely demolished that they could no longer be used by their inhabitants. Other houses were damaged to a lesser extent, and about a fourth of all the houses in the town were affected. The flood crushed the walls of the churchyards and swept away the church doors. The water was standing as high as $3\frac{1}{2}$ feet and 'two thumbs' in the church. Van der Goes also briefly mentioned the great damage in Vriesland, where so many people were drowned that they could not be properly buried. Holes were dug wherever possible, and the victims were buried in groups of three or four – a measure which must have been particularly devastating for communities where the proper burial procedures and a decent grave in holy ground were regarded as necessary for a smooth passage into the afterlife.[10] In his concluding remarks Van der Goes summarises the situation: 'the sufferings and the damages are so immense that words cannot describe them'.

The disaster of 1570 was by no means the only flood in the Low Countries in the sixteenth century, nor was it the worst with respect to loss of people, livestock, houses and lands. Due to what geographers and climatologists have termed the 'Little Ice Age' of the late sixteenth and seventeenth centuries, Europe underwent dramatic climatological changes during the early modern period. Average temperatures dropped, causing a series of severe winters with heavy storms, snowfalls and river inundations in spring. Prior to the All Saints' Flood there were serious floods recorded along the Dutch North Sea coast in 1502, 1509, 1530, 1532, 1551/52 and 1565. During the so-called St Elizabeth's Day Flood of 18–19 November 1421 – a catastrophe, which left deep scars on the Dutch landscape and on public memory, and which has often been compared with the All Saints' Flood – 500 square kilometres of land in Zealand and Flanders were flooded with seawater. Approximately 10,000 people died and twenty villages perished in the water.[11] The flood in early November 1570 was preceded by a storm flood in March of the same year and followed by a less disastrous flooding of the south-west coast of the Netherlands on 28–29 November. To make matters worse, many of the floods of the late sixteenth century were accompanied by severe winters with unusually low temperatures, long periods of frost and heavy snowfall.

The first half of the seventeenth century was less stormy, especially after 1630. Exceptions were the storm floods of 23 January 1610 and 8 March 1625 when recently drained dikes and *polders* (e.g. Beemster in 1610 and the Wormer and the Wieringerward in 1625) were again under water.

In general the south-west coastline fared better than the north. All the other floods of the first part of the seventeenth century, even when they covered quite a wide area, were of slight intensity. The two great storm surges of 1610 and 1625 were repeatedly compared by contemporaries and later authors with the notorious All Saints' Flood, but in general the situation did not match the catastrophe of 1570. Another series of disasters threatened the Dutch and the German North Sea coast from the second part of the seventeenth century onwards. In 1665, the central section of the coastline – North and South Holland – was seriously damaged by water. In 1682, the south-west suffered severe losses of people, livestock and land. In 1686, the area around Groningen was severely hit. Less serious, but more widespread were the floods of 1651, when nearly the whole of the Dutch coast was affected, and in 1662, when the southern part of the country suffered most damage. In 1671, the south-west Netherlands were heavily hit; in 1683, the north Netherlands suffered most from disaster.[12]

In private correspondence such as Van der Goes's letter or in diaries of others the flood of 1570 is often recorded in a rather detached and businesslike way, concentrating on the damages and losses to trade and commerce.[13] Metaphysical explanations and interpretations of the disaster were not attempted. Where supernatural involvement is mentioned, the authors thank God for not having caused further damage rather than seeing Him as the initiator of the disaster. Van der Goes, for instance, thanked God six times in his letter for the prevention of greater losses in lives and livestock, 'remembering that loss of goods is not loss of life'.[14] In their diaries Egbert Alting and Jan de Pottre both contemplated God's grace which had spared the world greater misery.[15] These remarks show a rather 'modern', i.e. rational, attitude towards natural disasters. It is difficult, however, to decide if these writers represent a general mentality of coastal inhabitants, who were used to floods and saw them as incidents merely caused by geographical and climatological circumstances. Here, further research into the reactions of the ordinary men and women, who have left little written evidence of their feelings and fears, would be helpful.

The discourse in the public press took another turn. One group of writers saw signs of God in the events of the flooding and interpreted the disaster as God's revenge for human sins and as a warning for their contemporaries to repent and to change their lives. This idea – that God manifests His will in the world by the use of nature – is at least as old as Christianity. The biblical story of the Flood sent by God to put an end to the sinful world (Genesis 6:9–8:21) was a well-known and often quoted tale in early modern times.[16] The analogy of the biblical Flood was also used in the few remaining contemporary pamphlets which describe the disaster of

Woodcut of the All Saints' Flood of 1570: frontispiece for Thiebolt
Berger's Jammerliche undershröckliche Zeitung, ausz Niderland
printed in Strasbourg in 1571 (Koninklijke Bibliotheek, the Hague)

1570. In Strasbourg, Thiebolt Berger printed a pamphlet on the floods in
1571. In his *Jammerliche underschröckliche Zeitung, ausz Niderland* a detailed
description of the damage to Holland, Brabant and Zealand is given (figure
2). An interesting detail is added with the account of the destruction of a
newly built Spanish fortification in Groningen. Here, the Spanish forces had
started to erect a fort, which collapsed in the floods. All the Spanish masons
and soldiers died, while the city itself remained relatively unharmed.[17] On
the frontispiece of the pamphlet a woodcut depicts the flood. Several men
and women are dramatically drowning, their hands helplessly raised to the
sky. A thunderstorm with heavy rain and hail comes down on the distressed
landscape and in the left-hand corner a sea monster is looming. However,
in the middle of this disastrous scene the Ark sails unharmed through the
waves and the dove with the green twig is just approaching its roof.[18] Both
this pamphlet and an earlier version with the same text, but without the
woodcut (dated 1570), offer a metaphysical interpretation of the disaster in
their concluding remarks. For the pamphleteers the flood was an expression of God's anger and a punishment for men's sinful and 'Epicurean' life.

Both texts refer explicitly to the biblical Flood, to the times of Sodom and Gomorrah, Nineveh and to the sinful Jerusalem. Lastly, the Bible is quoted (Matthew 24:13), referring to the Day of Judgement, when 'the sea and the waves roar'. Both texts end with a prayer and a warning that the people should give up their sinful life and should be well-prepared for the last day. These texts are part of the European tradition of early modern woodcuts and pamphlets, which deal with natural phenomena such as comets, eclipses of the sun, earthquakes, etc. The prints were often issued for religious purposes and used to underline sermons and exhortations for the sinful community of believers.[19]

Similarly, Johan Fruytier, the earliest contemporary interpreter of the flood, saw the hand of God at work in the disaster. He opens his aforesaid chronicle with a quotation from Habakkuk (3:8,9): 'Was Thine anger against the rivers? Was the Lord displeased against the rivers? Was Thy wrath against the sea, that Thou didst ride upon Thine horses and Thy chariots of salvation?' He then continues in his prologue with an outline of the aims of his writing: 'I had to tell those among you who do not live next to the sea, what I have seen with my own eyes and what witnesses and survivors have told me. My report shall serve as an admonition and as a warning of all those punishments which were sent upon us for our sins.' Fruytier's chronicle was widely read and went into a second edition (1622). Contemporaries and later historians frequently quoted from his work and often used his figures in their accounts of the victims. Godevaert van Haecht, a chronicler from Antwerp and a contemporary of Fruytier, quoted whole passages from his book, which he praised as 'very good'. Although his own intention in writing the *Kroniek ... Over de Troebelen van 1565 tot 1574 te Antwerpen en Elders* was to give a historical account of the events of 1565–74 rather than to admonish his compatriots to abandon their sinful lifestyle, he saw Fruytier's work as a useful and necessary exercise for his contemporaries. As most of Fruytier's admonitions were underlined by examples taken from the Bible, Van Haecht refrained from quoting the complete works, but only printed the prologue and seven stanzas describing the disaster. He suggested that his readers turn to Fruytier's original and to a serious study of the Bible for further advice. Van Haecht's own account of the flooding which precedes his quotations from Fruytier is centred around the economic distress it caused in Antwerp.[20] Thus, a second group of texts related to the flood used the disaster as a vivid example of God's activities in the world and his discontent with human behaviour.

In the works of Emmanuel van Meteren, another contemporary of the flood and one of the most prominent national historiographers of the late sixteenth and early seventeenth centuries, the interpretation of the disaster becomes part of the political debate of the time. Central to this debate was the revolt of the Dutch provinces against the Spanish monarchy and the question of the political and philosophical justification of such an insurrection. In the *Historie van de oorlogen en Geschiedenissen der Nederlanderen*, Van Meteren comments on the disaster of 1570 in the light of recent political events. He devotes three pages of the book to the description and interpretation of the flood. Here, he describes the height of the water in comparison to previous floodings in 1530 and 1552. He then gives a detailed account of the damage done in Antwerp and estimates the financial losses at 100,000 guilders. Van Meteren had known Fruytier's account, which he referred to as 'as a very artful description in verse'. He then comments on what was obviously a current debate at the time. The Spaniards, as he points out, saw in the inundation a sign of the wrath of the Saints, 'who on their holiday rose against the destruction of the churches and the breaking of their images'. The Dutch, however, were convinced that the Saints were not vengeful, but that the flood was a sign of greater upheavals – be they political, economic or natural – to come. Van Meteren himself is anxious to portray the flood as just one natural disaster among many: 'One has to know that the Netherlands, situated at the Spanish Sea, are frequently the victim of very severe floodings, which usually take place in winter at the New Moon, and are accompanied by a north-westerly wind. These disasters happened often in the past centuries.' He then presents a long list of previous floods starting with the year 850 when the Rhine flooded the Katwijk and Dordrecht area. He mentions the floods of 1176, 1230, 1375, 1400, 1420, 1508, 1509, 1530 and 1552. Thus, the All Saints' Flood appears as one inundation among others and in no way different from previous disasters, which, in general, are the result of the particular geographical and climatic circumstances in the Low Countries and not a supernatural punishment for the revolt against the political *status quo*.[21] This interpretation set the agenda for later writers.

Thus, Pieter Corneliszoon Hooft, probably the most prominent writer of the early Dutch Republic, followed this interpretation in his *Nederlandsche Histooriën* published in 1642. For the year 1570 he mentions the floods:

> On the first day of November a storm arose from the North-west, which threw this part of the Ocean, swollen by the springtide of the New Moon, towards the beaches of the Netherlands. This happened with such might and thunder that few dikes and sluices, which had been built for the protection of the land and the people, could withstand the water's power. It is well known that the North Sea has often and for a long time flooded the coastline with similar power and has swept away large parts of the land, churches and whole villages. But of all catastrophes caused by the water, which

humankind can remember this is the most disastrous both in terror and in
damages. The storm lasted twice twenty-four hours.

He then gives a detailed account of the damage, which borrows both from
Van Meteren and from Fruytier. Lastly, he mentions the different interpretations of the disaster both by the Spaniards and by the Dutch, with the
latter seeming the more plausible explanation to him.[22] Histories and chron-
icles written from a pro-Spanish perspective offered a different interpretation of the disaster.

Philip de Kempenaere, a Flemish barrister and city official from Ghent,
mentions the *Allerheiligenvloed* and the following severe winter with heavy
snow and ice in January 1571 both in his *Dagboek ... sedert het Begin der Godsdienstberoerten tot den 5en April 1571* and in its later version *Vlaemsche Kronijk*,
which is updated to include events to 15 July 1585.[23] In the later chronicle
he states that less than two weeks after the disaster, on 12 November, the
Bishop of Ghent admonished his parishioners in his Sunday sermon to
observe a day of prayer and to participate in the processions held in the city
as a penance 'for the punishment of the flood'.[24] Neither the day of prayer
nor the procession are mentioned in his earlier diary. As a member of the
magistracy De Kempenaere formally had to convert to Protestantism in
1580, which was confirmed by an official oath. However, in private he
remained a faithful Catholic. After the reconquest of Flanders he subscribed
to the city's petition to the Spanish King asking his pardon for their uprising against the Crown and the Catholic Church in 1585. Rewriting his first
Dagboek, he obviously felt more secure in revealing his personal interpretation of the flood.

That the interpretation of the flood is closely related to the political and
religious viewpoint of the respective author is rendered particularly evident
in the comparison of two histories of the Dutch provinces which were written in 1620 and 1621. The Flemish historian Adrianus van Meerbeck mentions the disaster in his *Chroniicke vande Gantsche Werelt, ende sonderlinghe vande
seventhien Nederlanden*, printed in Antwerp in 1620. For him the catastrophe
bears 'all the signs of God's anger with the sinfulness of humankind, which
he punished with the flooding'.[25] His northern contemporary, Pieter Bor
Christianszon, a barrister, later treasurer of North Holland and official historian for the province, also mentions the flood in his *Orspronck, begin ende
vervolgh der Nederlantsche Orlogen* (1621). In his description, however, there
is no word of God's wrath. On the contrary, in his detailed description of
the flood, Christianszon repeatedly thanks God for having saved the people
of his country from further losses.[26]

Joan Jacquinet, another historian with a decisively pro-Catholic position, took up the argument that the flood was a reaction to the Iconoclastic Fury. In his *Princelijcke Historie van haer leven ende daden van paussen, keysers, konningen, hertogen* (1653), he mentions the 'flood on All Saints Day 1570':

> In the same year [as the arrival of the Duke of Alva] on All Saints' Day God brought about such a severe storm and great floods from the North-west that people could not remember a more terrible disaster and greater suffering. God showed this sign of His anger with the whole Netherlands caused by the breaking of the images and the destruction of the churches. The storm and the floods lasted for twenty-four hours. Dikes and sluices could not withstand its force. Whole towns disappeared in the wild sea and no less than 100,000 people died.[27]

This aspect is also taken up by Joan Franc Verbruggen in his *Jaerboek der Stadt van Antwerpen*, 1719. Here he mentions under the date 1 November 1570 that 'on the first of November there was so great a flood that people might truly call it the Second Great Flood'.[28]

Even more than 200 years after the disaster, in his *Vaderlandsche Historie*, published in 1792, the historian Jan Wagenaar referred to the controversy: only the uneducated and ignorant saw the floods as a sign of God's and the Saints' anger caused by the Iconoclastic Fury, while *de Onroomschen* – the Protestants – interpreted it as a foreboding of further decisive events in the political world. 'Meanwhile', he concludes, 'people believe that this country, which for centuries has been suffering inundation and high tides, has previously been confronted with greater and more damaging floods than the current disaster.' He thus picks up van Meteren's argument, that the Netherlands were an area which was naturally prone to this kind of disaster.[29]

Whether seen as God's punishment, a political omen or simply a natural disaster, people could not help but be confronted with recurring floods of their land. What action did they take in response? Which means did they devise in the – often futile – attempt to prevent the catastrophe from happening?

Dike maintenance in the Low Countries dates back to the thirteenth century. In those days juridical and institutional measures were taken to sustain dikes, dams and newly reclaimed lands. Local drainage and polder boards were set up. These committees, which in Holland were called *heemraadschappen*, consisted of representatives from the villages, towns and the local nobility. Eventually the counts of Holland and Zealand gained growing influence on these boards, which, then, were presided over by one of

their nominees, the so-called *dijkgraaf* (dike-count). His function often
included the maintenance of the dikes and dams, and he acted as a regional
official with fiscal, juridical and political responsibilities.

The building of huge sea-dikes of earth and rubble in the thirteenth
century marked the starting-point of land reclamation and dike maintenance.
There was a gradual improvement in techniques and build-up in the pace
and capacity of *poldering* and draining, culminating in the early part of the
Golden Age (1590–1648). Thereafter, the interest in land reclamation and
dike-building declined and stagnated until the middle of the eighteenth century.

The system of local responsibility for the maintenance of dams and
dikes remained intact until the accession of Charles V. In 1544 a new, cen-
tralised system utilising hydraulic technology was introduced, which caused
much resentment and popular protest among the local authorities, who
objected to the imperial nomination of the dike-counts.

What actually happened to repair the broken dikes and to reclaim the
land that was drowned is difficult to reconstruct.[30] The provinces of Holland
and Zealand were especially shaken by the uprising against Spain, which
severely affected the maintenance of a routine in local and regional administration. Usually the cities and towns affected by flooding were exempt
from taxation for some time, while money was collected both in the area
and elsewhere to repair the damage. After 1572, when Holland and Zealand
proclaimed their independence from Spain, local and regional boards responsible for taking precautions against floods were set up, which in many
cases returned to practices in use before the Habsburg centralisation. On 2
March 1576 an order was issued for the town of Teerneuzen in Zealand,
where a special *waterschapsbestuur*, a new administrative unit for the maintenance and repair of the dikes and waterways of the area, was set up. This
new local board replaced the authorities of the *hogheemraad*.[31] In Zealand,
waterclerquen were responsible for the monthly collection of the communal
contributions to the defensive works. These taxes were set and spent locally,
which supported a spirit of independence and local responsibility in the
respective communities. In cases of emergency, for instance after a dike had
been pierced in defence of the Spaniards in spring 1577, the community of
Wolphaartsdijk was granted a special subsidy, which was financed by the
towns and villages of the adjacent islands of Zealand, since this effort was
regarded as a 'community project'.[32] In their regular meetings the *waterclerquen* not only set and registered the sums collected for the dikes but also
organised other matters such as the acquisition of the material necessary to
support the defensive works. On 11 November 1577, for instance, the trea-
surers of Walcheren ordered the purchase of 935 trees worth 600 guilders

for dike maintenance in the area. Two years earlier, on 22 June 1575, they had decided that the area could not give its annual contribution to the salaries of the academic personnel at the University of Leiden, since this year, dike maintenance should have top priority. It seems that the professors in Leiden accepted this loss of income without any complaints, which is yet another indication both of the importance of dike maintenance and of the relative autonomy of the local boards in dealing with their own financial affairs.[33]

How the task of dike maintenance and precautions against further flooding were perceived in the public literature of the time, can best be captured in Martin Boxhorn's *Chronijk van Zeeland*, which was printed in Middelburg in 1644. In part I: xxiii, Boxhorn, a clerk and historian from Zealand, gives a detailed account of the historical tradition of dike maintenance in the Low Countries and particularly in Zealand. In this context his description of the sea deserves further notice: 'The wrath of the sea can never be underestimated. The history of the previous centuries gives evidence for her unseemly lust to swallow up the land.'[34] In his text the sea has human contours. Wrath, lust and swallowing are words normally used to describe bad traits in human beings. The sea itself is active in the destruction of the coastline, of villages and human lives, which become 'the waves' cat-and-mouse game':

> the grimness of her anger, which makes the solid earth tremble and causes hills and high mountains to collapse has often buried whole towns and their inhabitants. The waters assembled to swallow up the richest land and with the roaring winds form a battle array to surmount the highest and strongest earth and the most fertile ground and the towns with their men, women and children become the waves' cat-and-mouse game.[35]

This description adds another interesting and important feature to early modern man's attitudes towards the sea. For the inhabitants of the coastline the sea was often perceived as an 'enemy', who 'does not rest nor sleep ... , but comes, suddenly, like a roaring lion, seeking to devour the whole land', as Andries Vierlingh, Holland's most eminent dike-builder in the late sixteenth and early seventeenth centuries, puts it in his *Tractaet van Dyck-agie*.[36] Thus, a constant awareness of a disaster and a preparedness to fight against the waves was a central element of the coastal inhabitants' mentality.

In Boxhorn's book, the reasons for the disasters were not 'godts getarde wraeke' – God's anger. Instead, he offers a catalogue of explanations of mismanagement, of putting personal interests before those of the community, of internal strife between the cities and towns affected by the floods and of appointing the wrong person to the wrong position.

Boxhorn points out that the communities were burdened with additional taxes and collections which basically helped the princes – and later the Spanish monarchy – to fight their wars. The office of dike-reeve was sold to the person with the greatest financial offer rather than given to men who were most experienced or had a closer interest in the area and would therefore invest in the maintenance of the dikes. The money necessary for this enterprise – called *Slimpenning*, *Dijkpenning* or *Watergelden* – was collected within the respective community according to the size of the land of each contributor. The mismanagement of the dikes started, according to Boxhorn, in the years 1500–50. He complains about the magistrates and the authorities of the cities and towns of Zealand and their 'disputes and strife … amongst each other' and the vanity of certain local magnates who spent more money on copying the courtiers of the Burgundian and Habsburg courts than on the maintenance of the dikes.

For Boxhorn, the remedy against this mismanagement is community action in the form of common financial contribution and the willingness to fulfil one's responsibility towards the community. Every coastal inhabitant should be expected to help with the necessary repair and maintenance works at the dike. They should bring their wheelbarrows, spades, carts and other tools to contribute to the work.

> that by the ringing of the bells and according to the ordinances of the dike-count or some of his sworn officials all country folk should be united from thence on without exceptions and excuses to come to the dikes with sledges, carts, wagons, baskets and bells and other tools and useful materials and should help to repair and to keep the dikes on severe pains. All workers, who are employed by the dike works are summoned to come whenever necessary, on severe pains, and should bring their spades, carts and cams for the maintenance of the dikes.[37]

Similar criticism had earlier been uttered by Andries Vierlingh. In his *Tractaet von Dyckagie* he criticised the appointment of officials, who were ignorant of the area, incompetent, and had been appointed through court favours.[38] Describing one emergency when a dike nearly broke, Vierlingh, like Boxhorn, propagates the ideal of the Dutch citizens united in their common fight against the sea. Thus, dike maintenance acquired the quality of a task for the community acting in solidarity.

For Dutch men and women in early modern times the sea was an essential part of their lives. This experience was often shaped by fear of floods and inundation and consequent losses of land, property and life. The reaction to the disasters of floods as they are preserved in diaries, letters, pamphlets and histories can offer at least a glimpse at the way people tried to cope with and make sense of this constant threat. In the late sixteenth and early seventeenth centuries, a period which was characterised by great political, economic and cultural upheavals culminating in the uprising against Spain and the eventual establishment of the seventeen United Provinces, floods could have a metaphorical significance. Some contemporaries tried to interpret them as signs of God's disapproval of their sinful lives and of their armed protest against the established powers of the Catholic Church and the Habsburg monarchy. The All Saints' Flood of 1570, which has been taken as an example of early modern 'disaster management', was popularised as the just punishment for a sinful lifestyle, but in the light of recent events in the Low Countries – the Iconoclastic Fury of 1566 and the rise of Protestantism – it became part of the political discourse on the war with Spain. Catholic and pro-Spanish writers saw in the floods a godly sign, while Protestant supporters of the Netherlands tried to convince their readers that – as a consequence of their particular geographic situation – the Low Countries were and had always been confronted with natural disasters caused by the sea.[39]

With regard to the preventive measures taken against further inundation and the maintenance of dikes and dams, the coastal inhabitants were advised to be aware of the constant threat of the dangerous sea. The sea was portrayed as an enemy, whose sole intention was the destruction of human efforts at land reclamation and a prosperous and peaceful life on the coast. The fight against the sea could only be won by communal effort, which required the mutual aid and assistance of all members of the community.

Notes

1 I would like to thank Bärbel Brodt and Angela Schwarz for their helpful comments on this chapter.
2 For a discussion of the sea as a breeding-ground for disease see Otto S. Knottnerus, 'Angst voor de zee. Veranderende culturel patronen langs de Nederlandse den Duitse waddenkust (1500–1800)', in Karel Davids et al., eds, De Republiek tussen zee en vasteland. Buitenlandse invloeden op cultuur, economie en politiek in Nederland, 1580–1800 (Leuven, 1995), 57–81.
3 See, for instance, Jean Delumeau, La Peur en Occident: XIVe–XVIIIe siècles (Paris, 1978); Alain Corbin, Le Territoire du vide. L'Occident et le désir du rivage (Paris, 1988); Manfred Jakubowski-Tiessen, Sturmflut 1717. Die Bewältigung einer Naturkatastrophe in der Frühen Neuzeit (Munich, 1992). Arno Borst, 'Das Erdbeben von 1348. Ein historischer Beitrag zur Katastrophenforschung', HZ, 233 (1981), 529–69. For a more general discussion on man and nature see Keith Thomas, Man and the Natural World: Changing Attitudes in Eng-

land, 1500–1800 (1983) and Simon Schama, *Landscape and Memory* (1995).

4 Recent histories of the Low Countries are Simon Schama, *The Embarrassment of Riches* (New York, 1987) and Jonathan Israel, *The Dutch Republic. Its Rise, Greatness and Fall 1477–1806* (Oxford, 1995).

5 Pieter Winsemius, *Chronique ofte Hist. geschiedenisse van Vrieslant etc.* (Franeker, 1622), 550–1. This and the following translations of the original documents are by the author.

6 Johan Fruytier, *Corte beschrijvinghe van de ellendighen ende seer beclaghelycken watervloet, di op den 1 Novembris 1570 in allen landen aen de Noerdtzee geleghen, is gesciet met afspoelinge van vele huysen, beesten en menschen met duysenten, op ryme gestelt door Johan Fruytier, di ook geen lange jaeren hierna en leefde etc.* (1571; 2nd edn Leiden, 1622).

7 See M. K. Elisabeth Gottschalk, *Stormvloeden en Rivieroverstromingen in Nederland* (Assen, 1975), 2: 701.

8 Gottschalk, *Stormvloeden*, 701.

9 The letter is printed in full in A. de Roever, ed., *Iets Over Den Allerheiligen-Vloed*, Oud-Holland 7 (1889), 189–94. The following quotations are taken from this edition.

10 See Manfred Jakubowski-Tiessen, *Sturmflut 1717* (Munich, 1992), 217–25. For further discussions of the importance of a proper burial in early modern times see Andrew Spicer, Ch. 10, in this volume.

11 For the folk memory of the St Elizabeth's Day Flood see H. van den Waal, *Drie Eeuwen Vaderlandsche Geschieds-Uitbeelding* ('s-Gravenhage, 1952), 1: 255–7.

12 For further details see Gottschalk, *Stormvloeden*.

13 See, for instance, *Dagboek van Jan de Pottre, 1549–1602*, Maetschappij der Vlaemsche Bibliophilen, 3rd ser., 5 (1864) and W. J. Formsma and R. van Roijen, eds, *Diarium van Egbert Alting, 1553–1594* ('s-Gravenhage, 1964).

14 Roever, *Allerheiligen-Vloed*, 191.

15 *Dagboek van Jan de Pottre*, 35–6; *Diarium van Egbert Alting*, 182.

16 See, for instance, *De Delftse Bijbel van 1477* (Amsterdam, 1977) and *De Nederlandse Statenbijbel 1637* (Amsterdam: Delft). For a further discussion of God's manifestations in nature see Gerhard Bott, ed., *Zeichen vom Himmel. Flugblätter des 16. Jahrhunderts* (Nuremberg, 1982); Wilhelm Heß, *Himmels- und Naturerscheinungen in Einblattdrucken des XV. bis XVIII. Jahrhunderts* (Leipzig, 1911); Hartmut Lehmann, 'Frömmigkeitsgeschichtliche Auswirkungen der "Kleinen Eiszeit"', in Wolfgang Schieder, ed., *Volksreligiosität in der modernen Sozialgeschichte* (Göttingen, 1986), 31–50.

17 If the author of the pamphlet added this episode to stress the fact, that not only the Dutch, but also their Spanish enemies were victims of God's wrath, is open to debate.

18 W. P. C. Knuttel, *Catalogue van de Pamfletten-Verzameling Berustende in de Koninklijke Bibliotheek* ('s-Gravenhage, 1889), 1: 1486–1620, no. 187, 'Jammerliche underschröckliche Zeitung ausz Niderland, ... van dem schaden, viler Landt, Stett, ... welche durch schröckliche Wassersnoth der Meers ... untergegangen seind ... . Anno MDCLXX, Getruckt zu Strasburg bey Thiebolt Berger 1571'.

19 Heß, *Himmels- und Naturerscheinungen*. Other disasters, such as fires, were also frequently exploited by preachers to appeal to their audience for a reflection on their lifestyle and for moral reforms. For a discussion of this aspect see also Penny Roberts' chapter on fire in French cities, Ch. 1, this volume.

20 Robert van Roosbroeck, ed., *De Kroniek van Godevaert van Haecht. Over de Troebelen van 1565 tot 1574 te Antwerpen en Elders* (Antwerp, 1929), 135–7. For the use of Fruytier's figures see also Pieter Corneliszoon Hooft, *Nederlandsche Histooriën* (Amsterdam, 1703), Book VI, 217.

21 Emmanuel van Meteren, *Historie van de Oorloghen en Geschiedenissen der Nederlanderen, en der zelver Naburen* (Gronichen, 1748), 525–7. Previously published with a few alterations as *Belgische ofte Nederlantsche Historie van onze tijden* (Cologne, 1595; Delft, 1599), and as *Commentarien ofte Memorien van den Nederlandtschen Staet/Handel Orloghen ende Geschiedenissen van onsen tyden* (n.p., 1608).

22 Pieter Corneliszoon Hooft, *Nederlandsche Histooriën sedert de overdraght der Heerschappye van Keizer Karel den Vyvden op Kooning Philips zynen zoon* (Amsterdam, 1642), 205–6.

23 Philip de Kempenaere, *Dagboek van Cornelis & Philip van Campene, Behelzende Het Verhaal Der Merkwaardigste Gebeurtenissen, voorgefallen te Gent sedert het Begin der Godsdienstberoerten tot den 5en April 1571* (Ghent, 1870), Frans de Potter, ed., and his *Vlaemsche Kronijk of Dagregister van al het gene gedenkweerdig vorgefallen is, Binnen de Stad Gent sedert den 15 July 1566 tot 15 July 1585* (Ghent, 1839).

24 Philip de Kempenaere, *Vlaemsche Kronijk* (Ghent, 1839), 87–8.

25 Adrianus van Meerbeck, *Chroniicke vande Gantsche Werelt, ende sonderlinghe vande seventhien Nederlanden* (Antwerp, 1620), 301.

26 Pieter Bor Christianszon, *Orsprong, begin ende vervolgh der Nederlantsche Oorlogen* (Leiden-Amsterdam, 1621), fol. 236.

27 BL, Add. MS, 17.89, Joan Jacquinet, *De Princelijcke Historie van haer leven ende daden van paussen, keysers, konningen, hertogen ect, 1653*, fos. 66v-67.

28 BL, King's Manuscript, 178, *Jaerboek der Stadt Antwerpen Bij een vergadert door Joan Franc Verbruggen, Het Eerste Deel 1719*, fol. 389v.

29 Jan Wagenaar, *Vaderlandsche Historie, vervattende de Geschiedenis der nu Vereeingten Nederlanden, inzonderheid die van Holland, van de vroegste Tyden af, uit de geloofswaardigste Schryvers en egte gedenkstukken samengestelt* (Amsterdam, 1792), 324.

30 The archives of the provincial governments of Holland and Zealand, particularly for the time before 1574, were to a great extent destroyed in the Second World War.

31 P. Dieleman, *Het Quartier van Ter Neusen* (Middelburg, 1959), 108.

32 RZ, SZ, Inv. no. 3227, p. 245. For further examples of the importance of community solidarity see Roberts, Ch. 1, and Naphy, Ch. 2, this volume.

33 RZ, SZ, Inv. no. 3227, waterclerquen 1576, 16 June, n.p.; see also Inv. no. 3227, p. 245, Dijkagie, 1577.

34 Martin Boxhorn, *Chronijk van Zeelandt* (Middelburg, 1644), 200.

35 *Ibid.*, 200.

36 Andries Vierlingh, *Tractaet van Dyckagie (1603)*, J. de Hullu and A.G. Verhoeven, eds ('s-Gravenhage, 1920).

37 Boxhorn, *Chronijk*, 202.

38 Vierlingh, *Traectaet*, 22, 49, 218–19.

39 This aspect has been largely neglected by Simon Schama. See Schama, *Riches*, 25–50.

5

The enemy within and without: an anatomy of fear on the Spanish Mediterranean littoral

BRUCE TAYLOR

The uniqueness of Spain's historical experience is owed, among other things, to the marked ethnic and cultural admixture that continued to characterise it into the early modern period as it had done throughout the course of the Middle Ages.[1] It was the history, the fact and the implication of this diversity which, to a considerable extent, shaped the mentality of the new and thrusting society that unfolded in Spain from the end of the fifteenth century, and conditioned its reaction to the wider European, Mediterranean and Atlantic worlds. The character of this new society, by turns innovative and conservative, confident and insecure, is nowhere more clearly revealed than in the *morisco* question – in the status of converted Muslims under Christian rule – and it is this that makes it one of the nodal issues of early modern Spanish and Mediterranean history. In this light, the decline of the pluralistic society that had characterised medieval Iberia until the end of the fourteenth century carries as much interest as its very creation in the conquest and coalescence of an earlier age. It is, therefore, to some of the underlying causes and aspects of this disintegration that we shall be turning our attention here.

In particular, this chapter will attempt to focus on one of the central aspects of the *morisco* issue in the context of early modern Spanish society: the pervasive and deepening climate of fear with which it became inextricably linked and intertwined, and which did not finally dissolve until the end of the eighteenth century.[2] It is fear, therefore, as both motor and corollary of change and experience that we shall here attempt to dissect.

In 1614 the people of Gibraltar wrote to Philip III informing him of the economic and physical travails they were suffering at the hands of the Muslim corsairs raiding their shores from the Barbary Coast.[3] The incursions were not new. In 1540 a large Algerian fleet had landed 900 pirates who proceeded to sack the town with exemplary thoroughness.[4] Attacks continued, but the 1570s still found Gibraltar's defences unimproved and it was only in the last decades of the century that steps were taken to remedy this situation. By the time the Gibraltarians composed their letter to the King, the town had erected nine watch-towers, these defended by forty-two sentries whose ranks were swelled during the summer months by a motley guard of local men.[5] However, these precautions did not prove altogether satisfactory, for, as the letter makes clear, the people felt secure 'neither at night nor during the day, neither in bed nor at mealtimes, neither in the fields nor in our homes'.[6] Corsair assaults continued unabated, with dozens of people carried away to North Africa each year and huge sums being required to ransom them from captivity. Gibraltar was clearly as exposed to pirate attack as anywhere on the Spanish coast during this period, but the same litany of panic and disaster can be found along the entire southern littoral, from the Balearics and Cadaqués in Catalonia to Ayamonte on the Atlantic coast and beyond.

By the beginning of the seventeenth century Gibraltarian fears were largely confined to the possibility of external attack, but this had not always been the case here, and neither was it elsewhere on the Spanish littoral at this time. In the Kingdom of Valencia, and in that of Granada until 1570, the terror among Old Christians that they might one day behold a sea covered with Barbary shipping was compounded by the widespread belief that their own neighbours in the *morisco* community were actively colluding with their coreligionists in North Africa. Indeed, far from being the product of hysterical bigotry, there is every indication that they were fully justified in holding this view. In September 1566, for example, the Andalusian coastal village of Benicanón was attacked by a party of corsairs with the collusion of local *moriscos*.[7] The attack resulted in the evacuation of ninety-nine *moriscos* and the capture of forty-three Christians from the same village. In another case, in October 1583, fifteen Valencian *moriscos* were executed for having 'guided the corsairs from the sea in the sack of Chilches and burnt the church' a month earlier.[8] As the Benedictine historian Dom Diego de Haëdo declared in his extraordinary *Topographia e historia general de Argel*, 'In this way they [the corsairs] have ruined the entire coast of Spain, relying to a very considerable degree on the assistance of the *moriscos* who live there, and who, being more Muslim than the Barbary peoples themselves, receive, succour, and inform them of all they wish and need to know.'[9] The impact of this combined internal and external threat on the life and *mentalité* of Old Christian and *morisco* alike, and the fears that underpinned it or were in turn generated by it, form the basis of this chapter.

However, it is important at this stage to underline the place of this phenomenon within the broader compass of Mediterranean politics and society from the end of the fifteenth century.[10] During the early modern period much of the Christian Mediterranean coast was plagued by incursions from Barbary pirates in what remains one of the most protracted, most disruptive and least recognised conflicts of the age. Naturally, the West did not remain passive in the face of this onslaught: Christian privateers operated throughout the period with the same violence and brutality as their Muslim counterparts.[11] The Spanish Habsburgs in particular replied with several large-scale military expeditions, but their efforts were in the main informed by criteria of defence and containment which were quite absent from the corsair mentality and that of their Turkish allies. Parts of southern France, Italy and Sicily were at times seriously affected by corsair activity, but it was Spain which remained the favourite target, and Spaniards who, more than any other nation, found themselves languishing in the *baños* and prisons of the Barbary Coast.[12]

The basis of this struggle lies in the gradual breakdown of relations between Christian Europe and Islam from the fall of Constantinople in 1453, and the 'clash of empires' that took place between Spain and the Turks during the sixteenth century.[13] However, that Spain should find herself at the interstices of this conflict reflects both her status as a major power in the Mediterranean and the presence of an unassimilated *morisco* minority within her borders following the fall of Granada in 1492. Unlike the Ottoman threat, the pirate raids that terrified the Old Christian population of Gibraltar and the rest of the Spanish littoral might not in themselves have been a major strategic concern to the Crown, far as they often were from the main centres of power. However, by the abdication of Charles V in 1556 the Crown had come to regard the *morisco* population who colluded with Spain's enemies as a serious danger to the corporeal and spiritual health of the State, and not least as a 'fifth column' that might provide the nucleus for a second Muslim invasion of the Peninsula.[14] These considerations serve as an important reminder of the international dimension of the *morisco* crisis that developed in Spain during the sixteenth century, and which informed the climate of fear that gathered over it and its frontiers.

By the end of the fourteenth century the so-called *convivencia* that had bound Christian, Jew and Muslim into an uneasy social and confessional pluralism was beginning to disintegrate.[15] The paradox of *convivencia* was that, in positing an uneasy social contract based on relative freedom of worship for religious minorities, it made permanent assimilation impossible. Throughout the fifteenth century the social and cultural tensions inherent in a system of limited toleration began to be reflected in a range of increasingly oppressive measures against Jews and converted Jews – *conversos* – in particular. In 1449 the first decrees touching on racial and religious purity – *limpieza de sangre* – were passed, and attempts made to assuage Old Christian fears of cont- amination by enforcing strict segregation between communities.[16] This men- tality culminated with the establishment by the Catholic Kings of the Inquisition in 1478 and, two years later, with the renewal of the *Reconquista* against the Kingdom of Granada, the last Muslim outpost in the Peninsula.[17] The Reconquest was made good with the fall of Granada itself on 1 Janu- ary 1492, to be followed on 31 March by the expulsion or forced conver- sion of the remaining Jewish population.

Despite fears that Spain's driving apostolic mission might be compro- mised, the Crown showed considerable restraint where the Granadine Moors were concerned, and opted for a policy of tolerant evangelisation that would preserve the existing socio-economic structure, and allow Castile to pursue her imperial destiny undisturbed. The terms of the capit- ulation were generous to the vanquished *mudéjares* – Moors under Christ- ian rule – guaranteeing them their religion, customs, laws and property.[18] Matters proceeded under the moderate first Archbishop of Granada, the Jeronymite Fray Hernando de Talavera, but the segregation policies of an earlier generation militated against any effective progress being made towards evangelisation. By 1499 hardliners were preparing to adopt a policy of forced conversion, and any hope of a peaceful continuum was dashed by the outbreak of revolts first in Granada and then in the Sierra de Alpujar- ras.[19] The prevailing view now was that the *mudéjares* had breached the capitulation treaty of 1492 and should be offered the same choice as the Jews: conversion or expulsion. Cheek by jowl with a mass of Old Christ- ian settlers and with little alternative but to comply, the majority of *mudé- jares* chose baptism to an unfeasible exile.[20] Mass conversions took place in Granada throughout 1501, to be followed by others in the rest of the Crown of Castile from 1502. However, though the neophytes were offi- cially granted near-equality with Old Christians, in solving one problem – that of religious plurality – the Crown had merely laid the foundations of another within the body of Christian society: that of a restive and unas- similated *morisco* minority.[21]

Though certainly the youngest and one of the largest, the *morisco* com- munity of the Kingdom of Granada was by no means the only grouping of conquered Muslims in Spain.[22] Elsewhere in Castile an older *mudéjar* com- munity lay thinly spread across the land, while in the Crown of Aragon, and Valencia in particular, a large rural proletariat played a key part in agrarian society.[23] Having been under Christian rule since the twelfth and thirteenth centuries, the *mudéjar* populations of the Crown of Aragon were generally, though not exclusively, less homogenous than their counterparts in the Kingdom of Granada, where a long tradition of independence was coupled with the memory of recent Muslim rule. In Valencia and Aragon a mainly rural population had been enserfed by the nobility to whom it paid feudal dues in return for protection and toleration. An economic rather than a religious imperative therefore governed the lives of the Aragonese *mudé-jares*, whose customs were preserved in order to maintain the livelihood of the seigneurs.

For the most part, the *mudéjares* of the Crown of Aragon occupied the Ebro valley and its tributaries, the dry uplands of the interior and the flood plains of the littoral, where they brought their irrigation techniques to bear on the cultivation of rice and mulberry bushes for the production of silk. Thus, whereas the *mudéjar* populations of the Crown of Castile were well represented in the towns, their Aragonese brethren tended to live confined to the land – baronial land above all – and often in complete isolation from Old Christians. Insufficient evidence survives to give accurate statistics for the *mudéjar* and *morisco* populations of Spain in this period. By the 1560s, however, 54 per cent of the population of the Kingdom of Granada was of Muslim origin, with *moriscos* amounting to over 30 per cent of that of Valencia and 20 per cent of that of Aragon in the late sixteenth century (about 150,000 and 50,000 respectively).[24] The *morisco* population of Catalonia remained under 10,000 during the entire period, while the Kingdom of Castile had, until after 1570, a proportionately even smaller community numbering only around 20,000 in 1502. By 1600 the *morisco* population of Spain amounted to over 300,000, perhaps 4 per cent of the whole.[25]

For the Valencian *mudéjares* the outbreak of the Revolt of the *Germanías* in 1519 spelled the end of a pattern of life that had remained substantially unchanged since the early fourteenth century.[26] Based on the grievances of urban artisans against the landed nobility, the leaders of the revolt saw the freeing of *mudéjares* from vassalage to the aristocracy as the most effective means of destroying their authority. The military support given by the Valencian *mudéjares* to their overlords inevitably converted the *Germanías* into a religious pogrom, and from 1520 onwards thousands were forcibly baptised in an orgy of apocalyptic fervour. However, although the Crown accepted that the majority of these conversions had been made under duress, the defeat of the *Germanías* in 1522 did not bring about a reverse of this situation. The Inquisition regarded all baptisms as valid, and in November 1525 Charles V ordered the conversion or expulsion of the remaining *mudé-jares* of Valencia and the Crown of Aragon. By 1526 Muslim Spain had officially ceased to exist, *convivencia* was at an end, and the Church found itself with the task of catechising tens of thousands of *moriscos* who were Christian in name only.[27] Like the rest of Spanish society, the task of assimilation was one which the mass of the clergy were poorly prepared to accept.

For the majority of Old Christians, the reality of the *moriscos'* Muslim background, the circumstances under which many of them had been brought under Christian rule and the doubtful sincerity of their conversions provided the obvious basis upon which they should be judged and treated. Apart from the capitulation treaties of the 1480s and that of Granada itself in 1492, the Spanish authorities never escaped from the nagging suspicion that the *moriscos* represented a terrible danger at the very heart of their society. And even here the underlying fear among Spaniards that the *mudéjares* might receive assistance from their coreligionists was reflected in several laws forbidding them from establishing contacts inside or outside the Peninsula or bearing arms in frontier areas.[28] From 1492 concern that Granada in particular might become a focus of anti-Christian sedition in Spain prompted a post-Conquest policy of resettlement and segregation that effectively ruled out any prospect of lasting coalescence.

The revolts of 1499 and 1500 and the conversions that followed them provoked a series of measures intended both to reaffirm earlier legislation and to move against those Islamic practices felt to undermine respect for Christianity. Unfortunately, the great wave of *mudéjar* conversions came in a period when the Church, increasingly committed as it was in the New World, was unwilling to launch a full-scale evangelising campaign in areas officially regarded as Christian.[29] With the *moriscos*, now surrounded by Old Christian immigrants, dissembling their religion, the government set about eliminating those social practices that were the outward manifestations of their Islamic belief and identity. Led by the Duke of Alba, in 1505 the Crown issued a blanket prohibition against Muslim baths, dress, weddings, circumcision, hair-styles, names and dietary laws, in fact almost the entire range of Moorish practice.[30] Though this proved impossible to enforce, the die was cast and from 1511 onwards the Crown passed a series of decrees in an effort to oblige the *moriscos* to abandon their traditional customs. These culminated in December 1526 with a comprehensive ban on *morisco* culture, including the use of Arabic.[31] However, the effect of these measures (and of the conversions themselves in the Crown of Aragon) was lessened by the signing of secret agreements between Charles V and *morisco* leaders in Valencia and Granada during 1526 and 1527.[32] These suspended the implementation of the aforementioned ban for forty years, and attempted, with rather less success, to restrict the activities of the Inquisition against Valencian *moriscos* in particular. Underlying this course of action was a recognition of the impossibility of the *moriscos* abandoning all their customs at once. However, it also reflected both the concerns of the aristocracy for their feudal rights and the incomes derived from these, and the widely-held conviction in both Church and State of the need for a proper programme of proselytisation. This was one destined never to come to fruition.

In Valencia particularly the landed nobility were cast as the protectors of a newly-converted *morisco* minority who, under a veneer of Christian practice, preserved their Islamic ways largely intact.[33] However, as the aftermath of the Revolt of the Alpujarras and the events of the *Germanías* had demonstrated, the pressure for the elimination of Islamic culture and the enforcement of Christian practice had widespread social support. The failure of the authorities to take the initiative in this led to continued and growing tension between *moriscos* and Old Christians over dress, language, customs and food in particular.[34] The cultural rupture dividing the two communities was reflected in a complete lack of integration which in turn fuelled mutual antagonism. For the *moriscos*, the effect of this was the development of a more cohesive society that was better able to frustrate attempts to bring about its conversion. Under these circumstances, the *moriscos* were predominantly and increasingly seen by Old Christians less as a rich field for evangelisation than as a growing threat to their own culture, a people unassimilated, ill-conformed, unpredictable and largely incomprehensible. And indeed, within a few years of their conversion, the actions of the *moriscos* themselves had begun to give tangible form to these fears and suspicions, eliciting ever more repressive measures against them from society at large.

Rejected by a society ever more intolerant of any form of cultural plurality, it is little wonder that the *moriscos* looked to the resurgence of Islam first under the Turks and then under Ottoman administration in North Africa to save them from an increasingly intractable situation in Spain.[35] In an Arabic poem sent to Sultan Bayezit II (1481–1512) in the early years of the sixteenth century, the Granadine *moriscos* explained how Christian persecution had obliged them to dissimulate in order to preserve their beliefs – in marked contrast to the tolerance shown to infidels under Islam – and ended by calling on the Turks to intervene on their behalf.[36] However, it was not the Turks so much as the Barbary corsairs in whom the *moriscos* found their staunchest allies during the sixteenth century.

The Barbary pirates had first turned their attention to the Spanish littoral at the end of the fourteenth century.[37] This activity, which found its justification in holy war, acquired a distinctively anti-Spanish character with the steady influx of Hispano-Muslims into North Africa that began in earnest during the conquest of the Kingdom of Granada. The intimate local knowledge they brought with them, the bitterness of their exile and the strengthened ideological base that grew out of this resulted in a major intensification of corsairing against Spanish shores from the end of the fifteenth century.[38] As the great Ottoman admiral and corsair commander Hayreddin Barbarossa indicated in the *Gazavatname* (his dictated memoirs) in the following century, the conquest of Granada had not only implied the imposition of Christian rule, but a concerted and unprecedented attempt to destroy Muslim society also.[39] It was on the basis of this 'cultural disengagement'[40] that the Barbary pirates now set out against Spain, and it was their depredations that influenced Ferdinand and Isabella's decision to carry their crusade to North Africa in 1497. However, early successes were not carried through, and the campaign represents a missed opportunity that had serious implications for Spain. As has been made clear, 'Spain's limited measures along the [Barbary] coast not only failed to curb corsair activity, but also provided a pretext and an opportunity for Ottoman penetration into North Africa.'[41] The principal result of this was the establishment of Algiers as a Turkish fief under Barbarossa from 1516.[42] The westward march of the Ottoman frontier therefore made the Algerian corsairs under Barbarossa and his successors an integral part of Turkish naval power and key players in the struggle both against and within Spain.

The onslaught that the Barbary corsairs now directed against the Peninsula was, as Friedman indicates, 'brought home to more Spaniards, in a more direct and personal way, and may have stirred up more religious and national feeling than any of the major wars in which Spain was involved in the sixteenth and seventeenth centuries'.[43] Equally, the phenomenon of captivity, and the fear associated with it, can be regarded, both individually and collectively, as the most tangible aspect of this continuing confrontation.[44] Captivity in North Africa, with all that this implied, represented a real concern for all sectors of Spanish society, not only those living on the coast or travelling by or near the sea, but for anyone with friends or relatives in captivity and burdened with the responsibility of raising money and arranging for their release.[45] It was, moreover, a fate from which no socioeconomic group could consider itself exempt, as surviving lists of ransomed captives make clear.

How many Spaniards were taken into captivity through corsair action in the early modern age? Clear data survives for only a fraction of those ransomed, let alone captured, but the sample is sufficiently large to give some impression of the circumstances under which people might lose their freedom to the Barbary corsairs. In a survey of 9,500 of the captives rescued by the two orders of redemption – the Mercedarians and the Trinitarians[46] – between 1575 and 1769, some 20 per cent had been captured on land or in immediate coastal waters, though the real figure was probably much higher, given that landsmen were never a priority of the ransomers.[47] Of these, 43 per cent had been captured in the vicinity of their homes. Seafarers were in especial danger: 26.6 per cent had been seized while fishing and a further 12.3 per cent while shipping merchandise in coastal waters. Another 3.7 per cent were seized while engaged in agricultural activities on the coast. The remainder of those ransomed were captured on the high seas or as the result of military actions. By the mid-sixteenth century it is possible that there were as many as 15,000–20,000 Spanish captives on the Barbary Coast, though this must only be considered a rough estimate.

So far as it is possible to tell, the only beneficiaries of corsairing in Spain were the ransoming agencies, most notably the Mercedarians and the Trinitarians, who enriched themselves – often at great risk, it has to be said – while making captive-taking such a profitable activity for the pirates. During the sixteenth century the Algerian and, indeed, much of the North African economy came to depend on the ransoms paid for Christian, and particularly Spanish captives.[48] By 1550 some 15,000 men were engaged in privateering in Algiers, and a century later the number of captives here had reached 25,000.[49] The frequency of Spanish redemption expeditions, the high prices they commanded (frequently paid in bullion) and the special circumstances prevailing in the Peninsula therefore made Spaniards the most sought after captives in the Mediterranean.[50] Voices were raised throughout the seventeenth century against organised redemptionism, which was seen, rightly, as a key inducement to the taking of captives and an intolerable drain of money to Spain's enemies.[51] However, ransoming activity continued unimpaired, and the prominent position occupied by these orders allowed them to craft skilful propaganda which intensified the fear and revulsion felt by ordinary Spaniards, both for the corsairs themselves and for the unspeakable horrors of confinement on the Barbary Coast. Clearly, for many, the fear of attack and captivity bore as great an effect as the reality of this taking place.[52]

Naturally, the volume of those captured and the circumstances under which they lost their freedom reflected the ebb and flow of events both in the Mediterranean and Spain itself. Already in 1515 Ferdinand the Catholic was authorising Catalan artisans' guilds to arm themselves against the threat of corsairs and marauding mudéjares, and two years later a second decree permitted the bearing of arms against any 'moors, enemies, robbers and corsairs'.[53] The expansion of Algerian corsair activity after 1516, the first major foray of the Turkish Navy into the Western Mediterranean, and the outbreak of the Germanías caused Barcelona to brace herself for an attack over the winter of 1519 which never materialised.[54] However, major corsair attacks were registered at Denia and Alicante in Valencia in 1518, at Badalona not far from Barcelona in 1527, at Parcent in Valencia in 1529, and against Minorca in 1535.[55] From now on the entire Catalan, Valencian and Balearic coast lived in a permanent state of undeclared war, while the ready availability of weapons compounded a growing banditry problem in Catalonia and contributed to a general sense of disorder. Frantic attempts were made to establish militias and defensive leagues between local towns, and improve coastal defences whose inadequacy had been amply demonstrated.[56] In 1527 and again in 1532 corsairs were able to land on the beach at Barcelona and take a number of captives under the nose of the Viceroy before withdrawing.

The capture of Tunis by Charles V in 1535 was a major success, but one the Emperor was unable to repeat against Algiers in 1541, and the pace of Muslim incursions against Spanish shores continued unchecked. The following year the Turkish fleet attacked Majorca and then wintered at Toulon before sallying forth again in 1543 with raids on Cadaqués, Rosas and Palamós in Catalonia.[57] Co-ordinated attacks by French soldiery against Perpignan were driven back by the Duke of Alba in 1542 and 1543, but the steady fall of Spanish *plazas* (fortresses) on the Barbary Coast boded ill for Imperial defence. By now too the Spanish littoral was in a state of near hysteria, and the prisons of Algiers were filled to overflowing with thousands of captives.

Inevitably, the commonly-held associations of most Spaniards between Muslims and captivity left an indelible mark on popular culture, and not least on Cervantes, who was himself a captive in Algiers during the 1570s.[58] The generous donations given to the orders of redemption by people from all walks of life may therefore reflect not only pity and generosity, but also fear that such a fate might be visited upon themselves. This very tangible amalgam of fears had a lasting effect not only on the mentality of Old Christians, but on the character of coastal regions in particular.[59] The sustained corsair threat led to the abandonment of large sectors of the Spanish littoral, and by 1600 long stretches of coastline had been deserted, with only those towns regarded as well fortified retaining their numbers. Though Valencia was less affected, the Granadan littoral was largely depopulated and the Murcian coast completely deserted except for Mazarrón and Cartagena. Local economies suffered commensurately, especially those dependent on fishing, and coastal trade and communications were badly disrupted, with many small boats being seized. Constant vigilance was necessary, with alerts often causing settlements to be temporarily evacuated, as in the case of Villajoyosa in Valencia which was sacked and burnt for three days in October 1543.[60] The costs of defence and replacing losses were

reflected in taxes on fish, meat, cattle and silk in many Mediterranean communities. The cost in human terms was incalculable.

   Naturally, the main psychological effect of this climate of fear was the
development of a siege mentality among ordinary Spaniards which added to
the xenophobic policy increasingly pursued by the State.[61] The accession of
Philip II in 1556 and the uncovering of Protestant cells in Seville and Valladolid ushered in an increasingly dogmatic approach to the dangers of religious deviation and an enhanced concern for the security of Spain's frontiers.
These concerns were given a greater immediacy by a renewed Muslim
onslaught in the 1550s. The death of Barbarossa in 1543 brought about a
temporary respite, but within a few years attacks were once more being
made against Spanish shores under a new generation of leaders and with
renewed ferocity. In 1551 Turgut Reis (Dragut) took Tripoli and in 1558
the Turkish fleet under Piali Pasha sacked Ciutadela on Minorca, capturing
or killing 5,000 people and causing Philip to consider the evacuation of the
entire island.[62] Naples was attacked in the same year and in 1560 the North
African *plaza* of Gerba fell to the Turks. Fears for a parallel *morisco* uprising
in Valencia were not realised, but disturbances along the Ebro in 1559
caused the Aragonese Inquisition to order the disarming of all New Christians.[63] The following year the King ordered the Duke of Segorbe, Captain-
general of Valencia, to muster forces on the coast to repel an imminent
Moorish attack, and permitted Old Christians to take possession of any
money or goods that escaping *moriscos* might attempt to carry away with
them on Saracen ships.

   To Old Christians the bitterness of these attacks was amplified by the
conviction that many of them were being made with the collusion of the
moriscos. In 1565, for instance, it became known that information from a
morisco deserter had caused Piali Pasha to launch a counter-attack during his
failed assault against Malta when he learnt that only 5,000 Spanish troops
had disembarked from the relief fleet.[64] Under these circumstances *moriscos*
increasingly came to be recognised as part of a uniform Islamic civilisation
that was at war with Catholic Christendom, and which represented an intolerable threat to the physical and religious integrity of Spain.[65] The effect was
to drive the Old Christians into an ever more repressive approach to the
morisco problem, and the *moriscos* into steadily more dogged defence of their
religion.

From the beginning, the main problem faced by the authorities was that of
making good the *moriscos'* nominal conversion. The Catholic Kings had
explained the expulsion of the Jews and the forced conversion of the *moriscos*
in terms of the preservation of religious unity.[66] Although the outward man-

ifestation of this policy, which itself remained broadly unchanged, was one of assimilation, the means employed to bring it to fruition altered considerably both in tone and in character with the passage of years. The approach of Fray Hernando de Talavera at the turn of the fifteenth century had recalled the *convivencia* of an earlier age, but by the 1520s only a handful of *moriscos* had actually embraced Christianity since the first conversions of a generation before.[67] Throughout most of their range, the *moriscos* preserved their Islamic faith largely intact, often under the supervision of *alfaquis* (fakirs). In Valencia particularly this circumstance owed much to the opposition of the seigneurs to missionary and inquisitorial activity, but nothing can obscure the *moriscos'* stubborn defence of their cultural and religious identity against every attempt to undermine it. In 1524, for instance, María la Monja of Arcos de la Frontera declared that 'not for all the world would she cease saying that she had been a Moor, so great a source of pride was it for her', and so it remained.[68]

With this frame of mind, it is little surprise that even the most heroic efforts of the missionaries to grasp Islamic culture as a basis for evangelisation came to nothing. All too often the approach taken by the clergy was that of uncompromising dogma, based on the assumption that Christianity was to be accepted without question with the Church itself as guarantor of divine truth.[69] Since the fundaments of the faith were reckoned to be beyond the *moriscos'* ability to understand them, no dialogue could or did take place. The result was often a mutual incomprehension in which each held the other in contempt and the *moriscos* found their Muslim belief strengthened. Where *moriscos* were exposed to Christian practice, their reaction was one of hostility or ridicule. Mothers went to great lengths to wash the holy water off their babies after baptism, while Muslim monotheism made the doctrine of the Trinity and the Eucharist repellent.[70] As one commentator declared of the *moriscos* 'they left Mass more Moorish than they had come'.[71] *Moriscos* increasingly took it as a point of honour not to learn their prayers, and indulged in gross blasphemy in church to the extent that clergy began to regard it as a sin to minister to them.[72]

This hostility was not then a matter of simple indifference, but of conscious opposition to Christian practice which the Inquisition regarded as a rejection of the authority of the Church.[73] As it became clear that the missionary endeavour had been a complete failure, so exasperation turned to desperation.[74] In this climate, religious authorities in particular increasingly came to view the *moriscos'* non-submission to ecclesiastical law as placing them beyond the pale of Spanish society. Determined to enforce assimilation, the ecclesiastical councils and synods of Granada (1526), Toledo (1539), Guadix (1554) and Madrid (1566) 'defined and redefined the dif-

ferences between the *moriscos* and the Old Christians so that the enemy might
be known'.[75] Already by mid-century the authorities had succeeded in identifying the major cultural differences that set the *moriscos* apart from the rest
of Spanish society. *Morisco* clothing, diet, social customs and above all language placed them beyond the bounds of social acceptability. Badly pronounced and ill-written Castilian signalled a rejection of the dominant culture
as much as adherence to Arabic language and letters. Public baths the synod
of Guadix denounced as 'nothing more than the houses of the devil'.[76]

The *moriscos* therefore became classed as *inhábiles*, a people naturally
ignoble and without honour: 'unworthy of governing or ruling ... As slaves
and the descendants of slaves they are naturally inclined to evil, they are
traitorous, sly, calculating, lying, envious and base.'[77] The majority of Old
Christians regarded them as at best crypto-Muslims living in virtual apostasy
and ready to return to their former religion at any moment, and at worst
as 'engaging in witchcraft, divination and other sinful forms of worship', as
well as conspiring with the mortal enemies of Spain.[78] By the end of the century even the ordinary pattern of their lives was viewed within the context
of a profoundly negative stereotype. The *moriscos*, it was said in 1589,
'marry among themselves and do not mix with Old Christians, none of them
enters religion or joins the army nor enters domestic service nor begs alms;
they live separately from Old Christians, take part in trade and are rich'.[79]
Thus, just as refusal to drink wine indicated attachment to Islamic practice,
so a *morisco's* industry reflected his innate avarice, his frugality pointed to
the meanness of those who lived marginalised from wider society, and his
fertility reflected the animal sexuality and racial menace that threatened to
make Old Christians a minority in their own country.[80] 'Their aim', it was
said in 1612, 'was to grow and multiply like weeds.'[81]

Small wonder, therefore, that efforts to promote unity between Old
and New Christian met with the same outcome as every other initiative
directed towards them.[82] Attempts at promoting mixed marriages were
apparently scuppered by the ill-will of Old Christians, while social realities,
notably the existence of *morisco aljamas* (segregated quarters of towns), prevented the interaction that might otherwise have eased the tensions between
the two communities. Beneath the revulsion of Old Christians for mixing
with *moriscos* was *limpieza de sangre*, the sense that Muslim blood was by definition unbleachably tainted, and represented a stigmatising threat to any
who communed with them. In this sense, the idea of intermarriage with
moriscos represented not only a threat to their honour as Old Christians, but
also to the honour of God Himself.[83] This underlying prejudice was to be
found even among those who advocated a greater degree of contact, yet
underlined the importance of distinguishing *moriscos* from the rest of society.

The *moriscos'* pride in their religion, culture and separateness was only strengthened by the oppression that attended the failure of every effort to convert them.[84] Disenfranchised by an alien law, persecuted and discriminated against in almost every sector of Spanish life, the *moriscos* reacted by turning inwards in the social as much as in the spiritual order.[85] Presided over by a council of elders, the extended Muslim family played a key role in maintaining the bloodlines and religious loyalties that bound *morisco* society together and preserved its cultural identity. Parents fostered a hatred for Old Christians and religious traitors in their children. Strict controls were placed on women and there was a minimum involvement in Christian institutions. The spiritual dimension of this internalised resistance was *taqiyya*, or dissimulation, by means of which *moriscos* could feign obligatory Christian worship while practising their own faith.[86] Faced by missionary attempts at religious instruction, the *moriscos* responded by organising their own teaching, mainly through clandestine readings of the Koran under itinerant *alfaquis*, supplemented by the work of *marabouts* in providing books and religious instruction.[87] The large numbers of books discovered to be in circulation by the Inquisition testify to the survival of Islamic religious culture, but even so the strain of repression began to show as much in the fabric of *morisco* society as in the nature of its religious observance.

The lack of a recognised leadership, for instance, provoked internal divisions that were exploited by the authorities, while the development of banditry reflected a widespread social disenchantment among *moriscos*.[88] However, it is in religious praxis that the impact of wider Spanish culture was most keenly felt, for as Islamic belief became more marginalised so it began to develop in conscious and then subconscious contraposition to Christianity, and acquire the devices and conceptual forms of the dominant religious culture.[89] With this inevitably came a syncretic approach both to Christian worship and, conversely, to Islamic religious practice. Where communities had largely ceased to speak Arabic, as had become the case in the Kingdom of Toledo by the 1540s, religious leaders took to making oral translations of Islamic texts into Castilian. Other didactic literature was composed in the dialogue genre of *alfaqui* and *morisco* that was borrowed from Spanish models of the period. Equally, elements of Christianity were reinterpreted in Islamic terms.[90] St John the Baptist was celebrated as a precursor of Mohammed rather than of Christ, while ironically a cult developed around St James the Great (Santiago), the 'Moor-slayer' (Santiago Matamoros), in the guise of Ali, one of the Prophet's companions who the *moriscos* transformed into paladins after the style of the *libros de caballerías* (chivalric romances) which enjoyed such a vogue in sixteenth-century Spain.

However, Muslim paradigms were not only invoked to obscure the sense of Christian teaching, but also to attack it. Thus, with a considerable strain on chronology, Jesus was made a relative of Mohammed by whom he was soundly confuted in theological disputation.

The *morisco* issue and the fears that attended it therefore took on the character of an internal polemic which lay at the heart of Spanish society, and to which the international conjuncture added a further dimension. So far as the *moriscos* were concerned, this was a polemic which, by force of circumstance, they were largely obliged to conduct in silence.[91] However, when views of Old Christians were expressed they were inevitably as scabrous as one might expect: inquisitors were described as 'thieving wolves whose trade is arrogance and greed, sodomy and lust, tyranny, robbery and injustice', and the Holy Office itself as 'a tribunal of the devil, attended by deceit and blindness'.[92] In a period racked by outbursts of Messianic and prophetic fervour among both Old Christians and *moriscos*, confrontation was fuelled by a mutually-held belief that each was the victim of a campaign of extermination by the other side.[93] Individual fears therefore escalated into collective phobias, with *moriscos* terrified that they might be castrated in retribution for their refusal to accept Christianity.[94] Old Christians, for their part, had visions of their children being spirited away by *moriscos* and brought up 'in this false sect'. Beyond their own connotations, these details provide an important reminder of the analogous and reciprocal nature of the fears and hatreds that drove *morisco* and Old Christian relations to and then over the brink of disaster during the sixteenth and early seventeenth centuries.

By the early 1560s internal conflict and external pressure were laying the foundations for an explosive climax to the *morisco* problem in Spain. In 1561, with millenarian hopes of liberation soaring, rumours circulated through the *morisco* community that Turkish attacks on the *plazas* of Oran and La Goleta would be followed by an invasion of Valencia.[95] To the Muslim threat was added that of the Huguenots with the outbreak of the French Wars of Religion in 1562. The waves of French immigrants pouring into Spain provoked fears of collusion between Huguenot bandits and *moriscos* which, in Philip's mind at least, were realised by the discovery of contacts with France in 1565. That same year the Granadine *moriscos* waited in vain for the arrival of another Turkish fleet to spark a rebellion in Andalusia.[96] That the Granada community was simmering with unrest owed much to the catastrophic decline of the silk trade, the mainstay of the *morisco* economy.[97] A prohibition on silk exports in 1552 was followed by heavy taxes on the raw material in 1561 and again in 1564. To all this Pedro de Deza, the hardline president of the *Audiencia* (high court) of Granada, added a *pragmática* in January 1567 which once again outlawed all remaining cultural differences between *moriscos* and Christians. At a stroke, Arabic writing, language, feasts, clothing and names were to be abandoned. The *moriscos'* sense of outrage is conveyed in the memorandum sent to the Crown by a local leader, Francisco Núñez Muley: 'Every day we are mistreated in every way, by both secular officials and clergy, all of which is so obvious that it needs no proof ... . How can people be deprived of their natural tongue, in which they were born and raised?'[98]

On Christmas Eve 1568 generations of fear and hatred erupted with the outbreak of the Revolt of the Alpujarras. The revolt, which came at a critical time in the fortunes of the monarchy, was conducted and eventually suppressed with the utmost savagery. Although the rebels elicited a disappointing response from the *Albaicín*, the *morisco* quarter of Granada, the call was taken up in the Sierra de Alpujarras and the revolt was not put down until the autumn of 1570.[99] The cultural and religious symbols of Christian society were singled out, and priests and *morisco* clergy in particular were massacred in an orgy of sectarian violence. Churches were attacked and profaned, iconoclasm was widespread and burlesque representations of the mass parodied Christian rites. Whipped up by the lower clergy and royal officials, Old Christians engaged in the same violence and brutality as the insurgents. Hostages were butchered and sold into slavery. A royal decree of October 1569 authorised a free-for-all against *morisco* property, and some of the most memorable passages of Diego Hurtado de Mendoza's *Guerra de Granada* depict Christian soldiery struggling home laden down with booty.[100] Royal fears for a simultaneous revolt in Valencia did not materialise, but 4,000 Berbers landed on the Andalusian coast to fight alongside the rebels and the possibility of Ottoman intervention was discussed in Constantinople.[101] By the time the revolt had been crushed in 1570 thousands had been killed, and thousands more had fled to the Barbary Coast to continue the war against Spain.

Before the revolt had been stamped out the Crown had taken steps towards a complete dismantling of *morisco* society in the Kingdom of Granada. Beginning in 1569, some 80,000 people – 90 per cent of the community – were stripped of their property and resettled throughout the Kingdom of Castile.[102] In return for eliminating the threat of large-scale collusion between local *moriscos* and Turks and cleansing the Alpujarras of bandits, the Crown had destroyed a distinctive feature of Granadine society, crippled its economy and transferred a disloyal and restive population into communities largely unprepared for such an eventuality.[103] The revolt over, attention now turned to Valencia and the Ebro Valley, where banditry became endemic during the 1570s and a large *morisco* population presented

a threat to the security of the region.[104] Lepanto may have quelled fears of
what Philip believed was an imminent Muslim invasion, but the activities of
the corsairs resumed with heightened zeal and, as the Spanish position in the
Mediterranean deteriorated once more, plans were prepared to move
moriscos away from the coast.[105]

In Castile, meanwhile, the wave of deportees bolstered and renewed
the faith of the existing *morisco* community, and the evangelising campaign
that opened here in the early 1570s therefore went hand in hand with a huge
increase in cases coming before the Inquisition.[106] The tone of the initiative
is captured in a memorandum of January 1573 which laid down, among
other things, an uncompromising observance of Christian practice, the
indoctrination of children and the breaking of family linkages which was so
bitterly resented among *moriscos*.[107] But the outcome was no different, for
the truth, as an inquisitor wrote to Philip in the 1590s, was that the *moriscos*
had no desire whatsoever to become Christians, and in this conviction the
missionaries were drained of all spirit.[108] A rash of uncovered conspiracies
and civil unrest increasingly began to turn government minds to a drastic
solution to the *morisco* problem. Permanent contacts were established with
France from the 1570s, and the civil war that broke out in 1585 between
the Aragonese *moriscos* and Old Christian *montañeses* (upland shepherds) was
marked by the involvement of Henri IV on the *morisco* side.[109] To the history of collusion with the Barbary corsairs and the Turks (though in this case
lessened by the Ottoman peace treaty of 1580) now came the reality of
alliance with heretics. The corsair onslaught itself acquired a new bitterness
with a succession of major raids and the desertion of thousands more *moriscos*
to North Africa, who in some cases returned to settle scores with their erstwhile enemies. At Teulada in Valencia, for instance, a band of corsairs singled out and killed Antonio Vallés, and included his wife and children among
their haul of captives.[110] In November 1606 the viceroy of Valencia reported
that eight corsairs attacking a village near Altea were recognised as having
defected to the Barbary Coast some years before.

Under such circumstances the Crown gradually came to the conclusion
that the time had come to consider the expulsion of a minority who could
not and would not be assimilated. Although debated from 1581, paradoxi-
cally it was the gravity of both the internal and the external situation that
prevented any action being taken.[111] A number of interim measures were
taken, with Philip restricting himself to improving frontier defences and
attempting to disarm the *moriscos* in what was largely a conciliatory policy
during the 1590s. However, information of *morisco* collusion with the English and Dutch fleets which sacked Cadiz in 1596 and of plots with Henri
IV in 1602 appear to have reopened the question of expulsion.[112] The sign-

ing of a succession of international peace treaties therefore provided the opportunity which war and conflict had thus far denied.

For many *moriscos*, tired of their minority status, the Barbary Coast became the promised land.[113] For others, however, their attachment to Spain ran deep, and as the missionary endeavour ebbed away many *moriscos* became anxious to avert the fate that clearly lay in store for them. In 1588 a number of forged tablets appeared in the Sacromonte of Granada purporting to add information to the Christian revelation.[114] Devised by two prominent *moriscos*, the so-called *libros plúmbeos* (lead books) represent a last desperate attempt to manufacture a syncretic Christianity that would be acceptable to Muslims. The problem of the Trinity was therefore addressed by redefining it in monotheistic terms – 'There is no God but God and Jesus, the Spirit of God' – while efforts were made to present the Arab conquest of the eighth century as the evangelisation of Spain.[115] But these devices could not possibly succeed, and in January 1602 the first outline plan for the expulsion was drafted. Vacillation and widespread opposition, particularly from the nobility, delayed the enactment of a policy recognised to constitute a serious moral and religious defeat for Spain, as well as an admission of practical failure. After all, as one inquisitor declared, 'they are Spaniards like ourselves', and voices were still being heard in 1607 in favour of more preaching and instruction.[116] However, these were drowned by the rantings of extremists like the *arbitrista* Gómez Dávila, who proposed to 'expunge once and for all the accursed line' of the *moriscos* by removing all children from their parents and placing them in Old Christian families 'all over the world'. 'Let us,' he said, 'pass a Sicilian Vesper on them before they do so on us.'[117]

In the end it was Patriarch Ribera, Archbishop of Valencia, who, embittered at the failure of fifty years' evangelical endeavour among the *moriscos*, turned into their most implacable foe and swayed opinions at court.[118] Citing fears of uncontrollable population growth and against the background of rumours of further conspiracy with the Berbers, on 9 April 1609 the decree of expulsion was signed by the Duke of Lerma.[119] Over the next four years some 300,000 *moriscos* – over 90 per cent of the total – were expelled, mostly to North Africa. In Aragon and Valencia in particular the demographic and economic impact was catastrophic, contributing in the latter case to a severe decline in the seventeenth century.[120] On the Barbary Coast, meanwhile, a new era of vengeful corsairing had dawned.[121]

As much as the social and religious realities which informed it, the story of Old Christian–*morisco* relations in early modern Spain is one of fears substantiated and phobias unstilled. It is also one of mutual incompre-

hension, of a *desencuentro* that extends beyond linguistic incapacity to a complete failure to assimilate the culture of the other.[122] Above all, it was the
failure of one party in particular to fulfil the evolving criteria of what it was
to be and to live as a Spaniard in the sixteenth century – and in so failing
becoming a threat to the other – that constituted the basis of this fear. The
analogous character of this relationship is therefore immediately apparent,
and can be seen in every sphere in which it developed: political, cultural,
social and above all religious. But there is also ambiguity, and in a charac-
teristically ambiguous passage from *Don Quixote*, the *morisco* Ricote applauds
Philip III's determination 'to expel the poisonous fruit from Spain, now free
of the fears in which our numbers held her'.[123] But, 'like a splinter,' says
Braudel, 'the *morisco* population was embedded right in the heart of Spain',
and so it remained, disembodied on the Barbary Coast.[124]

Notes

1 The best introductions to early modern Spain in English are J. H. Elliott, *Imperial Spain, 1469–1716* (Harmondsworth, 1970), John Lynch, *Spain 1516–1598: From Nation State to World Empire* (Oxford, 1991) and *The Hispanic World in Crisis and Change, 1598–1700* (Oxford, 1992). Another excellent study, beginning with the reign of Charles V, is Anto-nio Domínguez Ortiz, *The Golden Age of Spain, 1516–1659* (1971). An alternative per-spective is provided in Henry Kamen, *Spain, 1469–1714: A Society of Conflict* (1991).

2 On fear in Spain, see Augustin Redondo and Marc Vitse, eds, *L'Individu face à la société* (Toulouse, 1994).

3 Ellen G. Friedman, *Spanish Captives in North Africa in the Early Modern Age* (Madison, 1983), xvii.

4 *Ibid.*, 40.

5 *Ibid.*, xvii.

6 Cited in *ibid.*

7 Louis Cardaillac, *Morisques et Chrétiens: une affrontement polémique (1492–1640)* (Paris, 1977), 71.

8 Cited in Friedman, *Spanish Captives*, 11.

9 (Valladolid: Diego Fernandez de Cordova y Oviedo, 1612; repr. Madrid, 1929); 2: 87.

10 The classic study of the region in this period is Fernand Braudel, *The Mediterranean and the Mediterranean World in the Age of Philip II* (1972–73). On the *morisco* problem see in particular 2: 780–802.

11 See John B. Wolf, *The Barbary Coast: Algiers under the Turks, 1500–1830* (New York, 1979), 36, 42.

12 On capture, captivity and ransoming, see Friedman, *Spanish Captives, passim*.

13 The question of Spain's relationship with the Mediterranean and Africa is reassessed in Andrew C. Hess, *The Forgotten Frontier: A History of the Sixteenth-Century Ibero-African Fron-tier* (Chicago, 1978).

14 See Joan Reglà, 'La cuestión morisca y la coyuntura internacional en tiempos de Felipe II', in his *Estudios sobre los moriscos* (Barcelona, 1974), 193–218.

15 Angus Mackay, *Spain in the Middle Ages: From Frontier to Empire* (1977).

16 Hess, *Forgotten Frontier*, 129.

17 See Henry Kamen, *Inquisition and Society in Spain in the Sixteenth and Seventeenth Centuries* (1985).

18 *Ibid.*, 101.

19 *Ibid.*, 102.

20 Hess, *Forgotten Frontier*, 133–4.
21 Two pioneering works are still worth consulting, despite their faults: Henry Charles Lea, *The Moriscos of Spain* (1901), and the apologetic Pascual Boronat y Barrachina, *Los moriscos españoles y su expulsión* (Valencia, 1901). Two good modern studies are Antonio Domínguez Ortiz and Bernard Vincent, *Historia de los moriscos* (Madrid, 1978) and Cardaillac, *Morisques et Chrétiens*. The situation in Granada is explored in Julio Caro Baroja, *Los moriscos del reino de Granada* (Madrid, 1959), and Miguel Ángel Ladero Quesada, *Granada: Historia de un país islámico (1232–1571)* (Madrid, 1969).
22 See Henri Lapeyre, *Géographie de l'Espagne morisque* (Paris, 1959).
23 For the *moriscos* in the Crown of Aragon, see two articles by Tulio Halperín Donghi, 'Un conflicto nacional: Moriscos y cristianos viejos en Valencia', serialised in *Cuadernos de historia de España*, 23/24 (1955), 5–115; 25/26 (1957), 83–250, and 'Recouvrements de civilisation: Les Morisques du royaume de Valence au XVIe siècle', in *Annales. Économies, sociétés, civilisations*, 11 (1956), 154–82. For Aragon, see Gregorio Colas Latorre and José Antonio Salas Ausens, *Aragón en el siglo XVI: Alteraciones sociales y conflictos políticos* (Zaragoza, 1982). See also the summaries in Reglà, *Estudios sobre los moriscos*, 'Introducción', 24–40, and A.W. Lovett, *Early Habsburg Spain* (Oxford, 1986), 269–76.
24 Kamen, *Inquisition*, 104, 111.
25 Lovett, *Early Habsburg Spain*, 275.
26 See Ricardo García Cárcel, *Las germanías de Valencia* (Barcelona, 1975), Hess, *Forgotten Frontier*, 139–40, and Kamen, *Inquisition*, p. 103.
27 Kamen, *Inquisition*, 104.
28 Hess, *Forgotten Frontier*, 132.
29 *Ibid.*, 136. There were, however, some notable exceptions to this, not least the humanist Antonio de Guevara and the Franciscan Fray Bartolomé de los Ángeles in Granada and Valencia respectively; see Kamen, *Inquisition*, 104, 106.
30 Hess, *Forgotten Frontier*, 138.
31 Kamen, *Inquisition*, 103.
32 *Ibid.*, pp. 103–5 and Hess, *Forgotten Frontier*, 149.
33 Hess, *Forgotten Frontier*, 140–1.
34 Kamen, *Inquisition*, 106.
35 Hess, *Forgotten Frontier*, 127.
36 *Ibid.*, 136–7.
37 Friedman, *Spanish Captives*, xix.
38 *Ibid.*, 12.
39 Hess, *Forgotten Frontier*, 137–8.
40 Friedman, *Spanish Captives*, xxiv.
41 *Ibid.*, xx.
42 See Wolf, *Barbary Coast*, *passim*.
43 Friedman, *Spanish Captives*, xxiv–xxv.
44 *Ibid.*, xviii.
45 *Ibid.*, xxv–xxvi.
46 For the Mercedarians, see my *Armatures of Reform: The Mercedarian Order in the Spanish Golden Age* (forthcoming). On the Trinitarians, see Paul Deslandres, *L'Ordre des Trinitaires pour le rachat des captifs* (Paris, 1903); Friedman, *Spanish Captives*, ch. 5.
47 Friedman, *Spanish Captives*, 4–6. It should be noted that this sample of 9,500 captives represents but a fraction of those ransomed by the two orders of redemption, and their Discalced branches, in the period in question. The total may be nearer 50,000. Neither should the proportions of the ransomed be seen as a fair reflection of the profession and social status of those originally captured, nor the circumstances under which they were taken. For more on ransoming, see Fray Melchor García Navarro, *Redenciones de cautivos en África, 1723–5*, P. Fr. Manuel Vázquez Pájaro, ed. (Madrid, 1956).

48 Friedman, *Spanish Captives*, 3.

49 Wolf, *Barbary Coast*, 62.

50 It would seem from archival evidence that the average ransom in the sixteenth century was in the region of 100 ducats, but prices varied according to the importance of the captive. In 1527 the ransom of a Franciscan superior captured off Palamós in Catalonia cost 4,000 ducats, while those of the fishermen taken with him amounted to between 100 and 200 ducats each; see Núria Sales, Història de Catalunya *Els segles de la decadència. Segles XVI–XVIII* (Barcelona, 1989), 84.

51 Domínguez Ortiz, *Golden Age*, 301.

52 Friedman, *Spanish Captives*, xxv.

53 See Sales, *Els segles*, 70.

54 *Ibid.*, 71.

55 See Ferrán Soldevila and Ferrán Valls i Taberner, *Historia de Cataluña* (Madrid, 1982), 429.

56 Sales, *Els segles*, 3, 84–91.

57 Soldevila and Valls i Taberner, *Cataluña*, 430–1.

58 See particularly Cervantes's *Los baños de Argel* and *El trato de Argel*. On the theme of fear in popular culture, see Sales, *Els segles*, 33.

59 Friedman, *Spanish Captives*, 48–9.

60 *Ibid.*, 50.

61 *Ibid.*, xxv.

62 Soldevila and Valls i Taberner, *Cataluña*, 438.

63 Reglà, 'La cuestión moriscá', 201.

64 *Ibid.*

65 Hess, *Forgotten Frontier*, 143.

66 Cardaillac, *Morisques et Chrétiens*, 34.

67 Kamen, *Inquisition*, 106.

68 Cited in *ibid.*, 107.

69 Cardaillac, *Morisques et Chrétiens*, 37.

70 *Ibid.*, 28 and Kamen, *Inquisition*, 106.

71 Cited in Cardaillac, *Morisques et Chrétiens*, 32.

72 *Ibid.*, 31–2.

73 *Ibid.*, 29.

74 Kamen, *Inquisition*, 109. An excellent case-study based on the failure of the Jesuit mission to Granada in the 1560s is N. H. Griffin, '"Un muro invisible": *Moriscos* and *Cristianos Viejos* in Granada', in Hodcroft *et al.*, eds, *Mediaeval and Renaissance Studies on Spain and Portugal in Honour of P. E. Russell* (Oxford, 1981), 133–54.

75 Hess, *Forgotten Frontier*, 142.

76 Cited in *ibid.*, 143.

77 Cardaillac, *Morisques et Chrétiens*, 46–7, esp., 47.

78 Hess, *Forgotten Frontier*, 142–3.

79 Cited in Kamen, *Inquisition*, 109; the source is a report to Philip II on the *moriscos* of Toledo, and is by no means accurate.

80 Cardaillac, *Morisques et Chrétiens*, 67 and Hess, *Forgotten Frontier*, 151. On *morisco* meanness, see Reglà, 'Introducción', 27, and for fears of population growth, 'La cuestión morisca', 199–200.

81 Cited in Kamen, *Inquisition*, 111.

82 Cardaillac, *Morisques et Chrétiens*, 39–45.

83 Redondo and Vitse, *L'Individu*, 15–16.

84 Cardaillac, *Morisques et Chrétiens*, 67 and Kamen, *Inquisition*, 109.

85 Hess, *Forgotten Frontier*, 144.

86 Kamen, *Inquisition*, 110.

87 Cardaillac, *Morisques et Chrétiens*, 56–66.

88 Hess, *Forgotten Frontier*, 144.
89 Cardaillac, *Morisques et Chrétiens*, 59–62.
90 *Ibid.*, 32–4.
91 *Ibid.*, 20.
92 Both cited in Kamen, *Inquisition*, 109.
93 Cardaillac, *Morisques et Chrétiens*, 49–56.
94 *Ibid.*, 21. The suggestion that *moriscos* be castrated was in fact made in 1587 by Martín de Salvatierra, Bishop of Segorbe; see Kamen, *Inquisition*, 110–11.
95 Kamen, *Inquisition*, 108 and Reglà, 'La cuestión morisca', 204.
96 Reglà, 'La cuestión morisca', 201.
97 Hess, *Forgotten Frontier*, 145
98 Cited in Kamen, *Inquisition*, 108.
99 Hess, *Forgotten Frontier*, 145–8 and Kamen, *Inquisition*, 108.
100 The *Guerra de Granada* dates from the early 1570s: Bernardo Blanco González, ed. (Madrid, 1970).
101 For the situation in Valencia, see Sebastián García Martínez, *Bandolerismo, piratería y control de moriscos en Valencia durante el reinado de Felipe II* (Valencia, 1977); also in *Estudis. Revista d'història moderna*, 1 (1972), 85–167 and Joan Reglà, 'Valencia y los moriscos de Granada', in his *Estudios sobre los moriscos*, 245–57. For the Turks, see 'La cuestión morisca', 205.
102 See Kamen, *Inquisition*, 108–9, and Reglà, 'Introducción', 27.
103 Hess, *Forgotten Frontier*, 148.
104 See Reglà, 'La cuestión morisca', 205–8 and 'Valencia y los moriscos', 253.
105 Friedman, *Spanish Captives*, 7, Hess, *Forgotten Frontier*, 149. Though never brought into effect, plans to remove Valencian *moriscos* from the littoral and their Aragonese counterparts further into the hinterland were still being considered by the Crown in the 1590s; see Reglà, 'La cuestión morisca', 212–17.
106 Kamen, *Inquisition*, 109.
107 Hess, *Forgotten Frontier*, 150–1 and, on family linkages, 137.
108 Cardaillac, *Morisques et Chrétiens*, 43.
109 Kamen, *Inquisition*, 110, Reglà, 'La cuestión morisca', 209 and Lovett, *Early Habsburg Spain*, 206–7.
110 Friedman, *Spanish Captives*, 12.
111 Reglà, 'La cuestión morisca', 209–11.
112 *Ibid.*, 212 and Kamen, *Inquisition*, 110.
113 Cardaillac, *Morisques et Chrétiens*, 69.
114 Hess, *Forgotten Frontier*, 151, 154 and Kamen, *Inquisition*, 110.
115 Cited in Hess, *Forgotten Frontier*, 151.
116 Cited in Kamen, *Inquisition*, 111, 113.
117 Cited in Cardaillac, *Morisques et Chrétiens*, 49.
118 Kamen, *Inquisition*, 110.
119 *Ibid.*, 111.
120 James Casey, 'The Moriscos and the depopulation of Valencia', *P&P*, 50 (1970), 1–25 and his *The Kingdom of Valencia in the Seventeenth Century* (Cambridge, 1979).
121 Friedman, *Spanish Captives*, xxiv, 12, 24, 28.
122 See Cardaillac, *Morisques et Chrétiens*, 22, and Griffin, '"Un muro invisible"', 145–6.
123 Cited in Kamen, *Inquisition*, 112.
124 Braudel, *Mediterranean*, 2: 794.

6

Fear and friction in urban communities during the English Civil War

WILL COSTER

Richard Baxter, who served as a chaplain in the New Model Army, one of the most disciplined and godly of the many forces of the English Civil War, nevertheless did not have a particularly elevated opinion of the morals of soldiers. 'It must be an extraordinary army', he observed, 'that is not constituted of wolves and tigers, and is not unto common honesty and piety the same that a stews or whorehouse is to chastity.'[1] The dangers associated with armies were a constant theme on both sides of the pamphlet war that shadowed the military clash between King and Parliament from the summer of 1642 to the spring of 1646. These pamphlets listed and depicted the atrocities and outrages of soldiers, playing on the common alarm with which Englishmen viewed the armed forces that must have seemed to many to have descended as suddenly as a biblical plague.[2]

The immense historiography of the first civil war has only relatively recently turned towards the nature of the conflict within urban communities. The ground-breaking local studies of the 1960s and 1970s stressed dissenting voices within what had once been seen as Royalist and Parliamentary regions.[3] They also pointed to the importance of neutralism as a political creed.[4] However, their focus was naturally on the county community and not on the towns within it. Moreover, it has been the origins of the war that have remained the central debate in this field. The consequences, and particularly the course of the war, have been left to those interested on a military, technical and operational level. In recent years there have begun to emerge a number of detailed studies that have illuminated the role of towns in the war.[5] At the same time there appears to be the beginnings of a historiography that, on a more general level, appreciates the military as well as the political, social and psychological aspects of the conflict.[6] The aim of this chapter is to extend both these trends by focusing on the attitudes and responses of three contrasting urban communities at Chester, York and Leicester.

What, then, was the nature of the threat from the soldier to towns? Most obviously, the forces of both sides were an expense almost unknown in early modern England. Fear of the financial burden of armies was, as L. G. Schwoerer demonstrated over twenty years ago, one of the key elements in the hostility between Crown and the political nation in the build-up to the war.[7] It has generally been acknowledged that Parliament, possessing the key advantage of the capital, and with it the existing machinery of government, was by far the more successful in securing financial resources for its armed forces. Ronald Hutton's forensic examination of the Royalist war effort made clear the continued problems and many expedients adopted by the King in an attempt to maintain his armies.[8] Hostility to such exactions has been seen as a key element in the breakdown of royal authority and the rise of the clubmen in the latter stages of the war. These exactions ranged from the quasi-legal procedure of free quarter (where unwitting inhabitants found troops billeted on them without reimbursement, or in exchange for unreliable promises); through the requisitioning of necessary items such as horses and grain; to a straightforward process of plunder, often with the explicit or tacit approval of a commanding officer.[9]

Even in periods of relative peace, armies needed to absorb not only money and property, but also men. The loss of a few vagrants cannot have distressed some civic leaders too greatly, but the economic damage of widespread recruitment would have been almost as unwelcome to the authorities as to potential soldiers. The cost of occupation, or billeting, also included the destruction the very presence of an army could bring. Soldiers represented a unique concentration of population and with it a concentration of the risk of disease and death.[10] In addition, by disrupting the normal social order, with its reliance on ownership, deference and law, the armies of the Civil War attempted to substitute one based on the parallel hierarchy of loyalty, rank and discipline. However, given the need to relocate and arm much of the male population, such a transition was inevitably flawed. Although the presence of women as camp followers in the armies of the civil wars should be noted, soldiers themselves invert the model most modern commentators have postulated, of a society obsessed with women as an object of fear. In the seventeenth century, armies were an archetypal focus of a fear of men. Physical violence, and particularly sexual violence, was perhaps more gender-specific than concerns associated with early modern sexuality. Articles of war for both sides, and the few records of internal army discipline that have survived, both suggest that the violence inflicted by soldiers upon civilians, including theft, rape and murder, was a considerable concern.[11]

Nevertheless, the most dramatic danger to an urban community arose if it became the subject of a siege, or worse still, if it endured an assault. Capture carried with it the potential of ultimate destruction, which was entirely permissible under the laws of war prevalent in the early modern period.[12] Whatever the respective loyalties of members of a community, it can easily be seen why they were almost unanimous in attempting to avert this horror at all costs. Accounts of continental atrocities, such as the destruction of Magdeburg in 1631, were well known.[13] Closer to home, the fate of Protestant settlers in the Irish uprising of 1641 dominated perceptions of warfare. They also demonstrate the link between the fear of soldiers and that of popery and foreigners. This was a much greater problem for the Royalists, often depicted as Catholic or crypto-Catholic and as containing large numbers of Irishmen in their armies.[14] Accounts of the destruction of English towns, like Brentford in the early months of the war, reminded urban communities of the high stakes for which they were now playing.

Although there were over fifty set-piece battles in the first civil war, and numerous local raids and skirmishes, there were also large numbers of sieges and assaults.[15] In the 1645 offensive of the New Model Army alone there were forty-six such actions.[16] The indecisive nature of conflict in the field, added to the necessity of securing territory and resources through occupation, made urban communities particularly significant at a strategic level. In the first instance many towns held the county magazines of weapons and ammunition, intended for use by the closest thing to an army England possessed – the county militia and trained bands.[17] The vulnerability of English and Welsh towns also made them more probable targets. In 1642 most urban wall systems dated from the pre-gunpowder period.[18] The complex, low and deep fortifications of the *trace italienne*, so widely adopted in much of mainland Europe, were almost absent from the kingdom.[19] High and thin medieval walls, which were perhaps as much a status symbol as a military defence, were unsuitable for withstanding a serious seventeenth-century bombardment.[20] Most medieval towns had also experienced a suburban expansion that rendered their ancient fortifications irrelevant without the destruction of many private houses.[21] Thus urban communities were both particularly likely to be targets for civil conflict and vulnerable to a determined attack.

There was one final element of the military threat that applied to urban communities in this period – that is, the loss of their autonomy.[22] The existence within a town of a sizeable military force inevitably created a rival for local civil authority. Throughout the war, as borders shifted and the respective sides became more organised and determined, martial law would replace civil law. Thus in judging the strategies of urban corporations, we must consider their success in terms of the fate of the persons and property within their towns, but also in the light of a struggle to maintain the power and liberties of the local elite against armed force.

As John Morrill has observed, the local elite in Chester, as elsewhere 'identified civil war with economic disaster'.[23] Their response may, however, have been unique. The Corporation of Chester has been praised for its relative activity in the months preceding the war.[24] After a report in 1641 indicating that the once formidable medieval city walls were 'in many parts ruinous, some part fallen down and in other parts reddy to fall into further decay', the borough authorities ordered their repair funded by a special city tax.[25] The extent to which this was due to an accurate reading of the approaching storm, and to what degree happy chance, is debatable. In securing its defences an urban community was also making itself a more attractive object for rival armies. In the contest for the control of the militia which dominated the summer of 1642, the Corporation of Chester, unusually, chose to ignore both Parliament's Militia Ordinance and the King's rival Commission of Array.[26] Instead they attempted to exclude armed forces from the town, relying on its militia of around 100 men to enforce the policy. However, Chester's neutrality in the early months of the war was only possible in the absence of external force and was partly the product of deep divisions within the ruling elite.

　　Existing rivalry between factions, led by the Puritan Councillor William Edwards and Alderman William Gamull, had begun to harden into those between Parliament and King.[27] Generally, the Royalists under Gamull held the upper hand, but divisions were sufficient to prevent an assumption of control by either side for some considerable time. When the later Royalist commander Lord Strange appeared before the town in July, a tactic that had succeeded elsewhere in enforcing allegiance, the militia stood to and refused entry.[28] On 8 August Sir William Brereton, with the support of Edwards, attempted to carry out what amounted to a Parliamentary coup, by an appeal to the citizens and city militia. It failed and they were forced to leave, in what was to be the final throw for the local Parliamentarians. On 23 September the King arrived, but did not occupy the town. Nevertheless, the presence of the Court, and a growing armed force, consolidated the position of local Royalists. Staunch Parliamentarians quit the city for the suburbs, effectively excluding themselves from power.[29] When the royal army moved south towards Edgehill, and the first major clash of the war one month later, Chester was one of only three towns that were under firm Royalist control – its neutrality having collapsed as external pressure acted upon internal divisions.[30]

In judging the success of the confused strategy adopted by Chester we must note that it had avoided two early attempts to use armed force to take control of the city. Although this merely delayed the inevitable, its independence only ended when confronted by a major military presence, unlike the many towns that fell to local initiatives in the same period. The change of policy to Royalism was apparently favoured by the most powerful active grouping of the local elite. However, from this point local authority began to slip away from the existing institutions of the town. Until the spring, control of the city was taken over by a council sitting in the Bishop's palace. From early 1643, this council was itself to become effectively subordinate to Sir Nicholas Byron, the first military governor. Byron in his turn had his allegiances to the Royalist high command. Civilian institutions continued to exist and function, but as A. M. Johnson observes, 'the presence of a military governor meant that there existed two distinct forms of government in Chester'.[31] He also points to the frustration of the sidelined civil leaders, who 'resented their lack of authority to deal with abuses committed by the soldiers who, they alleged, went unpunished by their superiors'.[32] Two fears created by war had been realised for the elite of Chester – a loss of political authority and an inability to control the occupying soldiery. Now that it was a Royalist town the risks of blockade, and even attack, were significantly greater. The response was to improve Chester's fortifications by a series of outworks. Trench lines were reinforced every few hundred yards by square redoubts or bastioned forts, and by placing cannon at intervals.[33] Later, the chapel of St John and some hospital buildings outside the town were pulled down to prevent them being used as cover by the enemy.[34]

On 18 July 1643 the city suffered its first attack from the local Parliamentarians under Brereton. His retreat, after an under-strength bombardment of the outer defences, reveals the importance of the new fortifications. It was the occasion of considerable relief, expressed in the ringing of bells and rejoicing.[35] This was, however, only the beginning of a long involvement in the military conflict. Blockade, which threatened the very economic disaster feared by the civic leaders before the war, was interspersed with physical assaults on the defences. One of these, in August 1645, reached the suburbs and captured the city sword and mace.[36] During periods of close siege citizens were kept in constant terror by bombardment, sniping and attempted stormings. The final chapter of the city's conflict came in September 1645 after the Royalist disaster at Naseby. The retreating King reached the city, closely followed by cavalry of the New Model Army. The result was a further defeat at Rowton Heath, that destroyed what remained of the royal field army. It was a confused struggle, which, although largely outside of the town, spilled over into the suburbs and reached the walls.[37] The King fled and Chester was left to fend for itself.

A summons of surrender was rejected on 26 September. This time Brereton was able to complete the encirclement fully. Mines and counter-mines were exploded; there was a sporadic bombardment and numerous sallies and assaults.[38] On 10 December one defender recorded 'eleven huge grenadoes like so many demy-phaetons threaten to set the city, if not the world on fire. This was a terrible night indeed.'[39] Outside the city Brere-ton had intelligence that many of the poor within were starving, and sent another demand for surrender. In the end, it was the city authorities who reasserted their importance, convincing the Governor that further resistance was futile. Negotiations began on 15 January and the town surrendered on 3 February. Contemporary descriptions note the surprise of the victors on entering the town, finding 'the particular demolitions of it, now most grevous to the spectators and more woeful to the inhabitant thereof'.[40]

Thus Chester suffered considerably at the last, and many of the fears associated with armed occupation were realised. There had been a cost in both property and life, and the identity of the city had been subsumed under military command. The following period of Parliamentary control, although it saw the beginnings of economic recovery, not surprisingly, wit-nessed little improvement in the fortunes of the local elite.[41] Three days after the occupation a new governor was appointed and William Edwards returned as a colonel of foot in the city. The existing Aldermanic Bench and Assembly were severely purged and uneasy relations between the for-eign, Parliamentary authorities, and the native elite continued until the Restoration.

Ultimately, Chester's early policy of armed neutrality delayed the realisation of many fears of military occupation, but only for a few months. It had no answer to the presence of a significant armed force and was too divided to resist annexation. The unavoidable new policy meant the loss of local privileges and autonomy. This was coupled with the accident of geog-raphy that placed it in a fiercely contested zone of the country. Together, these factors created the constant threat of enemy action, and ultimately the town became the scene of a major conflict. However, there was one compensation in this picture of failure. The Parliamentarians, who block-aded the town and even occupied the suburbs, did not in the end take the city by the ultimate act of storm. This spared Chester the chaos and destruction of sack and, despite the horror and privations of the war, pre-served something through the conflict. This perhaps shows the wisdom of the city authorities in repairing their medieval walls before the war, which undoubtedly made the prospect of a final attack unwelcome to the enemy.

Similarly to Chester, York possessed a formidable set of medieval defences, but did not begin to see the improvement of its fortifications until September 1642.[42] This was despite the more urgent military threat posed to the city by invading Scots during the Bishops' Wars, and particularly in 1640 after the occupation of Newcastle upon Tyne. Lord Herbert urged the improvement of fortifications to the Crown, noting 'there being no town any where he knew in Christendom, of the greatness of York, that hath not its bastions and bulwarks'.[43] But his plan was dependent for labour and expense on the citizens of the town and was never acted upon.

Again, despite its traditional image as an archetypal Royalist city, the ruling elite of York were just as divided between sympathies to Crown and Parliament as that of Chester. Indeed the Aldermen may well have been more sympathetic to the Parliamentary cause. However, the newly-elected Mayor, Edmund Cooper, was more decidedly Royalist. Whatever the desires of its leaders, York was unable to adopt the neutralist policies of so many other towns. From 17 January until 16 August it was the base for Charles I's court in exile. Unsurprisingly York, unlike Hull three months later, was unwilling to set a precedent by refusing the King entry. Once occupied by the court York was used as a base for recruitment of military forces. The Grand Jury at the York Assizes had little choice but to accept the Royalist propositions, which called for local gentry to gather cavalry there for 24 August.[44] Such concentrations of force evidently led to panic in some quarters. A printed letter from one Parliamentary sympathiser indicates the susceptibility of Royalist forces to propaganda after the massacres in Ireland the year before.

> For their own parts, they are wickedly grown desperate, through the favours of so many men of note in Yorke, Noblemen, that they are not for the ruination of a whole kingdome, so themselves may imbrue their hands in innocent blood, which the Lord bee mercifull to us, if we owe to their mercy for this shall we see our wives ravished before our faces, our children's braines dashed out against the walls, and our lives exposed with so great losse to the adventure upon any oppisition of far more tyrannie possibly inflicted on us.[45]

Such paranoid correspondence probably read well in London, although how the Royalist forces were regarded in York itself is more difficult to discern.

The city authorities evidently treated them with caution. The offer by five Royalist gentlemen to advise on the safety of the city was refused, as the common council conceived 'the Cittie to be in noe danger'.[46] However, on 2 September, Henry Clifford, the Earl of Cumberland, was commissioned as Lieutenant-General of the Royalist forces in the North. Immediately he began to repair the city walls and fortify the town.[47] Fletcher argues that there was considerable tension between the town and the occupying military forces. He concludes that it was probably as a result of these dis-agreements that Cumberland quit York, leaving it virtually free to deter-mine policy. However, the watch set on the city (by which eighty citizens patrolled the walls, and the gates and ferry were locked up at night), which has been taken as indicative of a new policy of armed neutrality, predated Cumberland's departure.[48] Additionally, although unimpeded by a rival centre of command, there was still a considerable military presence within York, in the shape of the trained bands of the surrounding area. Neverthe-less, assured by Sir John Hotham, the Parliamentarian governor of neigh-bouring Hull, that no evil was intended them, the local elite may have attempted to move towards a neutral stance. This decision underlines the fragility of the King's support, even in the allegedly Royalist North. Although the pattern of policy differed significantly from that in Chester, clearly the aims of the two towns were very similar.

For this period there are signs of growing concern in York, evidenced in the attempts of the Mayor to safeguard the private plate of the leading citizens.[49] On 8 November four Aldermen were ordered to go to Cum-berland 'to show him that in respect what danger this Cittie now standeth wheither it be fittinge to move a treaty with my Lord Fairefax and the rest'.[50] The financial cost of defence was also mounting and the council was increasingly concerned about having to maintain the county-trained bands of the militia.[51] By the end of the month there were niggling worries about these soldiers felling and cutting the trees around the town.[52] However, problems may say as much about the lack of an organised local command as of the threat of a rival power base.

It was unlikely that a major urban centre such as York could escape the attention of rival military forces as warfare escalated elsewhere. Cum-berland resigned his commission on 30 November and it was taken up by the Earl of Newcastle. On 3 December Newcastle approached the city with 'a great army, ten pieces of Ordinance, and ammunition for the King's ser-vice'.[53] As in many towns neutrality simply collapsed, and the Earl was wel-comed with a civic reception. The problems the citizens had encountered with Cumberland and his forces were now multiplied by the more resolute Newcastle and his much larger, although not constantly present, army. The most obvious evidence of a new relationship was his insistence in the fol-lowing January, and again in 1644, that Cooper be re-elected as Mayor.[54] More worrying for the council, like most occupied towns, York now received its first military governor, Colonel John Bellassis. The Governor's first appearance in the records of this city is in a demand for provision for a garrison of 200 for three months – amounting to just under £550.[55] As a result of this the city plate had to be pawned, and concerns over payment of the trained bands the year before must now have seemed minor.[56] There were also a series of complaints which demonstrate the realisation of many of the fears associated with military occupation. There were petitions that 'market folkes be not hindered and robbed as they are repairing to the City', and that there should be 'freedom from the fre billitinge [of] soldiers any longer', at least for the Aldermen and Council of Twenty-Four.[57] On the positive side, orders to innholders that they sell oats, hay and other victuals at reasonable prices, indicate that military occupation brought not only fear, but also opportunity.[58]

There were, however, other compensations for the city. The presence of a large garrison, coupled with the relative success of the northern Royalists in the first two years of the war, insulated York from the most devastating effects of the conflict. However, in April 1644 the tide began to turn, as the Scots pursued the now Marquis of Newcastle south from Durham and combined with local Parliamentarians to confine the numerically inferior Royalists within the city walls. A blockade was begun, but the Parliamentarians lacked sufficient manpower to enforce it on all sides until the army of the Eastern Association, under the Earl of Manchester and his cavalry commander Oliver Cromwell, joined them towards the end of May.

Now the siege began in earnest, with bombardment and counter-bombardment; mining and counter-mining. Besides continual exchanges of fire and the threat of attack, we know that the conditions for the citizens and around 4,000 occupying infantry now rapidly deteriorated in terms of provision and hygiene. At this juncture the suburbs were set alight, probably to deny them to the attackers. There is also some evidence that members of the Aldermanic Bench had opened private, and therefore traitorous, negotiations with the enemy.[59] Nevertheless, like most citizens under siege, the local elite had little option but to support the occupying forces.

The siege was lifted when a relief force under Prince Rupert, nephew of the King, arrived on 1 May. However, the next day saw the Royalists decisively defeated at nearby Marston Moor, a battle which sealed the fate of the town and the region. According to the diary of Charles Slingsby, many quit the city rather than endure another siege, which began two days later.[60] This time there was little hope of relief and negotiations were soon opened. As at Chester, it was at this point that the civic elite began to reassert their authority over the military governor. The consequences of surrender could have been devastating and the civic leaders had much to lose. They were then fortunate that one of the besiegers, Lord Fernando Fairfax, was essentially a local man. Although this connection may have been exaggerated by later historians, it may have speeded events.[61] There was a meeting of the common council and terms were accepted. The articles were relatively generous in the circumstances, the Royalist garrison being allowed to march out with their colours and arms. They were also clearly designed to assuage the fears of the inhabitants. Article eight stated that the 'Citizens and Inhabitants may enjoy all their priviledges which formerly they did at the beginning of these troubles', and article thirteen that 'no building be defaced, nor any plundering, nor taking of any mans person, or of any part of his Estate, and that Justice, according to the Law within the Citie shall be administered in all cases by the magistrates, and be assisted there if need be by the garrison'.[62] It is, then, not surprising that on 25 July, nine days after the surrender, the city sent 'a butt of sack and a tunn of French wine' to Lord Fairfax, 'in regard of the great love and affection he hath shewed to us'.[63] However, relationships between city and the new governor inevitably remained problematic. As early as 13 August 1644, Fairfax was writing to the Lord Mayor, Aldermen and Sheriffs of the city to complain that they were not keeping the courts of justice correctly.[64] Interference in local affairs also continued, with Cooper being deposed as Mayor and Alderman Thomas Hoyle being appointed in his place.[65] Repairs to the city defences and the continued holding of private plate by the new Mayor are both reminders that at this stage a further attack by the Royalists, and consfications from the Parliamentarians, remained possibilities.[66] The costs of occupation were also considerable. In April 1646 an assessment of £317 was ordered to pay for repair of the walls and city property.[67] As late as November 1647, faced with payments for occupying soldiers, the Common Council was pleading 'the poverty of the Cittye by want of traide and by burneinge of the suburbs'.[68] However, the evidence suggests that this was the beginning of a period of accommodation between occupiers and the occupied. The worst trials of the city were now over and the final defeat of the Royalist forces meant the return of stability to the town.

The policy forced upon York was then relatively successful. Despite the dangers presented by its strategic location and regional importance as a capital of the North, the city seems to have escaped relatively lightly. But the competing fears of occupation and attack were in many ways both justified. York did endure a lengthy and damaging siege that caused considerable destruction and dislocation, but, like Chester, it escaped both storm and sack. As in Chester, neutralist policies were simply untenable as the city's leaders were forced to follow the wishes of whatever occupying power held sway. Again, the benefits of even medieval fortifications are highlighted by events in York; despite the many attacks of the Parliamentarian forces the walls were crucial in preventing the disastrous fall of the city without terms. Such terms secured the safety and stability of a town, when forced to change allegiance because of military events elsewhere.

In contrast to both Chester and York, Leicester seems to have possessed the advantage of relative unanimity in its loyalties. The petitions sent from the town and county to King and Parliament in the period immediately before the outbreak of war demonstrate a clear bias to the latter, particularly in matters of religion. One of these highlighted the increasing concern of the county 'situated in the middst of your kingdome of England, and in the middest of our great fears and apparent dangers'.[69] Support for the King was marshalled by the youngest member of the most prominent local family, Henry Hastings, based at Ashby de la Zouch on the western edge of the county. The Parliamentary cause was led by members of the Grey family, under the Earl of Stamford, based at nearby Bradgate.[70] In May 1642, the two county rivals became involved in conflict over the fate of the county magazine. The citizens of Leicester forced Hastings to withdraw and serious bloodshed was averted.[71] On 12 June the conflict was intensified as Hastings attempted to implement the King's Commission of Array. He came close to carrying out a coup, by persuading the Mayor, Thomas Rudyard, to ignore Parliament's conflicting commission to the Earl of Stamford. It was the reaction of Archdale Parmer, the High Sheriff, who condemned the King's commission that probably prevented the town becoming a Royalist centre.[72] Again Hastings retreated and the town maintained its independence. However, unlike Chester, Leicester seems to have been permeable to the enemy.

The town came close to losing its neutrality when Charles I arrived on 22 July. The King was received and addressed a large assembly at the Castle encouraging support and supply.[73] Unlike Chester, where a similar peaceful entry was to win over the town, support for the King among the ruling elite was insufficient to allow a monopolisation of power by the Royalists. The King was offered a mere 120 horses and men. He was refused control of the magazine, and in contrast to York, the Grand Jury for the Assizes actually complained about Hastings as a delinquent, and threw its support behind the Earl of Stamford.[74] With war yet undeclared Charles simply left quietly. The town, although clearly biased toward Parliament, found itself adopting a policy of unarmed neutrality. Most significantly, it resolved the problem of the magazine by agreeing to Royal demands to distribute it amongst the county trained bands, thus neatly pushing the problem on to other shoulders.

This was, however, a particularly worrying time for the town, lying in the logical path of the Royalist forces if they moved south after the effective declaration of war at Nottingham on 22 August. Any fears they might have about the dangers of such a situation were soon to be proved justified, when Prince Rupert stationed the Royalist cavalry at Queniborough, only five miles away. On 6 September he demanded £2,000 from the Mayor, by ten o'clock the next day, or he would 'appear before your town in such a posture with horse, foot and cannon, as shall make you know tis more safe to obey than tis resist his Majesties command'.[75] The result, unsurprisingly, was panic in the corporation. Immediately, £500 was handed over to six dragoons who appeared before the town and an appeal made to the King.[76] Charles expressed surprise at his nephew's conduct and excused the town from the demand. He did not, however, return the money already sent.[77]

The fragile position in which Leicester found itself became clear. It was fortunate not to have been occupied by the Royalist forces, who at this stage probably were anticipating a single decisive clash, not a lengthy war. When this did not occur, the danger of raiding from Royalist garrisons at Belvoir, and particularly from Ashby, meant a lower level of continual danger.[78] In the end the forces of Parliament under Lord Grey of Groby, the eldest son of Stamford, were the ones to secure the town with the acquiescence of the corporation. However, unlike Chester and York, the Parliamentary garrison in Leicester appears to have remained relatively small, at around 200 men.[79] Moreover, although the conduct of the war was in the hands of a county committee and a governor, clearly the corporation retained more authority than was the case elsewhere. It is tempting to feel this was in part because of the character of Grey, whom Clarendon described as 'a man of no eminent parts'.[80] However, although the area was hardly secure, it was not in the front line of conflict for most of the war. In these circumstances it is tempting to feel that members of the corporation decided simply to keep their heads down and hope for the best. The Chamberlain's Accounts and Hall Papers of the town make it clear that they were careful to keep good relations with Hastings at Ashby.[81] Nevertheless, in August 1644 Hastings's men were driven off by the Leicester garrison after they seized a cartload of plums and spices at nearby Belgrave. Again, in March 1644 the Leicester garrison clashed with the local Royalists at Hinckley, as they attempted to prevent local clergy from travelling to the town to sign the Solemn League and Covenant.[82] Events like this must have kept the citizens of Leicester in a state of insecurity. Ill-feeling against Royalist soldiers was perhaps exacerbated by local incidents, like the murder of Goodwife Woodlane from the parish of St Martin in Leicester in 1642. According to one pamphlet, a witness at the coroner's inquest pointed the finger at 'one Chumley, a cavalier trooper', who was alleged to have shot the heavily pregnant woman in the back.[83] Whatever the truth of the matter, the local presence of rival forces can hardly have calmed nerves. However, in the end it was the major Royalist field army that was to prove the greatest danger to the town.

In 1645, with the war going badly for the King, and to save his besieged wartime capital of Oxford, he turned to Leicester as a suitable distraction to draw off Parliament's recently formed New Model Army.[84] To them this was a Parliamentary town and they were aware that it was lightly garrisoned and possibly that it was poorly fortified. In the early stages of the war, locks had been repaired and chains put on gates.[85] Some repairs were carried out to bridges and gates, but there does not appear to have been any serious attempt to improve the fortifications. The first mention of any repairs or improvements in the corporation records was not until 1644 and there is some evidence that even this limited plan was never put into operation.[86] As late as April 1645 Colonel George Booth wrote to Lord Grey with considerable alarm, claiming "tis God's Providence alone in keeping it from the enemies knowledge, and suppressing their courage that is the town's defence'.[87] In particular, he was concerned that the urban elite, rather than fortifying the town, were concentrating efforts on their own houses in the walled suburb of the Newark. Only now were some houses in the suburbs to be pulled down and fortifications strengthened.[88] The garrison was also small and poorly armed. Despite bribing James Innes, a major in the Scots army, to divert his 200 dragoons to the town, only 2,000 troops of dubious quality could be assembled.[89] By 27 May Royalist forces were outside the town and the next day Prince Rupert, as commander, demanded surrender. While the corporation hesitated, the bombardment of the town began.

The fall of Leicester has been a byword for the atrocities that occasionally surfaced during the war. The poorly defended town was to suffer what Chester and York both escaped – a taking by storm. However, despite the undoubted relatively high cost suffered in human life and property, the claims of mass slaughter, used in Parliamentary propaganda and particularly at the King's later trial, need to be treated with extreme caution. Clarendon accepted that 'the conquerors pursued their advantage with the utmost licence of rapine and plunder', but attempted to exonerate the King.[90] Eyewitness accounts speak of hard fighting and considerable plunder, but the most balanced account from the Parliamentary side states that,

> I find some pamphlets speaking of the horrid cruelty of the insulting enemy putting man, women, and child to the sword. I know their tender mercies are cruelties, but give the devil his due, there was indeed many slaine at the first enterance and some that made little resistance, and some women and children amongst the multitude of the rabble of common soldiers, but I cannot learne of any such order given to destroy all, as is said by some.[91]

Although as many as 700 may have died in the struggle, most were probably soldiers, and the greatest loss to the town was in property.[92] Pamphlets mention 140 wagons of plunder being driven to Newark. Certainly the town mace, seals and archives were taken (although the last of these was later returned). Another £2,000 was exacted before a small garrison was left under Hastings as Governor.[93]

Royalist possession of Leicester was, however, to be short-lived. The strategy of attacking the town as a diversion succeeded all too well, and the New Model Army advanced to defeat the King decisively at Naseby in Northamptonshire on 14 June. Two days later, after a three-hour bombardment, Leicester surrendered and became a Parliamentary stronghold again. Despite grants from Parliament, the finances of the town and its economic fortunes remained fragile for some considerable time, but at least their occupation was to end in 1647. A year later the defences were slighted, making it largely untenable as a garrison.[94]

In one sense Leicester was more successful than many towns during the war. Like almost all urban centres it was eventually garrisoned by the forces of one side, but not until relatively late in the war. In turn this was partly a result of Leicester having taken the unusual step of dispersing the magazine, divesting itself of its role as a centre for military assembly. This contrasts with Chester, which initially attempted to use this resource for its own protection, and York, that allowed it to be used for the Royalist war effort. Once the war was under way Chester began to protect its independence, and York its status as a Royalist northern capital, through re-fortification, but Leicester avoided any such measure. Inactivity, and its lesser strategic significance, allowed the town to avoid serious attention from both sides for three years. However, by using its continued authority in negation of its role as a centre of military power, Leicester took a considerable gamble. Into such a vacuum a hostile force could easily be drawn. Such was the fate of the town in 1645.

The possible strategies available to urban centres balanced conflicting fears of armed force, between occupation and attack. In largely excluding the former, Leicester laid itself open to the latter. Given such alternatives, the horror with which seventeenth-century citizens regarded the prospect of civil war is hardly surprising. The fall of Leicester was no Magdeburg, but it became an English archetype of what urban communities had most to fear, if all restraints collapsed and military law replaced civil peace.

To urban communities, and particularly to their leaders, soldiers represented not simply a threat, but a total inversion of the social order. These were 'little commonwealths' based on political autonomy; rights of ownership; concepts of hierarchy, geographical immobility and the sanctity of the person. In contrast, armies consumed resources; presented an alternative social and political structure; and existed to move men for the overt purpose of delivering death and destruction. In a society without standing armies, war, and particularly civil war, did not simply threaten the social order, it was its antithesis.

Thus the fear of soldiers was based on a deep-seated horror of cancer in the body politic. The way in which so many English towns had neglected their fortifications indicates that this was an acute, rather than a chronic, condition. However, logic suggests that a continually present fear is not only likely to lessen, but that steps may be taken to find a solution. The reasons why many towns struggled to develop successful strategies for dealing with occupation and attack included the historic security of the kingdom, and the suddenness with which war descended. It is also clear that some towns were paralysed by terror, or chose to suppress their anxieties until they became unavoidable. In so doing they destroyed the positive function of fear as a spur to action. As the example of Leicester shows, in the English Civil War it was not fear itself, but a disregard for danger, that was to be most feared.

Notes

1 Cited in J. Adair, *By the Sword Divided, Eyewitnesses of the English Civil War* (1983), 163.
2 For example, one of the most prominent Royalist pamphlets, *Mercurius Rusticus*, was subtitled *The Counties Complaint of the Murthers, Robberies, Plundering, and Other Outrages Committed by the Rebels on his Majesties Faithful Subjects.*
3 The most important examples are A. Everitt, *The Community of Kent and the Great Rebellion* (Leicester, 1965); A. Hughes, *Politics, Society and Civil War in Warwickshire 1620–1660* (Cambridge, 1987); A. Fletcher, *A County Community in Peace and War: Sussex 1600–1660* (1975) and J. S. Morrill, *Cheshire 1630–1660: County Government and Society During the English Revolution* (Oxford, 1974). For an overview of the historiography, A. Hughes, 'Local history and the origins of the Civil War', in R. Cust and A. Hughes, eds, *Conflict in Early Stuart England* (1989), 224–53, is invaluable.
4 See particularly J. S. Morrill, *The Revolt of the Provinces: Conservatives and Radicals in the English Civil War* (1980), 36–42.
5 The best examples are M. Stoyle, *Exeter in the Civil War* (Exeter, 1995) and S. Porter, *Destruction in the English Civil Wars* (1994). However, the most important overview remains A. Fletcher, *The Outbreak of the English Civil War* (1981), 393–400.
6 C. Carlton, *Going to the Wars: The Experience of the British Civil Wars, 1638–1651* (1992). B. Donagan, 'Codes of conduct in the English Civil War', *P&P*, 118 (1988), 65–95.
7 L. G. Schwoerer, *'No Standing Armies!' The Antimilitary Ideology in Seventeenth-Century England* (Baltimore, 1974), 8–50. On the wider problem of taxation see Kümin, Ch. 7, this volume.
8 R. Hutton, *The Royalist War Effort 1642–1646* (1982), 145–203.
9 For estimates of the cost of these exactions on a county basis see J. Wroughton, *A Community at War: The Civil War in Bath and North Somerset 1642–1650* (Bath, 1992), 133–62.
10 E. A. Wrigley and R. S. Schofield, *The Population History of England 1541–1871: A Reconstruction* (Cambridge, 1989), 680–1. See also Gentilcore and Naphy, Chs 11 and 2, this volume.
11 J. Adair, 'The court martial papers of Sir William Waller's army, 1644', *Journal of the*

Society for Army Historical Research, 44 (1966), 214–15, and P. Young and W. Emberton, *The Cavalier Army: Its Organisation and Everyday Life* (1974), 172–86.

12 G. Parker, 'Early modern Europe', in M. Howard, G. J. Andreopoulos and M. R. Shulman, eds, *The Laws of War: Constraints on Warfare in the Western World* (Ithaca, 1994), 48.

13 S. H. Steinberg, *The 'Thirty Years War' and the Conflict for European Hegemony 1600–1660* (1966), 102–3.

14 This fear has is well covered in R. Clifton, 'Fear of popery', in C. Russell, ed., *Origins of the English Civil War* (1973), 144–67 and P. Lake, 'Anti-popery: the structure of a prejudice', in Cust and Hughes, *Conflict in Early Stuart England*, 72–106. See also A. D. Mills, 'The Earl of Derby's Catholic army', *Transactions of the Historic Society of Lancashire and Cheshire*, 137 (1987), 25–54; 29.

15 Carlton, *Going to the Wars*, 154–5.

16 P. Young, *Civil War England* (1981), 79.

17 L. Boynton, *The Elizabethan Militia, 1558–1638* (1967), 244–97.

18 C. Duffy, *Siege Warfare, The Fortress in the Early Modern World 1494–1660* (1979), 145.

19 G. Parker, *The Military Revolution: Military Innovation and the Rise of the West, 1500–1800* (Cambridge, 1988), 24–32.

20 The significance of walls as a defence against natural disaster is dealt with in Eßer, Ch. 4, and Roberts, Ch. 1, this volume.

21 On attitudes to the suburbs see comments in J. Youings, *Sixteenth-Century England* (1984), 68. However, as the cases of York and Leicester both demonstrate, Youings perhaps underestimates the numbers of the urban elite who had suburban residences.

22 On this concern see Kümin, Ch. 7, this volume.

23 Morrill, *Revolt of the Provinces*, 38.

24 P. Young and W. Emberton, *Sieges of the Great Civil War 1642–1646* (1978), 108–9.

25 *Ibid.*

26 A. M. Johnson, 'Politics in Chester during the Civil Wars and Interregnum 1640–62', in P. Clark and P. Slack, eds, *Crisis and Order in English Towns 1500–1700: Essays in Urban History* (1972), 204–37; 208.

27 Johnson, 'Politics in Chester', 207. For an alternative perspective see R. N. Dore, ed., *The Letter Books of Sir William Brereton*, SPODRLC, 2 (1990), 592–3.

28 Fletcher, *Outbreak of the English Civil War*, 394.

29 Johnson, 'Politics in Chester', 209.

30 Fletcher, *Outbreak of the English Civil War*, 399.

31 Johnson, 'Politics in Chester', 211.

32 *Ibid.*

33 Duffy, *Siege Warfare*, 157.

34 Young and Emberton, *Sieges*, 111.

35 J. Hall, ed., *Memorials of the Civil War in Cheshire and the Adjacent Counties by Thomas Malbon of Natwich, Gent., and Providence Improved, by Edward Burghall Vicar of Action Near Nantwich*, SPODRLC, 19 (1889), 64–5.

36 Young and Emberton, *Sieges*, 112.

37 Hall, *Memorials*, 182–3.

38 R. N. Dore, 'Sir William Brereton's siege of Chester and the campaign of Naseby', *Transactions of the Lancashire and Cheshire Antiquarian Society*, 67 (1957).

39 Cited in Young and Emberton, *Sieges*, 115. For the very real dangers posed by fire from such devices see Roberts, Ch. 1, this volume.

40 Young and Emberton, *Sieges*, 115.

41 Johnson, 'Politics in Chester', 220.

42 P. Wenham, *The Great and Close Siege of York: 1644* (Warwick, 1970), 7.

43 F. Drake, *Eboracum: or the History and Antiquities of York* (1736), 141.

44 Fletcher, *Outbreak of the English Civil War*, 389.

45 Anon., *Lamentable and Sad Newes from the North: viz Yorke, Lancaster, Darby, and Newcastle,*

Sent in a Letter from a Gentleman Resident in Yorke to his Friend Living in Lumbard Street. Also News from Leicester, how Colonell Lunsford, Captain Legg, and Mr Hastings Have Appeared in a Warlike Manner, with a True Discovery of their Intentions and the Manner of the Opposition by the Earle of Stanfoord Lord Lietenant of the County (1642).

46 YCA, CYHB, B.36, fos. 74v, 75.
47 Wenham, *Siege of York: 1644*, xvii.
48 Fletcher, *English Civil War*, 391.
49 YCA, CYHB, B.36, fol. 75v.
50 YCA, CYHB, B.36, fol. 77.
51 YCA, CYHB, B.36, fol. 77v.
52 YCA, CYHB, B.36, fol. 78v.
53 Drake, *Eboracum*, 141.
54 YCA, CYHB, B.36, fol. 81.
55 YCA, CYHB, B.36, fol. 95v. It had already been agreed to pay £3,000 to Newcastle to maintain his army; see fol. 88.
56 YCA, CYHB, B.36, fol. 98.
57 YCA, CYHB, B.36, fos. 87v, 86v.
58 YCA, CYHB, B.36, fol. 79v.
59 Wenham, *Siege of York*, 47.
60 D. Parsons, ed., *The Diary of Sir Henry Slingsby of Scriven* (1836), 144.
61 Wenham, *Siege of York*, 91–3.
62 The articles are reprinted in full in *ibid.*, 94–5.
63 YCA, CYHB, B.36, fol. 102v.
64 YCA, CYHB, B.36, fol. 105.
65 YCA, CYHB, B.36, fol. 106v.
66 YCA, CYHB, B.36, fol. 108v.
67 YCA, CYHB, B.36, fol. 180b.
68 YCA, CYHB, B.36, fol. 226.
69 E.g., Anon., *Two Petitions of the Knights, Gentlemen, Freeholders and Others of the Inhabitants of the County of Leicester* (1641). Quote from Anon., *His Majesties Letter to the Lord Major and Aldermen of the Citie of London with the Humble Knights, Ministers, Gentry, Free-holders and other Inhabitants of the County of Leicester to the King* (1642).
70 M. Bennett, 'Henry Hastings and the Royalist Cause in the East Midlands', in M. Palmer, ed., *The Aristocratic Estate: The Hastings in Leicestershire and South Derbyshire* (Loughborough, 1982), 35–55, at 35.
71 Anon., *News from Leicester* (1642).
72 Anon., *Lamentable and Sad Newes from the North*.
73 J. Wilshere and S. Green, *The Siege of Leicester: 1645* (Leicester, 1972), 11.
74 H. Stocks and W. H. Stevenson, eds, *Records of the Borough of Leicester, Being a Series of Extracts from the Archives of the Corporation of Leicester 1603–1688* (Cambridge, 1923), 317.
75 Stocks and Stevenson, *Leicester*, 317–18.
76 Stocks and Stevenson, *Leicester*, 318, 323.
77 Stocks and Stevenson, *Leicester*, 319.
78 M. Bennett, 'Leicestershire's Royalist Officers and the war effort in the county: 1642–1646', *Transactions of the Leicestershire Archaeological and Historical Society*, 59 (1983–4), 44–51.
79 Wilshere and Green, *Siege of Leicester*, 17.
80 W. Macray, ed., *The History of the Rebellion and Civil Wars in England Begun in the Year 1641 by Edward, Earl of Clarendon*, (Oxford, 1888), 2: 473.
81 Stocks and Stevenson, *Leicester*, 320, 323.
82 Bennett, 'Henry Hastings', 46.
83 Anon., *An Extract and True Relation of a Most Cruell and Horrid Murther Committed by One of the Cavaliers on a Women in Leicester Billetted in her House: Who Was Shot into the Back Being*

Within Five Weeks of the Time of Her Delivery (1642).

84 M. Ashley, *The Battle of Naseby and the Fall of Charles I* (Dover, NH, 1992), 61.

85 Stocks and Stevenson, *Leicester*, 325.

86 *Ibid.*, 334.

87 Wilshere and Green, *Siege of Leicester*, 17.

88 Stocks and Stevenson, *Leicester*, 336.

89 Wilshere and Green, *Siege of Leicester*, 18.

90 Macray, *Clarendon*, 4: 39.

91 Anon., *A Perfect Relation of the Taking of Leicester with the Severall Marches of the Kings Army Since the Taking Thereof* (1645).

92 Figure from Carlton, *Going to the Wars*, 155.

93 Stocks and Stevenson, *Leicester*, 337.

94 Wilshere and Green, *Siege of Leicester*, 26.

7

The fear of intrusion: communal resilience in early modern England

BEAT KÜMIN

The accumulation of powers by central institutions is one of the outstand-ing characteristics of early modern European history: cities and princes, from the Mediterranean to the Baltic Sea, strove to round off their landed possessions, to harmonise the legal and political systems within them, and to transform a society of vastly heterogeneous individuals into a more uni-form body of 'subjects'. Not all of them were equally successful, but the emergence of French and Prussian absolutism illustrates the enormous potential of the phenomenon. Religion, of course, played an essential part in the process. The resolute enforcement of confessional allegiances helped to create specific 'national' identities which distinguished the respective ter-ritories from their immediate neighbours.[1] Small wonder that historians have tended to concentrate on central government bodies, from which all changes were believed to originate. Local institutions, if noted at all, were scrutinised for their transformation and gradual acculturation.[2]

More recent research priorities, however, are changing this picture. There is a growing awareness of a long-standing tradition of interaction between villages and the outside world.[3] European state formation now appears more like a dialogue between forces 'from above' and 'from below'. Given the lack of bureaucratic penetration, governments had to rely on local agents and popular co-operation to meet their objectives. Social problems were identified at grass-roots level rather than in the princes' palaces, religious change had to be adapted rather than simply imposed and violent protest continued to upset many a modernisation agenda.[4] The classic functional differentiation of pre-industrial European society into nobles (who fight and govern), clerics (who worship and pray) and a third estate (who simply worked) clearly fails to reflect the com-plexities of medieval and early modern reality. For England, for instance, it has recently been emphasised that the strengthening of central powers derived not only from institutional change and legislative programmes, but just as much from impulses by humble local government bodies, even in the post-Restoration period.[5]

This chapter attempts to throw further light on the government of the *res publica anglorum* between the fourteenth and seventeenth centuries. It hopes to contribute to the ongoing search for a 'new' political history; one which explores the 'social depth of politics' and finds 'signs of political life at levels where it was not previously thought to have existed'.[6] In particular, it will highlight the remarkable vitality of the local communities in which the middling and lower sorts were organised.[7] For while the discovery of grass-roots input into high politics is an important new insight, it would be misleading to abandon the polarity 'state vs. community' altogether.[8] A balanced account of centre/locality relations must combine the evidence for co-operation and gradual integration with the sturdy determination of townspeople and villagers to retain a degree of local autonomy. While state involvement was accepted and often actively encouraged in some areas, expansive tendencies in others tended to meet with much less enthusiasm. In what follows, the emphasis will lie on this second, more 'parochial' aspect of the relationship: the fear of intrusion. Given the constraints of space, only the political sphere can be highlighted here, although contemporaries were clearly burdened by many other comparable anxieties: from very real threats of military invasion to more evasive fears about immigration, impending famine, disease or other natural disasters.[9]

From a European perspective, there is plenty of evidence to justify the approach. The Swiss Confederation, perhaps the most striking example of a communal constitutional model, always kept central institutions at bay: rural cantons and city-states deliberated their common affairs in regular diets, but reserved important decisions to the approval of their burghers' councils and assemblies.[10] Popular risings, which formed 'part of everyday life' in early modern Europe, were almost invariably co-ordinated by local communities; most had very mundane motives, but some fought for a utopian-free village or a confederate territorial organisation.[11] Many French parishes and *bailliages*, in turn, petitioned or pressed for a reduction in the number of royal officials and for permission to raise their own taxes.[12]

But how valid is this sort of enquiry in an English context? The conventional emphasis on a long-standing tradition of 'individualism' among the peasantry, on the 'early centralisation' of state institutions such as the Exchequer or the rule of Common Law and the unrivalled speed of (proto-) industrial development does not offer much encouragement.[13] And yet, there are some contrasting indications: first of all the existence of a substantial number of town corporations, whose powers and representative institutions differed only marginally from those of many a continental city.

Second, villagers not only played an important part in the juries of their lords' courts, but they needed to co-ordinate their economic activities and often assembled in a non-manorial capacity to decide a variety of common concerns. From the later Middle Ages, furthermore, the parish emerged as a focus for local institutionalisation, regulation and the accumulation of considerable communal resources.[14] In the early modern period, external and internal pressures increased considerably,[15] but one example, located a mere stone's-throw away from the Tower of London, indicates that local autonomy could well survive the Reformation changes. The royal peculiar of Holy Trinity Minories, a parish based on the precinct of a dissolved religious house, was exempt from regular taxation, enjoyed immunity from the interferences of the Bishop of London and arrests by outside authorities, appointed its own ministers and magistrates, licensed its own publicans and can be fairly described as 'a miniature kingdom of its own, acknowledging no allegiance to any authority whatever except the Crown'.[16] This was an unusual constellation, but the resilience of communal ties should not be underestimated. At Swallowfield in Wiltshire, for example, 'thoroughly political' meetings are documented in the 1590s, where we can observe a 'republican parity' (at least among the principal inhabitants) and a determination to tackle pressing socio-economic problems locally. Similarly, at Glatton in Huntingdonshire, communal assemblies with powers to pass and enforce by-laws survived independently of the manor court well into the early modern period.[17] A comparative focus on these local units can thus be justified and may help to bridge the historiographical gap between county studies on the one hand, which rarely 'go beyond rhetorical claims about the need to study governmental processes at village and parochial level', and individual micro-historical approaches on the other, whose typicality is often called into question.[18] The spirited defence of communal rights and autonomy shall be highlighted in a number of exemplary clashes between the Black Death and the Revolution, each of which – it goes without saying – can only be contextualised with the broadest of brushstrokes.

The Peasants' Revolt of 1381, to start with one of the most momentous upheavals in English history, owed much of its virulence to a sustained phase of 'intrusion of the state into the lives of every rural community'.[19] Taxation, legislation and jurisdiction all yielded cause for concern: continuing a trend towards greater fiscal exactions, the poll taxes of 1377–81 ignited smouldering discontent by shifting the burden towards the less prosperous segments of the population and stripping village elites of their established right to assess and collect the subsidies due from each community.[20] Government and Parliament also showed an unprecedented interest in economic regulation to counter the destabilising social effects of the Black Death. The labour laws – a prominent item on the peasants' agenda – are the prime example of how central norms were promulgated and enforced in the localities. Landlords, in turn, increasingly resorted to the State's coercive power to defend their feudal prerogatives; some of the rebels had personal experience of prosecutions in Westminster courts.[21] The chancellor, whose jurisdiction expanded greatly in the course of the century, was duly singled out (and killed) as a 'man false to the community' and castles, lawyers and royal officials appear as prime targets throughout the rebellion.[22]

The heterogeneous events cannot be forced into one single interpretative framework, but communal values, organisation and programmes played a very conspicuous part. According to the chronicler Thomas Walsingham, the rebels cherished no other concept more highly than that of *communitas*, which they identified with the established rights and privileges of their villages.[23] The first riots in the county of Essex were not individual skirmishes, but – as emphasised in the *Anonimalle Chronicle* – co-ordinated risings of whole communities guided by men experienced in local government. The king himself, startled by the rebels' entry into London, promised 'that each of you *by villages and townships* shall have letters patent'.[24] Not content with minor concessions, however, Wat Tyler and his followers demanded that 'there should be no law except for the law of Winchester' (a statute of 1285 which charged villages with the duty to set a watch) and that 'all things would henceforward be regulated by the decrees of the common people'. There was no need for any lordship other than that of the King in the State and that of a single prelate in the Church, with all ecclesiastical goods – apart from a 'sufficient sustenance' of conscientious clergy – to be divided 'among the people of the parish'. As for the discredited legal system, the peasants added that 'they should not be compelled to attend courts', with the exception of the local view of frankpledge.[25] This was by no means a rejection of all order and authority, but a belief in the superiority of a regime based on 'independent and self-governing village communities'.[26]

The rapid defeat of the rebels prevented the elaboration and testing of their vision. The poll tax experiment, however, was abandoned and other concerns continued to haunt the authorities. During Jack Cade's revolt of 1450, for instance, resentment of intrusion resurfaced: various articles of complaint charged sheriffs and King's Bench officials with 'the perpetuall destruction of the ... commons of Kent', ministers of the court of Dover with arbitrary imprisonment and 'divers estates' with interference in parliamentary elections, while attendance at distant Quarter Sessions caused people to be 'sore vexed in costs, and labour'. Once again, the anger was directed against intermediate officials, with the personal authority of the monarch unchallenged.[27]

During the early Tudor period, central government was reformed and – in the view of some historians – revolutionised. Energetic ministers over-hauled Westminster bureaucracy, former church responsibilities accrued to the State and legislative programmes became more ambitious.[28] Local com-munities were subjected to the religious whims of successive monarchs and charged with statutory poor relief, highway maintenance and military pro-visions. Enforcement was not left to chance, but entrusted to ecclesiastical visitors, royal commissioners and ever more powerful Justices of the Peace. The people, we are told, responded with a surprising degree of conformity: altars were stripped, re-erected and once more removed in accordance with successive instructions, local resources handed over to the Crown, popular religious practices abandoned and local taxes raised with great regularity. Parishes – to quote the bluntest assessment – turned into an instrument of a 'totalitarian regime'.[29] But did they really? There can be no doubt about the very real change of emphasis and the might of the government machin-ery, yet more and more evidence points to the existence of popular resent-ment. The statutes themselves remind us of how difficult it was to transform legislation into reality: many people 'willyngly … escape from taxacion' and 'neglect' their offices, some 'evyll disposed persons defraud the true mean-ing' of acts, while other rules proved impracticable because they 'are founde by Experience to be verie harde and extreme to many of the Queenes Majesties Subjectes'. Some parishes, for instance, delayed the introduction of compulsory poor rates for decades, relying on the careful management of private benefaction instead.[30]

Then there was open resistance. Fears that the dissolution of the monasteries would be followed by a confiscation of parish property helped to trigger the most dangerous rebellion in Henry VIII's reign, the Pilgrim-age of Grace in 1536. Here, as in the Western Rising thirteen years later, local communities resented the massive degree of interference in their cer-emonial life: on 6 June 1549 a town meeting at Bodmin protested against the new Protestant Prayer Book, while the parishioners of Sampford Courte-nay in Devon compelled their priest to celebrate mass, declaring 'that they would keep the old and ancient religion as their forefathers before them had done'.[31] Communal priorities, however, were not necessarily 'conservative'. The East Anglian rebels of the same year ostentatiously supported the new ecclesiastical regime, but rose against the manoeuvrings of their secular lords. The protest took the form of a 'confederation of aggrieved local com-munities that rallied around Kett's Demands in order to break the power of a predatory aristocracy' and aimed at a 'reformation', making landlords 'institutionally accountable' to their communities.[32] Subsequent resistance movements tended to reflect similar concerns: most were essentially local campaigns sparked off by seigneurial abuses, particularly where enclosures appeared as an unilateral, unnegotiated act by an outside intruder. At Blunham in Bedfordshire, for example, the village constable gathered the tenants of the Earl of Kent in the local parish church to fund a common purse and to organise the military defence of their commons.[33]

Returning to the religious field, there is a wealth of evidence to suggest that villagers and townspeople failed to co-operate with the State's appropriation of church property. The reformers' move was a kick in the teeth of generations of pious benefactors and threatened to undermine the spiritual provision and financial livelihood of countless parishes. When the monasteries disappeared in 1536–39, when chantries and fraternities were dissolved in 1547, and when royal commissioners toured the land to confiscate church plate in the early 1550s, officials were faced with a 'stampede to prevent theft by the Crown'.[34] At some point during Henry VIII's reign, the constable of Davidstow in Cornwall advised his parishioners to sell their best chalice before they would lose it to the authorities, and similar advice was heeded elsewhere: St Nicholas, Guildford, was forced to admit to the Edwardian commissioners that 'your orators not knowynge or conceyvynge any restraynt ... dyd sell ther saide churche plate' and if they now had to reimburse the Crown for its losses 'it wolde be to ther utter undoynge'.[35] Urban corporations, too, endeavoured to obtain possession of local ecclesiastical wealth before strangers could lay their hands on it: at Bristol in 1539, for instance, churchwardens loaned some of their silver plate to the city in an attempt to raise the necessary financial resources.[36] Large-scale transfer of property to the municipality may have ushered in a distinctive 'Age of Reformation' in many towns: the acquisition of former ecclesiastical possessions boosted revenues and led to a new wave of borough incorporations. Both promoted urban self-determination, although the benefits accrued above all to the local oligarchy.[37]

The most common strategy to protect local properties from the grip of the royal Exchequer, however, seems to have been concealment: in the Suffolk village of Cratfield, churchwardens and parish feoffees managed to retain practically all communal lands in spite of the fact that many had obvious 'superstitious' connotations, while a fresh search of the deeds of the London church of St Botolph Aldersgate revealed in 1559–60 that several tenements had been bequeathed for 'Lampes Lightes & soch like ... whereof the same [should have been] geven to the late Kinge Edwarde the vjth'.[38] As the latter example shows, the Crown tackled the problem by means of periodic investigations, but 'the activities of the concealment hunters often brought them into conflict with local communities and they must have caused deep resentment and ill-will'.[39] This evidence for 'non-conformity' can be added to the well-known attempts by conservative parishes to hide images and mass vestments in the hope of a future restoration of the old religion, to the survival of a strong conservative 'church papist' element among post-Reformation English congregations, and to the surprising resilience of features of local ceremonial life in an increasingly hostile environment. There can be little doubt that many people feared for the health of their souls. And yet, to repeat an important point, communal attitudes could also be 'progressive': a close study of the secretive Family of Love has discovered a degree of local religious tolerance which provides a sharp contrast to the persecution campaigns initiated by central authorities. Furthermore, where official guidelines were deemed to be insufficiently radical, town corporations and parishes could invest in lectureships and other forms of Protestant culture to satisfy their particular preferences.[40]

From the late 1620s centre/locality tensions approached a new climax and parishes turned into a 'battleground for rival visions of English society'. Under Charles I, the broad Calvinist–predestinarian consensus was challenged by a powerful clique of Arminian theologians for whom 'divine grace through prayer and sacraments were available to the entire Christian community'.[41] This change of emphasis went hand-in-hand with a renewed emphasis on the role of the clergy and a 'radical programme of liturgical and ecclesiological reorganisation', enforced by means of searching visitations, frequent prosecutions and a strong reliance on the backing of central courts.[42] A good example are the no fewer than 147 articles of inquiry which Matthew Wren, Bishop of Ely, put before his startled parishioners in 1638. Wren had just been translated from Norwich, where an anti-puritan campaign had left no doubts about his ideological allegiance.[43] Visitations, of course, were well-established forms of external intrusion, but the degree of detail and curiosity revealed in this document would have been unthinkable in the Middle Ages. A few examples may suffice: the bishop wondered whether the 'blessed Sacrament [had] been delivered unto any ... Communicants within your Parish, that did unreverently either sit, stand, or leane; or that did not devoutly and humbly kneele upon their knees, in plaine and open view, without collusion or hypocrisie?'[44] Churchwardens were under oath to provide 'true answer to all particulars therein demanded' and the returns echo the language of the inquiry in almost every detail (whether they were *adequate*, of course, is quite another matter). At St Edward's, Cambridge, the reply emphasised that 'there is not anie that takes the sacrament unreverentlie either setting, standing, or leaning. But humbly and devoutlie

kneeling upon their knees in open view without hypocrisie.'[45] Another article raised 'one of the most hated aspects of Church policy in the 1630s':[46]

> Have you in your Church … a convenient and decent Communion Table,
> with a carpet of silke … continually laid upon the Table at the time of
> Divine Service, and a fair linnen cloth … what did either of them cost? And
> is the same Table placed conveniently, so as the Minister may best be heard
> … . To that end doth it ordinarily stand up at the East end of the Chancell
> where the Altar in former times stood: the ends thereof being placed North
> and South … . Are there any steps or ascents in your Chancell up to the
> Communion Table; have you also a decent rail of wood … placed hand-
> somely above those steps, before the Holy Table, neere one yard high, and
> reaching crosse from the North wall to the South (except by the order of
> the Diocesan it be made with the ends returning unto the East wall) with
> two convenient doores to open before the Table; and if it be a Raile, are
> the Pillars … thereof so close, that doggs may not any where get in?[47]

To this, the same wardens replied that 'the table stand up at the east
end of the chancell thends thereof being placed north and south … there
are 2 steps in our Chancell to the Comunion table wee have a decent raile
of wood above the steps without a cover as yet reaching Cross from north
to south, the pillars are so close that no Doggs cann get in'.[48] St Edward's
clearly endeavoured to minimise disruption by presenting a picture of
'omnia bene', but elsewhere there were obvious tensions: Coveney and
Churcham conceded that they had 'no stepps nor raile to the communion
table', while Downham presented a 'William Segrave for abusing the
churchwardens and sidesmen'.[49]

Yet more explicit evidence of popular resentment emerged after the
recall of Parliament in 1640, when the wave of provincial petitions to the
House of Commons included a submission from 'divers of his Maties Subjects in the county of Cambridge' against the 'Tirannicall courses & Admin-
istracions of Do[r] Wrenn B[pp] of the Diocesse of Elie'.[50] The defence of
communal autonomy and customs is among the most conspicuous concerns:
hundreds of signatories complain against 'a certaine Book of Visitatorie articles to the number of one hundred fortie and seven which are enforced
upon us', against the Bishop's imposition of 'three or four supernumerarie
officers [in] everie parish whom he called assistants besides the ordinarie
churchwardens and sidesmen',[51] against 'the setting up of our communion
Tables altarwise … and the charge of all these things (being within the
chancell) levied by strict order upon the parishes whereas the chancell properly ought to belong to the Rector',[52] and against 'apparitors comeing to
take the keyes of our churches from the sexton'.[53] In this case, the plain-

tiffs went on to call for an abolition of episcopacy and the establishment of
a church government more in tune with scriptural models, but resentment
of 'these late superstition innovacions' was by no means the preserve of radical puritans.[54] Similar concerns emerge in petitions by loyal Prayer Book
Protestants who were happy to defend the rule of bishops in principle, but
dismissed the Laudian initiatives as an intolerable attempt to dismantle the
religious settlement they had come to cherish. Up and down the country,
parishes adopted a range of defensive strategies to counter the offensive:
more or less vociferous protest, cover-ups, delaying tactics and non-payment
of rates.[55] The rebuilding plans were controversial not only because of their
costs but also because they seem to have interfered with ongoing, local pro-
jects of church embellishment. On the whole, the two initiatives were difficult to reconcile, but once again grass-roots attitudes cannot be reduced to
one single party line. In some parishes, the drive for an increased 'beauty
of holiness' actually struck a chord with communal preferences.[56]

The enforcement of religious reform, of course, was not the only type
of external intrusion at the time. Early Stuart secular government was characterised by a similar 'increase of governance' and a long period of personal
rule by a monarch who decided on matters such as taxation and economic
monopolies without recourse to parliamentary advice.[57] Between 1629 and
1640 neither the people's spiritual welfare nor their material property
seemed to be safe from Charles I's grasp. At the same time, local and
national priorities clashed in the courts. Derbyshire mining law, to take but
one example, which allowed men of lowly social rank access to profitable
lead deposits, stood in the way of more privatised, commercial forms of
exploitation. In their attempts to challenge the customs, members of the
ruling elite turned to common law at the expense of the jurisdiction of
established local bodies.[58] The Westminster Court of Star Chamber, meanwhile, conducted a vigorous campaign against unlicensed publications: future
protagonists of the Civil War period such as the puritan pamphleteer
William Prynne or the Leveller leader John Lilburne suffered imprisonment
and physical violence for what they considered a legitimate campaign against
tyranny. Small wonder, then, that the *Camera Stellata* was among the first
casualties of the Long Parliament, which abolished the court in 1641.[59] Even
at the height of the pressure, however, communal activities did not simply
evaporate. Social historians stress the continuity of informal channels of local
conflict resolution by means of peer pressure and internal arbitration, with
presentments to external jurisdiction restricted to those sorts of cases which
the community failed to resolve satisfactorily.[60] Constables and churchwardens continued to be selected in accordance with local custom rather than
by outside appointment, and parish vestries still found some room for inde-

pendent regulative activities.[61] The constitutional debates of the 1640s were to reveal just how strong communal principles remained.

The collapse of censorship restrictions on the eve of the Civil War allowed the middling and lower sorts an unprecedented opportunity to participate in political reasoning. It is not surprising that they drew heavily on local models to resolve the predicament of the English State. The various Clubmen associations, peasant movements emerging in counties as diverse as Sussex and Worcestershire, are a case in point. Formed in 1644 and 1645 out of increasing war-weariness and fears of further outside interference, they devised an organisation with a 'sophistication that reminds us that however humble, these were men of independence long familiar with the processes of self-government'.[62] Shocked by a breakdown of order, by plunder, requisitioning and bad military discipline, they developed a programme based on local autonomy and a strengthening of the old communal offices. State bureaucracy had to give way to village custom, for 'what the clubmen resented more than anything else was outside interference in local affairs'.[63] The petition of the Sussex association of 26 September 1645 complained about

> the insufferable, insolent, arbitrary power that hath bin used amongst us, contrary to all our auncient knowne lawes, or ordinances of parliament, upon our persons and estates by imprisoning our persons, imposeing of somes of money, light horses, and dragoones, and exacting of Loanes by some particular persons stept into authority whoe have delegated their power to men of sordid condition whose wills have been lawes and Comands over our persons and estates, by which they have overthrowne all our English libertyes.[64]

What was needed now was a return to officers and institutions people could trust. The articles of the clubmen of the counties of Dorset and Wiltshire (25 May 1645) proposed the following:

> (1) Every town, tything, parish, and great hamlet, make present choice of three or more of the ablest men for wisdom, valour, and estate, inhabitants of the same, unto whom at all times they may repair for assistance and direction.
> (2) That the Constable, Tythingman and other officers of the town etc. in pursuance of the Statute in that case provided, set a constant watch of two at the least, and they every night well-armed and if required by day also; the number of watchmen to be increased according to the direction of the chosen able men and officers.[65]

There are some intriguing parallels with demands made in 1381, but in contrast to their fourteenth-century predecessors, the clubmen failed to combine local concerns with a wider, more revolutionary programme. For this, we have to turn to another, predominantly urban movement. Between 1647 and 1649 the Levellers rallied mass support behind their calls for periodical parliaments, a broad householder franchise and the accountability of all public officers. Given the simultaneous emphasis on religious tolerance and the references to all sorts of secondary authorities, the programme is normally related to Protestant congregationalism and influences from contemporary political thought.[66] Both undoubtedly played a part, but perhaps more on an abstract intellectual level, providing the ideological justification to advance a complete reordering of State and society. The actual proposals themselves, however, are borrowed from the Levellers' communal experience. London ward and parish government still supplied *prima-facie* evidence of householder-based regimes, periodical assemblies and the accountability of churchwardens and other local officials.[67] As a member of a parish vestry, the Leveller protagonist William Walwyn was perfectly familiar with the exercise of communal control. The records of St James Garlickhithe reveal how he was elected unto a committee of inquiry when 'divers parisheners desyred to bee acquainted how the estate of the parish and ... the rents and revenues of the Church & poores stocke now standeth'. His committee work resulted in the removal of the minister and a thorough investigation into parish finances.[68] Elaborating on the concept of popular sovereignty, Richard Overton emphasised that 'every man by nature [is] a King, Priest and Prophet *in his owne naturall circuite and compasse* whereof no second may partake, but by deputation, commission and free consent from him', and Lilburne added that everyman 'raignes and governs as much by God *in their inferior orbs* (of City, hundreds, wapentacks, and families) ... as Kings in their Kingdoms'.[69] This is why the programme proposed a radical process of decentralisation, a 'blueprint for a society of self-governing communities'.[70] Indirect taxation was to be replaced by the old subsidies, courts had to be erected 'in every Hundred in the Nation, for the ending of all Differences arising in that Hundred, by twelve men of the same Hundred, annually chosen by Free-men in that Hundred'. No one was to impose ministers on any congregation, but 'the parishioners of every particular parish' should have 'free liberty ... to chuse such as themselves shall approve'; neither should mayors or sheriffs be forced 'upon any Counties, Hundreds, Cities, Towns, or Boroughs; but the people ... shall chuse all their publike Officers' themselves. The revolutionary next step was to project the same principles on to the level of the State as a whole by allowing *all* the free-born of England (and not just a landholding elite) to select their MPs and to set clear limits to the discretion of any public functionary: 'no person whatsoever be permitted to exercise any Power or Authority in this

Nation, who shal not clearly ... receive his power from [Parliament], and be always accountable for the discharge of his trust, to the People in their Representers'.[71] English politics would have been turned upside-down. Small wonder that gentlemen such as Oliver Cromwell did all they could to marginalise and eventually defeat the movement.[72]

Communal principles, however, survived in their natural, local habitat. The resilience of the parish system in the face of presbyterian and sectarian challenges throughout the Civil War and Commonwealth is a striking example.[73] Stuart government may have resulted in an overall 'triumph of the gentry', but the lower sorts continued to stand their ground: in the early 1650s, John Lilburne turned his attention away from national campaigning to the plight of the Fenland rebels, who fought for their traditional rights of commons.[74] Local problems, furthermore, could still be tackled internally, without any state or gentry encouragement. In 1691, the Cambridgeshire parish of Lolworth resolved a number of agricultural issues by means of an agreement for 'good order' by 'all or at least the chief inhabitants'. Quarter Sessions often simply confirmed or approved such grassroots initiatives, for instance the understanding between the parishioners of Aston Clynton and those of the hamlet of St Leonard's in 1679, which specified that the latter was to pay one-fifth of 'all taxes, impositions, and rates which hereafter shall be imposed upon the said parish', or that between the inhabitants of Great and Little Brickhill of the same year, which determined their respective share in the maintenance of the local bridge.[75] State expansion was kept in check and England remained a localised society.[76]

The focus of this chapter has been on the fear of intrusion. However, as stated at the outset, centre/locality relations in our period cannot be subsumed under one single heading. Their character depended on the specific context and the balance of interests involved. While communal autonomy continued to be cherished and defended, Westminster courts and state institutions were readily used when their involvement promised to promote local concerns. From the late fourteenth century, for instance, parishioners appreciated equity jurisdiction as an informal and efficient new tool to deal with their legal problems.[77] During the Reformation period, many a community lobbied the highest authorities to prevent confiscation of their 'superstitious' assets: Long Melford in Suffolk sent four representatives 'to go to my Lord Protector & other of the Kynges councell to have ... the gyfte of Bowes Hall for a sc[ho]ol'.[78] Another good example is the persistent fight against oligarchical tendencies in communal government. Abuses in early modern urban administration, for instance, could be challenged in Star Chamber.[79] In the London parish of St Botolph Aldersgate, a newly established select vestry soon incensed the wider community by its assumption of ever more powers and a series of arbitrary financial exactions. In response, twenty-seven marginalised citizens initiated an 'Inquisition under the Great Seal' and other legal proceedings to protest against these abuses and to demand that 'the vestrie of the said parrish may bee publique as hath bin alwaies anciently accustomed'.[80] Even Arminian ordinaries, who ruffled so many feathers in the localities, could be called upon to protect communal government: their ecclesiological emphasis on an 'inclusive body based on participation in public worship', after all, mirrored parochial traditions much more closely than the sectarian preference for an 'exclusive grouping of proven true believers' at the other end of the theological spectrum.[81] The experience of St Lawrence Jewry is a case in point from the capital: after the vicar and a group of like-minded supporters had obtained a grant for the establishment of a select vestry in 1627, it was none other than William Laud who three years later – in his capacity as Bishop of London – ordered the return to a general meeting 'upon the humble peticion of the parishioners'.[82] At Tarporley in Cheshire, disgruntled members of the community protested at Quarter Sessions, in ecclesiastical courts, and ultimately by means of a petition to the King against their rector's disregard of 'many orders and customs which we have had in former times'. The State, clearly, could be a resource as well as an intruder.[83]

What other conclusions can be drawn from this brief survey? Even in a country as 'individualistic' and 'economically developed' as England, local communities retained their fundamental political and social role well into the early modern period. Tendencies towards greater integration and oligarchical government cannot be overlooked, but communal resilience prevented a complete erosion of popular participation. Central authorities were encouraged to enforce the rule of law, to defend the nation and to provide those sorts of services that simply transcended the powers of towns and villages. The monarch, quite in contrast to many of his representatives and lawyers, enjoyed great personal authority among his subjects, who often appealed to him directly when they found faults or negligence in the government machinery. This, both in England and on the Continent, was one of the driving forces of early modern state formation.[84]

And yet, while there was no absolute 'fear of intrusion', external authorities had to be aware of the limits of their powers. Excessive taxation, combined with attacks upon long-standing religious or socio-economic customs, set communal alarm bells ringing, most spectacularly in 1381, during the Reformation and in the run-up to the Civil War, when central interference reached particularly staggering levels. In such cases latent popular anxieties were transformed into very tangible fears about the loss of communal property, culture and self-government. Depending on the degree of resentment and the respective circumstances, villagers and towns-people responded with a variety of strategies, ranging from petitioning (either alone or as part of a county-wide initiative) and passive resistance (concealment, evasion, foot-dragging) to open rebellion (1381, the Pilgrimage of Grace). Given the sophisticated and balanced response to challenges by outside powers, local communities were anything but 'unpolitical' or 'ideologically barren' environments.[85] In contrast, the experience of intrusion and conflict helped the lower sorts to develop a potentially explosive, independent political consciousness based upon a qualified defence of local autonomy. In extraordinary circumstances, these principles broke out of their spatial confinement and inspired an alternative constitutional model for the nation at large (1381, the Levellers). However, while villages and towns shared a great number of structural similarities and priorities, there was no such thing as a uniform communal ideology: localities could develop 'conservative', 'progressive', 'puritan' or 'Royalist' sympathies, they could be ideologically united or divided; it all depended on their specific local context and, of course, the individual consciences of their inhabitants.[86] They could also change allegiances: by the early seventeenth century, many an erstwhile Catholic parish had developed into a staunch defender of the Church of England, whose 'ancient customs' needed to be protected against disruptive innovations.[87]

The wider political impact of communal fears of intrusion (and thus the chances of modifying or defeating national policies) varied greatly. Of crucial importance was the degree of support by local and regional elites. The fact that the Reformation was implemented more easily than the religious policies of Charles I did not only reflect differences in the level of popular resentment, but also a change of side by the gentry. Whilst they were happy to benefit from the large-scale dissolutions, the marginalisation of church authorities and the increasing powers devolved to them in their capacity as JPs in the sixteenth century, they clearly resented the monarch's personal rule, the threat to their properties and the influence of controversial theologians 100 years later. Early Stuart England was marked by an unprecedented coincidence of religious and political crises and in this environment, communal resilience developed synergies with fears among more powerful circles. Together, they proved an irresistible and ultimately revolutionary force, but villages, towns and parishes knew to defend their interests also in less favourable circumstances.

Notes

1 P. Anderson, *Lineages of the Absolutist State* (1974); H. Schilling, *Religion, Political Culture and the Emergence of Early Modern Society* (Leiden, 1992).

2 See, for instance, the influential works by J. Delumeau, *Catholicism Between Luther and Voltaire* (1977) and R. Muchembled, *Popular Culture and Elite Culture in France 1400–1750* (Baton Rouge, 1985).

3 R. M. Smith, '"Modernisation" and the corporate village community in England: some sceptical reflections', in A. Baker and D. Gregory, eds, *Explorations in Historical Geography* (Cambridge, 1984), 140–79.

4 Collections of recent research in W. Blockmans and J. P. Genet, eds, *The Origins of the Modern State in Europe* (Oxford, 1996) and P. Blickle, ed., *Gemeinde und Staat im Alten Europa* (Munich, 1997); for local modification of 'official' religious change see M. Foster, *The Counter-Reformation in the Villages: Religion and Reform in the Bishopric of Speyer 1560–1720* (Ithaca, 1992).

5 J. R. Kent, 'The centre and the localities: state formation and parish government in England, *c*.1640–1740', *Historical Journal*, 38 (1995), 363–404 (and literature cited in n. 2 above); M. Braddick, 'State formation and social change in early modern England: a problem stated and approaches suggested', *Social History*, 16 (1991), 1–17, esp. 5; a comprehensive survey of the historiography of centre/locality relations in early modern England, and a strong emphasis on the participatory character of the contemporary government system, in S. Hindle, 'Aspects of the relationship of the State and local society in early modern England with special reference to Cheshire *c*.1590–1630' (University of Cambridge Ph.D thesis, 1992), ch. 1 and p. 549.

6 P. Collinson, *De Republica Anglorum, Or, History with the Politics Put Back* (Cambridge, 1990), 15.

7 Here pragmatically defined as a 'small territorial unit with shared responsibilities, resources and broadly-based forms of political participation', without denying the existence of many other, and often overlapping, forms of neighbourhood, kinship or regional allegiances; see A. Macfarlane, S. Harrison and C. Jardine, *Reconstructing Historical Communities* (Cambridge, 1977), 12–13.

8 As proposed by Braddick, 'State formation', 5.

9 Potential French raids worried the inhabitants of Weymouth in Dorset when they left their dwellings to attend a distant parish church: A. Kreider, *English Chantries: The Road to Dissolution* (Cambridge, MA, 1979), pp. 57, 233; for seventeenth-century fears of military attacks, see Will Coster, Ch. 6, this volume. Anxieties about overpopulation and famine were important causes of popular protest: R. B. Manning, *Village Revolts: Social Protest and Popular Disturbances in England 1509–1640* (Oxford, 1988), 314, 316; see Roberts, Ch. 1, Eßer, Ch. 4, and Gentilcore, Ch. 11, this volume.

10 U. Im Hof, *Geschichte der Schweiz* (Stuttgart, 1981), ch. 4.4.

11 W. Schulze, 'Peasant resistance in sixteenth- and seventeenth-century Germany in a European context', in K. V. Greyerz, ed., *Religion, Politics and Social Protest* (1984), 62 (quote); P. Blickle, *Unruhen in der städischen Gesellschaft 1400–1800* (Munich, 1988), 87; A. Suter, *"Troublen" im Fürstbistum Basel 1716–40* (Göttingen, 1985), 333–9.

12 Examples cited in B. Hodler, 'Kommunale Partizipation an der königlichen Souveränität im Frankreich des 16. Jahrhunderts', in Blickle, ed., *Gemeinde und Staat* (forthcoming).

13 A. Macfarlane, *The Origins of English Individualism* (Oxford, 1978), J. Brewer, *The Sinews of Power: War, Money and the English State 1688–1783* (1989), 3–6; P. Hudson, *The Industrial Revolution* (1992).

14 For brief discussions of the origin and character of these communal units see, e.g., S. Reynolds, *An Introduction to the History of English Medieval Towns* (Oxford, 1977), C. Dyer, 'The English medieval village community and its decline', *Journal of British Studies*, 33 (1994), 407–29, and B. Kümin, *The Shaping of a Community: The Rise and Reformation of the English Parish c.1400–1560* (Aldershot, 1996).

COMMUNAL RESILIENCE IN ENGLAND

15 See the arguments for social polarisation and cultural differentiation developed in
K. Wrightson, *English Society 1580–1680* (1982) and D. Underdown, *Revel, Riot and
Rebellion: Popular Politics and Culture in England 1603–60* (1985).

16 E. M. Tomlinson, *A History of the Minories London* (1907), 165 and *passim*.

17 Collinson, *De Republica*, 30–1; W. A. Ault, *Open-Field Husbandry and the Village Community* (Philadelphia, 1965), 54 and appendix 211.

18 A. Everitt, *The Community of Kent and the Great Rebellion 1640–60* (1966) and K. Wrightson and D. Levine, *Poverty and Piety in an English Village: Terling 1525–1700* (1995) are
among the most prominent representatives of 'county' and 'village' studies; the quote
from Hindle, 'Relationship', 18.

19 C. Dyer, 'The social and economic background to the rural revolt of 1381', in R. Hilton
and T. Aston, eds, *The English Rising of 1381* (Cambridge, 1984), p. 36.

20 *Ibid.*, 36–8; J. R. Maddicott, *The English Peasantry and the Demands of the Crown
1294–1341* (1975).

21 R. Palmer, *English Law in the Age of the Black Death 1345–81: A Transformation of Governance and Law* (Chapel Hill, 1993); R. Hilton, 'A crisis of feudalism', *P&P*, 80 (1978),
3–19.

22 R. B. Dobson, ed., *The Peasants' Revolt of 1381* (Basingstoke, 1983), 174; N. Brooks,
'The organisation and achievements of the peasants of Kent and Essex in 1381', in
H. Mayr-Harting and R. Moore, eds, *Studies in Medieval History Presented to R. H. C. Davis*
(1985), *passim*.

23 S. Justice, *Writing and Rebellion: England in 1381* (Berkeley, 1994), 172.

24 Dobson, *Peasants' Revolt*, 17, 195 (quote from Henry Knighton's *Chronicon*; my italics);
Dyer, '1381', 17.

25 Demands made between 14 and 22 June 1381: Dobson, *Peasants' Revolt*, 165, 177, 310.

26 Dyer, '1381', 42; similarly Justice, *Writing and Rebellion*, 172–4.

27 'The complaints of the commons of Kent', articles 9, 12, 13, 15 and 'The requests of
the Captaine of the great assembly in Kent', article 5, all in Dobson, *Peasants' Revolt*,
340–2.

28 G. R. Elton, *The Tudor Revolution in Government* (Cambridge, 1953).

29 A. Tindal-Hart, *The Man in the Pew* (1966), 66; the impression of conformity emerges
even from revisionist accounts (R. Hutton, 'The local impact of the Tudor Reformations', in C. Haigh, ed., *The English Reformation Revised* (Cambridge, 1987), 137–8); for
a detailed description of mid-sixteenth-century change see Kümin, *Shaping of a Community*, ch. 6.

30 Quotes from *Statutes of the Realm* (1963), 4: 1 Eliz., c. 21, 14 Eliz., c. 5 and 11, 27
Eliz., c. 13; Boxford managed without rates well into the restoration period (CWA:
SufRO, Bury St Edmunds, FB77/E2/*passim*).

31 M. Bowker, 'Lincolnshire 1536', in D. Baker, ed., *Schism, Heresy and Religious Protest*
(Cambridge, 1972), 198–9; C. S. L. Davies, 'Popular religion and the Pilgrimage of
Grace', in A. Fletcher and J. Stevenson, eds, *Order and Disorder in Early Modern England*
(1985), 58–91; C. Haigh, *English Reformations* (Oxford, 1993), 174.

32 V. Magagna, *Communities of Grain: Rural Rebellion in Comparative Perspective* (Ithaca, 1991),
118; see the rebels' articles 11, 14, 21 demanding a reallocation of commons' profits to
tenants, a return to more reasonable copyhold rents, and checks on the selling of local
land: B. L. Beer, *Rebellion and Riot: Popular Disorder in England During the Reign of Edward
VI* (Kent, OH, 1982), 105–7.

33 Manning, *Village Revolts*, 309, 100–1 (Blunham, t. James I); similarly K. Lindley, *Fenland Riots and the English Revolution* (1982), 253.

34 W. G. Hoskins, *The Age of Plunder: The England of Henry VIII* (1976), ch. 6; E. Duffy,
The Stripping of the Altars: Traditional Religion in England c.1400–c.1580 (New Haven,
1994), 484 (quote).

35 PRO, Star Chamber Proceedings 3/2/20 (Davidstow); R. Roberts, ed., 'Further inven-

tories', *Surrey Archaeological Collections*, 24 (1911), 35.

36 M. Skeeters, *Community and Clergy: Bristol and the Reformation 1530–70* (Oxford, 1993),
    78; All Saints delivered 96 ounces of plate (BRO, P/AS/ChW/3: CWA, All Saints,
    1539–40).

37 Robert Tittler is engaged on a comprehensive study of the Reformation impact on the
    urban environment; in the meantime see his 'Reformation, resources and authority in
    English towns: an overview', in P. Collinson and J. Craig, eds, *The Reformation in the Eng-
    lish Towns* (Basingstoke, forthcoming).

38 K. Farnhill, 'Religious policy and parish conformity: Cratfield's lands in the sixteenth cen-
    tury', in K. French, G. Gibbs and B. Kümin, eds, *The Parish in English Life* (Manchester,
    1997) 217–29; GL, MS 1454: CWA, St Botolph Aldersgate, 1559–60.

39 C. Kitching, 'The quest for concealed lands in the reign of Elizabeth I', *TRHS*, 5th Ser.
    24 (1974), 63–78; David Thomas, 'Leases of crown lands in the reign of Elizabeth I', in
    R. W. Hoyle ed., *The Estates of the English Crown 1558–1640* (Cambridge, 1992), 182
    (quote).

40 Examples of hidden church treasures in Duffy, *Stripping of the Altars*, 490–1, 498ff; A.
    Walsham, *Church Papists* (Woodbridge, 1993); emphasis on the persistence of parish plays
    and other non-liturgical customs in A. Johnston and S. B. MacLean, 'Reformation and
    resistance in Thames/Severn parishes: the dramatic witness', in French *et al.*, eds, *The
    Parish in English Life*, 178–200; C. Marsh, *The Family of Love in English Society 1550–1630*
    (Cambridge, 1994); for Protestant initiatives see, e.g., P. Seaver, *The Puritan Lectureships*
    (Stanford, CA, 1970).

41 K. Fincham, 'Introduction', in his, ed., *The Early Stuart Church 1603–42* (Basingstoke,
    1993), 1, 10 (quotes); the seminal, but by no means unchallenged, study is N. Tyacke,
    Anti-Calvinists: The Rise of English Arminianism c.1590–1640 (Oxford, 1987).

42 J. Fielding, 'Arminianism in the localities: Peterborough diocese 1603–42', in Fincham,
    Early Stuart Church, 103 and *passim*. 'What is striking about the 1630s is the relentless
    pressure brought to bear by Laud and his bishops on the community': A. Foster, 'Church
    policies of the 1630s', in R. Cust and A. Hughes, eds, *Conflict in Early Stuart England*
    (1989), 195.

43 *DNB* (1900), 43: *sub nomine*.

44 *Articles to be inqvired of within the Diocese of Ely: In the first Visitation of the Rt Reverend Father
    in God Matthew, Lord Bishop of Ely* (Richard Badger, 1638) [STC 10197], ch. 2, art. 9.

45 W. M. Palmer, ed., *Episcopal Visitation Returns for Cambridgeshire* (Cambridge, 1930), 5
    (15 Jan. 1638/9).

46 Foster, 'Church policies', 203.

47 *Articles*, ch. 3, art. 3.

48 Palmer, *Returns*, 6.

49 *Ibid.*, 44 (quote from Coveney), 47 and 45 (quote from Downham).

50 Reproduced in *ibid.*, between 76–7; for other provincial petitions see, e.g., A. Fletcher,
    'National and local awareness in the county communities', in H. Tomlinson, ed., *Before
    the English Civil War* (1983), 154.

51 Assistants are known to have attended St Edward's presentments: Palmer, *Returns*, 4.

52 Ecclesiastical law supports this claim: W. Lyndwood, *Provinciale* (Oxford, 1679), 53.

53 These extracts from BL, Egerton MS, 1048, 24 (articles 1, 2, 5 and 13).

54 Palmer, *Returns*, 74.

55 J. Maltby, '"By this Book": parishioners, the Prayer Book and the established Church', in
    Fincham, *Early Stuart Church*, 128–31; for defensive strategies see Foster, 'Church poli-
    cies', 215–16.

56 Evidence for local embellishment from the 1590s in A. Foster, 'Churchwardens' accounts
    of early modern England: some problems to be noted, but much to be gained', in French
    et al., *Parish*, 74–93. Parish co-operation is stressed in P. White, 'The *via media* in the
    early Stuart Church', in Fincham, *Early Stuart Church*, 228–9.

57 Summary accounts in A. Fletcher, *Reform in the Provinces: The Government of Stuart England* (New Haven, 1986), 116ff, and D. Hirst, *Authority and Conflict: England 1603–58* (1986), 160ff.

58 A. Wood, 'Industrial development, social change and popular politics in the mining area of north-west Derbyshire c.1600–1700' (Ph.D. thesis, University of Cambridge, 1993), 161, 175.

59 William Haller, ed., *Tracts on Liberty in the Puritan Revolution 1638–47* (New York, 1934), 1: 9; Fincham, 'Introduction', 16.

60 J. Sharpe, 'Enforcing the law in the seventeenth-century English village', in V. Gatrell, B. Lenman and G. Parker, eds, *Crime and the Law* (1980), 97–119; Collinson, *De Republica*, 31.

61 J. Kent, *The English Village Constable 1580–1642* (Oxford, 1986), 57–71; vestry by-laws frequently fixed the duties of parish employees and the level of fees for certain communal services: see the survey of parochial customs in LPL, Carte Miscellanee, vol. 7.

62 D. Underdown, *Somerset in the Civil War and Interregnum* (1973), 107; for a more detailed analysis of the movements see his *Revel, Riot and Rebellion*, 156–9 and J. Morrill, *The Revolt of the Provinces: Conservatives and Radicals in the English Civil War* (1980), 98–110.

63 *Ibid.*, 106.

64 *Ibid.*, 198.

65 *Ibid.*, 199–200.

66 D. B. Robertson, *The Religious Foundations of Leveller Democracy* (New York, 1951); A. Sharp, ed., *Political Ideas of the English Civil War* (1983), 13–25.

67 V. Pearl, 'Change and stability in seventeenth-century London', in J. Barry, ed., *The Tudor and Stuart Town* (1990), 148–59.

68 GL, MS 4813/1: Vestry Minutes of St James Garlickhithe, fol. 54v (1640).

69 Richard Overton, *An Arrow Against all Tyrants* (1646), 69; John Lilburne, *Regall Tyrannie Discovered* (1647), 40 [my italics].

70 B. Manning, *The English People and the English Revolution* (1991), 410; decentralisation enjoyed support from a number of other radical writers: C. Hill, *Society and Puritanism in Pre-Revolutionary England* (1986), 428.

71 The quotations are from *The Foundations of Freedom* (1648) and *An Agreement of the Free People of England* (1649), both edited in D. Wolfe, ed., *Leveller Manifestoes of the Puritan Revolution* (New York, 1944), 303, 408, and from *The Earnest Petition of many Free-Born People* (1648) in W. Haller and G. Davies, eds, *The Leveller Tracts* (Gloucester, MA, 1964), 108.

72 The argument is developed more fully in my 'Gemeinde und Revolution: Die kommunale Prägung der englischen Levellers', in Blickle, *Gemeinde und Staat*, 359–94.

73 J. Morrill, 'The Church in England, 1642–9', in his, ed., *Reactions to the English Civil War* (1982), 89–114; C. Cross, 'The Church in England 1649–60', in G. Aylmer, ed., *The Interregnum* (1972), 99–120.

74 'Triumph of the gentry': Fletcher, *Reform*, 'Conclusion'; Lindley, *Fenland Riots*, ch. 6 (Lilburne); 'If the persistence of agrarian protest is any indication, a sense of community ... remained strong well into the middle of the seventeenth century': Manning, *Village Revolts*, 315.

75 CRO, L/65/4; W. L. Hardy, ed., *County of Buckingham: Calendar of Session Records 1678–94* (Aylesbury, 1933), 30, 433.

76 Brewer, *Sinews of Power*, xix; Hindle, 'Relationship', 555.

77 See the wide range of cases discussed in K. French, 'Local identity and the late medieval parish' (Ph.D. thesis, University of Minnesota, 1993), ch. 6.

78 SufRO, Bury St Edmunds, FL/509/1/15: Black Book of Long Melford, 1547–8.

79 Tittler, 'Reformation'.

80 Full text of the petition for a select vestry (by eight members of the parish elite in 1607) in *The Report of the Committee Appointed by a General Vestry* (1733), 9–13; last quote from

GL, MS 10,910: Inquisition under the Great Seal (6 Jan. 1630); a pending Star Chamber suit mentioned in LPL, Carte Miscellanee, vol. 7, no. 55.

81 Quotes from Fielding, 'Arminianism', 100.

82 LPL, Carte Miscellanee, vol. 7, no. 83.

83 The Tarporley case in Maltby, 'Parishioners', 121; emphasis on the state as a 'resource' in Hindle, 'Relationship', 28–9, and Braddick, 'State formation', 17.

84 Brewer, *Sinews of Power*, 22; Hodler, 'Kommunale Partizipation'.

85 Manning, *Village Revolts*, 310; Lindley, *Fenland Riots*, 253.

86 See the refusal of any sort of determinism in M. Spufford, *Contrasting Communities* (Cambridge, 1974).

87 'Too often local historians forget that people develop new ideas or change their minds under the pressure of events': A. Hughes, 'Local history and the origins of the Civil War', in R. Cust and A. Hughes, eds, *Conflict in Early Stuart England* (1989), 249.

8

The spectre of ignorance: the provision of education in the Swiss cities

KARIN MAAG

In the Protestant cities of the sixteenth century, one of the authorities' chief concerns and one of their greatest financial outlays was on education, to combat ignorance among the inhabitants. The fear of ignorance differs considerably from many of the other fears examined in this volume, as ignorance was not a visible phenomenon, and the fear of it generally manifested itself only in a positive form, as authorities sought to provide various forms of learning. Indeed, Luther thought that ignorance and lack of learning were all the more dangerous because they were hidden, unlike concrete threats like the Turks, fires and floods.[1] An analysis of the fear of ignorance is complicated by its different aspects, as magistrates and ministers were concerned not only about intellectual ignorance, but also about the lack of spiritual knowledge, and the negative consequences of each. But the reasons for the fear of ignorance were clear. In the city leaders' eyes, ignorance, whether intellectual or spiritual, was a source of anxiety, for it carried with it associated dangers of idleness, lawlessness and superstition.

Clearly, the remedy for ignorance was education, but as this was not open to all in the early modern period, one must consider whether the civic authorities' concern to provide education, both intellectual and religious, for their fellow-inhabitants may have been motivated by a combined desire to eradicate ignorance and its attendant dangers of idleness and lawlessness, and to foster the acquisition of knowledge appropriate to each inhabitant's needs and station in life.[2]

Hence the misuse of educational provision by parents and pupils was of grave concern to the civic authorities. On 16 September 1555, in a report on the use of church goods secularised by the Zurich authorities, complaints were made that

> there is a great problem in both [Latin] schools, in that they are overburdened with pupils. Parents are not sending their children to school to learn,

nor so that they pursue their studies further, but rather to keep them off the street, and out from their feet at home, and maybe only then because they might learn something, and so they let [their children] study.[3]

The educational council of Zurich disapproved of the parents' actions in this instance because the schools were then filled with students who were unsuited to the curriculum. Their parents were sending them to school with other purposes than learning in mind. Yet the authorities' distaste for the parents' use of the school as a form of day-care was not solely due to the parents' reluctance to see learning as its own reward.

Indeed, the civil and ecclesiastical authorities in Zurich, Geneva and other Reformed Swiss cities all advocated education and training, not only as ends in themselves, but as tools to combat ignorance. Their view of the purpose of education matched that of other urban leaders across Europe, many of whom sought to establish schools and colleges to eradicate ignorance and prepare young people to be good citizens and pious people.[4] The use of education and schooling as a means of improving the perceived poor standard of intellectual and moral life is clear in the 1616 school ordinances of the city of Berne: the schools were intended 'to put an end to the growing barbarity, general ignorance and helplessness, with the help and grace of God'.[5] Furthermore, in many cases, education was viewed as a key civilising influence, so much so that the behaviour of children who did attend school was favourably compared to that of children who had no access to schooling. For instance, in Geneva on 2 March 1591, the Consistory complained to the magistrates that the children who did not attend the *schola privata* or Latin school were badly behaved, created disturbances in church and on people's wedding nights, 'which causes great scandal among foreigners'.[6]

In the context of an early modern independent city, where inhabitants generally had to share the same creed and work together to maintain the city's rights and freedoms, ignorance created fear, for it cast a spanner in the works. Those who were ignorant in an intellectual sense, that is, without education or practical training in an apprenticeship, were dangerous, as their idle hands and brains could be put to use in breaking the city's code of discipline or laws.[7] Those who were spiritually ignorant, both lay-people and clergy, laid themselves open to heterodox beliefs, or were at risk of reverting to Catholicism. Ignorant clergy were a particular liability, as they could lead their flock astray through their own lack of learning. In order to prevent these results of ignorance, the magistrates and leading clergy in the cities did what they could to ensure that teaching, both intellectual and spiritual, as well as training and supervision were reinforced, so that the more ignorant inhabitants of their cities had as many opportunities as possible to become worthy individuals who could contribute more effectively to the city's life, rather than damage its social and confessional fabric. Indeed, the Reformers quickly moved away from any early ideas that education was in fact unnecessary, and that the inspiration of the Holy Spirit was sufficient for Christians. Luther in particular argued against this anti-educational view in his appeal to the councils of the German cities to establish schools, pointing out for instance the importance of learning Latin, Greek and Hebrew, so as to gain an accurate understanding of the Scriptures.[8]

The dangers of general ignorance or lack of skills was particularly prevalent among the young, who were at the start of their active working lives. It must be noted, however, that the preoccupation of urban authorities to ensure that young people were in school or learning a trade only really applied to boys. In the city leaders' eyes, girls at most needed to learn certain basic housekeeping skills like needlework. Schools for girls did exist, but only at a rudimentary level, and urban authorities tended to leave the matter of girls' schools aside, to focus on the central issue of boys' education. In Geneva, for instance, the Ecclesiastical Ordinances of 1541 prohibited the establishment of any other schools beyond the official one, but simply added, 'girls should continue to have their separate school, as has been done in the past'.[9] Because young men's sphere of activity was more public than that of women, their apprenticeships and education also took place in a more public context. Furthermore, as men generally were more active and visible in the city, the ignorance and ensuing idleness of young men, hanging about on the streets with nothing to do, was a greater threat to the city's stability than the ignorance of women, whose domain tended to be their household.[10]

The aim of magistrates and ministers was to create worthy inhabitants, able to fill their place in urban society. Hence, city ordinances condemned indolence and encouraged study or the learning of a trade. In his 1559 inaugural address for the opening of the Genevan Academy, Theodore Beza, its first rector, underlined the dangers of ignorance:

> What is the difference between a man who is totally unlearned and ignorant, and animals with no power of reasoning? [Aristotle], that well-known judge of the human condition, points out that there is nothing more dangerously unjust than an ignorant person, and therefore, there can be nothing more harmful, since injustice includes all forms of disorder.[11]

Hence Beza explicitly linked ignorance with disorder.[12] At the same time, the city leaders worked to create institutions which would train the most

promising young men for various careers. Thus, Zurich founded its academy, the *Lectorium*, in 1525, followed by Berne in 1528, and along the same
model, Lausanne in 1537. For its part, the Academy of Geneva opened in
1559. The most high-profile institution in the Swiss cities was however the
University of Basle, which was remodelled on Reformed lines in 1532. The
new statutes of Basle's university, dated 12 September 1532, outlined the
purpose of the university. It was intended to train 'pastors and teachers for
Christ's church, councillors and public servants for the councils, judges for
the courts, teachers for the youth, and doctors for the sick'.[13] Thus, study
at the University was clearly linked to a later career. Each of these academies
and universities had a feeder system, namely the Latin schools which existed
in nearly every Swiss city, including those without their own centre of
higher study, such as Schaffhausen, where the Latin school was reopened in
1527, and where an official German school was established in 1532.[14]
Although the curriculum of these establishments focused on the study of
Latin grammar and eloquence, on the study of Greek and Hebrew, and, in
the case of the academies and the university, on biblical exegesis and theological doctrine, these subjects were not intended as ends in themselves. It
was never a case of learning for its own sake. The Bernese school ordinances
from 1616 make this clear, stating,

> The purpose and goal of the school should be to train youth properly and
> well, first of all in the fear of God, pure religion, and Christian faith, then
> in the three principal languages: Latin, Greek and Hebrew, and in all liberal
> arts, insofar as is necessary for each one's future ecclesiastical or secular
> career, finally also in outward manners and behaviour, insofar as it helps in
> their contacts and coexistence with other men.[15]

Beza reinforced this theme in his inaugural address, pointing out that
education had a purpose that went beyond the academic curriculum.
Addressing the students, Beza said,

> Unlike the Greeks who used to go to their gymnasia to watch vain wrest-
> ling, you have come here to contribute to God's glory, to become the pride
> of your homeland and the support of your family, prepared by your knowl-
> edge of the true religion and all areas of learning. Never forget that you will
> have to account for your performance in this holy militia before the supreme
> commander.[16]

Thus Beza made a sharp contrast between the Greek model of study for its
own sake and the Reformed view of education as preparing its recipients for
specific tasks within the framework of the Reformed faith. Students were
expected to study diligently, to put what they had learned to use, and to
act as guides to others. In short, learning would dispel not only their own

ignorance, but that of others as well. In his speech, Beza added, 'It is also necessary for superior minds to be cultivated and improved thanks to a good education. The following statement is very true: "those who have studied, see twice as clearly".'[17]

In spite of these expectations, complaints about students' lack of diligence, linked to fears of disorder, were commonplace. On 19 August 1577 the magistrates of Geneva noted that although they had already raised the matter once with ministers, students were still running wild instead of learning. In order to control student behaviour more effectively, and encourage learning instead of ignorance, the authorities advocated measures such as having students matriculate, so that they would sign their names to an agreement regarding their code of conduct. This measure often remained unenforced, however, as on 11 May 1579, when the ministers reported that students were not matriculating nor attending classes and sermons. Instead, the ministers complained, the students gambled and drank.[18]

In order to have greater control over the students, and encourage those who would otherwise not have access to higher study due to lack of funds and opportunities, several cities organised a system of scholarships, to help these students meet the costs of their books, lodgings and food. The criteria for selection of scholarship students were generally an early aptitude for learning and good behaviour. In the 1560 ordinances on scholarships, drawn up by the educational council of Zurich, the scholarships were to be provided to boys chosen from among those in the vernacular school:

> As for the boys who are to go from the [German] school and be taken on as scholarship students, the *Schulherr* should keep an eye out, and inquire from the schoolmaster as to the most disciplined and hard-working boys, who have a good mind, like to study, and are particularly likely to do well.[19]

By supporting these pupils, the authorities assisted students who otherwise had little chance to stay in school because of parental poverty or lack of interest.[20] Thus the authorities' response to the fear of ignorance was not simply a verbal encouragement of education. Instead, they took concrete measures to ensure that education did flourish, and invested both time and money therein.

Apart from establishing or re-founding Latin schools and academies, the Swiss city leaders also copied another more recent trend in education, namely the process of yearly examinations. By examining students' performance on an annual or semi-annual basis, the authorities had greater control over students' progress, and a better idea of their performance. The use of relatively frequent examinations helped them to deal more rapidly with ignorant or idle pupils. Once again, the message to students was clear, namely that they were expected to learn. Those whose results were unsatisfactory knew that the authorities would take action against them. Boys who did badly in the examinations were scolded and urged to work harder. On 14 May 1565, for instance, the records of the Genevan Small Council state, 'At the *promotions*, we noted that the children have not done as well as in the past. It was decided that the syndics should go with the ministers to remind the pupils and regents of their duty.'[21] Those with scholarships were threatened with the loss of their funding and removal from the school if their results did not improve. The 1560 ordinances on scholarships from Zurich outlined the link between continued funding and good performance when they stated,

> These scholarships should never be increased or changed until after the yearly examinations, with strict orders that only those who have behaved themselves well, in a disciplined fashion, and have been hard-working should receive an increase. Those who have been lazy and have not worked hard should have their amount decreased or should even be removed altogether.[22]

Pupils whose poor performance was due to lack of effort were thus punished, whereas those whose intellectual abilities could not keep pace with the work were generally treated more leniently.

Indeed, the Zurich authorities for their part attempted to find the best career path for each student, rather than trying to force students into areas which did not match their abilities. The Zurich school ordinances of 1532 state,

> One should discover what each [pupil] is best at, so that the relatives and parents might also know how things stand with their child, what one can expect of him, so that one need not spend a long time teaching the humanities to those who would be much better at doing something else, which otherwise leads to a great waste of time, work, and money, and those who are profiting from their education would also be penalised and slowed down.[23]

In some cases, when it was clear that a student was not making any progress through lack of ability rather than lack of effort, the educational council then felt a certain measure of responsibility for the student, and did not simply remove him from the school. Instead they organised entry into an apprenticeship for him, indicating again how important it was for everyone to acquire appropriate training. For instance, on 6 April 1592, the *Schulherr* Rudolf Hospinian reported that Felix Brunner's studies were not progressing, as he had no talent for studying. However, as Hospinian added, 'he is otherwise a good boy'. The educational council decided to have Hospinian speak with the overseers of the Almosen fund, to ask for Brunner to be placed in an apprenticeship.[24] Thus, it is clear that the magistrates and ministers' dislike of and concern about ignorance did not go so far as forcing students into paths which outstripped their abilities.

To counter ignorance and foster learning among students, the ministers and magistrates also provided rewards to hard-working pupils, by giving them prizes. Geneva's *promotions* were attended by both leading magistrates and the city ministers, and the best students received small sums of money or books as prizes for their good results.

Thus, both the civil and ecclesiastical authorities worked hard to encourage learning among their city's inhabitants, by creating and reworking educational centres, by providing financial assistance to students, and by overseeing their progress through examinations and prize-giving. Yet the provision of education in the Swiss cities was not the authorities' only response to the problem of ignorance. Indeed, education, particularly in the Latin schools and academies, could not be the only solution, since it only touched a small proportion of the city's male children. Although the vernacular schools also attracted a number of children, the civic leaders had little to do with these schools, except in so far as to check that the teacher was in fact competent. For instance, on 19 March 1556, three years before the opening of the Academy, the Small Council of Geneva decided that the number of vernacular schools in the city should be fixed at six, and that those teaching in the schools were to be examined as to their ability.[25] By their very nature, the vernacular schools tended to be small, ephemeral, and offered only a basic curriculum of reading, writing and counting. Yet even these schools were a necessary stepping-stone to further study, as the educational council of Zurich, for instance, insisted that no boy could be admitted to the city's Latin schools without being able to read and write in German already.[26]

The proportion of pupils admitted to the Latin schools was likely to be smaller than the total enrolment in the vernacular schools, although this is difficult to verify, due to the absence of any pupil registers for the vernacular schools in particular. The number of local boys enrolling in the city academies of Berne, Geneva, Lausanne or Zurich was smaller still. In part, these decreasing numbers as one rises through the levels of schooling were entirely predictable. Although the city authorities saw education as one of the solutions to ignorance, the vernacular schools were better suited to the general population, who had no need of Latin or other more advanced subjects. Indeed, the writer of the report on the use of church goods in Zurich in 1555 advocated a greater use of vernacular schools for pupils who were not suited to the Latin school's curriculum:

such pupils would be more appropriately placed in a German school, and one should therefore not recommend the Latin school to them. Your Lordships [the magistrates] would do a great service to the city and church if you established a German school both in the upper and lower city, and two good and hard-working men could be paid by the church funds to teach reading, writing and the catechism.[27]

In contrast, those who enrolled in the Latin school and carried on to the academy were intended for careers in the ministry or teaching at an advanced level. Hence, the city fathers could not hope to reduce ignorance by advocating mass enrolment in the schools. The ministers, however, sometimes advocated a greater role for the first level of schooling. In 1572 for instance, on 14 January, the Small Council noted that the ministers wanted the schoolteachers of the vernacular schools, known as the *petites escolles*, to alert the *dizeniers*, or neighbourhood elders, to all the children who ought to be in school. The Council, however, was not interested in mandatory schooling, and said so, but added that those who did attend the schools should pay a small fee. On 21 January 1572, the ministers brought the matter up again, saying that parents should be made to send their children to school, and that the *dizaines* should be reorganised, so that all teachers could have means of support.[28] On 28 January, the magistrates agreed that each schoolmaster should receive the children from a specific *dizaine*, but significantly said nothing further on the matter of compelling parents to send their children to the vernacular schools.[29]

Although generalised schooling could not be achieved in these early modern cities, the civil and ecclesiastical leaders did however advocate another form of learning for everyone, namely religious education through catechism classes and mandatory church attendance.[30] School pupils went to church as a group, as shown by the Zurich school ordinances of 1532:

On every day of worship, while the bells are ringing, the pupils should assemble at the school, and one should read out the attendance list, so that those who are absent get pointed out and punished the next day. As soon as the bells stop ringing, they [the pupils] should then be led to church in an orderly fashion, and stand in one place together. A *Burgermeister* should be requested to leave a place for them in the chancel, alongside older people who are hard of hearing and those who may want to make sketches or take notes during the sermon. To prevent chatting or disorderly behaviour among the boys ... the schoolmaster or his representative should sit with them, so that they are not on their own. The pupils should be taken to the morning and evening services in this fashion.[31]

As for the catechism classes, the Genevan ecclesiastical ordinances of 1541 stated that 'All citizens and *habitants* were to bring or send their children to catechism classes on Sundays at noon.'[32] The authorities had a vested interest in ensuring that city-dwellers knew the basics of the faith, for their religious allegiance was meant to reinforce their political allegiance to their city and vice versa. In most cases, people were expected at least to be able to recite the Lord's Prayer, the Ten Commandments, and the Apostles' Creed, all in the vernacular, as using Latin was seen as a holdover from Catholic times. By insisting that everyone learn these basics of the faith, the authorities hoped to eliminate 'superstitions' tied to Catholic practices. The ministers focused their attention particularly on the young, the old, and servants.[33] Indeed, children's ability to learn new material relatively quickly had been duly noted by the church leaders, who then used children to transmit information to the older generations. In Geneva, for instance, in the 1541 Ecclesiastical Ordinances, the ministers noted, 'It would be good to introduce church singing, to help the people praise God and pray to Him. We shall start by teaching the small children, and over time, the whole church will begin to follow suit.'[34]

Those who could not show that they knew the requisite tenets of the faith risked being barred from communion, at least until they had made an attempt to learn the central prayers and creeds. The 1576 Ecclesiastical Ordinances of Geneva have a section outlining the examination carried out by the clergy of people's knowledge of their faith. This examination was to take place before the Easter communion.

> Because of the disorder of the papacy, many people were not taught when they were children, so that they have reached adulthood without knowing what it means to be a Christian. We have decreed that each household should be visited yearly, to examine each person very simply on their faith, so that at least no one will come to communion without knowing the grounds of their salvation.[35]

However, in spite of these actions, the authorities' efforts to ensure a basic level of religious knowledge did not always meet with success. In some instances, children stayed away from the catechism classes. On 12 March 1576, for example, the Small Council of Geneva complained that children who did not attend catechism classes caused problems, as they became similar to peasants. The Small Council decided to warn the elders to keep watch.[36] In order to reinforce the obligation to attend catechism sessions, the Bernese authorities in 1545 published an edict for the Pays de Vaud,

> Once again we order all fathers, mothers and guardians to send the children able to learn the Lord's Prayer, the Creed and the Ten Commandments to church on the day and at the time when the ministers hold the catechism

sessions. Otherwise, the penalty for the first three times is imprisonment, and the fourth time, banishment from the Bernese lands.[37]

Even when the children did attend, their actual understanding of the material they were learning off by heart may have remained superficial.

The third area of education which attracted the attention of the authorities was that of the clergy. Particularly in the first years after the establishment of the Reformation, the magistrates and leading Reformers were forced to use as ministers men whose training had not been as thorough as was thought desirable. These men were often former Catholic priests, who were hastily retrained if at all, and employed as Reformed ministers. The dangers of ignorant and doctrinally weak ministers were clear, as their hesitant spiritual leadership would not help their parishioners, and could even lead them into heresy. As the Reformation also moved the focus of worship services from the ritual of the Mass to the sermon, the authorities needed educated ministers, who could ably preach and faithfully transmit the teachings of Scripture to their people.

Urban leaders in the Swiss cities responded to the need to combat ignorance among the clergy in two ways. Firstly, in order to raise the standards of those already in a parish, several cities introduced forms of continuing education, in which active ministers attended regular training sessions largely focused on acquiring exegetical skills. For instance, in Geneva the ministers of the city and country parishes met weekly in the *congrégations*, during which each minister in turn provided an exegesis of a certain passage of Scripture, or defended a theological thesis. His colleagues then in turn added anything he had left out, in a fraternal spirit. Attendance at the *congrégations* was strongly encouraged, even for those in parishes outside the city, as the Ecclesiastical Ordinances of 1541 and 1576 reminded country ministers that they were not to miss more than one month's worth of these meetings at a stretch.[38] In Zurich, the continuing education sessions took the form of the *Prophezei*, in which ministers and students gathered daily except on Fridays and Sundays in the Grossmünster, Zurich's cathedral, to hear a Bible passage being read first from the Vulgate, then translated into Hebrew, then into Greek, and finally a German commentary and sermon on the passage would be given to an increased audience including interested townspeople.[39] Once again, these sessions were intended to strengthen the ministers' knowledge of Scripture and of its correct interpretation.

An ongoing commitment to private study, particularly of the Bible, was meant to be one of the hallmarks of a good minister. In Geneva, the ecclesiastical ordinances of 1541 noted 'Lack of study, especially in reading Scripture' as one of the faults of a minister that was to be the focus of fraternal admonition.[40] If however, a minister was incapable of making progress or uninterested in doing so, he risked being reprimanded or punished once the authorities were notified of his poor performance.

The second measure taken by the city authorities to prevent ignorance among the clergy was to ensure adequate standards of training and examination for prospective ministers. In Geneva, the Ecclesiastical Ordinances of 1541 noted,

> The examination consists of two parts, namely one of doctrine, so as to be sure that the candidate has a solid and accurate knowledge of Scripture and that he is able to communicate this knowledge accurately to the people for their edification ... . The second part deals with the life [of the candidate] namely whether his morals are sound and whether he has led a life beyond reproach.[41]

Indeed, after the Reformation, the Swiss cities moved to establish a more standardised form of training, involving study of Hebrew, Greek, the humanities and theology, normally focused on the Old and New Testaments. The students were examined on their knowledge at the end of their academic career, and then had to pass a second examination, often including a trial sermon, before being admitted as a candidate, known in Geneva and Lausanne as a *proposant*, and in German-speaking areas as an *Expektant*. Through this process of examination, the cities were able to weed out unsatisfactory students, who did not demonstrate sufficient knowledge of their subject.

By providing access to Latin schools and academies for talented pupils, by organising compulsory religious education through catechism sessions and church attendance, and by establishing standards for both established and incoming clergy, the civil and ecclesiastical leaders of the Swiss cities worked to encourage learning and knowledge instead of ignorance. Indeed, the ignorance which they feared went against both humanist and Reformation precepts, namely that one should study in order to become a good citizen, and that one should be able to give an account of one's faith. Without education, even at a basic level, neither of these two objectives could be attained.

Indeed, the fact that the urban authorities focused their attention not on intellectual education alone, but on religious education as well is significant, for the latter came closest to providing a generalised level of basic knowledge for all.

The authorities' efforts to dispel ignorance through schooling were not intended to encourage learning for its own sake. Instead, the dispelling of

ignorance served a wider purpose, since inhabitants who had access to learning and training appropriate to their background were thought to be able to
contribute more to the city than those who vegetated in ignorance and idleness. In the Reformed cities, learning, particularly in the religious sphere,
had become an obligation, for people were expected to be able to give a
basic account of their beliefs. For their part, the authorities also had a duty
to ensure that such education was available, and that the inhabitants took
part in it.

Notes

1 Martin Luther, 'To the Councilmen of all cities in Germany, that they establish and maintain Christian Schools', in Walther Brandt and Helmut Lehmann, eds, *Luther's Works*
   (Philadelphia, 1962), 45: 350.
2 On the need to train people only to the level appropriate to their station in life, see R.
   A. Houston, *Literacy in Early Modern Europe: Culture and Education 1500–1800* (New York,
   1988), 16–17.
3 STAZ, E II 341, fol. 3563 v. Fürtrag den wägen des kilchengüttern und anderen Sachen,
   Gethan Anno Domini 1555 den 16. Sept.
4 George Huppert, *Public Schools in Renaissance France* (Chicago, 1984), 32–3.
5 Friedrich Haag, *Die Hohen Schulen zu Bern in ihrer geistlichen Entwicklung* (Berne, 1903),
   44.
6 AEG, RC 86, 2 Mar. 1591.
7 On 27 April 1573, for instance, the Small Council of Geneva noted that some children
   from various quarters of the city were running wild, and ordered that they be caught and
   punished. AEG, RC 68, 27 Apr. 1573, fol. 94. Those who did not take part in schooling, even at a higher level, also risked contravening ordinances, as in the case of foreign
   students in Geneva on 20 January 1578, when the ministers Beza and Jean Chauvet complained that many students in lodgings were not attending classes, but were hanging
   around town, and were causing many scandals. AEG, RC 73, 20 Jan. 1578, fol. 12.
8 Luther, 'To the Councilmen', 358–9.
9 'Ordonnances ecclésiastiques de 1541', in Henri Heyer, *1555–1909: L'Eglise de Genève*
   (Geneva, 1909), 267.
10 The fear of idleness tied to ignorance appeared also in the French context. See Huppert,
   Public Schools, 41.
11 *Discours du Recteur Th. de Bèze prononcé à l'inauguration de l'Académie dans le Temple de Saint
   Pierre à Genève le 5 Juin 1559* (repr. Geneva, 1959), 13.
12 The dangers of disorder are also analysed in Coster, Ch. 6, this volume.
13 Andreas Muller, *Struktur und Soziale Funktion der Universität Basel* (Winterthur, 1955), 13.
14 Kaspar von Greyerz, 'Switzerland', in Bob Scribner, Roy Porter and Mikulas Teich, eds,
   The Reformation in National Context (Cambridge, 1994), 39.
15 Sammlung Schweizerische Rechtsquellen, Bern 12: 8. Quoted in Ulrich Im Hof *et al.*,
   eds, *Hochschulgeschichte Berns, 1528–1984* (Berne, 1984), 31.
16 *Discours du Recteur*, 23–5.
17 *Ibid.*, 13.
18 AEG, RC 72, 19 Aug. 1577, fol. 113; RC 74, 11 May 1579, fol. 82.
19 STAZ, E I 13 no. 21: Studentenamt (Stipendien). 1560 Ordnung wie man die Knaben
   an die Stipendia an der Stifft zu dem Grossmünster annemen un mit Inen umgan sölle.
   The *Schulherr*, normally a minister or professor, was the head of the educational council.
   The post was a two-year appointment.
20 Alice Denzler, in her pioneering work on the care of youth in the early Swiss confederation, points out that some pupils in the vernacular school received a one-year scholar-

ship from Zurich. This scholarship was kept to one year only, since a boy who could not learn to read and write in a year was not thought to be worth further investment. Alice Denzler, *Jugendfürsorge in der alten Eidgenossenschaft. Ihre Entwicklung in den Kantonen Zürich, Luzern, Freiburg, St Gallen und Genf bis 1798* (Zurich, 1925), 96.

21   AEG, RC 60, 14 May 1565, fol. 53. The *promotions* were the annual Geneva prize-giving sessions for pupils in the *schola privata*.

22   STAZ, E I 13, no. 21: Studentenarat (Stipendien).

23   STAZ, 'Ordination und ansehen, wie man sich fürohin mit den schuoleren, letzgen und anderen dingen halten soll in der schuol zum Münster (ze) Zürich 1532', in Emil Egli, *Actensammlung der Zürcher Reformation in den Jahren 1519–1533* (Zurich, 1879), 2: 822.

24   STAZ, E II 458, 6 Apr. 1592.

25   AEG, RC 51, 19 Mar. 1556, fos. 55v-56r.

26   Hans Nabholz, 'Zürichs höhere Schulen von der Reformation bis zur Gründung der Universität 1525–1833', in Ernst Gagliardi, Hans Nabholz and Jean Strohl, eds, *Die Universitt Zürich 1833–1933 und Ihre Vorläufer* (Zurich, 1938), 11.

27   STAZ, E II 341, fol. 3563v.

28   The *dizaines* were groups of Genevan inhabitants, each group dwelling in a particular sector of the city and being under the care of a specific elder.

29   AEG, RC 67, 14 Jan. 1572, fol. 5; 21 Jan. 1572, fol. 10; 28 Jan. 1572, fol. 14.

30   On catechisation and its background and impact, see for the English context, Ian Green, *The Christian's ABC: Catechisms and Catechizing in England c.1530–1740* (Oxford, 1996) esp., 13–44.

31   'Ordination und ansehen', in Egli, *Actensammlung*, 2: 821.

32   'Ordonnances ecclésiastiques de 1541', in Heyer, *1555–1909*, 272.

33   The 1576 Ecclesiastical Ordinances of Geneva specified that heads of households were to send their children, menservants, maids and wet-nurses to catechism classes. 'Les Ordonnances ecclésiastiques de l'Eglise de Genève passées et revues en Conseil Général le 2 Juin 1576', in Heyer, *1555–1909*, 287.

34   'Ordonnances ecclésiastiques de 1541', in Heyer, *1555–1909*, 271.

35   'Les Ordonnances ecclésiastiques ... 2 Juin 1576', in Heyer, *1555–1909*, 289.

36   AEG, RC 71, 12 Mar. 1576, fol. 39.

37   Henri Vuilleumier, *Histoire de l'Eglise Réformée du Pays de Vaud sous le régime bernois* (4 vols, Lausanne, 1927–33), 1: 354.

38   'Ordonnances ecclésiastiques de 1541' and 'Les Ordonnances ecclésiastiques ... 2 Juin 1576', in Heyer, *1555–1909*, 263, 281–2.

39   Jacques Figi, *Die Innere Reorganisation des Grossmünsterstiftes in Zürich von 1519 bis 1531* (Affoltern am Albis, 1951), 84.

40   'Ordonnances ecclésiastiques de 1541', in Heyer, *1555–1909*, 264.

41   *Ibid.*, 262.

9

Fear, purgatory and polemic in Reformation England

PETER MARSHALL

Did late medieval religion function primarily to deliver consolation to its practitioners, or to foster in them debilitating anxiety? Controversy over this question has been agitating Reformation historians for the best part of a generation, and is at root, of course, a debate about the causes of the Reformation itself.[1] Proponents of the model of a fear-laden pre-Reformation piety tend to identify the Church's penitential system as prime culprit: the mandatory confession of sins to a priest was an inquisitorial and guilt-inducing procedure; what is more, the logic of Catholic penitential teaching pointed to a fiery posthumous punishment in purgatory, where the satisfaction for sins not paid for by penances in this life would be relentlessly exacted.[2] In the English context, however, a considerable body of recent work, most notably by Clive Burgess and Eamon Duffy, has begun to question whether the prospect of purgatory was really such a fearful one for a great many laypeople, and has proposed alternative or at least complementary explanations for the vast and complex accretion of forms of commemoration and intercession which is so marked a feature of late medieval religious life.[3] No disparagement of the subtle and nuanced work of Burgess or Duffy is intended by noting that the attempt to write persuasively about the prevalence of fear in past societies, more especially on the 'metaphysical' fears associated with afterlife and judgement, can be a particularly hazardous historical endeavour.[4] Despite the temptation to apply the resources of information technology to the large numbers of surviving wills, individuals' fear of the conditions that awaited them after death offers no meaningful potential for quantification, and given the complexity of the cultural and psychological issues it comprehends, scope for only the most guarded attempts at qualification.[5] Whether or not most English Christians at the start of the sixteenth century lived in constant fear of the fate that awaited them in purgatory is arguably not only a question that can never satisfactorily be answered, but one that begs innumerable other questions within its own referencing. The intention of this chapter is to approach the issue in a manner both less ambitious and more unashamedly textual. It hinges on a recognition that in England in the first half of the sixteenth century discussion of the connection between soteriology and fear represented an important element of contemporary theological discourse. Of necessity a broad survey, it will attempt to explore how early English reformers made use of the topos of the 'fearfulness' of purgatory in their polemics against traditional orthopraxy, and how conservative writers responded to the charge. Further, it will seek to elucidate what the exchanges reveal, not only about literary strategies of persuasion and conversion, but about contemporary perceptions of the appropriateness and utility of the state of 'fear' in ordering people's relations with God and with their neighbours.[6]

In the early stages of the Reformation in England the validity of the Church's teaching on purgatory rapidly emerged as a major focus of controversy. Luther's ambivalence towards the existence of purgatory in the 1520s prompted treatments of the doctrine by English Catholic writers in their anti-Lutheran writings, but the doctrine became much more of a live public issue when the existence of purgatory was openly impugned in Simon Fish's populist tract, A Supplication for the Beggars, which was distributed in London in the early part of 1529.[7] Fish's short pamphlet provoked two weighty responses, Thomas More's Supplication of Souls (1529) and John Rastell's New Boke of Purgatory (1530). These were answered in their turn by John Frith's Disputation of Purgatory, a work which set the tone for much of the subsequent Protestant polemic against purgatory.[8] In the first half of the 1530s, controversy over purgatory intensified, as More continued the literary debate with other antagonists such as William Tyndale and George Joye, and as radical preaching on purgatory and prayer for the dead became increasingly common, much of it emanating from the evangelicals' rising star, Hugh Latimer.[9] In the last decade of Henry VIII's reign, literary and pulpit debates over the existence of purgatory and the value of suffrages for the souls there became more muted, not because the issue had ceased to interest theologians or laity, but because official policy had intervened to restrict the terms of the debate. The Ten Articles of 1536 undercut the traditional understanding of the place of post-mortem purgation by remarking that 'the name thereof, and kinds of pains there ... be to us uncertain by scripture', and the King's Book of 1543 went substantially further, insisting that it was impossible to know how masses or suffrages might benefit the dead, and stipulating that the King's subjects 'abstain from the name of purgatory, and no more dispute or reason thereof'.[10] Not surprisingly, some Henrician conservatives seem thereafter to have proceeded with circum-

spection, and to have avoided mentioning purgatory by name.[11] The accession of Edward VI signalled a renewed burst of Protestant agitation against
purgatory and intercession, achieving its logical triumph in the Chantries Act
of 1547, which abolished intercessory institutions and declared purgatory to
be a 'vain opinion'. Church of England formularies thereafter would reiterate this line.[12] Theological debate in the reigns of Mary and Elizabeth tended
to focus primarily on other concerns, but the existence or otherwise of purgatory remained a pertinent issue: the 1560s witnessed the production of
significant works by the exiled French Protestant, Jean Veron, and the English Catholic exile, William Allen.[13]

During the thirty years between the appearance of the treatises of John
Frith and Jean Veron, certain fundamental themes recurred repeatedly in
Protestant polemic against purgatory. In the first place, the reformers
regarded it as quite unwarranted by Scripture and would have no truck with
Catholic suggestions that it should be regarded as an 'unwritten verity' of
the faith.[14] When Catholics did attempt to prove their doctrine from the
Bible, Protestants were invariably contemptuous of their exegesis. Jean
Veron remarked sarcastically that it was no marvel if the papists could cite
a thousand places of the Scripture 'for whersoever me[n]tio[n] is made of
fire they make it to serve for theyr purgatorye'.[15] Furthermore, the reformers missed few opportunities to reiterate how intimately the doctrine and
development of purgatory was tied up with the authority of the Pope, a circumstance that undoubtedly allowed previously unorthodox views about the
fate of souls to make headway in the England of Henry VIII. Frith's translation of Luther's *Revelation of Antichrist* memorably observed that 'the Pope
is ... made the Kinge of them that are dead and raigneth in purgatorye'.[16]
Without doubt, however, the most substantial objection Protestant polemicists had to the theory and practice of purgatory was that it took away the
all-sufficiency of Christ's passion: by their reckoning, the only 'true purgatory' was the cross of Christ and His Precious Blood.[17]

In rehearsing their deep-seated theological rejection of purgatory, Protestant polemicists repeatedly seized upon the dread and fearfulness inher-
ing in the Catholic teaching, which, in the words of John Hooper, offered
nothing but 'the curse of that painful fire'.[18] From their unshakeable premise
that the object of such fear was illusory, indeed delusory, Protestant writers proceeded to explore its origins and rationale. Their diagnosis was
rapidly and confidently arrived at: fear of the fires of purgatory was deliberately inculcated into the laity by the clergy for the purpose of pecuniary
gain. The tone here had been set by Simon Fish's *Supplication*, which
itemised with specious precision the vast sums passing into the hands of the
priests, particularly the friars, and concluded that they had no 'other coloure

to gather these yerely exaccions ynto theyre hondes but that they sey they pray for us to God to delyver our soules out of the paynes of purgatori'.[19] The theme resonated through subsequent polemic in which the putative destination of souls was repeatedly epitomised as 'purgatory pick-purse'.[20] In this vein, John Frith sarcastically conceded the truth of the traditional *obiter dictum* repeated by Thomas More that the fire of purgatory was hotter than any earthly fire: 'it hath alone melted more gold and silver, for our spiritualty's profit, out of poor men's purses, than all the goldsmiths' fires within England'.[21] Only a desperate fear of fiery punishment in store could make sense of the level of investment in clerical services, and it followed that the clergy must be assiduous in promoting this fear. Dying men robbed their heirs of their inheritance, thought Tyndale, because the clergy 'fear them with purgatory', a theme endlessly rehearsed in Jerome Barlow's satire, *The Burial of the Mass*.[22] According to Miles Coverdale, the clergy manipulated 'this weak fear of pain to withdraw simple people from the whole love of Christ'.[23] In such polemics, one adjective more than any other was paired with purgatory, serving at once to explain and, it was hoped, to expel the fearfulness with which the concept was claimed to be indelibly imbued. Above all else, purgatory was 'feigned'. John Frith's *Disputacion of Purgatory* was predicated on the assumption that the papists had contrived to 'feign a purgatory'.[24] Frith's collaborator Tyndale excelled in references to 'that terrible and fearful purgatory they have feigned to purge thy purse withal', a purgatory 'as hot as their bellies can feign it', a 'feigned purgatory, where we must suffer seven years for every sin'.[25] Latimer noted that purgatory was infinitely profitable 'to the feigners of it'; Coverdale, that out of greed 'feigned they this horrible bog of purgatory'; Cranmer, that purgatory was simply 'feigned for lucre'.[26] In acknowledging the literary conceit of More's *Supplication of Souls*, in which the departed souls themselves present the argument, George Joye portrayed him as 'the proctour of purgatory fayning to have come fro[m] thence'.[27] Hooper epigrammatically linked a number of key themes in adducing a 'feigned purgatory that the scripture of God feareth no man withal'.[28] In a culture which, from our perspective, was habituated to a much heightened polarity of truth and falsehood, the 'feigning' of purgatory was intended to carry profoundly uncomfortable resonances. By revealing that the terrors of purgatory were no more than the hook for an elaborate confidence trick, Protestant writers sought not so much to persuade as to jolt, almost to embarrass their readers into abandoning their belief: Frith argued that 'their painful purgatory was but a vain imagination … a vain and childish fear which our forefathers had'.[29] Tyndale stressed that the only foundation for fear of purgatory was the 'poetry' of the Bishop of Rome, and concluded severely that 'fools be out of their wits to believe it'.[30]

In responding to this onslaught against purgatory in heretical works, traditionalist writers did not attempt to deny that contemplation of purgatory ought to evoke fear in the believer. The observation of a number of modern commentators that purgatory was a humane and consoling doctrine in so far as it permitted the greater mass of Christians to elude damnation was, for reasons which will become apparent, largely absent from contemporary Catholic polemic.[31] In fact, Thomas More did adduce purgatory as a source of consolation in his *Dialogue of Comfort against Tribulation*, but in a rather different sense: the believer suffering tribulation in this life could take comfort from the knowledge that it would reduce the penance that would otherwise be exacted in purgatory.[32] More's perception drew on a long tradition of the didactic and homilectic use of purgatory to encourage repentance and good works in this life. This was predicated upon the axiom that such works were infinitely more effective than post-mortem suffrages in securing relief for the individual's soul after he died, a formulation that perhaps received its most emphatic expression in the preaching of John Fisher.[33] When the concept of purgatory came under attack in the late 1520s, a rationale implicit in such teaching was more explicitly evoked: fear of purgatory was essential to restrain the people from sin. This argument was a central theme of John Rastell's *New Boke of Purgatorye*, which had ambitiously set out to establish purgatory 'by naturall reason and good philosophye'. In Rastell's view, the good order of a commonwealth depended equally upon laws to punish vice in this world and on 'a drede to be punysshed in an other world for offence done here'. Loss of purgatory would 'put away the drede of god from the most parte of the people in the worlde, and gyve them boldness to do and commytte offences and synnes'.[34] The same theme recurred throughout the polemical writings of Thomas More, who remained insistent that 'fere of payn to be suffred ... refrayneth men from the boldenes of synne'.[35] More's *Confutation of Tyndale's Answer* contained a merciless caricature of what would inevitably follow from the teaching of justification by faith: 'neyther purgatory nede to be fered when we go hens, nor penauns nede to be done whyle we be here, but synne and be sory and syt and make mery, and then synne agayne and then repent a lytell and ronne to the ale & wasshe away the synne, thynke ones on goddys promyse and then do what we lyste'.[36] As far as More was concerned, heretics were deliberately and irresponsibly propagating false teaching which served to undermine a necessary fear of purgation: 'of purgatory by two meanes they put men out of drede. Some by slepyng tyll domys daye, & some by sendyng all strayt to hevyn, every soule that dyeth & is not dampned.'[37] The reference to Luther's teaching on the 'sleep of the soul', and the diversity of opinion it engendered was a shrewd one, much canvassed by More in his writings. Already in the 1530s this teaching was a cause of controversy among English reformers, and was later to be repudiated decisively by the mainstream of English Protestantism.[38] After More's death, the argument that denial of purgatory 'bringes a man to carnall libertye' recurred in the preaching of Roger Edgeworth, and could even evoke an echo in those much less committed to the upholding of traditional orthodoxy: the humanist Thomas Starkey judged it to be folly to deny purgatory its place as 'a holesome tradition to the conseruation of the christian lyfe'. In a letter to Henry VIII in 1536 Starkey warned about the unsettling effects of radical preaching: 'with the despysing of purgatory, they began little to regard hell'.[39]

Given the centrality of such arguments to Catholic defences of purgatory, it is unsurprising that Protestant polemicists went to considerable lengths not only to deny that belief in purgatory was an effective deterrent against sin, but that, to quote John Hooper, 'it causeth men to live in a greater security and liberty of life'.[40] At best, purgatory was superfluous as a means of constraining man's propensity to sin. Frith and Tyndale both argued that if the unmistakable monitions of the Old and New Testaments did not induce men to reform themselves, fear of purgatory would hardly do so.[41] Indeed, the specious assurance of ultimate salvation that purgatory conveyed, combined with the myriad possibilities for ameliorating its pains, undermined any restraining effect it could possibly have. Frith envisaged the young saying to themselves, 'I will take my pleasure while I may, and if I may have but one hour's respite to cry God mercy, I care not, for then shall I go but to purgatory.' Meanwhile the older generation clung avariciously to their goods, confident that they too could cry 'God mercy', and that their executors 'shall redeem me thence well enough'. In a sweeping inversion of the argument of Rastell and More, Frith concluded that 'to believe purgatory is rather an occasion of reckless boldness than of the fear of God'.[42] Later writers worked the same vein: Hooper charged that Catholics 'thinke to redeem all their sins after death'; Bradford that 'it maketh no matter at all how thou live here, so thou have the favour of the pope and his shavelings'.[43] The respective efficacies as social constraint of the traditionalist and reformed views of the afterlife were juxtaposed in dramatic form in Jean Veron's dialogue *The Huntyng of Purgatorye to Death*. When a Catholic character expresses his fear that 'magnifying thus the grace & mercy of God ... shal minister an occasion unto many folke to do evell', his Protestant neighbour retorts that those 'thinking to make satisfaction in purgatory for their syns, do geve the[m] selves to all kind of abhomination & fylthynesse all their lyfe tyme'.[44]

To remark that such arguments seem hardly consistent with the line advanced by these same writers that the effect of purgatory was to terrorise the laity into giving to the clergy for the multiplication of commemorative services is perhaps to take us to the crux of the polemical campaign against intercession for the dead. The absurdity of a purgatory which could not exist, and which no one need fear, was best exposed by accentuating the dialectical confusion of fearfulness and easiness which, it could be argued, underlay the whole intercessory system. As Tyndale put it, 'what great fear can there be of that terrible fire, which thou mayest quench almost for three half-pence? ... Show the pope a little money, and God is so merciful that there is no purgatory.'[45] Hugh Latimer similarly suggested that the avail-ability of various means of indulgence must render facile the vaunted rigours of purgatory: 'if the bishop's two fingers can shake away a good part; if a friar's cowl, or the pope's pardon, or *scala coeli* or a groat, can dispatch for altogether, it is not so greatly to be cared for'.[46] In his commentary on the will of William Tracy, Frith pointed to the paradox of making elaborate preparations to alleviate 'the grievous pains of purgatory' when they might 'be quenched both with less cost and labour' if 'the Pope's pardon is ready at hand'.[47] English reformers proved particularly adept at drawing attention to awkward questions raised by the system of papal pardons, and at reiter-ating arguments which Luther had employed in 1517, and which indeed predated the Reformation itself: what motive, it was asked, other than squalid pecuniary advantage, could the Pope have for not releasing all the souls suffering in purgatory?[48]

If indulgences did represent such a sure and certain means of escaping speedily from purgatory, then the insistence of Catholic polemicists on the utility and beneficial effects of a healthy fear of its pains were inevitably undermined. In fact, some orthodox writers actively sought to play down the potency of pardons. The Bridgettine William Bonde suggested that it was wrong to rely on them too heavily, and Thomas More insisted that heretics exaggerated their comforting effects: 'that fyre is not so lyghtely quenched, that folke sholde uppon the boldenesse of perdons, stande out of the fere of purgatory': one could never be sure that some fault on the part of the purchaser or the beneficiary of the indulgence might not have impeded its validity.[49] Such caveats in a sense, however, served to strengthen the hand of More's opponents, for the cumulative effect of Protestant dis-cussion of post-mortem intercession for the souls in purgatory was not to make a consistent case that, objectively considered, it was too burdensome or too easy, but to imply that it was uncertain and contradictory, menacing yet somehow comical, and hopelessly compromised by the base motives of those who administered it. In *The Obedience of a Christan Man*, Tyndale remarked with mock astonishment that 'the very gods themselves, which sell their pardon so good cheap ... trust not therein themselves' but endow colleges, chantries and masses. In his *Exposition of Tracy's Testament*, he contrived to turn More's remarks on pardons to his own purposes, stressing the unreliability of indulgences 'which have so great doubts and dangers, what in the mind and intent of the granter, and what in the purchaser, ere they can be truly obtained with all due circumstances, and much less certitude than they have authority'.[50] In 1536, the year of Tyndale's death, Hugh Latimer appropriated the theme of uncertainty in his notorious sermon before Canterbury Convocation: that the souls in purgatory were in need of our help was at the very least 'ambiguous, uncertain, doubtful, and therefore rashly and arrogantly with such boldness affirmed in the audience of the people'.[51] In a funeral sermon of 1549, John Hooper took up the refrain, commenting on the confusion of those who imagined their friends' souls to be roasted in the fire of purgatory: 'even as they fear they wot not what, so seek they their remedy they know not how'.[52] By deftly and ironically seeming to invert this theme of uncertainty, Jean Veron's dialogue of 1561 further underscored the shiftiness and unreliability of popish claims: a Catholic preacher is portrayed as claiming an exact and perfect knowledge of the topography of the afterlife so that 'there is neyther halle, parlour, chau[m]ber, nor closed, there is neyther kytchen, cave, nor dongeon, there is neyther chymney, fornace, nor oven ... pothookes, fleshhookes, ketel nor cawderon, that he hath not so lively described unto us that I sawe the very thing before myne eyes.' It is significant that the effect is intended to be comic when Veron has his protagonist conclude that 'I now do quake and tremble to thinke on it.'[53]

To fear purgatory was thus irrational, a product of muddle and gullibility. It was also self-destructive, in so far as it was likely to lead one to rely on 'feigned' promises which promoted a false sense of security and consequently made the prospect of damnation more likely. A handful of Protestant polemicists were prepared to go further than this and argue that even if a fear of the torments of purgatory were able to restrain overt wickedness, it would have accomplished more harm than good. To John Frith, abstaining from evil purely for fear of punishment was in itself a morally culpable act: 'God's law requireth a thing to be done with a well-willing heart ... . If thou do it for fear, then workest thou not of love, but rather hatest both the thing that thou doest and also the law that constraineth thee unto it.'[54] A generation later, Veron similarly argued that good works done under compulsion were not truly meritorious, and posed the rhetorical question of whether one would account a man a friend 'that woulde be diligente aboute you, and do you servyce, onelye for feare?'[55] It was characteristic of Protestant writers to vindicate their own cause in terms of deliverance from the bonds of fear, the fear of death in particular, and conversely to claim that Catholic soteriology thrived on it like a parasite. 'If we should feign a purgatory', argued Frith, 'it were not possible to imagine a greater obstacle to make us fear and fly from death.'[56] Tyndale took a similar line: true Christians 'are delivered from fear of everlasting death', and are as bold with God 'as young innocent children, which have no conscience of sin ... which were impossible, if God now (as the bishop of Rome painteth him) did shake a rod at us of seven years' punishment, as sharp as the pains of hell, for every trespass we do'.[57] In his encomium for the early Protestant role-model, William Tracy, whose will of October 1530 famously and precociously denied the efficacy of intercession, Tyndale painted a picture of 'a perfect Christian man, and of such a one as needed not to be aghast and desperate for fear of the painful pains of purgatory, which whoso feareth as they feign it, cannot but utterly abhor death'.[58] By the mid-Tudor period it had become an axiom of the reformers that knowledge of the Gospel cast out fear of death, and an 'Exhortation agaynst the Feare of Death' (probably the work of Cranmer) was included in the Edwardian Book of Homilies of 1547.[59] A few years later, the concept received an emphatic endorsement in *The Sick Man's Salve*, Thomas Becon's Protestant redaction of the *ars moriendi* handbook. In this dialogue the dying testator, Epaphroditus, resists the blandishments of his neighbours to follow traditional funerary custom. Instead he affirms his faith in Christ, and roundly declares 'I fear the popish purgatory and the pains thereof nothing at all.'[60]

Thus far it would appear that in the period under discussion the treatment of purgatory by a range of Protestant writers, and some of the responses formulated by the defenders of Catholic orthodoxy, points to a dogged endorsement of the necessity of fear on the part of the latter, and a wholesale determination by the former to eliminate fear from the relationship between the faithful Christian and his Maker. Such an assessment would lend weight to the view that much of the popular appeal of first-generation Protestantism should be seen in terms of a liberation from scrupulosity and morbid anxiety. But there are grounds for caution here; indeed, there are good reasons for suggesting that the transcendence of fear should be acknowledged rather as an important strand in Reformation polemical and devotional discourse than as the defining characteristic of the movement or its essential point of departure from traditional pieties. In the first place, suggestions that the fear of death and punishment was a temptation Christians should strive to resist were hardly unique to reforming writers. Relieving the fearfulness of death had been one of the concerns of the fifteenth-century *ars moriendi* genre, a tradition maintained by the Bridget-

tine, Richard Whitford, who in 1537 published a treatise to demonstrate
how 'the fere or drede of deth [is] to be excluded, exiled, and utterly put
away'.[61] Roger Edgeworth was similarly persuaded that Christians should
endeavour to depart this life 'without al feare'.[62] Moreover, conservative
writers were capable of construing the fear of purgatory in more subtle and
nuanced ways than the Protestant caricature might suggest. In his sermons
on the penitential psalms, John Fisher presented the experience of such fear
as a necessary transitional phase, leading to contrition and repentance; fear
was inextricably linked with hope and 'noo thynge is more profytable to
the synner than to have a iuste moderacyon of them bothe'.[63] In devotional
works written in the Tower, both More and Fisher can seem as emphatic
as John Frith that love not fear should inspire the sinner's hope for salvation. In a short prayer, More sketched out his desire to be with God 'not
for thavoiding of the calamyties of this wretched world, nor so much for
the avoiding of the paines of purgatory ... as even for a very love to the'.[64]
In a *Spiritual Consolation* addressed to his sister, Elizabeth, John Fisher
lamented the times when he feared he might not have served God 'more
rather for his love, then for feare of his punyshement'.[65]

   If Catholic writers sometimes consciously stepped back from an all-
or-nothing endorsement of the desirability of fear of post-mortem punish- ·
ment, Protestant writers were equally capable of affirming its utility as an
instrument of social control, though of course with hell rather than purgatory as the object of apprehension. In his polemical exchanges with John
Rastell, Frith was at pains to deny the charge that he had given licence to
sin by impugning the existence of hell.[66] Cranmer's homily of 1547
remarked that Christians ought to fear damnation 'for it is an everlasting
losse, without remedy, of the grace and favor of God'.[67] Preaching in 1552,
Latimer proved as skilled in evoking the pains of hell as any indulgence
preacher the pains of purgatory, and affirmed that Christ wanted 'to make
us afraid thereof'.[68] Indeed, an important aspect of the Protestant rejection
of purgatory as a means of bringing men to repentance was to insist that
hell was a more terrifying and effective deterrent: as Tyndale pithily put it,
'to fear men ... Christ and his apostles thought hell enough'.[69]

   It should now be becoming apparent that religious writers of different persuasions employed the idea of fear for a variety of polemical, theological and devotional purposes. In the process they make clear that within
contemporary culture fear was an ambivalent, if not multi-faceted theme,
capable of diverse constructions and meanings. That any writer should
simply seek to banish fear on the grounds that it contributed to the misery
of the human condition was quite inconceivable. Franklin Roosevelt's
famous assurance that 'we have nothing to fear, but fear itself' would have

seemed preposterous, even blasphemous to the Tudor mind. The Scriptures on which all contemporary theologians relied were replete with striking monitions to accept and embrace fear: 'Fear God, and keep his command-ments', 'Happy is the man that feareth alway', 'Who would not fear thee, O King of nations?', 'Wouldst thou be wise, the first step is fear of the Lord', 'There is no want to them that fear Him', 'The fear of the Lord is clean, enduring for ever', 'Blessed is everyone that feareth the Lord', 'My flesh trembleth for fear of thee; and I am afraid of thy judgements', 'The fear of the Lord is the beginning of wisdom.'[70] But, confusingly, the Bible also taught that the spirit of God was not 'a spirit of slavery, to govern you by fear', and that 'perfect love casteth out fear'.[71] Long before the Refor-mation, in fact, scholastic theologians had elaborated sophisticated tax-onomies of fear, usually predicated on a basic distinction between 'servile' and 'filial' fear of the Lord, the former corresponding to the mere fear of being punished, such as a servant might feel towards his master, the latter approximating to the natural, reverential fear a child should have of dis-pleasing its father.[72] English Catholic writers of the early Reformation period deployed these concepts in varying ways. In *A Devoute Treatyse for them that ben Tymorouse and Fearefull in Conscience*, addressed to the sisters of Syon Abbey, William Bonde warned that only the 'holy feare of god' nourished charity, and that servile fear 'co[n]tentyth not god but rather yf it be undis-cretely usyd, moche dysplesyth hys grace'.[73] In his *Answer to a Poisoned Book*, Thomas More took an arguably more utilitarian view, accepting that 'though fere of hell alone be but a servyle drede', men already feared it too little rather than too much, a trend likely to be exacerbated by heretics present-ing its punishments in expressly metaphorical terms.[74] Roger Edgeworth's sermon 'intreating of the feare of God', preached probably in the early 1540s, more ambitiously laid out a tripartite structure for fear, compre-hending a 'carnall and worldly fear' of losses and gains in this life, a 'servyle fear' of the pains of hell, and a 'fillial and charitable feare' whence 'the former feare of punyshment vanysheth and goeth awaye'. Edgeworth took a fairly forgiving view of human infirmity: carnal fear was not damnable if it was simply a spontaneous reaction to pain, danger or deprivation. More-over, Edgeworth departed from the tradition that servile fear was also damnable, arguing that such fear of punishment developed a habit of justice and of doing good which would gradually develop into true filial fear.[75] Edgeworth's oration, like the scriptural meditations of John Fisher, and the pastoral treatises of Bonde and Whitford, was characteristic of Catholic dis-course in combining a fairly rigid typology of states of fear with a model of progression and improvement.[76] Such approaches encouraged the educated audiences they addressed to accept a construction of fear as an interlocking set of existential categories. Implicit also was the recognition that a laudable fear of God might slip into scrupulosity, that a natural fear of judgement might tip over into despair. Protestant polemic against purgatory, while at one level ignoring or caricaturing such subtleties and difficulties, in another sense paid service to them. At root, the objection to purgatory seems to have been not so much that it caused fear as a first principle, but that it misappropriated and corrupted a potentially godly and distinctly malleable set of impulses. In the prologue to his *Disputation of Purgatory* John Frith praised the perspicacity of his immediate forerunner Simon Fish for grasping that the common people 'was fallen into that frantic imagination, that they more feared the Pope and his decrees, which are but vanity, than God himself and his law, which are most righteous and eternal'.[77] Quite conversely, but no less pertinently, John Bradford was later to argue that with the easy availability of prayers, masses and pardons to smooth the way into heaven 'who will be so earnest to amend ... and live in a godly and true fear of God?'[78] In seeking to persuade the English people that preparation for the prospect of purgatory was fundamentally misdirected and misconceived, Protestant writers thus exploited the ambiguities of fear as a cultural construct, and co-opted the contemporary ambivalence towards 'fearfulness' into a set of polemical strategies that may have been the more effective because they were unsettlingly inconsistent. To suppose that medieval Christianity was sustained by an undifferentiated emphasis on fear, and that the aim and achievement of the reformers, like that of a modern psychotherapist with a disturbed patient, was to restore society to a condition of feeling at ease with itself, is to accept at face value a contingent aspect of their own propaganda. In fact, as far as the ontology of fear was concerned, the polemical sallies of rival theologians traversed an impressive area of consensus. Protestant and Catholic writers agreed that fear was in some sense a natural property of man, and could lead him in godly as well as ungodly directions. They usually accepted that fear of post-mortem judgement and punishment was unavoidable, and also that it served a useful social and religious function in reinforcing moral regulation in this world. More problematically, however, they also accepted that in itself such 'servile fear' was at best morally neutral, and that a purer form of 'fearing' God, a God who preferred service performed out of love than out of fear, was an attainable goal. If there appears to be a degree of tension in the simultaneous holding of all these assumptions and aspirations, it was a tension indelibly enscripted within the traditional teaching on purgatory. The doctrine's heady mix of fear, hope, self-interest, altruism, punishment, purgation and salvation rendered it of all the centrepieces of medieval theology, perhaps the most vulnerable to deconstruction and vilification. But in so far as English reformers shared the vision of a righteous God who decreed eternal punishments for the wicked and who expected fear to animate but not to overwhelm His servants, their alternative explanations of how God's ineffable justice might be made compatible with His infinite love would never be found universally convincing.

Notes

1 See in particular S. E. Ozment, *The Reformation in the Cities: The Appeal of Protestantism to Sixteenth-Century Germany and Switzerland* (New Haven, 1975), 22–32, and his *The Age of Reform 1250–1550* (New Haven, 1980), 216–22; L. G. Duggan, 'Fear and confession on the eve of the Reformation', *Archiv für Reformationsgeschichte*, 75 (1984); E. Cameron, *The European Reformation* (Oxford, 1991), 305–11; T. N. Tentler, 'The summa for confessors as an instrument of social control', in C. Trinkaus and H. O. Oberman, eds, *The Pursuit of Holiness in Late Medieval and Renaissance Religion* (Leiden, 1974), 103–26; J. Delumeau, *Sin and Fear: The Emergence of a Western Guilt Culture 13th–18th Centuries*, E. Nicholson, trans. (New York, 1990), esp. chs. 6–7; 10–11. (Delumeau, however, regards Protestant Christianity as almost equally inclined to inculcating fear: chs. 19–21.)

2 On the medieval development and rationale of the doctrine of purgatory, see J. Le Goff, *The Birth of Purgatory*, A. Goldhammer, trans. (Aldershot, 1984); P. Binski, *Medieval Death: Ritual and Representation* (1996), 181–99.

3 C. Burgess, '"A fond thing vainly invented": an essay on purgatory and pious motive in late medieval England', in S. J. Wright, ed., *Parish, Church and People: Local Studies in Lay Religion 1350–1750* (1988), 56–84; E. Duffy, *The Stripping of the Altars: Traditional Religion in England c.1400–c.1580* (New Haven, 1994), ch. 10, esp. 346–7; R. L. White, 'Early Print and Purgatory: the Shaping of an Henrician Ideology' (Ph.D. thesis, Australian National University, 1994), 21, 84, 109. These works intend to redress the bleaker assessments to be found in A. G. Dickens, *The English Reformation* (1989), 29–30; A. Kreider, *English Chantries: The Road to Dissolution* (Cambridge MA, 1979), 41–2, 91, 93 (the abandonment of purgatory 'brought joyful release from an acutely existential dread'.)

4 See the somewhat overwrought presentation of P. Camporesi, *The Fear of Hell: Images of Damnation and Salvation in Early Modern Europe* (Oxford, 1990), and of Delumeau, *Sin and Fear*. For a more circumspect approach, see C. M. N. Eire, *From Madrid to Purgatory: The Art and Craft of Dying in Sixteenth-Century Spain* (Cambridge, 1995), 78, 176–7; 189–95. See also the discussion of the methodological and conceptual difficulties in W. J. Bouwsma, 'Anxiety and the formation of early modern culture', in B. C. Malament, ed., *After the Reformation* (Manchester, 1980), 215–46.

5 For the dangers of attempting to use wills as the basis for a comprehensive assessment of religious mentalité, see in particular, among a burgeoning literature, Duffy, *Altars*, ch. 15; C. Burgess, 'Late medieval wills and pious convention: testamentary evidence reconsidered', in M. A. Hicks, ed., *Profit, Piety and the Professions* (Gloucester, 1990), 14–33.

6 A note on terminology is appropriate here. The following paragraphs will refer fairly indiscriminately to reformers–Protestants on the one hand, and to Catholics–conservatives–traditionalists on the other, but the intention is not to posit a rigid bipolarity of religious views on all contemporary issues or to promote anachronistic concepts of confessional identity. As a shorthand, 'Catholic' will usually be used to describe writers who accepted in its essentials the traditional conception of purgatory, 'Protestant' for those who rejected it in its totality.

7 For the early development of Luther's views on purgatory, see A. F. Mayne, 'Disputes about purgatory in the early sixteenth century' (M.Phil. thesis, University of London, 1975), 10–13. For references to the doctrine in the first wave of English anti-Lutheran

polemic, see Henry VIII, *Assertio Septem Sacramentorum*, in F. Macnamara, ed., *Miscellaneous Writings of Henry VIII* (n.p., 1924), 44; R. Rex, *The Theology of John Fisher* (Cambridge, 1991), 98–9; Thomas More, *Responsio ad Lutherum*, in *CWTM*, 5: 257–9. Fish's *Supplication* is reprinted as an appendix in More, *Letter to Bugenhagen. Supplication of Souls. Letter against Frith*, *CWTM* 7: 412–22.

8 More, *Supplication of Souls*; J. Rastell, *A New Boke of Purgatory whiche is a Dialoge & Dysputacyon betwene one Comyngo an Almayne ... & one Gyngemyn a Turke* (1530); J. Frith, *A Disputation of Purgatory*, in N. T. Wright, ed., *The Work of John Frith* (Oxford, 1978).

9 For the most pertinent passages, see Thomas More, *The Confutation of Tyndale's Answer*, *CWTM* 8: 90–1, 102–3, 210–11, 288–91, 372–5, 407, 578, 625, 702–3, 967–9, 1033–4; *The Answer to a Poisoned Book*, *CWTM* 11: 187–9; *The Apology*, *CWTM* 9: 72–4, 88, 101; William Tyndale, *Doctrinal Treatises and Introductions to Different Portions of the Holy Scripture*, H. Walter, ed., PS (Cambridge, 1848), 48, 122, 148, 158, 235–8, 243–9, 268–72, 302–3, 318–21, 330–1, 342, 424, 531; *Expositions and Notes on Sundry Portions of the Holy Scriptures, together with the Practice of Prelates*, H. Walter, ed., PS (Cambridge, 1849), 48–9, 159–62, 286–7; *An Answer to Sir Thomas More's Dialogue*, H. Walter, ed., PS (Cambridge, 1850), 27–8, 47, 121, 141–3, 180–1, 214, 273–83. G. Joye, *The Subversion of Moris False Foundacion* (Emden, 1534), fol. xxxvi^v. On contentious preaching, see Kreider, *English Chantries*, chs. 4–5. For Latimer's early contributions, see H. Latimer, *Sermons*, G. E. Corrie, ed., PS (Cambridge, 1844), 36–7, 48–51; *Sermons and Remains*, G. E. Corrie, ed., PS (Cambridge, 1845), 218, 235–9, 245–9.

10 C. Lloyd, ed., *Formularies of Faith put Forth by Authority during the reign of Henry VIII* (Oxford, 1856), xxxii; T. A. Lacey, ed., *The King's Book 1543* (1895), 156.

11 See, for example, a late 1530s sermon by the conservative preacher Roger Edgeworth: 'I will not contende aboute this vocable Purgatory ... but let A. be his name': R. Edgeworth, *Sermons very Fruitful, Godly and Learned*, J. Wilson, ed. (Cambridge, 1993), 128. Note also the studied avoidance of the term in a chapter contending that 'the masse is profitable to the deade' in Richard Smyth's *Defence of the Sacrifice of the Masse* (1546), fos. cxxvi ff., and the excision of overt references to purgatory in a 1540s reprinting of a medieval didactic work noted by J. F. Preston, 'The Pricke of Conscience (Parts I–III) and its first appearance in print', *The Library*, 6th ser. 8, no. 4 (1985), 313–14.

12 Kreider, *English Chantries*, ch. 8; E. J. Bicknell, *A Theological Introduction to the Thirty-Nine Articles of the Church of England* (1925), 347.

13 J. Veron, *The Huntyng of Purgatorye to Death* (1561); W. Allen, *A Defense and Declaration of the Catholike Churches Doctrine touching Purgatory* (Antwerp, 1565).

14 On this theme, see P. Marshall, 'The debate over "unwritten verities" in early Reformation England', in B. Gordon, ed., *Protestant History and Identity in Sixteenth-Century Europe I: The Medieval Inheritance* (Aldershot, 1996), 60–76.

15 Veron, *Huntyng of Purgatorye to Death*, fol. 280r.

16 J. Frith, *The Revelation of Antichrist* (1529), sigs. F 8r–v, cited in More, *Supplication of Souls*, lxxii. For other representations of purgatory as the 'kingdom' of the pope, see J. Bale, *The Complete Plays*, P. Happé, ed. (Cambridge, 1985–6), 1: 35; Tyndale, *Expositions and Notes*, 287.

17 Frith, *Work*, 90–1; Tyndale, *Answer to More*, 214; J. Hooper, *Later Writings*, C. Nevinson, ed., PS (Cambridge, 1852), 32; T. Becon, *The Catechism ... with other Pieces*, J. Ayre, ed., PS (Cambridge, 1844), 381, 414; Veron, *Huntyng of Purgatorye to Death*, sig. Av^v. See also C. R. Trueman, *Luther's Legacy: Salvation and English Reformers 1525–1556* (Oxford, 1994), 131, 142.

18 J. Hooper, *Early Writings*, S. Carr, ed., PS (Cambridge, 1843), 568.

19 Fish, *Supplication*, 419.

20 Frith, *Work*, 90, 183; Tyndale, *Doctrinal Treatises*, 122, 148, 237–8, 244–9, 302–3, 318, 342, 424; *Expositions and Notes*, 286–7; *Answer to More*, 47, 143, 214; Latimer, *Sermons*, 36, 50, 71; *Sermons and Remains*, 239, 363; T. Cranmer, *Miscellaneous Writings and Let-*

ters, J. E. Cox, ed., PS (Cambridge, 1846), 64, 182; J. Bradford, *Letters, Treatises, Remains*, A. Townsend, ed., PS (Cambridge, 1853), 280, 292; H. Bullinger, *The Decades: The Fourth Decade*, T. Harding, ed., PS (Cambridge, 1851), 395; Hooper, *Early Writings*, 570–1; M. Coverdale, *Remains*, G. Pearson, ed., PS (Cambridge, 1846), 270–1; Bale, *Complete Plays*, 1: 40, 70–1; Becon, *Catechism*, 174–5; *Prayers and Other Pieces*, ed. J. Ayre, PS (Cambridge, 1844), 129, 277.

21 Frith, *Work*, 183.

22 Tyndale, *Doctrinal Treatises*, 244; J. Barlow, *The Burial of the Mass*, in E. Arber, ed., *English Reprints* (1871), 133ff.

23 Coverdale, *Remains*, 475.

24 Frith, *Work*, 141.

25 Tyndale, *Doctrinal Treatises*, 302; *Expositions and Notes*, 287, 162.

26 Latimer, *Sermons*, 50; Coverdale, *Remains*, 475; Cranmer, *Miscellaneous Writings*, 182.

27 Joye, *Subversio[n] of Moris False Foundacion*, fo. xxxvi^v.

28 Hooper, *Early Writings*, 571.

29 Frith, *Work*, 90, 207.

30 Tyndale, *Expositions and Notes*, 159, 287. Frith also noted that those who believed in purgatorial punishment were 'fools': *Work*, 142. The theme, of course, was picked up in the contention of the Edwardian articles that belief in purgatory was a 'fond' thing: J. Ketley, ed., *The Two Liturgies … in the Reign of King Edward VI*, PS (Cambridge, 1844), 532.

31 D. Loades, *Revolution in Religion: The English Reformation, 1530–1570* (Cardiff, 1992), 23; R. Houlbrooke, 'Introduction', in Houlbrooke, ed., *Death, Ritual and Bereavement* (1989), 4; Burgess, 'Fond thing vainly invented', 63–4. Some Continental Catholic polemicists seem to have been readier to make the point: Delumeau, *Sin and Fear*, 384.

32 T. More, *A Dialogue of Comfort Against Tribulation*, *CWTM* 12: 37–8.

33 Duffy, *Altars*, 303, 339–40, 342; White, 'Early print and purgatory', 46, 60; G. R. Keiser, 'St Jerome and the Bridgettines: visions of the afterlife in fifteenth-century England', in D. Williams, ed., *England in the Fifteenth Century: Proceedings of the 1986 Harlaxton Symposium* (Woodbridge, 1987), 151; *Here begynneth a Lytel Boke, that speketh of Purgatorye* (?1531), sigs. Aii^r, Bii^v; J. Fisher, *English Works*, J. E. B. Mayor, ed., Early English Text Society extra ser. 27 (1876), 10–11, 15, 24, 362–3; M. D. Sullivan, ed., *A Critical Edition of 'Two Fruytfull Sermons' of Saint John Fisher, Bishop of Rochester*, University Microfilms Inc. (Ann Arbor, 1974), 39–40, 42.

34 Rastell, *New Boke of Purgatory*, sigs. Hiii^v–iv^r.

35 More, *Supplication of Souls*, 175. See also 199–200; *Dialogue Concerning Heresies*, *CWTM* 6: 377; *Confutation of Tyndale's Answer*, 90, 289–90, 967–8; *Answer to a Poisoned Book*, 187–8. It had been a cardinal principle of Utopian religion that subjects could not be trusted to obey the king if they had 'nothing to fear but laws and no hope beyond the body': *Utopia*, *CWTM* 4: 223.

36 More, *Confutation of Tyndale's Answer*, 90–1.

37 More, *Answer to a Poisoned Book*, 187.

38 More, *Dialogue Concerning Heresies*, 354, 365–6, 377, 544–5; *Confutation of Tyndale's Answer*, 288, 625, 702; *Apology*, 88, 101; *Supplication of Souls*, 177, 198; Tyndale, *Answer to More*, 180–1; Frith, *Work*, 490; G. Joye, *An Apology to W. Tindale*, ed. E. Arber, English Scholars Library, 13 (1883), 15; Ketley, ed., *Liturgies of Edward VI*, 537; Hooper, *Later Writings*, 63; Bullinger, *Fourth Decade*, 389–90; Becon, *Prayers and Other Pieces*, 182. See also Mayne, 'Disputes about purgatory', 55–60; W. A. Clebsch, *England's Earliest Protestants, 1520–1535* (New Haven, 1964), 219ff.

39 B. J. Verkamp, *The Indifferent Mean: Adiaphorism in the English Reformation to 1554* (Athens, OH, 1977), 110n; Kreider, *English Chantries*, 115.

40 Hooper, *Early Writings*, 566.

41 Tyndale, *Answer to More*, 28; Frith, *Work*, 122.

42 Frith, *Work*, 132. Such views were shortly afterwards subsumed into the government's

propaganda. The 1536 proclamation outlawing papal indulgences charged that as a result of them many of the King's subjects 'have been more encouraged to commit sin and to withdraw their faith, hope, and devotion from God': P. L. Hughes and J. F Larkin, eds, *Tudor Royal Proclamations, I. The Early Tudors* (New Haven, 1964), 237.

43 Hooper, *Early Writings*, 569; Bradford, *Letters, Treatises, Remains*, 290.

44 Veron, *Huntyng of Purgatorye to Death*, fos. 308r-v.

45 Tyndale, *Answer to More*, 28, 143.

46 Latimer, *Sermons and Remains*, 239. On the diffusion and popularity of the *scala coeli* indulgence, see Duffy, *Altars*, 375–6; N. Morgan, 'The Scala Coeli Indulgence and the Royal Chapels', in B. Thompson, ed., *The Reign of Henry VII: Proceedings of the 1993 Harlaxton Symposium* (Stamford, CT, 1995), 83–103.

47 Frith, *Work*, 250. For the importance of Tracy's will as a Protestant text, see J. Craig and C. Litzenberger, 'Wills as religious propaganda: the testament of William Tracy', *Journal of Ecclesiastical History*, 44 (1993), 416–31.

48 Fish, *Supplication*, 419; Tyndale, *Doctrinal Treatises*, 244; Frith, *Work*, 93; Latimer, *Sermons and Remains*, 339; Coverdale, *Remains*, 271. See also J. Bossy, *Christianity in the West* (Oxford, 1985), 56. The text of Luther's ninety-five theses is most conveniently available in E. G. Rupp and B. Drewery, eds, *Martin Luther* (1970), 19–25. More attempted to answer this objection in *Supplication of Souls*, 199–200.

49 W. Bonde, *Pylgrimage of Perfection*, cited in White, 'Early print and purgatory', 84; More, *Confutation of Tyndale's Answer*, 289–90.

50 Tyndale, *Doctrinal Treatises*, 330; *Answer to More*, 281. For Luther's view on the uncertainty of indulgences, see D. N. V. Bagchi, *Luther's Earliest Opponents: Catholic Controversialists, 1518–1525* (Minneapolis, 1991), 35.

51 Latimer, *Sermons*, 37.

52 Hooper, *Early Writings*, 561.

53 Veron, *Huntyng of Purgatorye to Death*, fol. 159v.

54 Frith, *Work*, 119–20, 132, 142.

55 Veron, *Huntyng of Purgatorye to Death*, fol. 310r.

56 Frith, *Work*, 141–2.

57 Tyndale, *Expositions and Notes*, 159.

58 Tyndale, *Answer to More*, 280–1.

59 *Certain Sermons or Homilies (1547)*, R. B. Bond, ed. (Toronto, 1987), 147–60. See also J. Frith [?], *Of the Preparation to the Cross, and to Deathe, and of the Comforte under the Crosse and Deathe* (1540), sig. k iv^v; Latimer, *Sermons*, 549; J. Bale, *Select Works*, H. Christmas, ed., PS (1849), 228.

60 Becon, *Prayers and Other Pieces*, 129. This work is discussed by N. L. Beaty, *The Craft of Dying: A Study in the Literary Tradition of the Ars Moriendi in England* (1970), 108–56.

61 Beaty, *Craft of Dying*, 7–8, 33–4; R. Whitford, *A Dayly Exercyse and Experyence of Dethe* (1537), quote at sig. A ii^r.

62 Edgeworth, *Sermons*, 307.

63 Fisher, *English Works*, 29–30, 113–14. For sensitive discussion of the interaction of fear, penitence and mercy in Fisher's thought, see Rex, *Theology of John Fisher*, 34–40; E. Duffy, 'The spirituality of John Fisher', in B. Bradshaw and E. Duffy, eds, *Humanism, Reform and the Reformation: The Career of Bishop John Fisher* (Cambridge, 1989), 205–10.

64 T. More, *Treatise on the Passion, Treatise on the Blessed Body, Instructions and Prayers*, CWTM 13: 230.

65 Fisher, *English Works*, 354.

66 Frith, *Work*, 226–7.

67 *Certain Sermons or Homilies*, 148.

68 Latimer, *Sermons and Remains*, 191.

69 Tyndale, *Answer to More*, 28.

70 Ecclesiastes 12:13; Proverbs 28:4; Jeremiah 10:7; Ecclesiasticus 1:16; Psalms 34:9;

19:9; 128:1; 119:120; 111:10. I quote from the Authorised Version and from Ronald Knox's translation of the Vulgate.

71 Romans 8:15; I John 4:18.

72 The *locus classicus* here is Aquinas's discussion in the *Summa Theologicae*, 2a2ae. 19: T. Gilby *et al.*, eds. and trans. (1964–81), 33: 43–85, which considered four potential classifications of fear in the light of scriptural, patristic and classical testimonies.

73 W. Bonde, *A Devoute Treatyse for them that ben Tymorouse and Fearful in Conscience* (1534), fos. ii^v–iv^r. See also *idem*, *The Pylgrymage of Perfeccyon* (1531), fol. 73.

74 More, *Answer to a Poisoned Book*, 187–8.

75 Edgeworth, *Sermons*, 163–4.

76 By stating at the outset that it will deal only with the 'dread terror' of God and not concern itself with 'authentic Judeo-Christian maxims' about the fear of the Lord, Delumeau's *Sin and Fear* (4–5) arguably imposes anachronistic limitations on its subject.

77 Frith, *Work*, 93.

78 Bradford, *Letters, Treatises, Remains*, 293.

10

'Rest of their bones': fear of death and Reformed burial practices[1]

ANDREW SPICER

The medieval Church provided a clear framework to reassure the dying and comfort the living. The services and masses for the dead provided a positive aid to the departed and helped them in their journey through purgatory. The sequence of ceremonies concerning the interment of the dead would begin the evening before the burial, when the corpse would be taken to the church. There the Vespers of the Office of the Dead (*placebo*) would be held and then, at some point after midnight, there would be the celebration of the Mattins Office of the Dead (*dirge*). This could be extended with extra psalms and antiphons such as the *Commendatio animarum*. The body was then buried after the Mass for the Dead or Requiem Mass. The whole sequence of services could then be repeated in seven and then thirty days after the burial, the week's and month's mind. After a year the services could be repeated again and could become an annual remembrance.[2]

The medieval Church's round of services served to undermine the fear and the anxiety which surrounded death. This was a very real fear because in a world where infant mortality was high, the harvest unreliable, disease and sickness commonplace and people, perhaps, more vulnerable to natural phenomena, death was always close. Furthermore the world of the departed was perceived to be close to that of the living. The souls of the dead lived in the churchyards which also served as a centre of social activity for the living. Folklore concerning the feast of All Hallows referred to the return of the dead to the land of the living.[3] The proximity of death makes this fear understandable. People feared dying suddenly, unprepared for their death. The actual act of death was feared as the dying came face to face with the sins they had committed and the consequent horrors of purgatory or hell. Popular legends about the agonies of death which haunted the resurrected Lazarus served to heighten this fear.[4] This awareness of death was increased by the popular practices and commemorations of the departed:

informing the neighbourhood, preparing the body, the funeral and burial rites, feasting. These made death and burial a matter for the whole community.[5]

With the Reformation there was a rejection of 'the exorbitance of superstitious exiquies ... as in their bel-ringinges, lampe-lighting, dirge singing, incense watering, letanie praying, soule-massing, vigilles keeping, and such other geare'.[6] The theological changes of the Reformation, in particular the denial of purgatory and of the efficacy of good works, meant that the institutionalised care and reassurance provided by the medieval church were attacked. In its place the Reformed Church emphasised the doctrine of predestination, as a result of which no human actions could serve to mitigate the consequences of death or to enable and assist the dead in achieving salvation.

While the practices and customs of the medieval Church were overturned, the fear of death was not so easily dispelled. People were still concerned about preparing themselves for death. The adaption of Holbein's 'Dance of Death' for a Protestant audience and the development of a Calvinistic *ars moriendi*, such as Thomas Becon's *The Sicke Mannes Salve*, represent an extension of the medieval culture concerning death and the associated fears.[7] The difficulty which the Reformed Church had in coping with this fear of death was reflected in the area of burial, where past customs and superstitious practices survived even amongst the faithful and devout.

The Reformed Church reacted against the complex round of rituals and masses of the dead of the medieval Church as well as the superstitious and popular practices associated with death. As a result the Reformed churches attempted to establish a simpler approach to burials. In Geneva, Calvin's Ecclesiastical Ordinances of 1541 stated that the dead were to be buried decently in the designated place, but those who were responsible for bearing the dead should swear an oath to prevent superstitious practices which were contrary to the Word of God.[8] The French synods also condemned the practice of prayers for the dead and several similar demands for simplicity with regard to burial were also made by the Walloon synods.[9]

In Scotland the First Book of Discipline expressed similar sentiments regarding burial and provided an almost complete attack upon the practices of the medieval Church.

> Buriall in all ages hath bene holden in estimation to signifie that the same bodie which was committed to the earth should not utterly perish, but should rise againe, and the same we would have kept within this realme, provided that superstition, idolatry and whatsoever hath proceeded of a false opinion, and for advantage sake may be avoided, and singing of Masse, *placebo*, and

dirge, and all other prayers over or for the dead, which are not onely superstitious and vaine, but also are idolatry and doe repugne to the plaine Scriptures of God. For plaine it is that everyone dyeth, departeth either in the faith of Christ Jesus or departeth in incredulity. Plain it is that they that depart in the true faith of Christ Jesus rest from their and from death doe goe to life everlasting, as by our Master and his Apostles we are taught. But whosoever departeth in unbeleefe, or in incredulitie, shall never see life, but the wrath of God abides upon him. And so we say that prayers for the dead are not onely superstitious and vaine, but doe expressly repugne to the manifest Scriptures and veritie therof. For avoiding of all inconveniences we judge it best, that neither singing nor reading be at buriall. For albeit things sung or read may admonish some of the living to prepare themselves for death, yet shall some superstitious think that singing and reading of the living may profite the dead. And therefore we think it most expedient, that the dead be conveyed to the place of buriall with some honest company of the kirk, without either singing or reading; yea without any kind of ceremony heretofore used, other then that the dead be committed to the grave, with such gravity and sobriety, as those that be present may seeme to feare the judgements of God, and to hate sinne which is the cause of death.[10]

The entry in the Book of Discipline went on to attack the practice of burial within the churches, as well as funeral sermons.[11]

The desire for simplicity and a break from the external observances of the medieval Church were also expressed in the wills written by those of Reformed beliefs. While the use of will evidence is controversial, there does seem to have been a rejection of the need for intercessors when appealing to God and a demand for simple burials in wills written by those of Reformed beliefs. An elder of the exile French Church in Southampton, Anthoine Jurion, personally wrote his will in 1578 and very clearly stated his beliefs:

That is first p'sentlye & untill the ower of my death I Recommend my soulle unto god in the name of his sonne Jesus christ deseringe hym to Reseve me to his mercye in exceptinge the death of his sonne for payment Recompence of all my sines & offences the which hym maye reserve me in his Blessed Realme. Secondlye I ordaine that when it shall please hym to call me oute of this lyffe that my bodye maye be buried honestlye according to the order of the Reformed church wher unto it hathe pleased god to call me of his good grace without worde of Idolatorye & superstition to the ende that beinge so laide in to the earthe from whence I came I maye Rest and staye in hope of this hapeye & Blessed Resurection the which shalt come in the Last daye in the which daye I beleve to rise in soulle & bodye to be Resevid unto lyfe everlastinge when I hope throughrewe faithe to in habite & lyve for ever with our lorde & saviour Jesus Christe.[12]

Similar religious beliefs were expressed by other members of the exile community and can also be seen in the wills written by their co-religionists on the Continent.[13]

While the Reformed churches could issue statements and decrees about their stance on death and burial practices, beliefs which their more faithful adherents were keen to express, it was an area which they repeatedly had to enforce. For the Reformed churches had not merely to combat the practices of the medieval Church but also the popular beliefs and superstitions which had developed around death and burial. In this whole area the task of the Reformed church was not easy, as they attempted to combat a somewhat irrational fear, the fear of death and of failing to achieve salvation. The Reformed churches also differed from country to country in their approach to the superstitious practices associated with death and burial.

In Scotland, a number of superstitions and traditions continued after the Reformation. One persistent custom which was repeatedly attacked and undermined was burial within the kirk itself. There were a number of different reasons given for attacking this tradition, both practical and religious. It was attacked in the First Book of Discipline in 1560 and was an issue which regularly came before the General Assembly and the government of the kirk. The anxieties concerning burial within the kirk were most eloquently and authoritatively expressed in the sermon delivered by William Birnie. This was subsequently published in Edinburgh in 1606, entitled *The Blame of Kirk-buriall tending to pervvade cemiteriall civilitie*.[14] In dedicating the pamphlet to the Marquess of Hamilton, Birnie wrote: 'There is nothing wherein the Antichristian crew is found more condemnable ... nor that by their lin-sey-wol-sey confusions, they have dared clamp the sincere twist of Gods trueth, with the tome clouts of their brain-sicke superstitions, instanced by their many fold sepulchromancy.'[15] Birnie was the minister at Lanark and may have been prompted to deliver this sermon as a result of his experiences as moderator of the Presbytery of Lanark.[16] In this position he seems to have become embroiled in a dispute over kirk-burial. In 1602 the Privy Council fined James Weir of Balshaw and others for burying his infant son within the kirk at Carluke and 'for any "offence or sklaunder" done by them to Mr. Williame Birny' and other ministers of the presbytery of Lanark.[17]

One of the reasons for attacking kirk-burial was that it was considered insanitary. The First Book of Discipline had stated that 'we think it neither seemly that the Kirk appointed to preaching and the ministration of the Sacraments shall be made a place of buryall, but that some other secret and convenient place, lying in the most free aire, be appointed for that use, which place ought to be walled and fenced about *and* kept for that use onely'.[18] An act of the General Assembly in 1563 concerning rural parishes had required that bodies be buried at a depth of six feet.[19] In the visitation of the diocese of Dunblane between 1586 and 1589, the visitors were to ensure that the kirkyard was suitably maintained for burials. There were complaints about animals grazing in the kirkyard at St Ninians and they emphasised the need to repair the kirkyard dykes.[20] The Reformed Church on Guernsey had also been concerned about such burials for similar reasons. They had complained about the problems of the smell from newly-buried corpses and the dangers of such burials at a time of plague.[21]

There were also structural considerations for opposing burial within the church. This could cause considerable disruption due to the need to move furniture and to break up the church floor. Injunctions were issued in several parishes during the visitation of Dunblane, ordering that burials should not take place within the kirk. At Logie the commissioners stated that 'the payment off the floir not equaly laid because off rasing the same for buriall. It is orderit that … the payment clos wyth all diligence after harvest and that na buriall be hereafter in the kirk'.[22] In the same parish in 1593 two men removed and broke up the local laird's pew because it was standing on the graves of their forebears.[23]

Birnie's *The Blame of Kirk-buriall* attempted to provide a reasoned and detailed criticism of kirk-burial which was seen to smack of superstition. This was necessary because 'the practise of manie in buriall processe, argues not onelie irresolution, but incredulitie, whereof kirk-buriall is a badge: as wherein by a sacrareligious conuersion they make Gods sanctuarie their Golgotha, that is the Kirk a caualrie or cairne of dead mens skulles'. Through using classical, biblical and patristic allusions and references, Birnie attempted to prove that kirk-burial was a sin and a profanation. He argued that it was one of 'many of the Papistical punkes hes secreetly slipped in the Kirk' and at various points claimed the practice was, in fact, not merely Papist but pagan. He went on to argue that whereas other abuses with regard to burial had been reformed, the superstition of burial within the kirk remained.[24] Birnie's attack on this ground was perhaps unfair as the Roman Catholic Church had itself complained at the Council of Basle in 1432 about churches being turned into cemeteries by incumbents seeking money.[25] Besides this polemical attack, Birnie did go on to identify and attack the reasons why kirk-burial persisted in spite of the kirk's assault.

In part, the popular recognition of the church as a holy place led to the continued desire to be buried inside the church. In 1598 Robert Bruce of Pitlathie was buried in the kirk of Leuchars by his friends and sons, despite attempts by the Presbytery of St Andrews to frustrate the burial within the kirk, which was a 'superstition to be detaistit of christians'.[26] Nor

was this an isolated incident. The burial of Sir William Hamilton of Sanquhar within the church provides an even clearer example of this abuse. The
General Assembly heard in 1573 that in the previous August, while the kirk
session was meeting, one John Hamilton with about 200 others broke into
the kirk of Mauchlin, where they threw aside the table boards which had
been used that morning for the Lord's Supper and there buried Sir William
Hamilton of Sanquhar. The placing of Hamilton's body would seem akin to
the medieval practice of being buried before the altar.[27]

Citing, among several examples, the money-changers driven by Christ
from the Temple, Birnie argued that burial within the kirk was in fact the
desecration of a holy place. If it was to remain a place 'holy for the seruice
of God', it should not be put to any other purpose.[28] Birnie could see serious
religious implications from such practices. To bury someone before the altar
[sic], he argued, was in fact only one step away from asking a priest to say
mass for the soul of the departed.[29] It was also, he argued, difficult to reconcile with the rejection of prayers for the dead. As the church was a house
of prayer and burial did not require prayer, the contradiction implied
'prayers for the dead. And so, by impropriating the Lord's prayer house to
be a burial kirk, we incure profanation.'[30] Furthermore, whilst praying in
the church, they further hinted at prayers for the dead by 'bowing their knee
no where else but on their forbeers bellies: which ceremony how sib it is
to the old superstition'.[31] This final argument is given credence by the situation in the Netherlands, where women defiantly kneeled and prayed at the
graves of their relatives, even during the services, well into the seventeenth
century.[32]

The kirk's limited success in preventing burial within the churches led them
to take stern measures against offenders. In 1588 the General Assembly was
forced to acknowledge that the acts prohibiting burial in the kirks were
'daylie brockin'. It therefore ordered that those responsible should be suspended from the benefits of the Church until they repented and that any
minister who gave his approval should be suspended from the ministry.[33]
The General Assembly had appealed to the King and his Council as early as
1573 to issue an ordinance prohibiting such burials. However, as this also
failed, the Assembly again requested, and in 1597 the king gave his support
for, an Act of Parliament.[34] Royal support against kirk-burial did not halt
the practice and in 1610 the presbytery of Peebles protested about burials
in the kirk of Innerleithen and requested an Act of the Council to prohibit
it. The Privy Council responded by forbidding burials within any of the presbytery's kirks on pain of £40 fine, except for those who had "ane heritable
rycht".[35] The presbytery at St Andrews attempted to eradicate the problem

with sterner measures and tried to excommunicate those who breached the order of the General Assembly. Baron Hay had buried his wife in the kirk of Forgoun in 1596 in spite of the order 'as of custom and of use'. It was only the intervention of the agent of the Convocation of the Barons which prevented Hay's excommunication.[36]

In order to deter burial within the kirk, the Synod of Lothian had proposed in October 1595 that those guilty of burying relatives in the kirk would in future be forced to dig up the corpse and publicly repent.[37] In the case of Adam Menzies of Enoch, the minister seems to have taken upon himself the responsibility for dealing with this breach of ecclesiastical order.

As the case of Baron Hay demonstrated, it was difficult for the kirk to apply the restrictions relating to kirk-burial to the more prominent members of society. This was particularly the case when people wished to bury their relatives in the churches where their ancestors had been buried for generations. James VI had even suggested that nobles should build sepulchres for themselves and their families in order to prevent burial within the kirk.[38] At Logie, the whole kirk session was censured for conniving at the burial of one Margaret Alexander.[39] In 1607 the Privy Council heard a complaint from Adame Menzies of Enoche, whose family had had an aisle in his parish church of Durisdeer for generations past. This aisle was used for hearing the Word and worshipping God but it was also used for 'the bureying of the deid bodyis thairin of the house of Enoch in all aigeis bigane'. Adam Menzies therefore buried his son in this aisle in accordance with 'his undoubtit rycht and continuall possessioun of his saidis antecessouris' in the presence of many parishioners and local gentry, 'in ane christiane and honnest maner'.[40]

Menzies protested to the Privy Council because the child had been disinterred with the connivance of the minister who claimed to have the support of the local presbytery. Menzies however recovered the body and again buried it in the family aisle, and in so doing incurred the wrath of the presbytery of Dumfries. The body was, however, again removed from the aisle. When the matter came before the Council the minister was reprimanded for dealing with the breach of an act of the kirk himself and without authority. Menzies was also given leave to return the corpse to its original resting-place in the aisle and was not required to answer the charges of the presbytery.[41]

As the cases of Sir William Hamilton and Adam Menzies demonstrated, the issue of kirk-burial could cause considerable distress and disorder. Such burials did not lead towards edification but, as Birnie claimed, 'now are become the occasion not onely of the brugling brags of men, but of the contemp also of Gods hous and servants'.[42] In the sixteenth chapter Birnie provided biblical and historical examples of burials which had been simply and soberly carried out.

The tradition of burying the dead amongst their forebears, as a justification for kirk-burial, was also criticised by Birnie in his essay. He claimed that such behaviour from those who were patrons of the church smacked of hypocrisy as they were prepared to give to the Church but then appropriate it for their own purposes, in this case burial. He questioned the traditional argument of the right to be buried with their forebears as this tradition had been broken in the past when their first ancestors were buried inside a church. It was not a legal requirement for such burials and, in fact, far from being a justifiable ancient custom, it was merely the continuance of an abuse.[43]

However, the authorities were not always prepared to acknowledge the wishes of the Kirk with regard to burial, and prominent figures continued to be buried within the kirk. In 1577 a complaint was made to the General Assembly that the Laird of Rossyth had been buried within the kirk. On questioning, it seems that the Provost and Bailies of Dunfermline had sanctioned the burial.[44] Knox himself had attended and preached at the burial of the murdered Regent Moray in St Giles's, Edinburgh, and his wife was subsequently laid to rest beside him.[45]

While kirk-burial certainly preoccupied the Reformed Church in Scotland, in the Netherlands the matter was viewed differently. A painting completed by Pieter Saenredam in 1637 illustrates the south aisle of the St Laurenskerk, Alkmaar. In the background a funeral procession has entered the church, the coffin borne aloft and preceded by a hatchard bearing the deceased's coat of arms. In the foreground a grave-digger rests on his spade and watches the procession; to his side is a mound of earth and around him the tools of his profession.[46] Although Saenredam did fabricate details in his paintings (two years earlier he had completed a painting of the same church which showed a man praying at a fictitious Catholic altar), there is an element of truth within this picture. This painting differs significantly from two other later paintings which also include funeral processions. In these, the funeral processions are more distant and less specific.[47] As Saenredam failed to illustrate the many burials which were quite literally taking place around him as he sketched in the churches of Utrecht, the detailed hatchment in the St Laurenskerk painting suggests that he was recording a specific funeral.[48]

Burials appeared in other paintings by other Dutch artists of church interiors throughout the seventeenth century. These tended to show an open grave, often with piles of earth and the grave-digger's tools strewn around about. Occasionally the grave-digger was also included in the painting.

These images sometimes appeared in the foreground of the painting or more subtly in the background.[49] It has been suggested that the image of the open grave and/or grave-digger represents the hope of everlasting life and is part of an allusion to the three virtues in the paintings. It is more likely to be either a *vanitas* symbol indicating the brevity of earthly life or a *memento mori*, a warning of impending death.[50] Whatever the artistic purpose of such illustrations within this genre, it is clear that burial within the church was an accepted practice in the Netherlands.

The reason for this difference is essentially a reflection of the thoroughness of the Reformation in these countries. In Scotland there was effectively a transfer from Catholicism to the Reformed Church; all were expected to be members and submit to the discipline of the kirk. In the Netherlands the Reformed Church, although the favoured and official church, did not achieve such status. The membership of the Reformed Church was made up of those who chose to submit to consistorial discipline. As a result Reformed congregations were often only comprised of a minority of the population. In this situation the legal and religious form of the parish took on a new significance. Whereas before the religious life of the parish had applied to the whole community, now it only related to a minority group. However, the responsibility for the church fabric and the churchyard remained with the parish community and was not the responsibility of the Reformed consistory.[51] Therefore alterations to the fabric of the church such as burials were outside the authority of the Reformed Church.

Although they were obliged to conduct baptismal and marriage ceremonies, they refused to take responsibility for burials. These were to be conducted without ceremony, and even the responsibility for recording those who were buried was to be delegated by the church to the grave-diggers.[52] Unlike in Scotland, the Dutch churches became burial grounds. As one Englishman observed, on 'finding a place where there have been none before, [they] make the grave as deep as possible and bury one upon another'.[53] Another Englishman provided a detailed description of a Dutch funeral which resembles the image that can be seen in the three paintings of church interiors which show such funeral processions.[54] A coffin, which is ridged and draped with a black cloth, is taken up from a bier by men in black gowns. They are preceded by the *aansprekers* (the ushers who have gathered the funeral company) bearing hourglasses who solemnly lead the procession into the church 'where they use no manner of ceremony or service over the grave, but immediately proceed to bury the corpse and those fourteen friends that bear the body thither do also fill up the grave'. The company then returned to the deceased's home to feast.[55]

The Reformed Church largely managed to desacralise the whole process of burial in the Netherlands. Although burials continued in the churches, clerics, if present in the company, had no part in the proceedings; they did not lead processions and did not deliver funeral sermons. This policy worked well in a country where, although technically outlawed, Catholicism had managed to establish a *modus vivendi* with the Reformed Church. The last rites could be held illegally out of the public eye and consecrated earth was spread in the graves of Catholics buried in Protestant cemeteries or churches.[56]

However, in spite of the apparent desacralisation of the burial service, the Reformed Church was unable to defeat superstition, particularly in the rural areas. A minister reported in 1586:

> I can scarcely find words to describe the superstitious practices used by the papists when they bury their dead. They have so many strange fancies about making the shroud, they place the body in this way or that in the charnel house, go the graveside or to the church to pray, assist or kiss the bier and make many unprofitable pilgrimages for the benefit of the deceased and, after the funeral, they lay on a veritable feast.[57]

Where the church commissioners were Catholic sympathisers, it was even possible in some cases for complete Catholic funerals to be held with all the accompanying trappings.[58] In the churchyards, 'superstitious and impotent crosses' remained and in another parish, youths who broke such crosses were charged with sacrilege by the local law officer in 1631.[59]

With the ringing of the bell at the burial of the dead could be seen the continuance of another Catholic superstition, a reminder to pray for the dead. It was for this reason that the church at Naaldwijk suspended bell-ringing in 1573.[60] In the city of Utrecht, this medieval practice was adapted by the Reformed Church. It was seen as a way of expressing communal grief, with the bells being rung at noon following a death and for an hour during the funeral procession. The church bells came to be seen as a *memento mori* to those who heard them, although the parishioners came to see this as an expression of grief.[61] In the same way the practice of feasting after the funeral continued after the Reformation. These also served to involve the community in the process of death and burial, as in the medieval world.

The Reformed Church in France faced different problems in the area of burial. The actual act of burial could generate a complex series of fears, especially if a Protestant was buried in a Catholic graveyard. Burial, as with other rites of passage, could serve as a catalyst for disorder and rioting. Natalie Zemon Davis recounted the story of a Protestant carpenter in Toulouse who attempted to bury his wife according to the Reformed rite but the body was seized by the Catholic mob and was buried. The corpse was recovered by the Protestants and then reburied. A fight with the Catholics ensued.[62] On the Catholic side there was the fear of desecration from burying Huguenots in a Catholic cemetery or graveyard. In the past, heretics, together with unbaptised children, lepers and Jews, were all buried in unconsecrated ground.[63] The Reformed, however, wished to maintain the tradition of being buried with their forebears. In some cases the Reformed were forced to compromise in order to satisfy the wish for relatives to be buried with their ancestors, although at times such trimming could result in riots and the desecration of the grave, if the deceased was a well-known heretic.[64] In some communities, the Reformed wanted to participate in Catholic funerals. The National Synod ruled in 1583 that they could accompany the corpse to the grave so long as the service was free from idolatry and superstition.[65] However, as in other Reformed traditions, the Synods found it difficult to eradicate superstitious practices.[66] The Synod, in fact, even had to combat new funeral customs; it ruled that the churches of Languedoc were to oppose the novelty of maids being carried to the grave accompanied by maids with garlands of flowers.[67]

During the religious wars, the Protestant communities had attempted to establish their own cemeteries, and this had been sanctioned by some of the edicts of pacification. This could, however, also lead to further unrest between the communities, as it did in Tours.[68] During the 1590s, under the influence of the Catholic League, the Reformed found some of their cemeteries taken from them and were denied burial in Catholic churches or cemeteries.[69] As a result, burial again became an issue for debate during the negotiations for a settlement in 1598. The Catholic Church opposed the burial of heretics in consecrated ground whether it was a cemetery, chapels in noble houses or churches where they were patrons. The Reformed disputed that one piece of land was more holy than another.[70] In the end the Edict of Nantes reiterated the earlier articles assigning the Reformed a place of burial.[71] However the desire to be buried with one's ancestors, in Catholic churches, remained strong; one noblewoman was buried in the choir close to the altar. These burials resulted in continued tension between the two communities as the Reformed attempted to exert their rights to be buried in churches while the authorities gave approval for them to be disinterred from their resting place.[72]

The burial practices of the Reformed Church should also be considered in one other area, that of the burial of those who were considered to be outside the Church. The medieval Church prohibited the burial of heretics, suicides and excommunicates in consecrated ground.[73] Although the Reformed Church did not recognise one piece of ground as being more holy than another, in practice the churches seem to have continued the distinction made by the medieval Church. The burial of excommunicates was a problem. The Colloquy in Jersey debated the matter in 1580 and the revised Discipline for the Channel Islands stated that those who were excommunicated were not to be buried in the churchyard unless it was ordered by the magistrates.[74] In Scotland they were to be buried without the company or a procession of the faithful members of the kirk.[75] A popular misconception on the Channel Islands was that women who had died in childbirth could not be buried in the churchyard. This led to people disguising themselves as the dead women so that they could be 'churched', and so suitably buried.[76] Suicides also continued to be buried separately; on Guernsey they were buried away from the community under a pile of stones.[77] In Scotland, the kirk session at Perth refused to bury a suicide who had drowned himself, demanding that he be buried on a small island in the river Tay.[78] Such contradictory behaviour serves to further highlight the continuing concern about the treatment of the dead after the Reformation.

The Reformed Churches clearly found it difficult to overcome the superstitions and religious practices of the medieval past. In some cases the churches were forced to adapt some traditions such as bell-ringing to their own purposes. Throughout, the communal nature of these traditions seems to sit uneasily with the independence and self-reliance that seems to be expressed in the wills produced by the Reformed. However the extent to which these medieval traditions survived and new ones were spawned suggests the difficulties which the Reformed tradition found in overcoming the anxieties and fears associated with death. The medieval Church, with its lengthy round of services, had offered a cathartic approach to death, but the desacralised burial of the Reformed Church went to the other extreme. In doing so, the Reformed failed to provide the reassurance that was needed to overcome this fear.

Appendix

The following paintings all include burial scenes, although this is not intended to be a comprehensive list:

Pieter Saenredam (c.1597–1665)

South aisle of the St Laurenskerk, Alkmaar, with a funeral procession, 1637, Penshurst, Major Philip Sidney.

Emanuel de Witte (c.1616–1691/1692)

Oude Kerk, Delft, 1654, Cat. No. 18.

St Janskerk, Utrecht, 1654, Cat. No. 93.

Oude Kerk, Amsterdam, Cat. No. 64.

Oude Kerk, Amsterdam, Museum Strassburg, Cat. No. 66.

Oude Kerk, Amsterdam, 165(4?), Cat. No. 44.

Oude Kerk, Amsterdam, Cat. No. 65.

Nieuwe Kerk, Delft, 1664, Residenz-Galerie, Salzburg, Cat. No. 28.

Protestant Church Interior, Museum Boymans-van Beuningen, Rotterdam, Cat. No. 131.

Protestant Church Interior, 166(1?), Cat. No. 101.

Protestant Church Interior, 1668, Museum Boymans-van Beuningen, Rotterdam, Cat. No. 112.

Protestant Church Interior, 1669, Rijksmuseum, Amsterdam, Cat. No. 109.

Nieuwe Kerk, Amsterdam, 1677, Museum of Fine Arts, Boston, Cat. No. 87.

Protestant Church Interior, Cat. No. 114.

Protestant Church Interior, 1680?, National Gallery of Scotland, Edinburgh, Cat. No. 113.

Oude Kerk, Amsterdam, Museum of Fine Arts, Springfield, Cat. No. 61.

Protestant Church Interior, 1677, Rijksmuseum, Amsterdam, Cat. No. 111.

Protestant Church Interior, 1679, Museum Strassburg, Cat. No. 106.

Protestant Church Interior, Staatliche Gemälde-galerie, Kassel, Cat. No. 108.

Protestant Church Interior, Rijksmuseum, Amsterdam, Cat. No. 102.

Protestant Church Interior, Museum der Bildenden Künste, Leipzig, Cat. No. 110.

Oude Kerk, Amsterdam, 16(80), Museum Boymans-van Beuningen, Rotterdam, Cat. No. 79.

Protestant Classical Church, Kunsthalle, Hamburg, Cat. No. 135.

Protestant Church Interior, 1687, Staatliche Kunstsammlungen, Weimar, Cat. No. 116.

Hendrik van Vliet (c.1612–1675)

Interior, St Laurenskerk, Rotterdam, 1652.

Interior, Pieters-kerk in Leiden, 1652, Herzog-Anton-Ulrich Museum, Brunswick.

View of the Interior, Oude Kerk, Delft, 1654, Museum der bildenden Künste, Leipzig.

Interior, Nieuwe Kerk, Delft, 1655, Pushkin State Museum of Fine Arts, Moscow..

Interior, Oude Kerk, Delft, with a Funeral Procession 1657, M. L. Wurfbain Fine Art, Oegstgeest.

Interior, Oude Kerk, Delft with the tomb of Maerten Harpertsz. Tromp, 1658 Museum of Art, Toledo, Ohio.

Interior, Oude Kerk, Delft, 1659, Museum der bildenden Künste, Sammlung Speck v. Sternburg, Lützschena, Leipzig.

Interior van de St Janskerk gezien naar het westen, toegeschreven aan Hendrik van Vliet, c.1661.

Interior, Oude Kerk, Delft, 1662, Staatliche Kunsthalle, Karlsruhe.

Interior, St Janskerk, Gouda, 1662, National Gallery, Melbourne.

Interior, Nieuwe Kerk, Delft with the tomb of William the Silent, 1667, Board of Trustees of the National Museums and Art Galleries on Merseyside, Walker Art Gallery, Liverpool.

Interior, Nieuwe Kerk, Delft, c.1660–62, Koninklijk Museum voor Schone Kunsten, Antwerp.

View of the Nieuwe Kerk, Delft, with the Memorial Plaque of Adriaen Teding van Berkhout, 1661, Stedelijk Museum Het Prinsenhof (on loan from the Stichting Teding van Berkhout), Delft.

Interior, Oude Kerk, Delft, 1669, Museum Stiftung Jakob Briner, Winterthur.

Church Interior, c.1670–75, Stedelijk Museum Het Prinsenhof, Delft.

Choir, Nieuwe Kerk, Delft, Narodowe Museum (officially attributed to Gerard Houck-geest), Warsaw.

Daniel de Blieck (?–1673)

Interior of the St Laurenskerk, Rotterdam, 1652, Peter H. Tillou Gallery, London.

Gerard Houkgeest (1600–1661)

Oude Kerk in Delft with the Tomb of Piet Heyn, 1650, Rijksmuseum, Amsterdam.

Interior of the Jacobskerk, The Hague, 1651, Kunstmuseum, Gemäldegalerie, Düsseldorf.

Cornelis de Man (1621–1706)

Interior of the Oude Kerk, Delft with Pulpit, 1660, The Art Institute of Chicago, Chicago.

Isaac van Nickelen (c.1630/35–1703)

De Grote of Sint-Bavokerk in Haarlem, 169?, Frans Hals Museum, Haarlem.

Sources: M. C. C. Kersten and D. H. A. C. Lokin, eds, *Delft Masters, Vermeer's Contemporaries. Illusionism through the Conquest of Light and Space* (Zwolle, 1996); National Gallery of Scotland, *Dutch Church Painters. Saenredam's 'Great Church at Haarlem' in context* (Edinburgh, 1984); *Perspectives: Saenredam and the architectural painters of the 17th century* (exhibition catalogue – 15/9–24/11/1991 – Museum Boymans-van Beuningen, Rotterdam); I. Manke, *Emanuel de Witte, 1617–1692* (Amsterdam, 1963); G. Schwartz and M. J. Bok, *Pieter Saenredam. The Painter and His Time* (New York, 1989).

Notes

1 The quotation comes from Donne's, 'Divine Meditations: Death be not Proud', *John Donne. The Complete English Poems*, A. J. Smith, ed. (1971), 313. My thanks are extended to Dr Jane Dawson (New College, Edinburgh) for her advice and comments on Scottish (especially Gaelic) attitudes to death and burial.

2 C. Gittings, *Death, Burial and the Individual in Early Modern England* (1984), 31–2. See also P. Binski, *Medieval Death. Ritual and Representation* (1996), 53–4.

3 J. Bossy, *Christianity in the West, 1400–1700* (Oxford, 1987), 33; N. Z. Davis, 'Some tasks and themes in the study of popular religion', in C. Trinkaus and H. A. Oberman, eds, *The Pursuit of Holiness in Late Medieval and Renaissance Religion* (Leiden, 1974), 331.

4 E. Duffy, *The Stripping of the Altars. Traditional Religion in England 1400–1580* (1992), 313–14, 340–1; J. Huizinga, *The Waning of the Middle Ages* (1955), 142, 145; R. Mandrou, *Introduction to Modern France 1500–1640. An Essay in Historical Psychology* (New York, 1976), 229–30; Davis, 'Tasks', 332. See also P. Marshall, Ch. 9, this volume.

5 Bossy, *Christianity in the West*, 27.

6 W. Birnie, *The Blame of Kirk-buriall, Tending to Cemeteriall Civilitie*, W. B. D. D. Turnball, ed. (1833), ch. 11.

7 Davis, 'Tasks', 334; N. L. Beatty, *The Craft of Dying. A Study in the Literary Tradition of the Ars Moriendi in England* (1970), 108–56; N. Z. Davis, 'Holbein's *Pictures of Death* and the Reformation at Lyons', *Studies in the Renaissance*, 3 (1956), 118–30.

8 *Registres de la compagnie des pasteurs de Genève au temps de Calvin*, J.-F. Bergier *et al.*, eds (Geneva, 1964), 1: 10.

9 J. Quick, ed., *Synodicon in Gallia Reformata* (1692), 1: 24, 131; *Livre Synodal contenant les articles résolues dans les Synodes des Eglises Wallonnes des Pays-Bas* (The Hague, 1896), 1: 4, 6, 10.

10 *The First Book of Discipline*, J. K. Cameron, ed. (Edinburgh, 1972), 199–200.

11 Funeral sermons were one area in which the practices of the Reformed churches differed, but it falls outside the scope of this chapter. See D. E. Stannard, *The Puritan Way of Death. A Study in Religion, Culture and Social Change* (Oxford, 1979), 103, 115–16, 129–31.

12 HRO, Winchester: Wills 1578/B/53.

13 A. N. Galpern, *The Religions of the People in Sixteenth-Century Champagne* (Cambridge, MA, 1976), 122–3.

14 This pamphlet is not paginated, so references are given to the relevant chapters.

15 Birnie, *Kirk-buriall*, Dedication.

16 Birnie had studied at St Andrews and later, Leiden. He was appointed to Lanark in 1597 and in 1612 was appointed Dean of the Chapel Royal. As a member of the Court of High Commission, he was concerned with the suppression of popery. *Fasti Ecclesiae Scoticanae. The Succession of Ministers in the Church of Scotland from the Reformation*, H. Scott *et al.*, eds (Edinburgh, 1915–), 3: 7.

17 *The Register of the Privy Council of Scotland*, J. Hill Burton *et al.*, eds (Edinburgh, 1877–), 6: 742.

18 *The First Book of Discipline*, 201.

19 T. Thomson, ed., *The Booke of the Universall Kirk of Scotland* (Edinburgh, 1839–45), 43.

20 *Visitation of the Diocese of Dunblane and Other Churches, 1586–1589*, J. Kirk, ed., Scottish Record Society, new Ser., 11 (Edinburgh, 1984), 3, 23, 30, 52, 53, 56, 59, 77, 84.

21 Priaulx Library, St Peter Port, Guernsey, *Papier ou livre des Colloques des Eglises de Guernezey (1585–1619)*, fol. 8v.

22 *Visitation of the Diocese of Dunblane and Other Churches*, 3, 14, 30.

23 M. Graham, 'Social discipline in Scotland, 1560–1610', in R. A. Mentzer, ed., *Sin and the Calvinists. Morals Control and the Consistory in the Reformed Tradition*, Sixteenth-century Essays and Studies, 32 (1994), 151.

24 Birnie, *Kirk-Buriall*, passim.

25 Bossy, *Christianity in the West,* 34. Burial of the unworthy within the church was also attacked by John Mirk in one of his homilies. *Mirk's Festial: A Collection of Homilies by Johannes Mirkus (John Mirk),* in T. Erbe, ed., *Early English Text Society,* 96 (1905), 297–9.

26 M. C. Smith, 'The Presbytery of St Andrews 1586–1605. A Study and annotated edition of the Register of the Minutes of the Presbytery of St Andrews. Vol. I' (Ph.D. thesis, University of St Andrews, 1985), 259–60.

27 The matter was referred to the Bishop of Glasgow. *Universall Kirk,* 272–3, 294.

28 Birnie, *Kirk-buriall,* ch. 19.

29 *Ibid.,* ch. 11.

30 *Ibid.,* ch. 17.

31 *Ibid.,* ch. 11.

32 A. Th. van Deursen, *Plain Lives in a Golden Age. Popular Culture, Religion and Society in Seventeenth-Century Holland* (Cambridge, 1991), 246.

33 *Universall Kirk,* 378, 733.

34 *Ibid.,* 280, 733, 937, 938.

35 *The Register of the Privy Council of Scotland,* 8: 425.

36 Smith, 'Presbytery of St Andrews', 189, 190, 191, 197, 201, 207.

37 *The Records of the Synod of Lothian and Tweedale, 1589–1596, 1640–1649,* J. Kirk, ed., Stair Society 30 (1977), 99.

38 *Universall Kirk,* 938. On the construction of burial aisles and monuments, see D. Howard, *Scottish Architecture from the Reformation to the Restoration, 1560–1660* (Edinburgh, 1995), 198–207.

39 Graham, 'Social Discipline in Scotland', 151.

40 *Privy Council,* 7: 315.

41 *Ibid.,* 7: 315–17, 337–8.

42 Birnie, *Kirk-buriall,* ch. 15.

43 *Ibid.,* ch. 19.

44 *Universall Kirk,* 388, 390.

45 D. Calderwood, *The History of the Kirk of Scotland,* T. Thomson, ed., Woodrow Society (Edinburgh 1843), 2: 525–6; Graham, 'Social discipline in Scotland', 151.

46 Pieter Saenredam, *South Aisle of the St Laurenskerk, Alkmaar with a funeral procession* (1637).

47 Hendrik van Vliet, *Interior of the Oude-Kerk, Delft with a Funeral Procession* (1657); Isaac van Nickelen, *De Grote of Sint Bavo-kerk in Haarlem* (169?).

48 G. Schwartz and M. J. Bok, *Pieter Saenredam. The Painter and His Time* (New York, 1989), 154.

49 See Appendix.

50 R. Ruus, 'Functions of Architectural Painting, with Special Reference to Church Interiors', *Perspectives: Saenredam and the Architectural Painters of the 17th Century* (Museum Boymans-van Beuningen, Rotterdam, 15 Sept.–24 Nov. 1991), 47; B. Heisner, 'Mortality and faith: the figural motifs within Emanuel de Witte's Dutch church interiors', *Studies in Iconography,* 6 (1980), 110–12, 113, 117–21.

51 A. C. Duke, *Reformation and Revolt in the Low Countries* (1990), 259.

52 Van Deursen, *Plain Lives,* 263.

53 C. D. van Strien, *British Travellers in Holland during the Stuart Period. Edward Browne and John Locke in the United Provinces* (Leiden, 1993), 216. I am grateful to Dr A. C. Duke for this reference.

54 Pieter Saenredam, *South Aisle of the St Laurenskerk, Alkmaar, with a Funeral Procession* (1637); Hendrik van Vliet, *Interior of the Oude Kerk, Delft with a Funeral Procession* (1657); Isaac van Nickelen, *De Grote of Sint-Bavokerk in Haarlem* (169?).

55 Van Strien, *British Travellers,* 217.

56 B. J. Kaplan, *Calvinists and Libertines. Confession and Community in Utrecht, 1578–1620* (Oxford, 1995), 270. An example of a *beaardingskistje,* which contained the consecrated earth which was scattered in the coffin, dating from 1651, is on display in the Museum

   Amstelkring, Amsterdam.
57 Quoted in Duke, *Reformation*, 228.
58 Van Deursen, *Plain Lives*, 245–6.
59 Duke, *Reformation*, 259, 260.
60 Van Deursen, *Plain Lives*, 244.
61 Duke, *Reformation*, 260; Kaplan, *Calvinists*, 285–6.
62 N. Z. Davis, 'The rites of violence', in Davis, ed., *Society and Culture in Early Modern France* (Oxford, 1987), 171. For other examples, see E. Benoît, *Histoire de l'Edit de Nantes* (Delft, 1693–95), 2: 346–7; P. Benedict, *Rouen during the Wars of Religion* (Cambridge, 1981), 64; P. Roberts, *A City in Conflict. Troyes during the French Wars of Religion* (Manchester, 1996), 89–90; Kaplan, *Calvinists*, 263; R. G. Dottie, 'The recusant riots at Childwall in May 1600: a reappraisal', *Transactions of the Historic Society of Lancashire and Cheshire*, 132 (1983), 9–11. I am grateful to M. Luc Racaut for this last reference.
63 Binski, *Medieval Death*, 56.
64 Roberts, *Troyes*, 88–90.
65 Quick, *Synodicon*, 245.
66 J. Garrisson, *Protestants du Midi, 1559–1598* (Toulouse, 1991), 250.
67 Quick, *Synodicon*, 204.
68 J. Pannier, *L'Eglise Réformée de Paris sous Henri IV* (Paris, 1911), 390; D. Nicholls, 'Protestants, Catholics and magistrates in Tours, 1562–1572: the making of a Catholic city during the religious wars', *French History*, 8 (1994), 23.
69 B. S. Tinsley, *History and Polemics in the French Reformation. Florimond de Raemond: Defender of the Church* (1992), 57–8.
70 Benoît, *Nantes*, 1: 232.
71 Pannier, *L'Eglise*, 386–87; G. Hanlon, *Confession and Community in Seventeenth-Century France. Catholic and Protestant Coexistence in Aquitaine* (Philadelphia, 1993), 22.
72 Benoît, *Nantes*, 1: 364–5, 379; 2: 97–8, 257, 278, 449, 473–4; Hanlon, *Confession*, 154, 166–7.
73 Mandrou, *France*, 231; Binski, *Medieval Death*, 56.
74 CUL, MS Dd 11.43 Jersey Colloquy Minutes, 1577–1614, fol. 4v; G.E. Lee, *Discipline Ecclésiastique des Iles de la Manche 1576 et 1597* (Guernsey, 1885), 14.
75 W. McMillan, *The Worship of the Scottish Reformed Church, 1550–1638* (1931), 296.
76 D. M. Ogier, *Reformation and Society on Guernsey* (Woodbridge, 1996), 121; J. Stevens, 'Les funerailles à Jersey', in *Du berceau à la Tombe: Les rites de passage. Revue du Département de la Manche*, 26 (1984), 267.
77 St Peter Port, Greffe Archives, *Crime (Livre des enquestes)* 2: fos. 1–1v, 6v–8. I am grateful to Dr Ogier for this reference and also for a preview of his book which is cited above.
78 McMillan, *Worship*, 295.

11

The fear of disease
and the disease of fear[1]

DAVID GENTILCORE

On 28 July 1615 a peasant named Dionisio Spisani appeared before an episcopal investigation being held in the diocese of Bologna. A notary was
taking down depositions in the wake of a spate of miracles which had
occurred upon the discovery of an image of Our Lady in the church of the
hospital of Santa Maria della Vita.[2] Dionisio, from Lavoletto, just outside
Bologna, told the notary of a miracle the Virgin had performed on his wife,
Domenica. The young couple had been married for just one year and
Domenica was four or five months pregnant when, on her way to meet her
husband at a neighbour's house, 'she saw I don't know what, that passed
before her eyes, and she heard a footstep (*pestaria*) in the trough near our
house, and she was afraid of this, and started to run, and ran into the
[neighbour's] house'. When Dionisio arrived at the neighbour's, his wife
told him nothing of the fright she had suffered. She only told him that they
should go home to bed, 'and she showed no sign of having any complaint
whatsoever'.

That was on Friday 10 July. Six days later Domenica, her husband and
several other women were threshing grain. Towards evening Domenica
returned home, only to fall senseless to the ground at the doorway of their
house. None of the threshers knew of this until some of them went back
to the house to fetch something to drink, and saw her lifeless on the
ground. Taking her for dead, they began screaming and Dionisio ran home
to investigate the cause of the commotion. They carried her inside and put
her on the bed. Half an hour later Domenica came to her senses, began
speaking and got up out of bed, as if nothing had happened. Then, half an
hour later, standing at the doorway, she was again taken ill, and they put
her to bed, where she remained until the following Monday.

By then it appeared to all that Domenica was possessed, 'because she
screamed and hit herself and did things'. They tied her up so she would
not hurt herself. But Dionisio, obviously suspecting something was amiss,

had sent one of his brothers-in-law to a priest in Bologna on Sunday. Don Stefano was well known for an oil of his which had the power to reveal whether people were bewitched (*guasti*) or not. Then, at lunchtime on Tuesday, Domenica said that she wanted to go to Bologna, to the church of Santa Maria della Vita. She jumped down from bed and went into the street, wearing just 'her blouse, apron and open bodice', and started running in the direction of Bologna. They caught up with her at Lavoletto's church and forcibly led her inside. A female relative then brought some of her clothes and dressed her, after which they departed for Bologna.

On the way there, and especially as the party approached the church of Santa Maria della Vita, Domenica shouted out, over and over, 'Mary, I'm coming; Mary, I'm coming.' Once inside, Domenica knelt before the altar of Our Lady, where she began

> shouting, cursing, screaming and throwing herself on the ground, and in this way she fell backwards for about an hour's time with several fainting spells, and three times she snuffed out a candle from the altar with her left hand, and at the third snuffing out of the said candle the demons finished leaving her, and my wife fell backwards and remained senseless for about a quarter of an hour.

When she came to she calmly said that she had been freed from the Devil by the Madonna della Vita. The party, together with all those who had gathered in the church, gave thanks to Our Lady for the miracle. They then returned home. Dionisio concluded his account before the notary by noting that his wife, 'by the grace of God and the Blessed Virgin, has never again done anything like what she did then and is healthy and sane'.

It would be all too easy to interpret this event from the point of view of modern biomedicine and label Domenica's disease as some sort of psychosomatic syndrome or disorder. This label would serve as a clinical explanation for her behaviour. But in so doing we would miss the opportunity the account provides to explore the ways in which illness was perceived in early modern Italy – a world where fear-induced diseases and possession were part of normal, comprehensible, experience, a world where a fright could be implicitly linked to the onset of other symptoms and, finally, demonic possession and insanity.

An account like Dionisio Spisani's allows microhistorians to engage in their favourite pastime: taking an apparently irrational, unusual event to unravel a whole complex of beliefs and practices. My effort is a contribution towards putting culture back into medical history and medicine and healing back into culture. An early work in the field of medical anthropology stressed the need to produce 'culturally oriented studies of illness'. I have taken to heart the suggestion that one should study 'an illness – its genesis, mechanism, descriptive features, treatment and resolution – as an event having cultural significance'.[3] Disease is not simply a set of symptoms. Revolving around it are the complex and elaborate ways in which illness itself is perceived and responded to, how it is diagnosed, which healers are sought out, if any, how such choices are made, and what therapeutic procedures are performed. One way out of the endless labyrinth of cultural possibilities – all cultural phenomena related to the illness experience – is to focus on one particular set of symptoms or illness. This approach has been advocated as a way of supplying context to the social history of medicine, 'by tracing as many of the threads as possible that lead from and to any given medical focus, by being conscious of doing so, and by conceptualising the relationships discovered in this way'.[4] In this chapter I shall be exploring fear, as both an emotional response to illness and as illness itself. The 'period eye' of treatise-writers, physicians and sufferers – most of all the sufferers – will be extended by means of the related studies of medical anthropologists, in an unashamed use of the regressive method to shed light on somewhat obscure aspects of the past.

The records that form the basis of this study, the miracle narratives, are a useful source for exploring personal ideas about illness. Their richness allows us more than a passing nod to the experience-centred approach favoured by some folklorists.[5] The narratives detail the entire illness episode, from the moment when the illness was first perceived, or when an accident occurred, through attempts to deal with it and, of course, culminating in miraculous intervention after these attempts fail.[6] Illness episodes, as recounted to the bishop's notary, like stories of illness told to family and friends, privilege specific moments: (i) the discovery of illness or the occurrence of a traumatic accident; (ii) initial attempts to respond to this; (iii) the decision to have recourse to the Virgin when these fail; and (iv) the miraculous intercession.

    Dionisio Spisani's simple account is noteworthy in several respects. Like the other depositions in the investigation, its spontaneity and relative lack of structure would suggest that it is a fairly accurate rendering of the deponent's own words. Striking too is the sufferer's independence of mind: it was Domenica who diagnosed what was wrong with her, decided on the appropriate treatment and determined when a cure had been accomplished. Sadly, we do not have Domenica's own words. Given the inferior legal status of women, the voice of her closest male relative may have been deemed sufficient. And yet, in most of the other incidents narrated in the course of the investigation, we have depositions from several people: the

sufferer or victim, as well as family and friends. In the case of Domenica
Spisani, the investigation may not have seen the incident as worthy of further investigation; or it may have been that only her husband was able to
come to Bologna to testify (as far as we know, Domenica was still pregnant).

Any image depicting the Virgin Mary or the saints was worthy of ven-
eration. Italian cities were full of images, not only in the private domain,
but in the public world: images on walls, at street-corners, in wayside altars
and, of course, in churches.[7] When miracles, centred around a particular
image, began to occur the Counter-Reformation Church authorities were
quick to investigate the situation.[8] The Church sought to ensure that any
cult developing around the image was of an orthodox nature, that the miracles reported were genuine and that the often substantial donations were
not being put to illicit or fraudulent uses. The situation could be especially
difficult when the image was painted on a privately-owned building or town
wall and the local bishop had to proceed through regular legal channels,
sometimes in opposition to other interest groups (for whom financial considerations might outweigh devotional ones). Things were much more
straightforward when the image was found in a church, already under episcopal jurisdiction. There was nothing unusual about these investigations;
indeed, they were almost routine. Around the time of the investigation
which concerns us here, there were four Marian images in Bologna and its
hinterland which had occasioned similar spates of miracles and which had
likewise been the focus of episcopal investigations.[9]

The church of Santa Maria della Vita itself was attached to a large hospital, run by the confraternity of the same name, and located in the heart
of Bologna, between via Clavature and via Pescharia, parallel streets running east from the Piazza Maggiore.[10] The presence of a miraculous image
in a hospital church is a convenient reminder of the close ties between natural and supernatural forms of healing. Yet despite the proximity of hospital and image, only one of the *miracolati* had stayed at the hospital.[11] Most
of the witnesses had absolutely no connection with the hospital; it was the
image's reputation that had drawn them into the church. The miraculous
image fitted conveniently into the confraternity's ongoing struggle for status
and prestige. It was already one of the city's largest property-holders when,
in 1585, Pope Sixtus V conferred upon it the rank of archconfraternity,
making it the focal point for a group of ten lesser city confraternities.[12] The
image would be used to bolster this important position still further. The
miracles associated with it would be used as advertising to spread the
image's fame, attracting devotees to the church. Although I have referred
to the handsome manuscript collection of depositions as an 'investigation',

the status of the image was never really in dispute. The words of the patri-
cian confrères were not called into question. They were present and over-
saw things — even stage-managed them — from the start, much in the way
a Religious Order might. Their support of the image, the awe it inspired in
the confrères, was typical of Counter-Reformation devotion. It was indeed
a long way from the attack on the cult of saints, especially invocation of the
Virgin, made by one of their own members in the very different religious
climate of the 1540s.[13]

Even the discovery of the Marian image was retold as a prodigious
event, a foretaste of the wonders to come. The image was already on the
way to acquiring its own discovery narrative, its own oral tradition, linking
it to — and explaining — the subsequent miraculous events. Whilst scraping
the walls in preparation for whitewashing, a painter uncovered a fresco
depicting the Virgin's face. He was so moved that, as he worked, 'my heart
wept in my body and tears started to come to my eyes and my insides were
touched'.[14] Eventually an entire image of the Virgin was revealed, seated 'in
great majesty', holding the infant Jesus (Figure 3). What in our times would
bring art scholars to investigate a previously unknown work, in seventeenth-
century Bologna attracted devotees from throughout the city. The miracles
began with the confraternity's chamberlain, whose baby boy was cured.
Soon the church was filled with people from dawn to dusk, 'offering that
most holy image vows and presents of gold and silver, of various types and
shapes, small and large'. Sixty or seventy masses were being said every day,
many with musical accompaniment, according to private requests. Rich
tapestries and hangings now adorned the walls, the gifts of devotees. An
altar was installed beneath the image, the altar of St Francis and the Blessed
Riniero (the confraternity's beloved founder) having been moved to the
other side of the church to accommodate it.[15] The crowds of people present
in the church, attracted by the image, forms a constant setting for many of
the illness episodes narrated in the depositions.[16]

The depositions were recorded in the sacristy of the church by the
archbishop's notary, Pirro Belliosso. They were taken over a two-year
period, from October 1614 to November 1616, based on the miracolati who
presented themselves. In a typical example, one woman 'recounted [her
miracle] to that priest who collects donations inside by the door, and he
then fetched a doctor to whom we likewise said what I have said above to
you [the notary], and he then fetched you, the notary'.[17] Witnesses and miracolati came from a variety of social backgrounds, from noblemen and colle-
giate priests, with patrimonies of several thousands of ducats, through to
landless peasants, with barely a lira to their name.[18] It is impossible to say
how much the notary himself influenced the testimony and how much of the

A depiction of the image of Santa Maria della Vita, which forms the
frontispiece to the miracle collection compiled by the Bolognese
archconfraternity. (Archiginnasio di Bologna, *Fondo Ospedali,* no. 28.)

words are those of the deponents. Belliosso does ask the occasional question and translate the proceedings into Tuscan Italian (although traces of Bolognese remain).[19] But most of the depositions consist of uninterrupted narration, complete with the occasional repetition and *non sequitur* typical of oral speech.

What is striking throughout the miracle narratives is how the word fear, *paura*, is used in relation to disease. The title of this chapter is not just a play on words, but is meant to evoke this ambivalent usage. The 'fear of disease' is primarily about the anxiety or anguish that accompanies severe illness, whilst the 'disease of fear' is primarily about sudden fright or alarm. In either case, 'fear' (*paura*) is the term most often applied to the resulting emotional responses or states.[20]

It might be helpful, at this stage, to unravel further the interwoven conceptual threads before we proceed. In his 1920 study *Beyond the Pleasure Principle*, Sigmund Freud distinguished between fright, fear and anxiety, according to the relationship between the subject and the danger.[21] Thus 'fright' refers to the state we fall into when suddenly confronted by a dangerous situation for which we are not prepared. 'Fear' presupposes a definite object of which one is afraid. Whilst 'anxiety' refers to a state characterised by expecting and preparing for a danger, even if unknown or imagined. Freud stressed the fact that common usage tended to employ the three terms interchangeably, virtually as synonyms. This was an error he wanted to clarify. However, it is precisely the confusion in usage that can tell us much about the relationship between fear and disease in early modern Italy.

It should come as no surprise that the people of early modern Italy feared disease. Fear is a constant and central feature of individual and collective existence. We are conscious of our own mortality. However, although we realise that we are part of the world and must submit to its rules, nowhere in the world do people accept sickness and death as perfectly natural and thus not requiring special notice or explanation.[22] Fear is a response to the spirit of self-preservation and the instinct for survival. Faced with some sudden and threatening occurrence, an intense emotive state is triggered, which can have serious mental and physical consequences. This much is organic and more or less unchanging. For this reason, studying fear as an end in itself would not be very revealing.[23] The emotive reaction only becomes of interest to the historian when we explore it as a cultural expression, studying the range of beliefs and practices that surround it (as exemplified by the contributions to this volume).

In search of signposts, it seemed natural to turn to psychology. Surprisingly (at least to one outside the discipline), the fear of disease is so much taken for granted that it has rarely been the subject of serious study. It only acquires interest, it would seem, when the fear becomes extreme, irrational: a phobia.[24] Even illness phobia, the fear of a single symptom or illness, has been little studied, despite its frequency.[25] What is of relevance here is the way illness phobias are part of the culture surrounding disease. They reflect the preoccupations present in the culture at large or in a community or family subculture. The response to pain and disease takes place within an elaborate cultural context in which sufferers, their families and communities respond in socially patterned ways. Thus previous family history of disease may sensitise family members to particular illnesses or parts of the body. Moreover, generalised anxiety, depression or loneliness can serve to lower the threshold at which people ask for help, leading to increased illness behaviour.[26]

Discussion of fear in early modern Europe has found fruitful ground in dealing with collective experiences: for example, aspects of community reactions to plague as explored by Jenner, Chapter 3, and Naphy, Chapter 2, in this volume. The miracle narratives allow us to shift the emphasis to the individual experience. What I wish to discuss here is not so much fear of the possibility of illness as the feelings of dread and anxiety that accompany the sudden onset of symptoms and the possibilities that emerge from this. This emotion presupposes an ability to anticipate possible events. The lack of a precise, circumventable threat, however, may prevent any decisive action.[27] A sense of foreboding pervades all the accounts, occasionally erupting into terror, especially during the first two phases of discovery and initial responses. It may be as straightforward as a man telling his wife: 'I am afraid that I have ruptured myself', after a fit of coughing upon getting up out of bed.[28] Since a hernia could mean wearing a wooden and canvas truss, perhaps for the rest of one's life (in preference to risky surgery), this was not to be taken lightly. Or it might consist of an explicit linking of disease to death, as when a boy miraculously cured of 'pustules, flux and bad fever' recounts that he had been ill 'for a while, and I was dead sick, and I was afraid I would die'.[29] There is also fear as panic, not knowing what to do. After Ercole Manzoni's young son received a splinter in his eye,

> his eyes turned very black, and I said to him 'see if you can open your eyes a little', which he wanted to do but could not, but started screaming very loudly, and because his mother and I were weeping and we did not know what to do about it, I said to my wife 'I do not know what to do.'

The only response, Ercole decided, was to kneel and pray to the Virgin, beseeching her intercession on the boy's behalf.[30]

The lack of fear may be as remarkable to the modern reader as its presence. Fear is not the only emotional response to illness. This is especially the case when the sufferers and their families have diagnosed the complaint as non-life-threatening. It is surprising the extent to which the sick and their families learn to live with symptoms that we might consider intolerable, secure as we are in the knowledge that they can be dealt with effectively. One woman, Margarita Galliani, recounted feeling a mixture of disgust and shame at the fistula growing next to her daughter's right eye. 'It was a sickening thing to see, so that sometimes I was ashamed to take her out of the house with me, since it turned the stomachs of those who looked at her', she commented. And yet, though the fistula continued to grow for a further nine years, she had nothing done about it, because two physicians had told her that the fistula would have to be burnt, and Margarita was afraid for the child's eye. The miracle cure resolved her dilemma.[31]

Medical practitioners figure only rarely in this collection of miracle narratives.[32] Instead, the narratives evoke the importance of the family unit and a close circle of relatives, friends and neighbours in dealing with disease. Following the eruption of the symptoms into everyday life, the first response is diagnosis. Usually, in the early modern period, this is self-diagnosis (though this must be taken to include the circle of family and friends). Identifying the problem, its origin and nature, offered sufferers a degree of control that was in itself therapeutic. Diagnosis is the beginning of the healing process, paving the way for further therapeutic action. Indeed, one cause of fear was not being able to identify the nature of the illness because it meant that no beneficial action could be taken. The simple words 'and I didn't know what this illness was', uttered by a suffering father about his sick child, belie an ongoing intense anguish.[33]

The therapeutic process itself could involve a whole range of healers. Early modern Europe was a medically pluralistic society. However, it was the sick themselves, and their family and friends, who chose the forms of treatment. This may include rejecting treatment, as we have just seen with the young girl's troublesome fistula. The possibility of a miracle cure offers an alternative. In the miracle narratives, sacred healing supplements natural forms. Miracles served a vital role in supplementing the relatively limited technical abilities of early modern physic and surgery. One speciality of the image of the Madonna della Vita was hernias. A maker and seller of 'trusses, ligatures and bags' for hernia sufferers, with a workshop in Bologna, is even among the deponents. 'And', he boasted, 'I am always around the square to sell the said trusses, and I have made them for gentlemen, townsmen and paupers' (we can hear traces of the mountebank's patter).[34] As we noted above, there was not much that could be done about hernias. There were surgical interventions, but these were dangerous, painful and of dubious success. And let us not forget that linked to a fear of illness was the fear of medical treatment (think of prevailing modern-day attitudes to dentists). Hernia trusses were thus a fact of life for many. Our maker of trusses was in fact a medical practitioner. Sufferers would come to his shop and he would ascertain the nature of the hernia by feeling the swelling.

A fifty-year-old coachman named Giovanni de Berti recounted how he had suffered a hernia twenty-three years earlier and was forced to wear a truss. 'Jesus, how I suffered ... even though I had the truss my guts would come down and come out through the rupture I had and very often in the evening they were so large and swollen outside that I had to lie down ... and I could not put them back inside without great difficulty.' When he heard of the miracles the Madonna della Vita was performing he started recommending himself to her, and praying before the image each morning, hearing two or three masses. No medical practitioner figures in the account. It is Giovanni who decides he has been cured. 'And my continual going to her and beseeching her that she do as I have said [i.e., 'free me from my infirmity'] lasted until I saw and understood for myself that I no longer have that defect and am completely cured.' He adds by way of proof that despite coughs and sneezes and going without the truss for four days his 'guts no longer descend' and his side is smooth (which he shows the notary).[35]

What sort of rapport did sufferers establish with the Madonna? As ever in religion, devotion mingled with practical needs. Choices about healers – natural and supernatural – were of crucial importance. We must not think, however, that once this was decided on the practitioner was necessarily allowed to take over. Sufferers and their family and friends were never passive. Following on from self-diagnosis, patients would proceed to tell practitioners what they wanted done. It was common to reach an agreement on the treatment – the forms it would take, its duration and its cost – often formalised into a notarised contract between the two parties, practitioner and patient. Payment was only forthcoming at stipulated stages in the treatment, the larger part being withheld until the treatment was finished and, most important, successful.[36]

Sufferers could approach Our Lady and the saints in exactly the same way. Scholars have often been at odds to explain the way devotees beseeched the Virgin for a miraculous cure, bribing her with the promise to go on pilgrimage or leave a votive offering at the shrine in exchange for her intercession, which she could not refuse. Demands of this sort smacked too much of the mechanical efficacy of magical rites to be an example of faith and piety.[37] But there is a way out of this impasse. The bargaining between saint and devotee may be better depicted as akin to the healing contract between practitioner and patient, into which both parties enter voluntarily. In the words of the hernia victim Giorgio Bellioti: 'I pledged myself (mi avodij) to the most holy Madonna della Vita, that if she healed and liberated me from this hernia illness I wanted to have two masses said for her and bring her two candles.'[38] There is nothing mechanical or automatic about the arrangement; believers still put themselves into the hands of the divine. But the interests of both parties had to be served. And like the healing contract, 'payment' was made only after the successful outcome.

What factors induced the young Domenica Spisani, pregnant for the first time, to put down her illness and possession to a fright she had experienced? How could a fright lead to illness in early modern Italy? To begin with, there was no doubt that strong emotions could affect the body, resulting in disease. Judging by the late twentieth-century rise of stress as a factor in diseases, and medical labels like 'post-traumatic stress disorder', it might seem as if we had just discovered the close interconnection between mind and body. But of course the holistic approach is not new to medicine. The close connection between mind and body, alien to Enlightenment thought, was reintroduced early this century when the body began to be regarded as a psychosomatic unit. It was a way of accounting for very real but variable complaints like peptic ulcers, migraines, asthma and, more recently, hypertension. 'Pschysomatic' may have been a new term, but it was an ancient concept.

For early modern Europeans the body affected the mind and the mind affected the body. The same bad humours that caused disease would, according to Robert Burton, trouble the spirits, 'sending gross fumes into the brain'. These, in turn, would disturb the soul and all its faculties, bringing about fear and sorrow, the 'ordinary symptoms' of melancholy. Conversely, 'the mind most effectually works upon the body, producing by his passions and perturbations miraculous alterations, as melancholy, despair, cruel diseases, and sometimes death itself'.[39] Based on the still-dominant Hippocratic corpus, conditions like mania, characterised by excitement, and melancholy, characterised by depression, were still seen in essentially biological terms. Melancholy, for example, was by definition an excess of black bile. The key to health lay in the maintenance of bodily balance, avoiding excess or extremes. The emotions or passions, as one of the Galenic six 'non-naturals', had to be carefully managed in order to conserve or restore health.[40] Francis Bacon was drawing on this tradition when he wrote: 'as for the passions and studies of the mind, avoid envy, anxious fears, anger fretting inwards, subtile and knotty inquisitions, joys and exhilarations in excess, sadness not communicated'.[41]

Strong emotions – anger, fright, impressions, delusions, imagined things – were thus major causes of illness. 'With all these phenomena', Barbara Duden has pointed out, 'there occurred an exchange between outside and inside, and the inner body mediated what happened to it in the outside world'.[42] This was as much part of the popular tradition as of the learned in the early modern period. Given the acknowledged power of the imagination, early modern Europeans – basing themselves on classical tradition – realised that the fear of disease could be as harmful as the disease itself. (The illness phobias of twentieth-century pschoanalysis are not completely new.) Such was the power of the emotions, and the link between mind and body, that fear of a disease could result in one's becoming sick with it.[43] In Robert Burton's words:

> Men, if they but see another man tremble, giddy, or sick of some fearful disease, their apprehension and fear is so strong in this kind, that they will have the same disease. Or if by some soothsayer, wise-man, fortune-teller, or physician, they be told that they shall have such a disease, they will so seriously apprehend it, that they will instantly labour of it.[44]

Aside from the way Burton pluralistically puts physicians on a par with various cunning folk, what is striking about this passage is the reality of the resulting complaint. Fear could even lead to death itself. Burton continues: 'I have heard of one that, coming by chance in company of him that was thought to be sick of the plague (which was not so), fell down suddenly dead. Another was sick of the plague with conceit.'[45]

Plague was a special case, where individual fear could not be separated from the collective response. A late sixteenth-century Modenese chronicle, detailing the disastrous effects of plague, remarked that many more died of 'hunger, fear and torment' than of the disease itself.[46] The idea was ancient in origin and still widely held. Ludovico Antonio Muratori, in his 1721 treatise on dealing with plague, pointed out at some length that

> the strong passions of the heart, ruling contagion, can be called the first grave-diggers of man. All the physicians proclaim with one voice that one should flee from rage, melancholy and terror as from plague itself ... . Once the imagination is wounded and the spirits and humours put into disordered movement by some frightening spectacle, the pestilential poison is all too easily taken, and even without the plague death sometimes occurs from pure consternation and black humour.[47]

The sources of fear during plague were many and frequent. In normal times the sick were surrounded by relatives, healers and priests, all bringing comfort. But during times of plague, human relations were inverted, as Jean Delumeau has pointed out. Gone were the rituals uniting sufferers with those attending them. Instead, plague victims were shut in their own homes or removed to lazarets outside the town walls.[48] In the words of Muratori:

> It is too easy for one to lose courage and die of fright, seeing and hearing the ministers of the lazarets and grave-diggers go about with horrible faces, bizarre clothes and frightening voices and bear away the sick and the healthy, living and dead, as long as there is something to pilfer. Nor can one describe the horror caused by the frequent ringing of their bells.[49]

The power of the emotions and human imagination, by means of their effects on the blood, also lay behind explanations of how sorcery and fascination worked. For the professor of philosophy at Padua and Bologna, Pietro Pomponazzi, the power of the soul and its imagination and emotion first altered the blood and spirits in the human agent's own body. The blood and spirits then produce vapours and exhalations which act upon the victim's body by subtle and insensible means, but all the more potent for that, through the pores.[50] It was in this way that one person could transmit disease to another.

It was acknowledged that the more violent and sudden the emotion, the greater the effect on the body. Especially pernicious were what Burton referred to as 'terrors and affrights'. Their effect was to 'suddenly alter the whole temperature of the body, move the soul and spirits, strike such a deep impression, that the parties can never be recovered, causing more grievous and fiercer melancholy than any inward cause whatsoever'. The fright thus 'impresses' itself upon the spirits, brain and humours to such a degree that, in particularly serious cases, letting all the blood out of the body would not suffice to remove the impression.[51]

Blood, and its flow, was the key. The blood was the site of diseases of the soul, the *animi passiones* that caused imbalances and perturbations in human equilibrium. From the time of the ancients, every student of medicine had known that the blood flowed from the heart to the head, ebbing back by the same path. Life and health were linked to the blood's quality and purity. Being bled was part of a seasonal routine, an element in every kind of treatment, to restore or maintain the body's humoural balance. The Capuchin friar and nurse Felice Passera da Bergamo wrote that

> of the soul [blood] is the chiefest instrument, of the humours it is the most noble; it is it that gives our bodies strength and beauty; it is it that generates the spirits and nourishes our flesh; it is it that is justly called nature's treasure, whence originates the proverb that, wishing to say that something is very dear, it is said that it costs blood.[52]

As it emerges from the eighteenth-century patient histories Duden has studied, fright was caused by sudden, unexpected, unusual events: a mouse that jumped at a pregnant woman, thunderbolts, a violent quarrel, a sudden illness or death, a ghost. Young girls were victims more often than older women, and pregnant women and women in childbed were especially threatened. Fright 'struck the limbs' and drove the blood to the heart. It caused the monthly bleeding to stagnate. Women also requested a prescription against fright for afflictions like heart constriction, anxiousness and fearfulness. Bloodletting was the common remedy for fright, to counter the blood blockage, as well as remedies to re-establish the menses.[53]

The 'looseness' of women's blood meant that they were more vulnerable to diseases caused by the emotions. Their blood was also less pure than that of men. Women were considered defective, incomplete men, in need of the regular purging action of the menses. Nowhere is this more clearly expressed than in the words of the Modenese physician Giovanni Marinello in his 1574 treatise on the diseases of women. Following Aristotle, he wrote that woman, 'for her frigidity and humidity [is] a weak man and as if made by accident', who each month had to expel all the accumulated 'excessive' excrement and 'superfluous humours'.[54] But male treatise-writers could, and did, come to the opposite conclusion regarding menstruation. Lodovico Domenichi, writing in praise of the female body, suggested that it provided an enviable regular cleansing of the body and a means of maintaining its balance. He did not see menstruation as a sign that women were less clean to begin with. Indeed, because men did not experience the benefits of menstruation, they remained 'still less clean and pure' than women. For Domenichi menstruation was a divine gift bestowed on women. But God's gift did not end there. Menstrual blood also had health-giving powers of its own. Domenichi advocated its use as a medicine to cure quartan fever, the bites of rabid dogs, elephantiasis, melancholic frenzy and insanity. Whereas the Milanese physician and natural philosopher Girolamo Cardano, writing at the same time, referred to its traditional, Aristotelian, capacity to harm everything from growing crops to mirrors, this was inverted by Domenichi, who praised its virtues in putting out fires, calming storms and waves, undoing spells and keeping away evil demons.[55]

In any case, popular and learned traditions overlapped to the extent that they shared the knowledge that pregnant women were the most susceptible of all to the effects of the emotions and the imagination. This extended to the child they were carrying. The idea that a woman's imagination, especially when fixed on something, could impress itself upon the foetus has a long pedigree and was of great interest to early modern medicine. 'A woman's strong imagination and fixed thought has the power to shape the creature's body in likeness and image to the desired object', the

Roman physician Girolamo Mercurio states in his 1596 midwifery treatise.[56] Likewise Ambroise Paré, in his lively work on the subject of monstrous births, noted that from the time of conception to the full formation of the child – thirty-five days for boys and forty-two days for girls – the pregnant woman was advised to avoid looking on monstrous things in order not to give birth to a 'monster'.[57]

As far as Domenica Spisani was concerned her fear was both an emotional reaction and an illness. The unexpected hearing of a footstep, the fainting spells in the doorway, indeed the final possession itself, were part of the same cultural construction. Even today in many regions of Italy, the word *paura* is used to denote an illness the origins of which are interpreted as lying in a fright or shock experienced by the sufferer.[58] Cause and effect go under the same name. A person can be suffering from fear because they experienced fear. The distinction between fright, fear and anxiety fades, the instantaneous violence of the former leading to the diffuse permanent state of the latter.[59] In this social construction of the emotions, fear is domesticated. It is rendered manageable by the labelling process.

The concept of *paura* is more than just a means of making sense of the individual's response when confronted by material dangers, and even more than the short- and long-term physiological symptoms that might result. For *paura* can also denote the agents who lie at the root of these afflictions. It can personify fears into figures as diverse as ogres, ghosts and demons.[60] It can extend to certain topographic sites, places associated with witches and ghostly apparitions. And, on a symbolic, mythical level, fear can also take the form of animals and trees, becoming objectified in the process.[61] In earlier centuries any of these phenomena could have been seen as diabolical, manifestations of evil spirits at work. Sudden noises at night could easily be put down to 'evil spirits', a conclusion reached by two women of Gallipoli when one night they heard plates crashing on the ground and pounding noises. They eventually realised that the noises were caused by someone who had broken into their house. However, as they told the court notary who came to their house to record their accusation: 'we would have come [to the tribunal] in person, without troubling you [the notary] to come here, had we not been ill as you see, because of the shock and fear which still keeps us in a serious condition'.[62] We do not learn from Dionisio Spisani's account whether his wife thought her fright was caused by an evil spirit. But if this was Domenica's conclusion it would make the subsequent possession easier to understand.

The traumatic situation can result from various incidents, from a single sudden and violent noise to a fall, from the sight of a serpent to an encounter with a ghost. To be labelled as *paura* – and not, say, sorcery or the evil eye, which can cause similar ailments – the sufferer must have the tell-tale symptoms as well as a plausible antecedent causal event. This may be recent, as in Domenica Spisani's case, or hidden somewhere in the long-term memory. Diagnostic procedures may be complex, subject to negotiation. Diagnosis is first and foremost an attempt to determine causation. Hence Dionisio Spisani's recourse to the Bolognese priest's holy oil, which was able to determine the presence, or absence, of a spell. In Domenica's case it meant, apparently, that her symptoms were caused, not by magic, but by some other agent.

In Italy *paura* is a cultural survival. Although it is 'popular' now, in the sense that it survives in poorer, rural areas of the peninsula, its ancestry is part of a cultural tradition shared with learned medicine. Similar conditions associated with fear and fright are to be found throughout the world – in the Philippines, India, China, Bali – part of ancient and well-articulated medical traditions.[63] But the Italian version is most similar to the semantically-related *susto* (literally, shock or fright) of South America.[64] In Italy, what was once ascribed by humoural tradition to the experience of all strong emotions is now, in popular culture, limited to a single emotion. The effects of fear are still explained in terms of the blood. It undergoes a stoppage at the moment of the event. When it resumes movement thereafter its flow is slower, its colour lighter and its consistency more watery. When the fright is particularly intense, or is not dealt with in time, it can lead to *feluspersu* (*fiele sperso;* literally, shed bile), which is the discharge of bile into the blood.[65] As we have seen, the linking of fear to an excess of black bile – melancholy – goes back to the ancients, and is to be found in the Hippocratic corpus.[66] The experience of fright brings with it a sense of loss. This loss is identified with the world of spirits. One informant remarked that 'when you get a fear, it's as if a spirit has left you, it's as if you got a fear from a spirit'.[67] Here the spirit is both cause and effect. As far as Italian sufferers of *paura* are concerned, what leaves the body it is some sort of vital spirit or substance, borne through the body by the blood.

Corresponding to these internal effects are a wide range of external symptoms: tiredness, lack of appetite, insomnia, unease, abulia, paleness, nervous imbalance, paralysis, fevers, intestinal worms, cessation of the menses and, in children, an interruption of growth. As in the case of magic spells or the evil eye, the aetiology is not specific to a single symptom or disorder. In fact virtually any disease can be labelled *paura*, as long as it can be traced to fear or shock. If not treated, they can have fatal consequences.

Paura is thus used to account for a wide range of complaints and illnesses, just as melancholy was in the early modern period. It is generally the case that the nature of the fright does not seem to be at all in proportion to the seriousness of the resulting symptoms. Rather than dismiss this as simply the ambiguous and uninformed rationale traditional societies have about disease causation, there may be an explanation that can be accepted by modern biomedicine. The standard psychological reasoning is that repressed anxieties and emotions are projected on to an objective fright by the sufferer, according to a precise cultural code. This offers the sufferer an outlet and model for resolving the crisis. Even more intriguing, the medical anthropologists exploring *susto* in southern Mexico found that the lack of appetite, debility, tiredness, apathy and weight loss typical of *asustados* served to weaken the body's resistance to other attacks, such as infectious processes or complications. *Asustados* were found to be more in need of medical attention than the population as a whole, suffering from a wide range of biological illnesses. They were also more severely affected by these illnesses: they brought a greater disruption to the patients' daily lives and activities, as well as a greater risk of death.[68] If *susto* is not a purely biomedical phenomenon, then neither can it be conceived solely as a unique form of social behaviour. That is to say, a *susto* complaint does not simply serve to legitimise 'time off' from the exigencies of everyday social roles, where the sufferer benefits from the socially accepted 'sick role'. Rather, *asustados* are forced to the sidelines by excessive demands – social, physical, psychological – on their adaptive resources.[69]

In early modern Europe the traditional treatment for a fright was to have the sufferer bled, although Cardano advocated the gem hyacinth, either worn about the neck or taken in a potion.[70] Following the Gallipoli episode referred to above, one of the town's barbers suggested that instead of letting blood all the patient had to do was take two eggs and then some hyacinth in a strong glass of wine. [71] If a sufferer today diagnoses *paura* then treatment can only come from specialist folk healers. The healer begins by confirming the diagnosis, feeling the sufferer's pulse at the wrist or temples. Treatment has more in common with traditional remedial forms involving the sacred than with those of early modern medicine. Although treatments vary, they all reflect the fact that fear must be charmed out of the body. One response is to prepare a potion made from wine into which a red-hot key is immersed. This is left outside overnight before being consumed by the sufferer. The drink may symbolically reflect the blocked blood, loosened and freed by the sizzling heat of the key, to say nothing of its specific opening function.[72] Another common treatment consists in making the sign of the cross on the patient, reciting an exorcising formula. The healer also massages and rubs the sufferer, until the latter perspires and the flesh reddens, the aim being to free the blood. The treatment may also benefit from being performed at certain times of the day: mid-afternoon, so that the fear will come to an end with the day, or during the same lunar phase as the initial incident.[73] In Sardinia the treatment consists in returning the victim to the place where the original fright took place, having them roll on the ground, outlining a cross with their body and reciting a ritual formula.[74]

The early modern period has been characterised as a period of increasing fear, when Europe was besieged by widespread witch crazes and possession panics. A reading of the witchcraft treatises of the period, at least, does conjure up a 'limitless fear of the devil present everywhere, author of madness and organiser of artificial paradises', in the words of Jean Delumeau.[75] The investigation of our Marian image was held just when the fear of Satan was reaching its apex, according to Delumeau's chronology. And, in fact, several of the miraculously-cured people who testify were liberated by demons through the intercession of Our Lady.

Let us conclude by examining the final link in the chain of Domenica's illness episode: demonic possession. What could have brought it on? According to her own diagnosis, the fright was clearly the trigger. Domenica was especially vulnerable, given her advanced state of pregnancy. A demon may have taken the form of the footstep that so startled her, taking possession of her body at that initial moment. Or she may have concluded that she had become possessed later on, given the nature and severity of her subsequent suffering. It is impossible to be sure. Yet the link between a fright and possession is not so far-fetched as it may seem. Some 168 patients of the English cleric and astrological physician Richard Napier became mentally ill after having experienced a fright. Of those, just over one-tenth suspected demonic possession or bewitchment.[76] A link between fright, madness and possession was thus perceived to exist.

The miracle narratives in the Bolognese collection reflect commonly-held knowledge that illness involved more than the body itself, for the body was inextricably tied up with the entire cosmos. As we have seen, disease came from the outside, brought on by external forces and unusual events. The sick and those caring for them would look to perturbations in human society, in the world of the spirits and in the heavens. Whether or not this meant an increased level of anxiety and dread amongst early modern Europeans, as is often alleged, is debatable. Clearly there were more potentially harmful disease-causing agents to fear, but there were also ways of dealing with and responding to them.

Witches were one such agent of disease. Demonologists concluded that witches depended on the fear they inspired to achieve their results. According to the Milanese demonologist Francesco Maria Guazzo, writing around the time of our investigation, 'nearly all witches who have been questioned on the matter have confessed that the greater their fear the greater their boldness in doing evil'.[77] But the demonologists themselves had the most to fear. The witches they described were only capable of evil: 'for hardly ever do they drive a sickness from one man without transferring it to some other man, so that often they give a man health at the expense of another's health'.[78] Where such views about spells and counter-spells predominate, people can quite literally be scared to death.[79] But such views were not typical of the population as a whole in early modern Italy. Whilst Italian wise women were certainly feared for the spells they could cast, they were also sought out for their ritual remedies. Left untreated, a spell could kill. But, the point is, it *could* be treated. The fear of sorcery and the disease that could result was not a limitless terror, because there were ways of dealing with it. Like illness, sorcery was part of everyday lived experience. There were established procedures for counteracting the threats, for appeasing the cunning folk behind them, for restoring harmonious social relations.

We could view possession in much the same way. The Devil was another agent behind disease, and the belief that demons could cause almost any mental or physical illness was widespread throughout Europe. We find it in the patients of Napier, active during the early seventeenth century, just as we find it amongst the people treated by the Piedmontese exorcist Giovan Battista Chiesa, active in the final years of the century.[80] For the latter, in fact, the Devil was the direct cause of most illnesses. Chiesa was said to have declared that 'out of ten thousand people more than nine thousand would be oppressed [by demons]'. Clearly, the appearance of Satan in one's everyday affairs was a terrifying prospect. But there were recognised responses, known to be effective. The Catholic Church made extensive use of exorcisms as therapy, one of the many 'ecclesiastical remedies' against disease.[81] Indeed, the use of exorcism to treat disease seems to have been on the increase in Italy during the first half of the seventeenth century (just when the ritual was dying out in Napier's England). The approach taken by exorcists in such cases was very matter-of-fact, almost routine: a question of applying the established ritual until the body of the possessed was liberated.

If our Bolognese miracle narratives are anything to go by, it would seem that the fear generated by demonic possession was far greater for the possessed people's family and friends than for the possessed themselves. Whatever the possessions may have been — and this is not the place to make amateur medical guesses — the victims seem to have been too involved, too weak, too out of body to remember much of the chain of events surrounding the possession, exorcisms and eventual cure. Accounting for this forgetfulness, one of the Bolognese exorcists involved concluded his deposition by noting that 'the liberated person remains forever injured by the departed spirits either in mind or in another part of the body'.[82] This is also a nice way of reminding us that the mind was considered an organ like any other.

Giulia di Gurioli's account of her own experience is brief and to the point, even though she apparently suffered for over twenty years. In fact she talks at length about her stomach pains, before finally remarking, 'it was that most holy Virgin who liberated me, because before I was liberated I would drag myself on the ground, scream and swear and in short I was possessed, but I do not remember these things now'.[83] Her friend's version of events, by contrast, was lengthy and detailed. The seventy-year-old widow Nicola Tosarelli recounted that Giulia was exorcised for her possession by two monks, in her house, though without success. While they were performing the exorcism Nicola heard terrible noises in the house, 'so that it seemed as if the world was coming down'. During this period Giulia would sometimes spend the night at Nicola's house, though 'she shouted and screamed so much it was frightening'. Finally Nicola took Giulia to the church of Santa Maria della Vita. They went up to the altar and Nicola began to say a Salve Regina. 'And at that moment [Giulia] fell to the ground and started to roll over and hit her head on the ground, and seeing this I fled away.' Nicola ran to the exit, but turned around when she heard voices saying 'ugly beast, get out of this body and depart with God'. When she saw a group of people holding Giulia down, whilst she continued to hit herself and scream, Nicola returned home. Despite her terror, she returned to the church later, preceded by her daughters, and found Giulia 'sitting down, all beaten and in disarray'. And she asked Giulia if she was 'free from those spirits' and she said she was.[84]

The same fear of the possessed is expressed by the employers of the servant Domenico Brusati, the Bentivoglio family. When 'it was discovered that I had spirits on me' (delli spiriti adosso) the family did not want him in the house. Domenico had to spend the night in the church of Santa Maria del Carmine. He lost his speech as a result of the possession, which a priest diagnosed as having been occasioned by a fall. 'I fell to the earth as if dead', Domenico recounted, 'so that I could hear nothing of what people were saying to me, since I fell at four hours after nightfall and that same evening on St John's day [24 June], they discovered three spirits on me, one named Giacopello, one Staforte and the other Chiaveghino.'[85] As with disease, identifying and naming the spirits clearly made possession easier to deal with. Also worth noting about this account is how the shock of a traumatic phsyical event, like strong emotional sensations, can lead to possession.

In the same way that the Madonna della Vita supplemented the activities of Bolognese medical practitioners, filling in for their failures or limitations, so she supplemented the activities of canonical exorcists. Exorcists could not satisfy the demand for exorcisms, due in part to the greater role attributed to Satan in causing illness. The widespread belief in the reality of the Devil meant that demonic possession was not dismissed out of hand or necessarily identified with madness. Madness and possession were separate phenomena, though closely related to one another. One could be used to explain the other. Symptoms of mania or melancholia could be the result of possession. Conversely, Satan could take advantage of these conditions – particularly melancholy – to lead souls away from God.[86] There was thus a considerable grey area. This explains why Dionisio Spisani stressed the incident where his wife had run out into the street half-naked: a public state of undress had been considered a sign of mania from ancient times. And, at the end of his account, Dionisio noted that his wife had remained sane (*in cervello*) since the time she had been liberated from possession.

This chapter has sought to unravel the various strands that form the thread of logic behind Domenica Spisani's interpretation of, and reaction to, the events that befell her in July 1615. The focus has been on cultural definitions of fear, especially as linked to the experience of disease in early modern Europe. Domenica's experience is an example of fear tamed. She responded to her fright, illness and possession according to the cultural explanations she shared with her family and the society around her. Her explanatory system conjured up a whole range of ideas and phenomena to give an identity to her suffering: emotion and imagination, blood flow, demons, magic, the Devil. And whilst these phenomena were doubtless the cause of much real fear, they also allowed her to label her affliction and respond to it.

Notes

1 Research for this chapter was made possible by a Wellcome Trust University Award in the history of medicine at the University of Leicester. Versions of the chapter were presented at the Anglo-American Conference (Historical Institute, London, July 1996) and at a conference on 'Religion, health and suffering' (Wellcome Institute for the History of Medicine and the School of Oriental and African Studies, London, September 1996).

2 'Sanctae Mariae de Vita miraculorum et gratiarum processus', *Processus*, 28, fos. 76v–79.

3 Horacio Fabrega, *Disease and Social Behavior: An Interdisciplinary Perspective* (Cambridge, MA, 1974), 39–43.

4 Ludmilla Jordanova, 'The social construction of medical knowledge', *Social History of Medicine*, 8 (1995), 361–81, at 372.

5 David Hufford, *The Terror that Comes in the Night: An Experience-centered Study of Supernatural Assault Traditions* (Philadelphia, 1982), ix–x, xviii–xix.

6 For a fuller discussion of the source, see David Gentilcore, 'Contesting illness in early

modern Naples: *miracolati*, physicians and the Congregation of Rites', *P&P*, 148 (1995), 117–48.

7 Edward Muir, 'The Virgin on the street corner: the place of the sacred in Italian cities', in Stephen Ozment, ed., *Religion and Culture in the Renaissance and Reformation* (Kirksville, 1989), 25–40.

8 The resulting quasi-judicial procedure has been used by historians to reveal much about both the nature of belief and the demands of the Catholic Church. See Paola Vismara Chiappa, *Miracoli settecenteschi in Lombardia tra istituzione ecclesiastica e religione popolare* (Milan, 1988); Adriano Prosperi, 'Madonne di città e madonne di campagna. Per un'inchiesta sulle dinamiche del sacro nell'Italia post-Tridentina', in S. Boesch Gajano and L. Sebastiani, eds, *Culto dei santi, istituzioni e classi sociali in età preindustriale* (Rome, 1984), 615–47; William Christian, *Local Religion in Sixteenth-century Spain* (Princeton, 1981), 70–126; Pierroberto Scaramella, *Le Madonne del Purgatorio: iconografia e religione in Campania tra rinascimento e controriforma* (Genoa, 1991), 170–95.

9 Gianna Pomata, *La promessa di guarigione. Malati e curatori in antico regime: Bologna XVI–XVIII secolo* (Rome, 1994), 192, n. 79.

10 The church is best known today for its late fifteenth-century Pietà, scuplted by Niccolò dell'Arca. The confraternity's origins went back to the flagellant movement of the thirteenth century, and it had founded the hospital in 1289. As the confraternity had expanded, becoming one of the city's richest and most prestigious, it had developed its charitable acitivities, expanding the hospital. The salaried physician and surgeon were obliged to treat sick confrères and labourers employed by the hospital free of charge. By 1555 it had fourteen paid staff and it also elected two confrères each week to visit the hospital twice a day as *visitatori dei poveri*. For sources regarding the hospital and its confraternity, see G. G. Forni, 'Sette secoli di storia ospedaliera in Bologna', *Sette secoli di vita ospedaliera in Bologna* (Bologna, 1960), 3–28; Nicholas Terpstra, *Lay Confraternities and Civic Religion in Renaissance Bologna* (Cambridge, 1995), 4–5, 148–9; Pomata, *La promessa di guarigione*, 184 n. 10; Christopher Black, *Italian Confraternities in the Sixteenth Century* (Cambridge, 1989), 186.

11 Domenico Brusati was liberated from demonic possession. Whether he had been taken in by the confrères because of his demonic possession or his indigence is hard to say. *Processus*, fos. 45v–48v.

12 Terpstra, *Lay Confraternities*, 220.

13 In 1543 the grocer Girolamo Rainaldi argued that confrères should not invoke the saints or Our Lady, but have recourse to Christ alone. He eventually retracted his views. A. Rotondò, 'Per la storia dell'eresia a Bologna nel secolo XVI', *Rinascimento*, 13 (1962), 137 ff; in Black, *Italian Confraternities*, 61.

14 Deposition of Sansone Zanetti, *Processus*, fol. 27v.

15 Deposition of Ercole de Garzaria, *Processus*, fos. 89v–90. Where surnames are given only in Latin I have made no attempt to re-Italianise them.

16 On passing the church, one witness asked his coachman 'what the great gathering of so many people was, going in and out of the church, and he replied … that for maybe 300 years an image of the Virgin had been covered up and had now been discovered and was performing great miracles'. Deposition of Carlo Capponi, *Processus*, fos. 53–53v.

17 Deposition of Lucia dalla Villa, *Processus*, fos. 123v–125v.

18 The deponents number 75, narrating 36 separate miracles, which can be broken down as follows: 5 cases of children falling into wells or water, 5 accidents involving carts or animals, 3 examples of demonic possession, 3 hernia cases, 2 for urinary gravel (*mal d'orina*), 9 involving various other complaints. Of the deponents, 27 are women, one of whom is a midwife; tradesmen and shopkeepers number 12, peasants and gardeners 9, nobles and *gentiluomini* 6, servants 3; priests and monks 7; 24 of the witnesses are *miracolati*, recounting miracles which have occurred to them. Close to 100 years later, in 1710, the image was the focus of another investigation: 'Ristretto informante circa il

preteso miracolo della restituzione della lingua ad Antonio Prandi per intercessione della Beata Vergine della Vita', Biblioteca Universitaria, Bologna, ms. 207 B, b.viii; cit. in Pomata, *La promessa di guarigione*, 184–5, n. 12.

19 For instance, in *nezza* for niece (instead of *nipote*), *cancua* for feeding trough (instead of *conca*), *ara* for threshing floor (instead of *aia*), and *aventasone* for hernia (instead of *allentatura*). My thanks to Piero Camporesi for his help with terms not appearing in Bolognese dialect dictionaries.

20 'Anguish' (*angoscia*) does make an appearance, but it is used in its (now archaic) literal sense of a feeling of suffocation, breathlessness or choking (from the Latin *angustiae*, meaning a straightness or tightness). Deposition of Angelica Caccianemici, *Processus*, fol. 105v.

21 Sigmund Freud, *Beyond the Pleasure Principle* (1961), 6–7.

22 Yi-fu Tuan, *Landscapes of Fear* (Oxford, 1980), 87.

23 Augusto Placanica, 'Pensiero colto e mentalità popolare davanti alla paura da catastrofe', in Laura Guidi, Maria Rosaria Pelizzari and Lucia Valenzi, eds, *Storia e paure: immaginario collettivo, riti e rappresentazioni della paura in età moderna* (Milan, 1992), 134–45, esp. 134.

24 For example, the intriguingly titled book by Oskar Pfister, *Christianity and Fear. A Study in History and in the Psychology and Hygiene of Religion* (1948). Discussion is limited to pathological fears which Christianity, as a religion of love, should be ideally placed to alleviate. However, especially in its Catholic guise, it seems more concerned with their promotion. With venomous rage, Pfister concludes that 'there is no field of life except the pathological one where fear dominates as thoroughly and, in the expert's eyes, as ostentatiously as in Catholicism' (271). Though there is a clear Protestant bias, this same negative conclusion would later lead Jean Delumeau to study the role of the Catholic Church in encouraging a sense of fear in the faithful during the early modern period.

25 Hypochondriasis, which concerns fears of multiple bodily symptoms and a variety of illnesses, has received much more attention, both in literature and in scientific studies.

26 Isaac Marks, *Fears, Phobias and Rituals: Panic, Anxiety and their Disorders* (Oxford, 1987), 410–11.

27 Tuan, *Landscapes of Fear*, 5.

28 Deposition of Daniello de Borelli, *Processus*, fol. 12.

29 Deposition of Giovanni Fusari, *Processus*, fol. 36v.

30 Deposition of Ercole Manzoni, *Processus*, fol. 30.

31 Deposition of Margarita Galliani, *Processus*, fol. 41.

32 In contrast to the canonisation processes conducted by the Congregation of Rites in Rome, where physicians have a privileged role as guarantors. See Gentilcore, 'Contesting illness', 132–9.

33 Deposition of Bartolomeo dallo Spirito, *Processus*, fol. 120.

34 Deposition of Niccolò de Dialaitis, *Processus*, fol. 79v.

35 Deposition of Giovanni de Berti, *Processus*, fos. 34v–35.

36 On the healing contract, see Pomata, *La promessa di guarigione*, esp. chs 2, 4 and 6.

37 Giovanni Battista Bronzini, '"Ex voto" e cultura religiosa popolare', *Rivista di storia e letteratura religiosa*, 15 (1979), 3–27.

38 Deposition of Giorgio Bellioti, *Processus*, fol. 104v.

39 Robert Burton, *The Anatomy of Melancholy, what it is, with all the kinds, causes, symptoms, prognostics, and several cures of it*, repr. of London 1651 folio edn, pt. 1, sect. 2, mem. 3, subs. 1.

40 The other five non-naturals were food and drink, sleep and waking, air, evacuation and repletion, motion and rest.

41 Francis Bacon, 'Of Regiment of Health', in Sydney Humphries, ed., *Bacon's Essays* (1912), 178. My thanks to Mark Knights for drawing this reference to my attention.

42 Barbara Duden, *The Woman beneath the Skin: A Doctor's Patients in Eighteenth-Century Germany* (Cambridge, MA, 1991), 142.

43 On the role of the imagination as a factor in disease, see Esther Fischer-Homberger, 'On the medical history of the doctrine of imagination', *Psychological Medicine*, 9 (1979), 619–28.

44 Burton, *Anatomy of Melancholy*, pt 1, sect. 2, mem. 3, subs. 2.

45 *Ibid.*, pt 1, sect. 2, mem. 3, subs. 2.

46 Cited in G. L. Basini, *L'uomo e il pane. Risorse, consumi e carenze alimentari della popolazione modenese nel Cinque e Seicento* (Milan, 1970), 83.

47 Ludovico Antonio Muratori, *Li tre governi, politico, medico ed ecclesiastico, utilissimi, anzi necessari in tempo di peste* (Milan: Vigoni e Cairolo, 1721), 119.

48 J. Delumeau, *La Peur en Occident: XIVe–XVIIIe siècles* (Paris, 1978), 114.

49 Muratori, *Li tre governi*, 97.

50 Pietro Pomponazzi, *De naturalium effectuum causis sive de incantantionibus* (Basle, 1556); in Lynn Thorndike, *A History of Magic and Experimental Science* (New York, 1941), 5: 103.

51 Burton, *Anatomy of Melancholy*, pt 1, sect. 2, mem. 4, subs. 3.

52 Felice Passera da Bergamo, *Pratica universale della medicina ovvero annotationi sopra tutte le infermità più particolari che giornalmente sogliono avvenire ne corpi umani* (Milan: Malatesta, 1693), 20; in Piero Camporesi, *Il sugo della vita: simbolismo e magia del sangue* (Milan, 1988), 28.

53 Duden, *Woman beneath the Skin*, 147–8.

54 Giovanni Marinello, *Le medicine pertinenti alle infermità delle donne ... nuovamente da lui ampliate e ricorrette* (Venice, 1574), 95. The book and its author are discussed in Maria Luisa Altieri Biagi, Clemente Mazzotta, Angela Chiantera and Paola Altieri, eds, *Medicina per le donne nel Cinquecento. Testi di Giovanni Marinello e di Girolamo Mercurio* (Turin, 1992).

55 Girolamo Cardano, *De subtilitate libri xxi* (Nuremberg: Petreius, 1550), ch. 12, 'De hominis natura et temperamento'; Lodovico Domenichi, *Della nobiltà delle donne* (Venice: de' Ferrari, 1549), 98r, 113r.

56 Girolamo (Fra Scipione) Mercurio, *La commare o riccoglitrice* (Venice: Ciotti, 1606), book I, ch. 12; reprinted in Biagi *et al.*, *Medicina*, 94.

57 Ambroise Paré, *On Monsters and Marvels (1573)* (Chicago, 1982), 38–42.

58 The exact term varies according to linguistic area: in Sardinia, for example, it is generally referred to as *assustu* or *azzichidu*, in Sicily as *scantu*.

59 Italo Signorini, 'Eziologia folclorica: la "paura", le "arie", il malocchio', in Tullio Seppilli, ed., *Le tradizioni popolari in Italia. Medicine e magie* (Milan, 1989), 43–8, esp., 44.

60 Clara Gallini, 'Immagini di paura: una lettura antropologica', in Guidi *et al.*, *Storia e paure*, 30–42, esp. 32.

61 Olivio Galeazzi, 'La paura nelle Marche: un esempio di culturalizzazione integrale del patologico', *Storia e medicina popolare*, 6 (1988), 16–34, esp. 23.

62 'Contro Sac. Diego Picciolo per esser entrato di notte tempo in casa di Faustina Basile e Grazia Suarez forzando la porta', 1732, ACV, Gallipoli, *Processi Penali*.

63 Charles Hughes, 'Glossary of "culture-bound" or folk psychiatric syndromes', in R. Simons and C. Hughes, eds, *The Culture-bound Syndromes: Folk Illnesses of Psychiatric and Anthropological Interest* (Dordrecht, 1985), 469–505.

64 Also known as *espanto, pasmo*, or *perdida de la sombra*, it is to be found in Mexico (and amongst Mexican-Americans), Peru, Argentina, Colombia and Guatemala. The most detailed exploration is Arthur Rubel, Carl O'Nell and Rolando Collado Ardon, *Susto, a folk illness* (Berkeley, 1984).

65 Patrizia Ritarossi, 'La paura', *Storia e medicina popolare*, 6 (1986), 7–24, esp. 8.

66 'Aphorisms', sect. vi, no. 23, in Geoffroy Lloyd, ed., *Hippocratic Writings* (Harmondsworth, 1983), 229. The survival of Hippocratic interpretations of disease into the present century has not been adequately studied, but see George Foster, 'Humoral pathology in Spain and Spanish America', in Antonio Carreira, Jess Antonio Cid, Manuel Gutiérrez Esteve and Rogelio Rubio, eds, *Homenaje a Julio Caro Baroja* (Madrid, 1978), 357–70.

67 Ritarossi, 'La paura', 18.

68 Rubel et al., Susto, 82–5, 98, 104.

69 Ibid., 122.

70 Cardano, De subtilitate, ch. 7, 'De lapidibus'.

71 Deposition of Luca Mauro, 'Contro Sac. Diego Picciolo'.

72 Signorini, 'Eziologia folclorica', 46.

73 Ritarossi, 'La paura', 15–16.

74 Gallini, 'Immagini di paura', 35.

75 Delumeau, La Peur, 237.

76 Michael MacDonald, Mystical Bedlam: Madness, Anxiety, and Healing in Seventeenth-Century England (Cambridge, 1981), 250.

77 Francesco Maria Guazzo, Compendium maleficarum (1608, 1626; repr. 1929), bk. 2, ch. 12, p. 124.

78 Ibid.

79 For a very personal account, see Jeanne Favret-Saada, Deadly Words: Witchcraft in the Bocage (Cambridge, 1980), esp. 78–91.

80 Both kept detailed records of their activities. On the former, see MacDonald, Mystical Bedlam; on the latter, see Giovanni Levi, Inheriting Power: The Story of an Exorcist (Chicago, 1988), ch. 1.

81 On the use of exorcisms against disease, see Mary O'Neil, 'Sacerdote ovvero strione: ecclesiastical and supersitious remedies in 16th century Italy', in Stephen Kaplan, ed., Understanding Popular Culture (Berlin, 1984), 53–83; D. Gentilcore, From Bishop to Witch: The System of the Sacred in Early Modern Terra d'Otranto (Manchester, 1992), 107–13.

82 Deposition of Don Stefano Mucia, Processus, fol. 49v.

83 Deposition of Giulia di Gurioli, Processus, fol. 56.

84 Deposition of Nicola Tosarelli, Processus, fos. 56v–58.

85 Deposition of Domenico Brusati, Processus, fos. 45v–48v.

86 Theologians of the time frequently linked melancholy with the sadness and torpor of the cardinal sin sloth (accidie), which the Devil used to his advantage to lead people away from the service of God. Jean Delumeau, Le Péché et la peur: la culpabilisation en Occident (Paris, 1983), 189–208.

12

The fear of the King is death: James VI and the witches of East Lothian

P. G. MAXWELL-STUART

On 1 September 1589, Anne of Denmark set sail for Scotland from Copenhagen and got as far as Elsinore. For the next six days North Sea storms drove the flotilla back and forth until, on 7 September, it was forced to put in at Mardø on the Norwegian coast. The succeeding five weeks are a story of leaking vessels, continuing storms, further attempts to reach Scotland, and finally the Princess's decision to weather it out in Oslo while some of her ships made their way back to Copenhagen. On 8 October, King James wrote to Anne in French, apparently the language they had in common, and then in the second half of the month – sources differ about the precise date – set sail himself for Norway to fetch back his bride. He, too, was subjected to storms but eventually came to Oslo where he and Anne were married on 23 November. They stayed there until 22 December when they left and made their way by stages into Denmark. Once there, they were married again in Kronborg on 21 January and stayed in Denmark until 21 April. Upon setting to sea on their homeward voyage they were attended yet again by storms but arrived safely in Leith on 1 May, thus ending their Scandinavian adventure.[1]

Scotland managed to survive the King's prolonged absence, and he seems happy to have been away, for it is noticeable how rarely he attempted to contact his Council. A month after his arrival in Norway there was no news from him, nor week by week after that until a message arrived at Leith on 15 December to say that James would be absent until the spring. Even so, communications were still being sent to Oslo long after the King had left.[2] The round of royal engagements during this period included a prolonged visit to Tycho Brahe's home at Uraniborg where James noticed a picture of George Buchanan, his former tutor, and a lengthy conversation with the leading Danish theologian of the day, Niels Hemmingsen. The principal subject of their discussion appears to have been predestination.[3] But while the King was enjoying an extended break from his fraught and dangerous existence in Scotland, Peder Munk, the Danish admiral who had been in charge of Anne's flotilla, was eager to clear himself of any accusations of negligence consequent upon the embarrassments of the previous winter. A court case brought by him against Christofer Valkendorf, the governor of Copenhagen and the man responsible for keeping the Royal Navy in repair, threw up charges of witchcraft against several named women who were supposed to have raised the storms which delayed Princess Anne; and one of them, Ane Koldings, may have gone on trial in Copenhagen two days before James and Anne left for Scotland. In spite of this, however, the general consensus of those involved with the earlier voyages was that the problems they had encountered were entirely natural.[4]

In Scotland, meanwhile, there was absolutely nothing to suggest an upsurge of potentially treasonable witchcraft. On 28 April 1590, Meg Dow was put on trial for witchcraft and infanticide, found guilty, and later executed; on 7 May, the Haddington Synod had begun to investigate a complaint of witchcraft (first raised the previous September) against Agnes Sampson; on 22 July, Lady Fowlis and Hector Munro were finally tried on charges of witchcraft and murder going back as far as 1577; and several witches were arraigned in Edinburgh on charges relating to the Laird of Wardhouse. The matter of these trials involved the murder of children and adults, poison, personal abuse, elf-shot, sorcery, devilish incantations, and consultation with witches – nothing in the least unusual, and none of it touched the King or Queen at all.[5] Early in November 1590, however, all that changed. The Bailiff Depute of Tranent in East Lothian, David Seton, became suspicious of his maid, Gellie Duncan, who was frequently absent overnight from his house. She had a reputation as a remarkable healer and this, although harmless in itself, might always be liable to trigger a suspicion of witchcraft. After torture, applied by Seton, and the discovery of a witch's mark on her throat, Gellie Duncan was put in prison, where she began to tell a tale which soon involved a large number of others, both men and women. Two names quickly surfaced as particularly significant, those of Richard Graham and Francis Stewart, Earl of Bothwell; and two confessions transformed the investigation from local to national interest. First, it was alleged that a group of Scottish witches had deliberately sought to delay or destroy the King and Queen on their homeward journey and also made later attempts to kill the King by means of witchcraft and poison. Secondly, it was said that these treasonable attempts had been made at the request of the Earl of Bothwell.

Now, the trials of 1590–91 have been the subject of comment before, and two points have been repeated so often that they are in danger of turning into received wisdom. The first is that although a belief in witches was common in Scotland before the King's visit to Scandinavia, witchcraft was treated with a degree of scepticism, and penalties for its practice were not always inflicted according to the rigour demanded by statute law; but while James was in Denmark, he came into contact with Continental theories about witchcraft and upon his return home began to have them applied with a certain degree of ferocity. Torture, it is suggested, was used in witchcraft cases for the first time, and investigators started to look for the apparatus of the witch-mark, the *Sabbat*, flying through the air, and the Satanic pact, all of which characterised Continental theory but none of which had played a part hitherto in Scottish opinion. This proposition, I shall maintain, is broadly mistaken and has little evidence to support it.[6]

The second is that these East Lothian trials were similar in nature to an earlier type of witch-trial, 'in which the accusation of witchcraft was used, sometimes cynically, as a means to convict, or make popular the conviction of, a particular person'.[7] This, too, is somewhat dubious.[8]

Let us take first the suggestion about Denmark as a turning-point. As Larner has pointed out, there is no evidence that James was interested in witchcraft before 1590.[9] There are no books on the subject in the list we have of his library, nor was Buchanan in the least sympathetic to occult studies. Indeed, in his astronomical poem, *Sphaera*, he warns of the dangers of astrological prophecy and magic. Nor were there many books on witchcraft printed in or imported into Scotland: we know only of two. Alchemy was much more popular.[10] In *c*.1580, James may have been present at a performance of Montgomerie's *Flyting* which contains humorous scenes of elves and fairies and witches. Certainly he knew the work, for he quotes from it in an essay on poetic skills, written in 1584. If Montgomerie could use the subject for Court entertainment, it follows that James must have known enough about it to appreciate the plot, and the likelihood that he was entertained by it suggests he did not find witchcraft frightening at this stage.[11]

Nor would the situation in Scotland have particularly encouraged untoward fear. Certainly it is true that the Act of 1563 forbade anyone to use witchcraft, sorcery, or necromancy, to claim any powers thereby or knowledge thereof, or to seek help, response, or consultation of anyone claiming to be a witch, the penalty for both witch and client being death. But the wording of the statute treats the reality of witchcraft with a reticent scepticism, calling it 'a heavy and abominable superstition' and referring to witches as abusers of the people. So, as Legge points out, it is curious that all subsequent witch-trials in Scotland should have been founded on an enactment which seems to have been aimed at nothing worse than the fraudulent assumption of 'supernatural power'.[12] It is also true that the Act was not always enforced to the letter, the General Assembly of the Kirk, for example, on 12 August 1573, ordering merely that witches do penance in sackcloth. But the Satanic pact was known in Scotland at least as early as 1552 when a reference to it appears in a catechism,[13] and in none of the extant papers relating to the East Lothian witches (or, indeed, to any others at this date) is there any suggestion that they were attending anything like a Continental *Sabbat* or that they travelled thither by flying through the air. What, therefore, might James have learned from his Danish experience?

The Danish Church's attitude to witchcraft before and after the Reformation remained more or less unchanged. Ecclesiastics were not particularly interested in witchcraft, although some priests were known to practise it, and so they did not busy themselves unduly with fighting the phenomenon unless it was linked in some way with harmful magic (*maleficium*).[14] Denmark, in fact, seems to have regarded cunning folk and maleficent witches more or less as two separate species. Its two key witchcraft statutes of 1547 and 1576 declared: (i) that no evidence obtained from a dishonest person could form the basis wherefrom a third party might be convicted, and that torture could not be employed until after the final sentence; and (ii) that no one convicted by a jury could be executed until an appeal had been heard.[15] Neither of these is typical of Continental practice. It is also important to note that Danish trials almost invariably concerned themselves with specific offences committed by sorcery, and they scarcely bothered with the notion either of the *Sabbat* or of the Satanic pact.[16] Two of the characteristic features of Continental theory were therefore little regarded in Denmark.

Now, while James was there, he had a lengthy conversation with Niels Hemmingsen. Could this have made a difference to his attitude to witchcraft? Hemmingsen was the most important Danish Reformation theologian of his day, with an international reputation. He wrote a book on magic and related subjects, *Admiratio de Superstitionibus Magicis Vitandis*, published in Copenhagen in 1575, but although (as one might expect) he accepted the reality of the existence of witches and sorcerers who were able to effect *maleficium* against both people and animals, he was not very sure whether witches could fly through the air and absolutely denied the reality of the *Sabbat*: 'statuendum est illusionem diabolorum esse'. Hemmingsen's influence on the next generation of Danish clergy was immense and, in the words of Johansen, 'as there was no other Danish source where the vicars could read about these subjects, it must be regarded as unlikely that they would have described the organisational side of the witch-system from the pulpit'.[17] Had James and Hemmingsen talked about or touched upon witchcraft, therefore, it is most unlikely that Hemmingsen would have said anything to convert James to standard Continental witch-theory. But in any

case, if the surviving minutes of their discussion give an accurate account
of what was said, it is clear the subject never arose at all. So it is difficult
to see how James could have been influenced in this regard by his Danish
experience.[18]

That leaves Norway as a source for consideration. James was there for
nearly two months. Could he have picked up Continental theory during
those eight weeks? From 1536 Norway was considered by Denmark to be
a Danish province. After the Reformation, the priests were gradually
replaced by Lutheran pastors, many of them Danish, trained in both Germany and Denmark. Some of these, at least, followed quite closely the concepts of witchcraft and demonology common elsewhere on the Continent,
and a set of circumstances peculiar to Stavanger in 1584 led the local Bishop
to obtain passage of a law that all forms of witchcraft – in other words,
cunningness as well as malefice – should be punishable by death. Torture,
however, was forbidden and a right of appeal allowed. Moreover, this legislation applied only to Bergen and Stavanger, and was not extended to the
rest of Norway until 1593. What is more, it was never introduced into
Denmark. In Norway, moreover, in the last decades of the sixteenth century, several women were acquitted of the charge of witchcraft after they
had sworn a co-oath, that is, an oath to a person's innocence sworn by the
accused together with twelve, six, or three others.[19] The situation, therefore, is not quite the same as that of Denmark, although we might perhaps
ask whether it was those pastors who had studied in Germany (as opposed
to Denmark) who waged war more fiercely against witches and sought to
explain their existence by notions they had picked up abroad. Nevertheless,
the Danish account of James's journey through Norway gives no indication
that he or his hosts concerned themselves with witchcraft. If anything, the
King was more interested in theology, the kind of topic he took up later
with Hemmingsen.

The evidence relating to James's stay in Denmark, then, does not suggest that he absorbed or even discussed Continental theories of witchcraft
and demonology. It is possible he did so in Norway, but there is no evidence to support that notion and in consequence we must question whether
he came into contact with the subject at all in either country.

Had he done so, and had he been profoundly affected by it, we should
expect to see some sign of that influence when he returned to Scotland.
Such signs, however, are missing, as the schedule of royal events suggests.
May was preoccupied with Anne's coronation, her state entry into Edinburgh, and entertainment of the Danes who had come to Scotland with her.
In the second week of June, the Earl of Worcester arrived bearing official
messages from the English Court. He stayed for about a week.[20] On 4 July,

a woman from Lübeck arrived with a prophecy for James, that he was the 'prince of the north' of whom noble deeds were foretold. Robert Bowes wrote to Burghley that

> she had sought the King of Scots at Elsinore, but coming after his departure took her voyage hither. She brings a Latin letter ... [and] she had conference with the Queen in her own language, 'having no other tongue than the Dutch' [i.e. German] ... The King and country think her a witch; yet he is purposed to hear her.[21]

Bowes describes her as a 'gentlewoman'. It would be interesting to know whether the Latin letter was her own or entrusted to her by someone else. But she was obviously respectable, which probably played a part in her gaining an audience with the Queen. James may have thought she was a witch, but his curiosity and eagerness to listen to her clearly stem from the contents of the letter and her announcement that he was destined to be a great prince, rather than from any special interest in witchcraft.

Throughout May, June and July the women arrested in Copenhagen were examined and put on trial. Ane Koldings was tortured: the others may or may not have been. One hanged herself in prison.[22] On 25 June, Burghley received word from Copenhagen that a witch (probably Ane Koldings) had been burned for bewitching Princess Anne's attempted voyage to Scotland the previous autumn. No news of this, however, appears to have reached Scotland until 23 July.[23] In August there was a little flurry of witch-activity in Scotland: an excommunication, one or two trials for witchcraft, in one of which the panel was acquitted of all charges. But nothing in any of them would have been of especial interest to James.[24]

Still, this does not mean to say that the King's existence was entirely tranquil. Papists, Jesuits, pirates, and quarrelsome Scottish lords, took up much of his attention on his return as, one may note, they did that of the kirk. Robert Bruce's sermons in St Giles's, for example, in 1589 and 1590, are much occupied with the threat posed by papistry and when he talks of the Devil, the context makes it clear that he is referring to Catholic activity in Scotland.[25] But of immediate interest, in view of the later witch-trials, must be James's relationship with the Earl of Bothwell between May and November 1590. We can follow the course of it in CSPS. In the middle of May they are in amity, then Bothwell takes the huff and departs from Court. In June he returns, quarrels, and departs again. This time the King is irritated. In July Bothwell is involved in Court intrigue, prepares to leave Scotland for Germany, but stays and is reported to be very friendly with the Chancellor and to have been reconciled with the Master of Glamis. In August he is lodged overnight in Edinburgh Castle. In September he is

appointed Lord Lieutenant of the Borders. In October he and the King are
blowing somewhat cold, and by the end of the month Bothwell is said to
be at Kelso on local business.[26] The important point to note is that none of
this is serious enough to engender in the King a desire to destroy Bothwell
politically or personally. So when Bothwell's name turned up in the East
Lothian witchcraft investigations, as it did very quickly, the King may have
been irritated or even angered, but not necessarily to the point where he
would want to go as far as engineering Bothwell's death.

By 11 November, Richard Graham and other witches had been
arrested and lodged in the Edinburgh Tolbooth.[27] Thereafter, investigations
proceeded apace. As we have seen, this sequence of events was triggered
by a local incident – David Seton's suspicions about the behaviour of his
maid, Gellie Duncan. Gellie confessed that she had heard Bothwell's name
in connection with Agnes Sampson at a convention of witches in Prestonpans. She also said that the King, too, had been named, but after a fashion
she did not fully recollect; and that Agnes Sampson had said, 'The King is
going to see his wife, but I shall be there before them.' Some of these
details were confirmed by Donald Robinson and Janet Straton, two more
of the accused.[28] Agnes, questioned by William Schaw, the Master of the
King's Works, and John Geddie, confessed to a number of different witch-
conventions including the latest (and subsequently most notorious) at North
Berwick on 31 October 1590.[29] According to the pamphlet, *Newes From Scotland*, published in London in 1591 and giving an apparently reliable account
of events, Agnes was further examined by the King himself both before and
after torture. She told him details of the meeting at North Berwick, including the Devil's expressed rage at the King of Scotland. She also drew him
on one side and 'declared unto him the very words which passed between
the King's Majesty and his Queen at Oslo in Norway the first night of their
marriage, with their answer each to other'.[30] It is hardly surprising that
James was mightily disturbed. The anecdote raises interesting questions.
How did she know what was said? James and Anne almost certainly
exchanged remarks in French, the language they had in common. Did Agnes
repeat them to James in French, or did she use a Scots translation? Either
would have seemed extraordinary, but the former perhaps even more so.
What is the connection between this episode and the cryptic remark attributed to her by Gellie Duncan, that when the King arrived in Scandinavia
to meet Princess Anne, she would be there before them?

Altogether Agnes Sampson was accused of 102 articles and confessed
to 58 which included the usual cures, raising of storms, attempted magical
murder, and trafficking with the Devil.[31] But both from her testimony and
from that of the other witches, it emerged most damagingly that there had

been three separate attempts to kill the King and Queen. First, cats had been bewitched and thrown into the sea at Leith and Prestonpans with a view to raising a storm and thus delaying the Queen's journey to Scotland and drowning both her and her company.[32] Secondly, a picture of James was made from wax and passed from witch to witch to be enchanted. Donald Robinson describes the process clearly. At a convention in Acheson's Haven at which there were more than twenty people present,

> Agnes Sampson brought the picture to the field. She delivered it to Barbara Napier. From Barbara it was given to Euphemia MacCalyean. From Euphemia to Meg Begton of Spilmourford. It passed through eight or nine women. At last it came to Robert Greirson. From him to the Devil. They spoke all 'James the Sixth' amongst them, handling the picture. The Devil was like a man. Agnes Samson said there would be both gold and silver and victuals gotten from my lord Bothwell.[33]

Thirdly, a toad was hung up by its heels, 'dripping between three oyster shells and nine stones, cooking slowly for three nights'. The poison thus extracted was to be dropped, along with other magical items, on some pathway along which the King would walk; or placed on a ceiling so that it might fall on the King's head or body. The object, clearly stated, was to kill the King,[34] and curiously enough, Agnes seems to have had indirect access to James's bedchamber. *Newes From Scotland* tells us that she required a piece of the King's dirty linen whereby to work this magic, 'which she practised to obtain by means of one John Kers who being attendant in his Majesty's chamber, desired him for old acquaintance between them, to help her to one or a piece of cloth as is aforesaid'.[35] Kers in fact refused, but it is an interesting question how the two people became acquainted at all. The answer is likely to involve magical consultation. Item 31 of Agnes's dittay informs us that she cured the late Robert Kerse in Dalkeith. He was gravely tormented by both witchcraft and disease which had been laid upon him when he was in Dumfries by a Westland warlock, and Agnes assumed the sickness herself until Robert Kerse recovered.[36] Was this Robert Kerse a relation of John Kers, and did Agnes make her request to John in the knowledge that he was under a family obligation to her? We are also told by Melville that Richard Graham was a Westland man.[37] Is there any connection between him and the male witch who tormented Robert Kerse? The possibilities of interconnection between the parties need to be pursued further.

The evidence of intent to kill the King might well be worrying, but it depends how seriously the King took it. In the cases of Gellie Duncan and a male witch, John Fian, he seems to have been more curious than alarmed. Gellie was supposed to have played the jew's harp at the convention of

North Berwick, and James had her brought to play the same tune to him. Fian, too, was fetched into the King's presence, on 24 December, to demonstrate magical frenzy, which he did to remarkable effect.[38] James was probably also aware that several of the witches contradicted themselves, admitting – presumably after the pain or fear of torture had diminished – that their former testimonies had been 'false and feigned'.[39] To be sure, any reservations the King may have had did not interfere with the judicial procedures: nor could they have been allowed to do so. These witches were deeply involved in treason. So Agnes Sampson was duly executed on 28 January 1591, and when, soon after, certain witches escaped and fled into England, David Seton of Tranent was despatched to get them back.[40] But James's behaviour so far does not strike one as that of a man in a panic, although what must have lodged in the King was Agnes Sampson's apparent knowledge of the private conversation between himself and the Queen on their wedding-night in Oslo. If nothing else about this witch-investigation was frightening (as opposed to worrying), that point surely was. But the person who may have frightened him thereby was Agnes Sampson, not the Earl of Bothwell, and she was easy to kill. Had Bothwell been shown, at this stage, to be much more than a suspicious irritant?

The principal witness against him was proving to be somewhat unreliable. Richard Graham, a witch well known to Bothwell and to several of the East Lothian witches, had been warded in the Edinburgh Tolbooth since at least 11 November 1590. This did not please him at all. He sent a letter to William Schaw, Master of the King's Works – an interesting comment on his acquaintance with important people – to give to James himself. A précis of its contents, signed by Schaw and Durham of Duntarvie, runs as follows:

> In the first part of this bill he declared his hard handling in the Tolbooth and want of entertainment in meat and clothing against conditions made to him.
>
> He declared that conditions were made that he should be warded in the castle of Stirling and entertained, himself and a servant, honestly for his surety against his jewels.
>
> He desired, saying that he had kept conditions to them in saying that which he was desired or promised, that they would keep conditions to him in warding and entertainment in clothing and meat as is above said.
>
> This bill was publicly read at the Master [of] Household's table before the Master of Works presented the same to the King's Majesty.[41]

This is an extraordinary document. It suggests, unmistakably, that there was some kind of arrangement made between Graham and a person or persons unknown to deliver a certain story in relation to the matters under investigation. The story he was telling is fairly obvious, but was it true, either in part or in whole? Had the arrangement he mentions existed from the start, or did Graham become involved later on? Who was manipulating the evidence in this business, and how deeply was Bothwell engaged?

That he was engaged to some degree there is no doubt. For while it is true that Bothwell's name does not appear in the official dittays of John Fian, Agnes Sampson, Barbara Napier, Euphemia MacCalyean or *Newes From Scotland*, it does crop up frequently in the manuscript records. Gellie Duncan, for example, confessed that she had heard he had promised Agnes Sampson gold, silver and food for herself and her children; and Donald Robinson said more or less the same – Bothwell was paying them to bewitch a picture intended to destroy the King. Moreover, a connection is well established between Bothwell and Richard Graham. Graham is supposed to have said that Bothwell sent him money on several occasions during his imprisonment,[42] and in the account of the dittay against Bothwell and the decision of the jury at his trial, which is dated 10 August 1593, details are given of alleged meetings between the two men in Edinburgh and Crichton on various occasions since 1582. According to Graham's depositions these occasions numbered twenty. Bothwell admitted four and flatly denied two.[43]

But how far can anyone rely on what Graham is reported as having said? His letter to James is not the only indication that something mysterious was afoot. A document entitled 'Certain infallible reasons wherefore of law nor practice Richard Graham's depositions cannot make faith against my lord Bothwell' lists twelve points supported by marginal notes referring to legal sources. The body of the paper is scribbled and nearly illegible, with a title clearly written in a different hand, but out of the scrawl one can gather the main thrust of this *aide-mémoire*, which is (a) that Graham's testimony is unsupported by other witnesses; (b) that he was not sworn to tell the truth; (c) that he had been subject to threats; (d) that he was a depraved individual whose evidence should therefore not be believed.[44] It has the look of a hasty memorandum drawn up by one of Bothwell's defence advocates. We know that all three were dissatisfied by the contradictions in Graham's depositions and that they made other submissions to the court which suggested that Graham's evidence was not admissible.[45] In addition, Barbara Napier wrote to Bothwell, perhaps in April 1591, urging him 'to stand fast, showing that his enemies had devised his dittay'.[46] This letter was opened and read by several people before being burned, but its contents were conveyed by Robert Bruce to the King. Bruce may, of course, have given the King a tendentious version, but James would have added this information to that store of impressions he had started to form of the reality or otherwise of Bothwell's guilt.

The fact of the matter is, James at this stage seems to have been in two minds about the whole affair, even though he himself had sent for Graham and listened to what he had to say.[47] An accumulation of small points in 1591 hints at his uncertainties. He was eager to know what the Queen thought about how things were going and, according to Robert Bowes, the English ambassador, 'seems to look for advice from her'.[48] Most tellingly, he wrote to Maitland, 'the rest of the inferior witches, off at the nail with them' – that is, they are completely confused. Nevertheless, he wanted Graham kept in prison with 'his ordinary allowance' while he considered further what he should do about his evidence.[49] As for Bothwell, the King listened to the Earl's impassioned self-defence and found himself no further resolved. But he was eager to see justice done and to preserve Bothwell's children from any consequences attendant upon their father's being found guilty. On the other hand (an important clue to his state of mind), he remarked that he 'will be loath to be the instrument that the Devil or any necromancer shall be found true in their answers'.[50] Bothwell was now lodged in Edinburgh Castle (17 April) – scarcely surprising in view of the seriousness of the charges against him. His trial was set for 6 May, but by 5 May the King was saying that 'the evidence against Bothwell for conspiring his death was so weak as the assize of the nobility would hardly be satisfied to declare him guilty'.[51]

His wavering is understandable. He was being told from various quarters not only that the evidence against Bothwell was deeply flawed, but also that it was questionable whether that evidence was admissible in a court of law. This presented such a problem that James had to assemble the Lords of Session and other lawyers to determine what the answer might be.[52] The King was also under pressure from the kirk. On 6 June, Robert Bruce urged him in a sermon to 'execute justice upon malefactors, although it should be with the hazard of his life'.[53] The remark may have been general, but the political circumstances made its import clear, although James seems to have wondered whether it would not be better for Bothwell to take himself into exile and thus solve the problem.[54] The trial and condemnation of Euphemia MacCalyean on 8 June did nothing to help.

At this critical juncture, however, when the King was increasingly nervous about the extent of the witchcraft in East Lothian and the evident desire of a large number of witches to kill him and the Queen, and when his mind towards Bothwell seems to have been somewhat divided, a novel figure suddenly appeared with the evident aim of dispelling the King's irresolution. On 14 June a witch called Kennedy, who came from Reddon in

Roxburghshire and had recently been in England, had a private audience
with the King and told him that Graham was right and that the Earl was
indeed guilty of trying to engineer the King's death by witchcraft.[55] The
result was enough to tip the tremulous scales. To be sure, James still hesitated to set the Earl at liberty, but on 19 June, uncomfortably aware that
he was being in some measure manipulated, he remarked waspishly that 'he
would not have so many kings in this realm, neither should Bothwell be
delivered in time and manner as they had promised'.[56] Nevertheless,
arrangements were made to release Bothwell on bail and grant him liberty
on certain stipulated conditions. These included the requirement that he go
at once into exile overseas. Robert Bowes observed in a letter to Burghley,
'thus Bothwell has found the King's mind more resolute than he or others
looked for'.[57]

On 21 June, Bothwell was informed of the King's decision. That night
he broke out of the Castle and fled south; and at once he was proclaimed
traitor, with his possessions and estates declared forfeit.[58] From this point,
the effect wrought by Kennedy starts to become more evident. Relations
between James and Bothwell rapidly deteriorated and it is obvious that the
two men had become frightened of one another. Each fed the other's fear
and thus Bothwell's downward spiral into ruin began in earnest. The nobility, as one might expect, split into faction. James and Bothwell pursued each
other round the south and east of Scotland and into the Borders until, on
27 December, while James was at Holyrood, Bothwell and his supporters
broke in and tried to seize the King's person.[59] The raid was unsuccessful,
but it destroyed whatever lingering doubts the King may have had about
Bothwell's intention to kill him. In January 1592, he instructed the Scottish
ambassador in England to tell Elizabeth that 'some of our most unnatural
subjects [have been] led by the abominable author who betrays himself guilty
of that sorcery and witchcraft devised against our own person'.[60] Bothwell's
subsequent behaviour, wilder and less predictable with each passing month,
served only to confirm this conviction.

His eventual trial in August 1593, however, resulted in an acquittal,
largely because he had excellent defence advocates and the jury and court
were packed with his supporters. But was the Earl actually innocent? The
whole episode, from Princess Anne's attempts to reach Scotland in 1589 to
this theatrical judicial performance in 1593, is in need of thorough investigation.[61] Nevertheless it is clear that, far from being a political assize to
which witchcraft had been added in order to stimulate prejudice against the
accused, the trial was about witchcraft rather than anything else. In essence
it was no different from any other Scottish trial – no Continental theories
in evidence – in which a witch was accused of murder or attempted murder

by magical means. The difference in this and the other East Lothian cases is that the intended victims apparently included the King and Queen, and this point strikes one as odd. These witches were principally healers of the sick, raisers of storms, and murderers of unwanted relatives. Why should they suddenly venture into potentially fatal high politics? For what reason, and *cui bono*? Bothwell himself blamed the Chancellor, Maitland, and it is interesting to note that Maitland seems to have known Richard Graham. On one occasion Bothwell met him at the Chancellor's house. The three men went riding and during the course of their excursion, Graham showed the others an enchanted stick, so Maitland cannot have been in any doubt about Graham's status as a student of magic.[62] But one cannot start to blame Maitland on the strength of Bothwell's word alone. Here is another point for further investigation, along with the further question, if there was some kind of conspiracy against the Earl of Bothwell, was it planned from the start or did someone take advantage of the witchcraft investigations to involve Bothwell to his possible destruction? One may ask further whether this was not the cause treason was added to a series of witchcraft trials — to add a fatal prejudice against the accused. If Bothwell were actually guilty of consorting with witches, he would fall (technically) under the provisions of the Act of 1563, although had he done no more than consult witches, or practise witchcraft himself, it would have been difficult to cause a man of his standing more than some temporary embarrassment. He was, when all was said and done, the King's cousin. But if his consultation and practice had involved the King and Queen, that would be treason and the case would be transformed.[63]

Should that be so, the most intriguing question is, who did the adding? To that there is, unfortunately, no immediate answer. But one can be in no doubt that both the King and Bothwell were being manipulated. Someone was playing on their fear of each other for his own ends, and in the end he was successful. The extent to which the King became afraid is a matter for further investigation. The examinations of 1590–91 uncovered an extensive and organised body of witches operating in East Lothian. As the extent of this became clearer; as the realisation that a large number of women was routinely exercising maleficent as well as beneficent power within a few miles of Edinburgh became obvious; and as the knowledge that these people forming a coherent, regulated group numbering at least 100 persons, probably more, had ventured into the realm of politics and treason, lodged in the King's consciousness, one can see how his initial relative insouciance could turn into something like panic. Conspiracies against him by nobles might be frightening, but they had happened before and were composed of human beings with human motives and human power. They did not represent a combination of factors unknown. The East Lothian witches, on the other hand, did and in consequence the suggestion that they and their master, Satan, were allied with the increasingly unstable Earl of Bothwell might well have been enough to play ruinously upon the King's unhappy nerves.

Out of this fear came his book, *Daemonologie*, published in 1597 but obviously planned and prepared some time before. A manuscript of it survives, in the margin of which appear three sets of initials, EM, RG and BN, each set accompanying, so to speak, a descriptive phrase in the text. EM may well refer to Euphemia MacCalyean, her phrase being, 'rich and wordly wise'; BN, 'given over to the pleasures of the flesh', could be Barbara Napier; and RG, 'fat or corpulent', may be plausibly identified as Richard Graham.[64] The presence of these three sets of initials, if they have been correctly attributed, will therefore suggest that the *Daemonologie* was directly inspired by the events of 1590–93. Indeed, the book may have been intended as an accompaniment to the *Newes from Scotland* which appeared in 1591;[65] and in as far as it can be read as a political as well as a demonological work[66] – the intellectual offspring from a war of nerves conducted between the King and an unknown puppet-master – one must acknowledge that it had a long-term, widespread, potentially insidious influence stretching far beyond the local, transient turmoil which produced it.[67] If Kings are afraid, the rest of the body politic suffers too.

Notes

1 The sequence of events is laid out in B. Liisberg, *Vesten for Sø og Østen for Hav* (Copenhagen, 1909), 9–15. Copenhagen GkS 2586, fos. 8v–21v. T. Riis, *Should Auld Acquaintance Be Forgot* (Odense, 1988), 1: 264–5. All dates in this chapter are given in the New Style.

2 *CSPS*, 10: 195, 197, 198, 204, 212, 216. D. Moysie, *Memoirs of the Affairs of Scotland* (Edinburgh, 1830), 81. *CSPS*, 10: 223, 241, 847–8.

3 Riis, *Acquaintance*, p. 121. *CSPS*, 10: 281.

4 Liisberg, *Vesten for Sø*, 21–2, 95. Riis, *Acquaintance*, 266, and n. 16. James himself proclaimed to the people of Scotland in October 1589 that 'the contrarious winds stayed [the Queen]' and that 'she was stayed from coming through the contrarious tempests of winds and ... her ships were not able to perfect their voyage through the great hurt they had received', in G.V.P. Akrigg, ed., *Letters of James VI* (Berkeley 1984), 98. Cf. W. Murdin, ed., *Collection of State Papers, 1571–1596* (1759), 637.

5 SRO, JC26/2/27. Pitcairn, *Criminal Trials in Scotland*, 1.1–2 (Edinburgh, 1833), 1.2: 186. J. Kirk, ed., *The Records of the Synod of Lothian and Tweeddale* (Edinburgh, 1977), 12, 22. Pitcairn, *Trials* 1.2: 191–204. *CSPS*, 10: 365.

6 'It is quite clear that James encountered the witch theory while in Denmark', A. H. Williamson, *Scottish National Consciousness in the Age of James VI* (Edinburgh, 1979), 61. Cf. C. Larner, *Enemies of God* (Oxford, 1983), 69, 198; E. J. Cowan, 'The darker vision in the Scottish Renaissance', in I. B. Cowan and D. Shaw, eds, *The Renaissance and Reformation in Scotland* (Edinburgh, 1983), 127, and T. D. Whyte, *Scotland Before the Industrial Revolution* (1995), 226. The suggestion had actually been made a long time before by F. Legge, in 'Witchcraft in Scotland', *SR*, 18 (1891), 261. One should bear in mind that

this is supposed to refer only to Lowland witchcraft. Highland witchcraft was quite different and neither its beliefs nor its practices played any part in the Lowland situation. For a good example of a case in 1588/89, see J. G. Campbell, *Witchcraft and Second Sight in the Highlands and Islands* (Glasgow, 1902), 27–30.

7 Larner, *Witchcraft and Religion* (1984), 10. Cf. Whyte, *Scotland*, 226.

8 One may also note that Cowan's particular claim that Bothwell was not implicated until April 1591 is actually wrong; 'Darker vision', 130.

9 Larner, *Witchcraft and Religion*, 8.

10 G. F. Warner, 'The library of James VI in the hand of Peter Young, his tutor, 1573–1583', in *Miscellany of the Scottish History Society* (Edinburgh 1893), 1: ix–lxxv. The only two books on occult subjects are the *Poimander* attributed to Hermes Trismegistus, and Agrippa's *De Vanitate Scientiarum*, which is actually a repudiation of his own former interest in them. I. D. MacFarlane, *Buchanan* (1981), 527–31. The *Sphaera* was published in Paris in 1585. For the animadversions therein against magic and astrology, see Book 5.42sq. M. A. Bald, 'Vernacular books imported into Scotland, 1500 to 1625', *SHR*, 23 (1926), 260–1.

11 J. Simpson: '"The weird sisters wandering": burlesque witchery in Montgomery's Flyting', *Folklore* 106 (1995), 9, 10–11, 17.

12 *SR*, 18 (1891), 260.

13 'For without doubt, all witches, necromancers and suchlike, work by operation of the Devil under a pact, condition, bond or obligation of service and honour to be made to him', T. G. Law, ed., *The Catechism of John Hamilton* (Oxford, 1884), 50.

14 K. S. Jensen, *Trolddom i Danmark, 1500–1588* (Copenhagen, 1982), 30. Cf. *Idem*, 'Med trolddom som saadan, var ikke noget kirken specielt focuserede paa', 27; and J. C. V. Johansen, 'Faith, Superstition, and Witchcraft in Reformation Scandinavia', in O. P. Grell, ed., *The Scandinavian Reformation* (Cambridge, 1995), 187–8, 211.

15 J. C. V. Johansen, 'Denmark, the sociology of accusations', in B. Ankarloo and G. Henningsen, eds, *Early Modern European Witchcraft: Centres and Peripherics* (Oxford, 1990), 340–1.

16 G. Henningsen, 'Witchcraft in Denmark', *Folklore*, 93 (1982), 134.

17 Johansen, 'Denmark', 362–3. Jensen, *Trolddom*, 20–5. He regarded witchcraft as a denial of God and a pact made with the Devil. H. E. Naess, *Med Bål og Brann* (Stavanger, 1984), 93.

18 See the brief comment in Copenhagen GkS, 2586, fol. 22, and *CSPS*, 10: 281. It is true that in his *Daemonologie* James cited Hemmingsen as an authority on witchcraft, but the most likely explanation for this lies in the existence of Hemmingsen's book on magic rather than in any conversation with the King himself.

19 Naess, *Med Bål og Brann*, 109, and 'Norway, the criminological context', in Ankarloo and Henningsen, *Early Modern European Witchcraft*, 368, 373–5. Johansen, 'Faith, superstition, and witchcraft', 195, 200, 205.

20 Moysie gives a useful summary of these and other preoccupations at the time; *Memoirs*, 83–5.

21 *CSPS*, 10: 348. There is no warrant in the sources for Cowan's use of the word 'crazed' to describe her 'Darker vision', 129.

22 Liisberg, *Vesten for Sø*, 46, 50, 54, 55, 59, 60–1.

23 R. B. Wernham, ed., *List and Analysis of State Papers: Foreign, Elizabeth* (1964), 1 (Aug. 1598–June 1590): no. 752. *CSPS*, 10: 365.

24 *Register of the Privy Council*, Appendix, 14: 373 (Neving MacGhie). Pitcairn, *Trials*, 1.2: 206–9, the trials of Jonett Grant, Bessie Roy, William Leslie, and Violat Auchinleck.

25 *Sermons Preached in the Kirk of Edinburgh* (Edinburgh, 1591), 171, 202–3, 308, 317. In a list of things he considers wrong with contemporary Scotland, he makes no mention of witchcraft, *ibid.*, 288. See also *Acts and Proceedings of the Kirk of Scotland*, part 2 (Edinburgh, 1840).

26 *CSPS*, 10: 295, 297–8, 315, 328, 335, 348–9, 359, 365, 368, 375, 391, 404, 411.

27 G. P. MacNeill, ed., *The Exchequeur Rolls of Scotland* (Edinburgh, 1903), 22: 160.

28 SRO, JC 26/2/2.

29 SRO, JC 26/2/3.

30 *Newes From Scotland* (1591), 12–15, at 15.

31 *CSPS*, 10: 467. There are fifty-three articles in the record of her dittay made by Pitcairn, *Trials*, 1.2: 231–41.

32 SRO, JC 26/2/3 (Agnes Sampson's examination). Pitcairn, *Trials*, 1.2: 236–7 (Agnes Sampson's dittay); 254 (Euphemia MacCalyean's dittay). Cf. *Newes From Scotland*, 16–17.

33 SRO, JC 26/2/2. Cf. SRO, JC 26/2/2, the testimony of Barbara Napier.

34 Pitcairn, *Trials*, 1.2: 245 (Barbara Napier's dittay). Cf. *Newes From Scotland*, 16.

35 *Newes From Scotland*, 16.

36 Pitcairn, *Trials*, 1.2: 234.

37 Sir James Melville, *Memoirs of his own Life by Sir James Melville of Halhill, 1549–1593* (Edinburgh, 1827), 216. Cowan's suggestion that Richard may have been a Graham of Netherby is unsupported by evidence, 'Darker vision', 129.

38 *Newes From Scotland*, 14, 20–1.

39 As, for example, did Donald Robinson and Janet Straton in the presence of examiners and notaries, SRO, JC 26/2/23 (4 July1591).

40 *CSPS*, 10: 464, 457.

41 SRO, JC 26/2/17. Unfortunately, this document bears no date.

42 SRO, JC 26/2/16. Cf. JC 26/2/2. *CSPS*, 10: 502, 504. *Warrender Papers* 2: 159 (June–July 1591).

43 SRO, JC 26/2 [*Earl of Bothwell's Conspiracy*]. *Border Papers*, 1: 486–7 (12 Aug. 1593), referring to Bothwell's speech in his own defence at his trial two days earlier.

44 SRO, JC 26/2/9.

45 *Border Papers*, 1: 487. Cf. the statement in the *Warrender Papers* that 'other miscreants, of both sexes, were also sought for, were threatened with torture and bribed with hope of pardon to depone against him', 2: 159.

46 *CSPS*, 10: 506 (27 Apr.).

47 *CSPS*, 10: 502.

48 *Ibid*. It is unlikely that James learned Continental demonology from Anne. It is true she had been brought up in Germany, but only until she was five. Thereafter she was in Denmark. E. C. Williams, *Anne of Denmark* (1970), 2–3. Had she taken any interest in witchcraft – and there is not the slightest evidence that she did – the ideas she might have passed on to James would have been Danish rather than German. Anne was in her fifteenth year when she married James and the two began their marriage in much mutual affection. Therein, probably, lies the reason for James's talking to her about his problems and listening to her comments and advice.

49 *CSPS*, 10: 510.

50 *CSPS*, 10: 504.

51 *CSPS*, 10: 506, 511.

52 *CSPS*, 10: 519–20, 522.

53 D. Calderwood, *The History of the Kirk of Scotland,* 8 vols (Edinburgh 1842–49), 5: 129.

54 *CSPS*, 10: 509, a letter from James to Maitland, incorrectly dated to April. The reference to Barbara Napier's pregnancy (510) makes it clear that the date should be post-8 May. Bothwell was still in possession of a passport he could use; *CSPS*, 10: 501.

55 *CSPS*, 10: 531.

56 *Ibid*.

57 *CSPS*, 10: 533.

58 *CSPS*, 10: 534–5. *Privy Council*, 14: 643–4.

59 Melville, *Memoirs*, 156–8.

60 *Warrender Papers*, 2: 168.

61 I am currently preparing a monograph on the subject, *Satan's Conspiracy: James VI and the Witches of East Lothian*, in which the questions raised by and in this chapter will receive closer attention.

62 *CSPS*, 11: 61–2, Bothwell's answer to calumnies (7 Feb. 1592). *Border Papers*, 1: 487.

63 Bothwell's relationship with Graham is intriguing. If they met anything like as frequently as Graham alleged they did, one must conclude that Bothwell was deeply involved in consultation with a known witch, at the very least. He also acted as one of the prolocutors for the panel (counsels for the defence) in a witchcraft trial in Aberdeen in August 1590. See Pitcairn, *Trials*, 1.2: 209. He may have done this for a variety of reasons, but the association with witchcraft would merely add fuel to the later fire, however unjustly.

64 See R. Dunlap, 'King James and some witches: the date and text of the "Daemonologie"', *Philological Quarterly*, 54 (1975), 40–2.

65 Dunlap, 'King James', 43.

66 As Stuart Clark argues, 'King James's *Daemonologie*: witchcraft and kingship', in S. Anglo, ed., *The Damn'd Ar* (1977), 156–78, especially 164–6.

67 The latest person to write about the North Berwick incident, Deborah Willis, sees James as a man frightened by the possibility that women had a special 'female' access to supernatural power, and his subsequent behaviour in regard to the North Berwick witches as part of an attempt to assert himself against the supposed power and omniscience of the 'mother' by appropriating that power and omniscience to himself, *Malevolent Nurture* (Ithaca, 1995), 117–58.

Suggested reading

General reading

Anglo, S. ed., *The Damn'd Art* (1977)

Ankarloo, B. and Henningsen, G., eds, *Early Modern European Witchcraft* (Oxford, 1990)

Blamires, A., ed., *Woman Defamed and Woman Defended* (Oxford, 1992)

Bossy, J., *Christianity in the West. 1400–1700* (Oxford, 1987)

Bouwsma, W. J., 'Anxiety and the formation of early modern culture', in B. C. Malament, ed., *After the Reformation* (Manchester, 1980)

Braudel, F., *The Mediterranean and the Mediterranean World in the Age of Philip II* (1972–73)

Camporesi, P., *The Fear of Hell: Images of Damnation and Salvation in Early Modern Europe*, L. Byatt, trans. (Oxford, 1990)

Carlton, C., *Going to the Wars: The Experience of the British Civil Wars, 1638–1651* (1992)

Clark, P. and Slack, P., *English Towns in Transition 1500–1700* (Oxford, 1976)

Cowan, I. B. and Shaw, D., *The Renaissance and Reformation in Scotland* (Edinburgh, 1983)

Delumeau, J., *Sin and Fear: The Emergence of a Western Guilt Culture, 13th–18th Centuries*, E. Nicholson, trans. (New York, 1990)

Deursen, A. T. van, *Plain Lives in a Golden Age. Popular Culture, Religion and Society in Seventeenth-Century Holland* (Cambridge, 1991)

Domínguez-Ortiz, A., *The Golden Age of Spain, 1516–1659* (1971)

Douglas, M., *Purity and Danger* (1966)

Duffy, C., *Siege Warfare, the Fortress in the Early Modern World 1494–1660* (1979)

Duffy, E., *The Stripping of the Altars: Traditional Religion in England c.1400–c.1580* (New Haven, 1994)

Dunant, S. and Porter, R., *The Age of Anxiety* (1996)

French, K., Gibbs, G. and Kümin, B., eds, *The Parish in English Life 1400–1600* (Manchester, 1997)

Goldberg, P. J. P., ed., *Women in England, c.1275–1525* (Manchester, 1995)

Holt, R. and Rosser, G., eds, *The English Medieval Town: A Reader in English Urban History 1200–1540* (1990)

Horrox, R., ed., *The Black Death* (Manchester, 1994)

Huizinga, J., *The Waning of the Middle Ages* (1955)

Kümin, B., *The Shaping of a Community: The Rise and Reformation of the English Parish c.1400–1560* (Aldershot, 1996)

Larner, C., *Enemies of God* (Oxford, 1983)

Larner, C., *Witchcraft and Religion: The Politics of Popular Belief* (1984)

Lutz, C., *Unnatural Emotions* (Chicago, 1988)

Lutz, C., and White, G., 'The anthropology of emotions', *Annual Review of Anthropology*, 15 (1986), 405–36

Lynch, J., *The Hispanic World in Crisis and Change, 1598–1700* (Oxford, 1992)

Marwick, M., ed., *Witchcraft and Sorcery* (1982)

Schama, S., *Landscape and Memory* (1995)

Thomas, K., *Religion and the Decline of Magic. Studies in Popular Beliefs in Sixteenth- and Seventeenth-Century England* (1971)

Thomas, K., *Man and the Natural World: Changing Attitudes in England, 1500–1800* (1983)

Tuan, Yi-fu, *Landscapes of Fear* (Oxford, 1980)

Willis, D., *Malevolent Nurture* (Ithaca, 1995)

Chapter 1

Friedrichs, C. R., *The Early Modern City, 1450–1750* (1995)

Goudsblom, J., *Fire and Civilization* (1992)

Heller, H., *Labour, Science and Technology in France, 1500–1620* (Cambridge, 1996)

Jones, E. L., Porter, S., and Turner, M., *A Gazetteer of English Urban Fire Disasters, 1500–1900* (Hist. Geog. Research Series, 13, 1984)

Roberts, P., 'Arson, conspiracy and rumour in early modern Europe', *Continuity and Change*, 12 (1997), 9–29

Ruff, J. R., *Crime, Justice and Public Order in Old Regime France. The Sénéchaussées of Libourne and Bazas, 1696–1789* (1984)

Underdown, D., *Fire from Heaven: Life in an English Town in the Seventeenth Century* (1992)

Chapter 2

Briggs, R., *Witches and Neighbours* (1996)

Carmichael, A. G., *Plague and the Poor in Renaissance Florence* (Cambridge, 1986)

Cipolla, C. M., *Cristofano and the Plague* (1973)

Kors, A. C. and Peters, E., eds, *Witchcraft in Europe 1100–1700* (Philadelphia, 1972)

Monter, E. W., *Witchcraft in France and Switzerland* (1976)

Naphy, W. G., *Calvin and the Consolidation of the Genevan Reformation* (Manchester, 1994)

Roper, L., *Oedipus and the Devil: Witchcraft, Sexuality and Religion, 1500–1700* (1994)

Chapter 3

Darnton, R., *The Great Cat Massacre and Other Essays in Cultural History* (1984)

Lake, P., 'Anti-popery: the structure of a prejudice', in R. Cust and A. Hughes, eds, *Conflict in Early Stuart England* (1989)

MacDonald, M., '*The Fearefull Estate of Francis Spira*: narrative, identity and emotion in early modern England', *Journal of British Studies*, 31 (1992), 32–61

Slack, P., *The Impact of Plague in Tudor and Stuart England* (Oxford, 1990)

Underdown, D., 'The taming of the scold: the enforcement of patriarchal authority in early modern England', in A. Fletcher and J. Stevenson, eds, *Order and Disorder in Early Modern England* (Cambridge, 1985)

Chapter 4

Corbin, A., *The Lure of the Sea: The Discovery of the Seaside 1750–1840* (1995)

Lambert, A., *The Making of the Dutch Landscape: An Historical Geography of the Netherlands* (1985)

Schama, S., *The Embarrassment of Riches: An Interpretation of Dutch Culture in the Golden Age* (New York, 1987)

Chapter 5

Casey, J., 'The Moriscos and the depopulation of Valencia', *P&P*, 50 (1970), 1–25

Casey, J., *The Kingdom of Valencia in the Seventeenth Century* (Cambridge, 1979)

Friedman, E. G., *Spanish Captives in North Africa in the Early Modern Age* (Madison, 1983)

Griffin, N. H., '"Un muro invisible": *Moriscos* and *Cristianos Viejos* in Granada', in Hodcroft *et al.*, eds, *Mediaeval and Renaissance Studies on Spain and Portugal in Honour of P. E. Russell* (Oxford, 1981), 133–54

Hess, A. C., *The Forgotten Frontier: A History of the Sixteenth-Century Ibero-African Frontier* (Chicago, 1978)

Kamen, H., *Inquisition and Society in Spain in the Sixteenth and Seventeenth Centuries* (1985)

Wolf, J. B., *The Barbary Coast: Algiers under the Turks, 1500–1830* (New York, 1979)

Chapter 6

Bennett, M., *The English Civil War 1640–1649* (1995)

Donagan, B., 'Codes of conduct in the English Civil War', *P&P*, 118 (1988), 65–95

Morrill, J. S., *The Revolt of the Provinces: Conservatives and Radicals in the English Civil War* (1980)

Porter, S., *Destruction in the English Civil Wars* (1994)

Schwoerer, L. G., *'No Standing Armies!' The Antimilitary Ideology in Seventeenth-Century England* (Baltimore, 1974)

Chapter 7

Collinson, P. and Craig, J., eds, *The Reformation in English Towns* (Basingstoke, forthcoming)

Dobson, R. B., ed., *The Peasants' Revolt of 1381* (Basingstoke, 1983)

Dyer, C., 'The English medieval village community and its decline', *Journal of British Studies*, 33 (1994), 407–29

Fincham, K., ed., *The Early Stuart Church 1603–42* (Basingstoke, 1993)

Kent, J. R., 'The centre and the localities: state formation and parish government in England, c.1640–1740', *Historical Journal*, 38 (1995), 363–404

Magagna, V., *Communities of Grain: Rural Rebellion in Comparative Perspective* (Ithaca, 1991)

Manning, B., *The English People and the English Revolution* (1991)

Sharpe, J., 'Enforcing the law in the seventeenth-century English village', in V. Gatrell, B. Lenman and G. Parker, eds, *Crime and the Law* (1980), 97–119

Smith, R. M., '"Modernisation" and the corporate village community in England: some sceptical reflections', in A. Baker and D. Gregory, eds, *Explorations in Historical Geography* (Cambridge, 1984), 140–79

Tomlinson, E. M., *A History of the Minories, London* (1907)

Chapter 8

Green, I., *The Christian's ABC: Catechisms and Catechizing in England c.1530–1740* (Oxford, 1996)

Houston, R. A., *Literacy in Early Modern Europe: Culture and Education 1500–1800* (New York, 1988)

Huppert, G., *Public Schools in Renaissance France* (Chicago, 1984)

Strauss, G., *Luther's House of Learning: Indoctrination of the Young in the German Reformation* (Baltimore, 1978)

Chapter 9

Burgess, C., '"A fond thing vainly invented": an essay on purgatory and pious motive in late medieval England', in S. J. Wright, ed., *Parish, Church and People: Local Studies in Lay Religion 1350–1750* (1988)

Duggan, L. G., 'Fear and confession on the eve of the Reformation', *Archiv für Reformationsgeschichte*, 75 (1984)

Eire, C. M. N., *From Madrid to Purgatory: The Art and Craft of Dying in Sixteenth-Century Spain* (Cambridge, 1995)

Le Goff, J., *The Birth of Purgatory*, A. Goldhammer, trans. (Aldershot, 1984)

Kreider, A., *English Chantries: The Road to Dissolution* (Cambridge, MA, 1979)

Ozment, S. E., *The Reformation in the Cities: The Appeal of Protestantism to Sixteenth-Century Germany and Switzerland* (New Haven, 1975)

Chapter 10

Beatty, N. L., *The Craft of Dying. A Study in the Literary Tradition of the* Ars Moriendi *in England* (1970)

Binski, P., *Medieval Death. Ritual and Representation* (1996)

Birnie, W., *The Blame of Kirk-burrial, Tending to Cemeteriall Civilitie*, W. B. D. D. Turnball, ed. (1833)

Caciola, N, 'Wraiths, revenants and ritual in medieval culture', *P&P*, 152 (1996), 1–45

Gittings, C., *Death, Burial and the Individual in Early Modern England* (1984)

Stannard, D. E., *The Puritan Way of Death. A Study in Religion, Culture and Social Change* (Oxford, 1979)

Chapter 11

Duden, B., *The Woman beneath the Skin: A Doctor's Patients in Eighteenth-Century Germany* (Cambridge, MA, 1991)

MacDonald, M., *Mystical Bedlam: Madness, Anxiety, and Healing in Seventeenth-Century England* (Cambridge, 1981)

Levi, G., *Inheriting Power: The Story of an Exorcist* (Chicago, 1988)

Favret-Saada, J., *Deadly Words: Witchcraft in the Bocage* (Cambridge, 1980)

Marks, I., *Fears, Phobias and Rituals: Panic Anxiety and their Disorders* (Oxford, 1987)

Simons, R. and Hughes, C., eds, *The Culture-Bound Syndromes: Folk Illnesses of Psychiatric and Anthropological Interest* (Dordrecht, 1985)

Chapter 12

Bald, M. A., 'Vernacular books imported into Scotland, 1500 to 1625', (SHR), 23 (1926), 254–67

Dunlap, R., 'King James and some witches: the date and text of the "Daemonologie"', *Philological Quarterly*, 54 (1975), 40–6

Grell, O. P., ed., *The Scandinavian Reformation* (Cambridge, 1995)

Henningsen, G., 'Witchcraft in Denmark', *Folklore*, 93 (1982), 131–7

Riis, T., *Should Auld Acquaintance Be Forgot*, vol. 1 (Odense, 1988)

Simpson, J., '"The weird sisters wandering": burlesque witchery in Montgomery's Flyting', *Folklore*, 106 (1995), 9–20

Williams, E. C., *Anne of Denmark* (1970)

Williamson, A. H., *Scottish National Consciousness in the Age of James VI* (Edinburgh, 1979)

Index